Superior Customer Value

In The

NEW ECONOMY

Concepts and Cases

SECOND EDITION

Superior Customer Value

In The

NEW ECONOMY

Concepts and Cases

William C. Johnson • Art Weinstein

CRC PRESS

Boca Raton   London   New York   Washington, D.C.

Library of Congress Cataloging-in-Publication Data

Johnson, William C. (William Charles), 1954-
    Superior customer value in the new economy : concepts and cases / William C. Johnson
and Art Weinstein.--2nd ed.
        p.   cm.
    Rev. ed. of: Designing and delivering superior customer value / Art Weinstein and
William C. Johnson
    ISBN 1-57444-356-9 (alk paper)
    1. Customer services--Management. 2. Consumer satisfaction. I. Johnson, William C. II.
Weinstein, Art. Designing and delivering superior customer value, 1999. III. Title.

HF5415.5.W442 2004
658.8′12—dc22   2004041820

Visit the CRC Press Web site at www.crcpress.com

© 2004 by CRC Press LLC

No claim to original U.S. Government works
International Standard Book Number 1-57444-356-9
Library of Congress Card Number 2004041820
Printed in the United States of America 1 2 3 4 5 6 7 8 9 0
Printed on acid-free paper

DEDICATION

To my mother, who understood value when she gave sacrificially
through the years

WCJ

As always, to Sandee and Trevor, with love

AW

PREFACE

Designing and delivering superior customer value is the key to successful business strategy in the 21st century. Value reigns supreme in today's marketplace and marketspace; customers will not pay more than a good or service is worth. Consider the remarkable success of service and information providers such as Amazon.com; Dell Computer; eBay; FedEx; General Electric; Hewlett-Packard; Intel; JetBlue Airways; Lexus; Nordstrom; Wal-Mart; and Yahoo! — these companies truly know how to maximize value for their customers.

According to the Marketing Science Institute, *managing customers* and *understanding customers* are top-tier research priorities — ranked third and fifth, respectively — for the years 2002 through 2004. The nine most important subtopics comprising the former area are:

- Customer retention
- Measuring the lifetime value of a customer
- Customer relationship management (CRM)
- Managing loyalty to brand, channel, and employees
- Customer expansion
- Customer loyalty measurement
- Customer acquisition
- Managing customer experiences
- Managing customer relationships

The four key subtopics in the latter area include:

- Understanding/anticipating customers' needs
- Assessing the value to customers of firms' actions
- Customer experiences
- Communicating customer knowledge within the firm[1]

These topics and much more are explored in the second edition of *Superior Customer Value in the New Economy.*

Market-focused management posits that organizations should provide outstanding value to customers because they are the most important organizational stakeholders. A recent study of chief marketing and financial officers in *Fortune* 1000 firms affirmed this proposition. Of 16 organizational goals mentioned, both groups of top executives rated customer satisfaction as the primary business goal. The CMOs rated customer value creation second, while the CFOs listed this third (long-term profit was cited second for CFOs and third for CMOs).[2]

We have been researching, consulting, speaking, and writing about customer value in service markets for more than 8 years. In addition, we have developed and teach the definitive MBA course on the subject entitled "Delivering Superior Customer Value." We are truly convinced that developing the right value proposition (combining service, quality, image, and price or S-Q-I-P™) must be the top priority for management.

A customer-driven business culture stresses service management; continuous quality improvement; product and process innovation; and the use of Internet-based technologies to provide focus and direction for the organization and ensure that outstanding customer value will be offered. This, in turn, results in enhanced market performance. Unfortunately, caught up in the daily pressures of running complex service and information-based organizations, many managers lose sight of customers' needs and wants. As a result, the delivered experience often falls far short of customer expectations.

Great companies consistently meet and exceed customer desires. This book offers a blueprint for benchmarking world-class service providers and how to respond more effectively to customer demands. The second edition of *Superior Customer Value* was produced from the latest thinking of the business and academic communities. It summarizes and extends leading marketing and management work in the crucial area of customer value (CV).

Building on a three-pronged approach to the study of CV — concepts, cases, and in-chapter applications — the book serves as a comprehensive, integrative, and highly practical marketing management resource. It explores important marketing planning and strategy issues that emphasize relationship management strategies to keep customers satisfied and delighted, as well as "best practices" on customer service, organizational responsiveness, and market orientation. This perspective positively affects value-creating organizations and management in fast-changing and highly competitive global service industries.

Superior Customer Value was written to provide marketing practitioners, managers and executives, and scholars (professors and graduate students) with an informative, state-of-the-art guide to designing, implementing, and evaluating a CV strategy in service and information-based organizations. The material appearing in the book has been discussed at length in our MBA course "Delivering Superior Customer Value." In addition to the thousands of MBA students who have been exposed to these ideas, hundreds of managers have benefited from our interpretation of the new customer value paradigm via executive seminars and marketing doctoral courses.*

Each chapter in this book includes useful figures, tables, customer value checklists and insights, end-of-chapter discussion questions, and additional reference material. *Superior Customer Value* is organized into five parts:

Part I — *Customer Value – the Building Blocks* (Chapter 1 through Chapter 3) is the foundation material. This section examines critical business issues such as the importance of creating value for customers, customer orientation, and value-creating processes and operations.

Part II — *Creating Value through Services and e-Commerce* is offered in Chapter 4 through Chapter 6. In addition to our revised chapter on service quality, this section features two new chapters on the service-dominant new economy and online service quality.

Part III — *Planning and Implementing a Winning Value Proposition* (Chapter 7 through Chapter 9) explains how to build successful value propositions, pricing techniques, and strategies for adding and promoting value.

Part IV — *Delivering Long-Term Superior Value to Consumers* (Chapter 10 through Chapter 11) wraps up the text/concepts portion of the book with important material on customer retention and relationship marketing.

Part V — *Customer Value Cases* provides 18 detailed, "hands-on" examples of how successful organizations create value for their customers. This section opens with a framework for analyzing business cases via the customer value funnel approach introduced in Chapter 1. More than half of the cases are completely new for the second edition of the book. These include:

Boston Market
Delicato Family Wineries
Dow Corning

---

* For further discussion regarding the design of the MBA course "Delivering Superior Customer Value," see Weinstein, A. (1998) How to create an innovative MBA course, *Mark. Educator*, Spring, 6.

Edward Jones
FedEx
"Herding Cats" across the supply chain
JetBlue Airways
Lexmark International
Office Depot
Walgreens

Popular returning cases from the first edition of the book, most of which have been revised, include:

The Grateful Dead
Harrah's Entertainment
Nantucket Nectars
Newell–Rubbermaid
Pizza Hut
Publix Super Markets
StatePride Industrial Laundry
Time Insurance

Each case reveals an in-depth look at a dominant customer value theme (e.g., responding to change, being customer oriented, customer loyalty, etc.) and offers end-of-case questions to guide the analyses. The cases provide excellent learning opportunities to model effective customer value behavior and practices.

We look forward to learning more about your customer value marketing experiences. Feel free to contact us to discuss any of the material in our text.

Bill Johnson and Art Weinstein
Professors of Marketing, H. Wayne Huizenga School of Business and Entrepreneurship
Nova Southeastern University
3301 College Avenue
Ft. Lauderdale, FL 33314-7796
1-800-672-7223 (phone)
1-954-262-3965 (fax)
billyboy@huizenga.nova.edu
art@huizenga.nova.edu

REFERENCES

1. *2002–2004 Research Priorities*, (2002), Cambridge, MA: Marketing Science Institute, http://www.msi.org/msi/rp0204.cfm.
2. Hall, P.L. and Williams, T.G. (1998) Marketing/finance executives' personal and business value perspectives: implications for market-focused management, *Int. J. Value-Based Manage.*, 95, 125–157.

ACKNOWLEDGMENTS

Many individuals provided valuable input toward the preparation of *Superior Customer Value in the New Economy*.

First and foremost, we thank our Nova Southeastern University associates. In particular, Randy Pohlman, dean of the Huizenga School reenergized us to think about customer value in marketing in a new light. Preston Jones, associate dean of academic affairs, has provided us encouragement and the freedom to pursue meaningful teaching and research activities.

Second, we thank our support team. Sylvia Lanski developed the concept for the book cover. She and Barbara Ireland provided assistance with various figures and word processed some of the case studies. Some of Isabell Layer's computer graphics from the 1999 first edition were reproduced in this book.

Third, we acknowledge the following people for generously sharing their outstanding case studies and other contributions. In alphabetical order, thank you to

Sally Baack
Eric W. Balinski
Barry Barnes
Hilton Barrett
Jim Barry
Jamie J. Bodouva
Nicholas W. Bodouva
Norapol (Paul) Chinuntdej
Jude Edwards
Robert Fast
John Feather
Trevor Fried

Armand Gilinsky, Jr.
Brett A. Gordon
Pam A. Gordon
Mariana Ilca
Jerry Johnson
Bahaudin (Dean) Mujtaba
Ram Reddy
Edward Schwerin
Alan Seidman
Murray Silverman

Fourth, we thank the thousands of MBA students who have benefited from taking the "Delivering Superior Customer Value" course at NSU since 1996. In addition, hundreds of doctoral students and executive seminar participants in marketing have provided us a tremendous learning laboratory to sculpt and fine-tune our customer value-based marketing philosophy.

Finally, we especially thank you for reading *Superior Customer Value in the New Economy*.

THE AUTHORS

William C. Johnson is professor of marketing in the H. Wayne Huizenga School of Business and Entrepreneurship at Nova Southeastern University, Ft. Lauderdale, Florida. He earned his Ph.D. in 1985 from Arizona State University. Dr. Johnson is the coauthor of *Total Quality in Marketing*; *Business Process Orientation*; and *Supply Chain Networks and Business Process Orientation: Advanced Strategies and Best Practices* (CRC/St. Lucie Press) and has published widely in marketing journals and trade publications. He has consulted for companies in the health care, industrial chemical, soft drink, and telecommunications industries, as well as small businesses. Dr. Johnson has had experience in international education, giving seminars to businesspeople from Brazil, Taiwan, China, Thailand, and Indonesia.

Art Weinstein is professor and chair of marketing in the H. Wayne Huizenga School of Business and Entrepreneurship at Nova Southeastern University, Ft. Lauderdale, Florida. He earned his Ph.D. in 1991 from Florida International University. Dr. Weinstein is the author of *Defining Your Market* and *The Handbook of Market Segmentation,* 3rd Edition (Haworth Press), as well as more than 50 scholarly articles and papers on customer-focused topics and marketing strategy issues. He was the founder and editor of the *Journal of Segmentation in Marketing.* Dr. Weinstein has consulted for many high-tech and service firms.

CONTENTS

PART II: CREATING VALUE THROUGH SERVICES AND E-COMMERCE

PART III: PLANNING AND IMPLEMENTING A WINNING VALUE PROPOSITION

PART V: CUSTOMER VALUE CASES: A PRIMER AND QUESTIONS FOR ANALYSIS

1

CUSTOMER VALUE —
THE BUILDING BLOCKS

1

CUSTOMERS WANT TOP VALUE

It's not the employer who pays the wages. Employers only handle the money. It is the customer who pays the wages.

Henry Ford

As marketers, we should be committed to the proposition that the creation of customer value must be the reason for the firm's existence and certainly for its success.

Stanley F. Slater, Colorado State University

According to *Fortune* magazine, Citigroup; FedEx; General Electric; Intel; Johnson & Johnson; Microsoft; Nestle; Nokia; Singapore Airlines; Sony; Toyota; and Wal-Mart are among the most admired companies in the world. Stellar corporate reputations are based on eight criteria[1]:

- Innovation
- Financial soundness
- Employee talent
- Use of corporate assets
- Long-term investment value
- Social responsibility
- Quality of management
- Quality of products and services

Such criteria are evidenced by companies that practice customer value (CV) thinking. Designing and delivering superior customer value propels organizations to market leadership positions in highly competitive global markets.

The Internet explosion of the middle- to late-1990s was characterized by a frenzy of entrepreneurial activity and new business concepts; billions of dollars raised in (often misdirected) venture capital; a soaring stock market; and a marketing mindset advocating e-commerce. Exciting e-businesses such as Amazon.com, Cisco Systems, Dell Computer, eBay, Expedia, Priceline.com, and Yahoo! achieved remarkable success by pioneering innovative and better ways to create value for customers with changing needs and wants. These businesses survived the dot.com meltdown of 2000 by creating winning strategies based on superior value for their customers. Unfortunately, most of the start-up Web-based companies lacked a solid business model, strong value proposition, and a long-term focus and, ultimately, they failed.

In the new economy, tradeoffs are not necessary. Customers want fair prices and acceptable quality; *good value* and their business to *be valued*; innovativeness and image status; physical goods and value-added services; and retail shopping malls as well as online merchants. As Barnes and Noble learned, customers want "bricks and clicks" — the ability to buy books in the *marketplace* (store) or the *marketspace* (www.bn.com).

In the 1980s, the battle for customers was won or lost based on quality alone. As TQM (total quality management) became the rage in business, quality gaps diminished and companies focused on customer service. Enhanced customer value synthesizes and extends the quality and customer service movements and has emerged as the dominant theme for business success for 21st century companies.[2] Although this philosophy is commendable, not all companies have embraced it. The unprecedented number and magnitude of recent bankruptcy proceedings is evidence of not placing the customer first. For example, Arthur Andersen, Enron, K-Mart, United Airlines, and WorldCom were rocked by major accounting scandals; ethical gaffes; greedy top executives; misreading market needs; and/or shoddy management practices.

Managing customer value is even more critical to all organizations in the new service and information-based economy. Progressive companies that create maximum value for their customers will survive and thrive; they will be able to carve sustainable competitive advantages in the marketplace. Firms that do not provide adequate value to customers will struggle or disappear. By examining relevant customer value and marketing concepts and applications, this opening chapter accomplishes four objectives:

- To explain why CV must be the overall basis for business strategy
- To offer several key CV implications for forward-thinking managers

- To discuss the attributes of value-creating organizations
- To explain how the customer value funnel (CVF) can be used to improve managerial decision-making (see appendix at chapter's end)

THE IMPORTANCE OF CUSTOMER VALUE

Great companies do not simply satisfy customers; they strive to delight and "wow" them. Superior customer value means continually creating business experiences that exceed customer expectations. Value is the strategic driver that global companies, as well as mom-and-pop small businesses, utilize to differentiate themselves from the pack in the minds of customers. How is it that Lexus can sell sport utility vehicles for $65,000 and Taco Bell can offer meal combinations for less than $4.00 and both are considered good values? Value is the answer — and value is defined by your customers. Companies that offer outstanding value turn buyers ("try-ers") into lifetime customers.

What Does Value Really Mean?

The concept of customer value is as old as ancient trade practices. In early barter transactions, buyers carefully evaluated sellers' offerings; they agreed to do business only if the benefits (received products) relative to the cost (traded items) were perceived as a fair (or better) value. Thus, value is "the satisfaction of customer requirements at the lowest total cost of acquisition, ownership, and use."[3]

According to a dictionary definition, *value* means relative worth or importance. Furthermore, it implies excellence based on desirability or usefulness and is represented as a magnitude or quantity. On the other hand, *values* are the abstract concepts of what is right, worthwhile, or desirable.[4] Management's values have an impact upon how an organization creates value and, ultimately, its success. The legends about the Frito-Lay sales rep stocking a small grocery store's potato chip rack in a blizzard and Art Fry's "intrapreneurial" initiative that brought Post-It to 3M reinforce organizational cultures.

Value may be best defined from the customer's perspective as a tradeoff between the benefits received from the offer vs. the sacrifices to obtain it (e.g., costs, stress, time, etc.). Value is created when product and user come together within a particular use situation. Thus, each transaction is evaluated according to a *dissatisfaction, satisfaction*, or *high satisfaction* experience in terms of the value received. These service encounters affect customer decisions to form long-term relationships with organizations.

As an area of formal marketing study, value-based thinking has evolved in its approximate 60-year life — it originated at General Electric after World War II. Value-driven marketing strategies help organizations in ten areas[5]

- Understanding customer choices
- Identifying customer segments
- Increasing competitive options (for example, offering more products)
- Avoiding price wars
- Improving service quality
- Strengthening communications
- Focusing on what is meaningful to customers
- Building customer loyalty
- Improving brand success
- Developing strong customer relationships

According to Woodruff and Gardial, a three-stage value hierarchy exists that consists of attributes, consequences, and desired end states. These levels of abstraction describe the product or service; the user–product interaction; and the goals of the buyer (person or organization), respectively. For example, a new-car buyer may seek attributes such as comfortable seating; an easy-to-read instrument panel; smooth shifting; a *Consumer Reports* endorsement; no pressure sales tactics; and a good service/warranty program. At higher levels of abstraction, buyers may want driving ease, no hassles, reliability (consequences), and, ultimately, peace of mind (desired end state).[6]

Service, Quality, Image, and Price: the Essence of Customer Value

Providing outstanding customer value has become a mandate for management. In choice-filled arenas, the balance of power has shifted from companies to value-seeking customers. CV can be expressed in many ways. The S-Q-I-P approach states that value is primarily a combination of service, product quality, image, and price. Top-notch companies often differentiate themselves and create legendary reputations largely due to singular attributes. Although a focus on key attributes is advisable, firms must meet acceptable threshold levels with respect to each dimension; formidable global competition provides little room for weakness in any area.

The service factor must reign supreme in value-creating organizations. Nordstrom, Ritz-Carlton, and Southwest Airlines are renowned for unparalleled customer service. Extensive field studies in Europe, the U.S., and Asia by Cap Gemini Ernst & Young (a worldwide leader in management and information technology consulting) found that global consumers value courteous and respectful employees and honesty more than merchandise quality or low prices.[7] In addition, a recent study by CustomerRespect.com found that only 41% of *Fortune* 100 companies responded to an Internet communication within 2 days; 22% eventually responded; and, amazingly, 37% never responded. (The insurance sector was the most responsive; drug companies were the least responsive). Thus, this research indicates that nearly 60% of giant companies fail to take their Web presence seriously.[8] Furthermore, as Chapter 10 will demonstrate, customers defect for service reasons about 70% of the time.

Hewlett-Packard, Lego, and Rubbermaid are obsessed with product quality and innovation. Ben & Jerry's and Harley-Davidson's cult-like followings are attracted to the ice cream and motorcycles, as well as to what the organizations stand for (image). Brands-Mart and Wal-Mart are committed to offering great prices. Successful retailers such as Home Depot, Victoria's Secret, and Walgreens (see case study) realize that price is only part of the value equation — value is the total shopping experience. This includes such customer benefits as dominant product assortment; respect for customers; time and energy savings; and fun, as well as fair prices.[9]

Because tradeoffs exist among the S-Q-I-P elements, companies cannot expect to be market leaders in all areas. The cost of developing and sustaining a four-dimensional leadership position would be overwhelming. Clearly, customer value is a much richer concept than just a fair price; superb service, top quality, and a unique image are also highly valued by target markets. Realize that CV is a multidimensional construct. Varying emphases on S-Q-I-P explicate a company's value proposition (see Chapter 7). Customer value insight 1.1 explains how Speedpass creates value for customers.

──────── ▼▲▼ ────────

CUSTOMER VALUE INSIGHT 1.1:
HOW *SPEEDPASS* CREATES CUSTOMER VALUE[10]

ExxonMobil's Speedpass taps into the service dimension of saving time by creating strong relationships with users based on brand equity. A preprogrammed tiny Speedpass wand (small enough to fit on a keychain) is waved at gasoline pumps or retail cash registers to expedite transactions. Primarily used at gas stations, this radio frequency identification technology cuts about 30 seconds of precious time from typical $3 \frac{1}{2}$ minute service encounters. Although this may not seem significant, in today's convenience-seeking society, more than 5 million customers said it matters to them; management expects five times that number to sign on by 2006.

Speedpass drivers average one additional visit per month to Mobil stations and spend about 3% more than other customers. Because Speedpass is easier to use than credit or debit cards, ExxonMobil hopes that its very loyal users will use it to buy a variety of goods and services in the near future. Speedpass is now accepted at 440 Chicagoland McDonald's restaurants and is being test-marketed at Stop and Shop Supermarkets. Drugstore chains, video stores, and other national partnerships are being explored. The ever-growing Speedpass database is likely to attract high-profile retailers. In turn, this expanded buying network will appeal to the next generation of Speedpass holders and thus customer value is created for all participating parties.

▲▼▲

CUSTOMER VALUE: MARKETING MANAGEMENT IMPLICATIONS

Maximizing customer value is an evolving challenge for service marketers. Visionary companies are responding to the new breed of smarter, more demanding customers by rethinking some of their traditional job functions, using customer value-based decision-making and stressing customer retention strategies. To adapt more effectively and efficiently to customers, new types of value providers (value adders) are often needed. Some changes may seem to be cosmetic; however, in reality, they are sound strategic responses to the changing business environment and the need to deliver superior value to customers. Consider these four examples:

- Procter and Gamble, the quintessential consumer marketer, recently renamed its sales force the customer business development (CBD) group. Selling is now only a small part of the CBD rep's job function. More important marketing activities include assisting customers in reducing inventory; tailoring product and price offerings in each market; and creating suitable co-marketing promotional plans.[11]
- Merck, Xerox, and other *Fortune* 500 companies have created market segmentation managers.
- Micro Motion's (a Colorado-based division of Emerson Electric that specializes in the production of mass flowmeters) differentiation strategist is charged with the responsibility of enhancing the company's customer service activities.
- Vacation Break, a Ft. Lauderdale travel provider and developer of vacation ownership resorts (acquired by Fairfield Communities in the late 1990s) called its front desk receptionist the director of first impressions.

A customer value decision-making framework offers management a unique and potentially superior way of understanding business problems and opportunities. For example, the customer value funnel (see the appendix for this chapter) is a systematic, multifaceted, integrated, and rich tool for making customer-focused marketing management decisions. Managers can consider value-based criteria such as economic values; relevant values of the various constituencies; maximizing value over time; value adders (or destroyers); value-based segments; and value tradeoffs to improve their business analyses. An initial list of six important customer value issues for managers to ponder is summarized in customer value checklist 1.1.

─────────────── ▼▲▼ ───────────────

CUSTOMER VALUE CHECKLIST 1.1:
GUIDELINES FOR CREATING CUSTOMER VALUE[12]

Do your goods and services really perform?
Do your company and its people give more than what is expected?
Does your firm stand behind its work with service warranties?
Are your pricing policies realistic?
Do your advertising and promotional materials give customers the necessary facts?
Do you use frequent-buyer programs, toll-free numbers, and membership clubs to build customer relationships?

─────────────── ▲▼▲ ───────────────

The adoption of customer value in management's mission and vision statements means that customer retention (relationship management) becomes the primary vehicle for market success. Amazon.com's digital franchising concept links more than 40,000 Web sites and pays "associates" 5 to 15% of any revenues they generate. This clever cyber-based marketing strategy resulted in a 50% increase in new accounts; repeat customers accounted for 60% of all orders.[13] Enhanced customer value goes beyond isolated transactions and builds long-term bonds and partnerships in the marketplace. Strong customer–corporate ties change buyers to advocates. Increased customer loyalty results in increased usage frequency and variety. Perhaps more important, however, is the fact that delighted customers play an important word-of-mouth, public relations role that creates new business opportunities via referrals.

Conversely, bad-mouthing by dissatisfied customers can be not only harmful, but also the death knell to a company. Consider a case in point: one unhappy buyer at a computer superstore determined that this company lost $50,000 of his business (direct lifetime value) and another

$350,000 (indirect lifetime value) due to negative word-of-mouth comments to his family and friends.

THE VALUE-CREATING ORGANIZATION

Organizations should be viewed as value-creating entities. Customer-responsive organizations create value by solving individual customer problems. Delighted customers perceive a high value relative to the economic cost and hassle of obtaining a solution.[14] A strong competitive advantage can be gained through consistently providing superior customer value. As Figure 1.1 shows, value-creating firms such as Dell Computer score high in purpose (they understand their business and customers' desires) and high in process (they know how to utilize internal procedures to respond to customers effectively and efficiently).

Unfortunately, many organizations do not master purpose (customer focus) as well as process (customer support) activities. Typical of many government agencies, the Internal Revenue Service (IRS) represents a bureaucratic organization. Although the IRS does a reasonably good job processing tens of millions of tax packages annually, they rank relatively poorly on the purpose dimension. Recent developments in electronic filing (e-file); fax-on-demand tax forms and instructions; TeleTax phone service; and a Web site are all steps in the right direction. This organization has a long way to go, however, to overcome an unfavorable image. Most Americans perceive the tax system as overly complex, imprecise, time consuming, and, at times, unfair or even unnecessary.

Segmentation, targeting, and positioning (STP marketing) and the 4 Ps — product, price, promotion, and place — are focal points for value creation actions in the firm. These strategic controllables have major implications for attracting (conquest marketing) and keeping (retention marketing) customers. Sometimes, companies may go too far in one direction at the expense of the other. For example, in the 1990s, America

High	WELL-INTENTIONED	VALUE-CREATING
PURPOSE		
Low	ADVERSARIAL	BUREAUCRATIC
	Low　　　　　　**PROCESS**　　　　　　**High**	

Figure 1.1   The Value Matrix (Adapted from Capowski, G. [1995], *Manage. Rev.,* **May, 34.)**

Online's solitary focus on the former cost the company millions of dollars in bad press; dealing with customer complaints, dissatisfaction, and defections; and legal fees. During this period, the company was viewed by its existing clients as adversarial (AOL's sales orientation is discussed further in Chapter 2). In spite of difficulties in the AOL–Time Warner marriage, America Online has made solid improvements on the purpose and process dimensions. If it is to remain a market leader, AOL must commit to becoming a value-creating company.

On the other hand, some companies try really hard, but just cannot seem to get it quite right even though they are well intentioned. A foreign car repair specialist may do an excellent job of scheduling appointments with busy professionals only to find that the service technicians generally take longer than expected to fix cars or they routinely run out of stock on key auto parts.

The value matrix is a most useful tool for management. Where would you place your company and your major competitors in the four quadrants? If your answer is anything other than creating value, clearly you have some homework to do. Because markets are dynamic, the status quo will not do; even value-creating organizations must constantly work at getting better to stay on top.

SUMMARY

To succeed in the 21st century, service organizations must do a great job of creating customer value. Developing strong bonds with customers creates loyalty, which leads to high customer retention rates. Each firm must find the right mix of value ingredients to satisfy and delight its target markets. Designing and managing customer value is critical for business executives in today's highly changing and competitive markets.

Next, the two dimensions introduced in the value matrix will be explored. Chapter 2 explains what customer orientation means (purpose) and Chapter 3 reviews how to plan and execute customer operations (processes) effectively.

CUSTOMER VALUE ACTION ITEMS

1. What is meant by CV? In general, what do customers truly value in: (1) the marketplace and (2) the marketspace? Provide an example of how a specific retailer and an e-tailer create value for their customers.
2. How does Dell Computer design and deliver value for customers? How can Hewlett-Packard compete successfully against Dell in the

PC market? As market niche players, what can Apple or Gateway do to offer superior value to customers?

3. Based on the S-Q-I-P approach, analyze five airlines (your choice) based on the following CV dimensions: service, product quality, image, and pricing. Rate the airlines as above average (+), average (0), or below average (–) on each component, and then compute overall CV scores for each of them.

4. Using the value hierarchy framework (attributes, consequences, and end states), conduct a value analysis of a hotel chain and an online travel facilitator.

5. Identify three "best practices" from service industries/firms that a cable television or cellular phone provider can adapt to deliver better value to its customers.

6. Identify three companies that stress conquest marketing and three others that emphasize customer retention. Are these the appropriate strategies for these organizations? Why or why not?

7. How can your organization improve with respect to purpose (customer focus) and process (customer support) activities?

8. Identify a decliner, adapter, and star in the restaurant industry. What value-based strategies should these restaurants use for repositioning and/or future growth?

APPENDIX: ANALYZING BUSINESS SITUATIONS — THE CUSTOMER VALUE FUNNEL APPROACH*

To compete successfully, organizations must evaluate all pertinent actors and factors in a market. This briefing develops a managerial perspective featuring a four-stage customer value funnel (CVF) framework. The CVF approach is a valuable tool for understanding and assessing business dynamics and situations. You are encouraged to utilize the questions at the end of this section when analyzing the case studies in Part V of this book.

Management's objective should be to maximize value over time, realizing that customer values have a major impact on business processes and performance. Thus, the enhanced customer value approach offers management an alternative view of how to compete effectively in dynamic and volatile markets. This value maximization premise means that corporate success should be evaluated in a new light. Business performance should be built on a dual foundation of paramount value concepts: (1) anticipating and responding to the relevant values of all constituencies

---

* This section builds on ideas by Weinstein, A. and Pohlman, R.A. (1998) *Adv. Bus. Stud.*, 6(10), 89–97.

(e.g., customers; stakeholders and employees; collaborators, competitors, suppliers, and regulators; and society) and (2) value maximization — how economic value and knowledge are created and applied throughout an organization to best serve its target customers. Although the former element is largely qualitative in nature, the latter is mostly a quantitative dimension. This approach provides an insightful basis for designing a value-based model for managers to assess business situations as they enter the 21st century. The conceptualization of the value-driven model is developed in the subsequent section.

The Value Funnel

The CVF captures and summarizes the salient attributes of the two sets of customer value concepts in action (see Figure 1.2). As the framework illustrates, organizations must deal with a set of macro issues as well as customer-specific concerns to excel in business. Viewing the four levels of the model — global business community; market; organization; and customers — through a broad to narrow lens ultimately impacts the performance of a business unit.

The interdependency of the four levels is readily apparent. The dotted lines (between levels) indicate that each successive level is part of the preceding one. For example, there would be no companies without customers; similarly, organizations are part of markets, which, in turn, are part of the global business community. The values of the major "players" in the model must be carefully scrutinized as to value identification and congruency, and value delivery options (these are the relevant values). From the top down, the value drivers are what are valued by: (1) society (level I); (2) suppliers, partners, competitors, and regulators (level II); (3) owners and employees (level III); and (4) customers (level IV).

A realistic assessment of opportunities to create value (value maximization) throughout the funnel is the next step. Organizations consist of value providers. If the delivered value of these employees exceeds the expectations of customers (perceived value), positive net transaction experiences result. This leads to ongoing satisfaction and increased customer loyalty. In these cases, organizations are faring well in their moments of truth (points at which value transfer occurs). Thus, isolated favorable transactions evolve into continued long-term relationships.

The value over time (lifetime value) of a customer is measurable and, in many cases, substantial. For example, leading supermarkets typically generate about $50,000 from households ($100 per week for 50 weeks for 10 years); Ford Motor Company estimates the lifetime value of an average customer at more than $250,000; and the Ryder system expects about $9 million from logistics customers (3 years at $3 million per year).

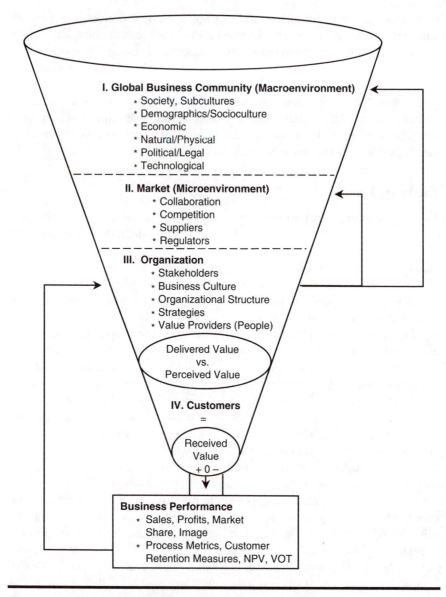

Figure 1.2   Customer Value Funnel

For the most part, the funnel model represents a downward flow with each successive level a component of the level above (e.g., markets are part of the global business community, organizations are part of markets, etc.). However, the feedback loops evidenced in levels I, II, and III demonstrate that market intelligence and knowledge are an ongoing, iterative, interactive, and integrated process. If business performance does not meet corporate objectives, strategic or tactical changes are mandated. The organization (level III) can adjust internally via rethinking its overall direction; implementing training and development initiatives; revising business plans; etc. Often, however, external adaptations are required due to changes taking place in the macro/global or micro/market environments.

In sum, the customer value funnel offers executives and students of the market a tool to help achieve a competitive business edge. The long-term value of the organization is maximized by being in harmony with the relevant values in the marketplace and the energy of value providers is harnessed to deliver excellence in all endeavors. Realize that the value paradigm is still in the formative stage. A strength of the customer value approach is that it is pragmatic and consistent with the managerial need for integrating business functional areas. The information presented in this book can provide a springboard for creation and refinement of marketing/customer value management strategies.

Finally, think about how your organization uses competitive differentiation to take maximum advantage of market opportunities. As a framework for analysis, five guiding CVF questions can help you assess relevant customer value issues.

QUESTIONS

1. Identify the relevant macroenvironmental factors (level 1). What impact do these issues have on the focal organization?
2. Discuss the market factors (level 2). How do collaboration, competition, suppliers, and regulators affect the performance of the focal organization?
3. Explain how the focal organization (level 3) creates value for its customers. What strategic changes are required to deliver outstanding value to its customers?
4. Do customers (level 4) perceive value as unsatisfactory, satisfactory, or superior? Why? Which of the attributes that customers value are not receiving adequate attention by the organization?
5. Critique the organization's business performance based on traditional (e.g., sales, profits, market share, and image) and value-based (e.g., process metrics, customer retention measures, net present value, value over time) performance criteria. What can the organization do to improve its performance?

REFERENCES

1. *Fortune* (2002) Global most admired companies — 2002 all-stars, www.fortune.com/fortune/globaladmired, March 4.
2. Fagiano, D. (1995) Fighting for customers on a new battlefield, *Am. Salesman*, February, 20–22.
3. DeRose, L.J. (1994) *The Value Network*, New York: AMACOM.
4. *Random House Webster's College Dictionary* (1992) New York: Random House, Inc.
5. MacStravic, S. (1997) Questions of value in health care, *Mark. Health Serv.*, Winter, 50–53.
6. Woodruff, R.B. and Gardial, S.F. (1996) *Know Your Customer: New Approaches to Understanding Customer Value and Satisfaction*, Cambridge, MA: Blackwell Publishers.
7. Anon. (2002) Global consumers value honesty and respect more than quality products and low prices, *Bus. Wire*, April 23,   .
8. Daly, D. (2002) 2002 online customer respect study of *Fortune* 100 companies, www.CustomerRespect.com, October 25.
9. Berry, L. (1996) Retailers with a future, *Mark. Manage.*, Spring, 39–46.
10. Hammonds, K.H. (2001) Pay as you go, *Fast Company*, November, 44–46, and www.speedpass.com.
11. Conlon, G. (1997) Procter & Gamble, *Sales Mark. Manage.*, October, 59.
12. Power, C. et al. (1991) Value marketing: quality, service, and fair pricing are the keys to selling in the '90s, *Bus. Week*, November 11, 132–140.
13. Nakache, P. (1998) Secrets of the new brand builders, *Fortune*, June 22, 167–170.
14. Davis, F.W., Jr. and Mandrodt, K.B. (1996) *Customer Responsive Management: The Flexible Advantage*, Cambridge, MA: Blackwell Business.

2

BEING CUSTOMER ORIENTED

Focus everything — all assets, all decisions on your customers.
They are the ultimate arbiters of success or failure.

Jack Smith, former Chairman/CEO/President of General Motors

You can drive your business or be driven out of business.

B. C. Forbes

"We need to be more customer oriented." Undoubtedly, you have heard
this management mantra or a variation of this theme recently. Executives
use terms such as *customer driven, customer focused, market driven,
market oriented*, and so forth* to motivate their people to do a better job
serving the customer. Although the idea is sound, too often it is just "lip
service" or talk rather than a major investment in improving all facets of
the organization and its business culture. A true customer-orientation basis
creates and maximizes customer value, which in turn leads to increased
market performance.

This chapter explores how a CV-based organization can clarify its purpose by implementing a customer-focused foundation to build long-term

---

* Several writers have said that the terms *market oriented, market driven, customer
focused, customer orientation*, etc. are synonymous. For example, see Slater, S.F.
and Narver, J.C (1995) Market orientation and the learning organization, *J. Mark.*,
59 (July), 63; Nwankwo, S. (1995) Developing a customer orientation, *J. Consumer
Mark.*, 12(5), 6; and Shapiro, B.P. (1988) What the hell is "market oriented"? *Harvard
Bus. Rev.*, November–December, 120. Although we acknowledge this perspective,
recent literature (developed in this chapter) shows that customer orientation is an
extension of market orientation and needs to be considered as a separate area of
study.

profitability. First, examples of service companies that excel in this area are reviewed; next, the changing concept of marketing in business is examined. Then, sales-oriented companies are compared to market-driven and market-driving firms. The chapter concludes with practical managerial guidelines for creating a customer-centric organization.

CUSTOMER COMMITMENT: HOW MARKET LEADERS DO IT

Great companies such as Dell Computer, FedEx, Nordstrom, and Southwest Airlines are extremely market oriented and masterful at creating and delivering value to their highly satisfied, loyal customers. Consider three examples revealing how this key objective is accomplished:

■ Dell's customer-friendly Web site now generates more than $50 million a day in business.
■ Federal Express changed its name and repainted its trucks to read FedEx because that is what customers called them ("let's FedEx this package to Omaha").
■ Nordstrom's sales associates have been known to buy products from a major competitor, Macy's, to satisfy an unfulfilled customer's request.

The spirit of Southwest Airlines is readily apparent. The Southwest culture creates customer value and lasting goodwill. On one entertaining flight from Baltimore to Ft. Lauderdale, Southwest flight attendants played games with the passengers (for example, the passenger with the most credit cards, oldest penny, and best memory won cases of peanuts); joked about the captain's age; and encouraged passengers to smile and wave to passengers on the nearby American plane upon landing.

Greatness in marketing and customer service is a function of attitude, not resources. Consider the entrepreneurial tale of Hal and Sal. Hal, owner of a small diner/coffee shop, not only greets his regulars warmly by name (often with hugs and occasionally kisses) but also frequently sits with them at the table for a couple of minutes to show his genuine concern for how they are doing. Sal, a sidewalk newspaper vendor, gives his customers upbeat morning cheer; sports and news updates (including opinions); and even credit when they do not have $0.35 in change that day.

Other companies do not do a very good job as marketers — you probably can identify several such firms. Consider when you have been put on hold endlessly when calling for technical support; when you have been ignored or treated indifferently when visiting a retail site; or when you have been sold inferior goods or services. Second-rate firms sometimes survive in the short term; however, they will not last in the long run unless they change their philosophy and start creating superior value for their customers.

THE MARKETING CONCEPT REVISITED

The marketing concept is that guiding business doctrine advocates a company-wide effort (*interfunctional coordination*) to satisfy customers (*customer orientation*) and organizational objectives (in particular, *profitability*). The traditional marketing concept — summarized as *customer satisfaction at a profit* — has been the cornerstone of the marketing discipline for more than 40 years. This philosophy worked well in the 1980s and early 1990s because most companies stressed conquest marketing (getting new business) over retention marketing (keeping customers).

In today's mature and highly competitive global markets, a changing twofold objective exists: focus primarily on maintaining and upgrading customer relationships (including generating referral business) and, secondarily, grow the business by finding new customers. In many cases, this might mean investing 80% or more of the marketing budget on customer loyalty and retention programs; the balance would be directed to activities designed to win new customers (note that many companies currently have this ratio reversed).

Given the 21st century environment and the new service economy (see Chapter 4), a revised marketing concept is called for. This philosophy states that all organizations must provide socially responsible business experiences that meet or preferably exceed customer expectations while creating long-term value for all stakeholders (for example, owners, employees, customers, etc.).

SELLING VS. MARKET ORIENTATION

Why do many companies fail to understand their customers' needs and wants? A major reason is that many organizations are not market oriented. Companies have different degrees of commitment to marketing. As Figure 2.1 illustrates, a five-stage continuum from production driven to market driving exists. Henry Ford pioneered the idea of mass production, which led to mass marketing ("give them any car they want as long as it's a black Model-T"). Many medical clinics still practice this production orientation nearly a century later. Other companies become enamored with their products (for example, many computer software firms) and employ a product orientation without carefully discerning customer problems. The selling orientation is widely used by automobile dealers, insurance firms, media companies, and network/multilevel marketers.

Production → Product → Sales → Market Driven → Market Driving

---

Figure 2.1 Business Orientations

How does a sales-oriented company differ from a market-oriented firm? As Table 2.1 shows, a sales-oriented firm bases market decisions on what the top executives think customers want. It often has a strong core product and/or an established, deep product line and spends heavily on advertising and selling to win new business. Attracting customers (conquest marketing) is the major objective of the firm.

America Online used a sales orientation to build a customer base exceeding 25 million subscribers in about a decade. However, in the late 1990s, when AOL permitted unlimited access for a flat $19.95 monthly fee, it entered a logistical nightmare as the increased customer base took advantage of unprecedented levels of online service usage. Many existing customers became dissatisfied with the provider because they experienced log-on failure rates at times as high as 50%. In the bleakest period, the company had customer turnover rates exceeding 20% a month. Finally, in an attempt to become market oriented, AOL added tens of thousands of new lines to deal effectively with the increased customer traffic generated. Given AOL–Time Warner's mind-boggling $99 billion loss in 2002

Table 2.1 Becoming Marketing Oriented

Marketing Variables	Sales Oriented	Market Oriented
Starting point	Organization	Target markets
Marketing focus	Product/service	Customer needs
Customer focus	New business (attraction)	Existing customer base (growth and retention)
Competitive edge	Lowest delivered cost	Superior quality or service
Product strategy	Generic product	Augmented product
Promotional strategy	Selling/advertising	Integrated marketing communications (IMC)
Pricing strategy	Maximizing profit margins	Profitable use of resources
Marketing objective	Sales volume	Customer satisfaction
Planning approach	Reactive	Proactive
Time perspective	Short term (tactical)	Medium and long term (strategic)

The statements below describe norms that operate in businesses. Please indicate your extent of agreement (1 = strongly disagree; 2 = disagree; 3 = neither agree nor disagree; 4 = agree; or 5 = strongly agree) about how well the statements describe the actual norms in your strategic business unit.

	SD	D	N	A	SA
Our business objectives are driven primarily by customer satisfaction.	1	2	3	4	5
We constantly monitor our level of commitment and orientation to serving customer needs.	1	2	3	4	5
We freely communicate information about our successful and unsuccessful customer experiences across all business functions.	1	2	3	4	5
Our strategy for competitive advantage is based on our understanding of customers' needs.	1	2	3	4	5
We measure customer satisfaction systematically and frequently.	1	2	3	4	5
We have routine or regular measures of customer service.	1	2	3	4	5
We are more customer focused than our competitors.	1	2	3	4	5
I believe this business exists primarily to serve customers.	1	2	3	4	5
We poll end users at least once a year to assess the quality of our products and services.	1	2	3	4	5
Data on customer satisfaction are disseminated at all levels in this business unit on a regular basis.	1	2	3	4	5

Figure 2.2 The MORTN (Market Orientation) Scale (From Deshpande, R. and Farley, J.U. [1998], *J. Market Focused Manage.*, 2, 213–232.)

and the departure of two top executives, Steve Case and Ted Turner, it will be interesting to see if the company can devise a plan to return to profitability.

A market-oriented firm carefully researches and evaluates its target markets to provide products that satisfy or exceed customer needs. They invest in an integrated marketing communications program (discussed further in Chapter 9) that allows them to grow, but the principal marketing objective is customer retention. A highly reliable, 10-item summary scale for market orientation is provided in Figure 2.2. Marketing managers can use this valuable tool to assess their current level of market focus as well as think about how their organization can improve in this critical area.[1]

Customer retention is so critical because it has a direct impact on the bottom line. A 5% decrease in customer defections can lead to a 25 to 50% (or more) increase in profitability. Although 10 to 15% customer defection rates are common in many industries, Leo Burnett does a stellar job in this area with a remarkable 98% customer retention rate in one of the most hotly contested market sectors — advertising.[2]

Coca-Cola, General Electric, Procter & Gamble, and Sony are renowned for their marketing prowess (market orientation), which has been perfected over the years. Marketing is a relatively newer phenomena for many service organizations (banks, hospitals); professional service firms (accounting firms, attorneys, consulting organizations); information-based companies (high-tech companies, telecommunications firms, mailing list houses); and nonprofit organizations (museums, park and recreation departments, universities).

Regardless of the type of company, a market orientation provides the impetus for building an organizational culture that puts customers first; creates superior value for your customers; and leads to increased, overall business performance (see CV insight 2.1). Employees of market-oriented companies become value adders; they know the importance of listening and responding to customers. DuPont's Adopt a Customer program is one example of a successful customer-focused initiative. Workers visit customers monthly, learn the customer's needs, and are their representatives on the factory floor.[3]

Market-driving companies go beyond accepting given market structures and behaviors. Rather than working in the status quo (i.e., existing customer preferences and current competitive sets), truly innovative firms try to shape or change markets by eliminating, adding, or modifying the players in a market and their functions.[4] Companies such as Amazon.com, CNN, FedEx, IKEA, Southwest Airlines, Starbucks, and Wal-Mart rewrite industry rules and compete in new market arenas. Their unique business ideas and systems deliver large leaps in customer value.[5] For further insight into the market-driving concept see the Lexmark International case study.

CV Insight 2.1: Market Orientation — Findings and Implications

Managers intuitively know that becoming market oriented favorably affects business success. Although much academic research has been conducted on this subject in the past decade, evidence of the consequences of a market orientation (MO) on business performance (BP) is still in the formative stage. A meta-analysis by Dawes found that 14 studies used subjective measures of performance and 12 of those were significant. In contrast, only three of the six studies that used objective measures (e.g., ROI, sales growth, profit margins, market share, etc.) found a significant or marginally significant relationship between MO and BP.[6]

In a research study conducted in cooperation with the Tennessee Association of Business, Barrett and Weinstein found a highly significant correlation between MO and BP.[7] According to Narver and Slater, market orientation consists of three major components: (1) customer orientation; (2) competitor orientation; and (3) interfunctional coordination. Their research showed a strong link between MO and BP.[8] Kohli and Jaworski argued that the market orientation construct comprises intelligence generation, intelligence dissemination, and responsiveness[9]; thus, market orientation involves learning about customers and competitors.

British Airways and Ford have a strong market orientation; these organizations view themselves through their customers' eyes; know how to detect or predict underlying customer concerns; use formal customer-based performance measures; and have action-oriented implementation mechanisms in place.[10] Successful companies like GE, Merck, and Sony are marketing driven but are equally adept at technological innovation. Preliminary evidence indicates that these balanced companies outperform ones stressing only marketing, selling, innovation, price, or production.[11] Yet, in another recent study, only 15% of a multinational sample of large businesses qualified as truly market driven.[12] Clearly, managers have their work cut out for them.

Firms operating in competitive industries are most likely to benefit from a market orientation. In a multistate study of hospital executives, "responsiveness to competition" was the only MO issue that correlated with three hospital performance dimensions: financial performance, market/product development, and internal quality.[13] Also, market orientation inputs are valuable for formulating an initial definition of your market as well as staying in touch with your customer base.

————————————▲▼▲————————————

Developing a Customer-Oriented Organization

Market-driven and market-driving companies go beyond target marketing to delight buyers. According to Sheth et al., "customer-centric marketing emphasizes understanding and satisfying the needs, wants, and resources of individual consumers and customers rather than those of mass markets or market segments."[14] The new customerization framework is contrasted with the "old" marketing model in Table 2.2. How do companies become customer oriented? It begins with the business culture; consider top management's values; employees; interdepartmental dynamics; organizational systems; and response to the environment. A dual customer (satisfy/delight the buyer) and competitive (marketing has been likened to war) emphasis is needed, as well as a long-term view. The Japanese are known for long-term marketing plans (some last 25 to 100 years) that often will outlive the executives in the company sculpting the strategy.

Table 2.2 Traditional Marketing vs. Customer-Centric Approach

Marketing Function	Traditional Marketing Model	Customerization Model
Customer relationship	Customer is a passive participant	Customer is an active coproducer
Customer needs	Articulated	Articulated and unarticulated
Segmentation	Mass market and target markets	Customized segments and "segments of one"
Product innovation driver	Marketing and R & D	Customer interactions
Product offerings	Product modifications	Customized products and services
Pricing	Fixed prices, discounting	Value-based pricing
Promotion	Advertising, personal selling, sales promotion, public relations	Databases, Internet, integrated marketing communications (IMC)
Distribution	Retailing, direct marketing	Augmented by online distribution and third-party logistics services
Competitive advantage	Marketing power	Customers as partners

Source: From Wind, J. and Rangaswamy, A. (2001) *J. Interactive Mark.*, 15 (Winter), 20.

Customer orientation subscribes to Regis McKenna's philosophy that marketing is too important to be left to the marketing department. It is the responsibility of everyone in the organization. For example, the tremendous success of Southwest Airlines is based on a strategy emphasizing three key factors: shared goals, shared knowledge, and mutual respect.[15] Customer orientation is a service organization practicing Japanese-style marketing — putting the customer first. In fact, the Japanese word *okyaku-sama* literally means "honored customer" or the "customer is God."[16] Is the customer really king in the U.S.? When leaving an American restaurant, sometimes one is barely acknowledged; in contrast, it is not uncommon at a Japanese dining establishment to have several parties graciously bow farewell in thanks for the customer's patronage.

Recognize that today's customers are quite smart and sophisticated; they are looking for companies that: (1) create maximum value for them based on their needs and wants and (2) demonstrate that they value their business. Road Runner Sports (which bills itself as "your #1 running source") is a San Diego-based distributor of running shoes, running fashion accessories, and related running-oriented products. Using a direct mail catalog as their main marketing tool, Road Runner sells a complete line of specialized products to highly loyal customers (many are members of their Run America Club) at very competitive prices.

John Naisbitt, author of *Megatrends*, noted that "in today's Baskin-Robbin's society everything comes in at least thirty-one varieties." The new value-seeking customers often possess the following attributes: they are choice seeking, demanding, and knowledgeable; they believe that loyalty must be earned; and they are price conscious, concerned about the environment, and convenience oriented (often time impoverished). Astute marketers recognize and respond to these issues when designing value propositions and marketing strategies. Furthermore, customer-oriented firms know how to use mass customization techniques; databases/marketing information systems; research; integrated marketing communications (IMC); and the human touch (getting close to customers) to develop personalized marketing relationships that build long-term loyalty and ensure customer retention.

At times, excellent companies such as General Motors, IBM, Kodak, and Sears have become complacent. Management and employees lose their competitive edge and enthusiasm and become satisfied with the status quo. Fortunately for the market, strong rivals emerge, such as Toyota, Dell, Fuji, and Wal-Mart; these companies provide a loud wake-up call to action and force once invincible giants to change or fade away. To overcome complacency and stay relevant in the market, organizations must avoid marketing myopia; be creative in programs and processes; adapt to and be flexible with changing market conditions and tastes; and use a *kaizen* (continuous improvement) philosophy.

Creating a Bias for Action

Great companies go beyond satisfying customers: they are able to predict customer needs and wants and practice anticipatory marketing. These organizations invest in research, get close to the customer, innovate, and accept reasonable business risks. According to Barrett, there is a five-stage *bias for action* continuum (see Figure 2.3)[17]:

Nonresponsive → Reactive → Responsive → Proactive → Anticipatory

Figure 2.3   The Bias for Action Continuum (Adapted from Barrett, H. [1996] *Mark. News*, Oct. 7, 4.)

- At the nonresponsive level, awareness of external stimuli is limited (for example, IBM initially ignored the PC market).
- At the reactive level, the firm is aware of the stimuli, but only after repeated prodding does it reply (e.g., Xerox was slow in developing competitive strategies to win back the low-end sector of the copier market from Canon in the 1980s).
- Most companies are at the responsive level. Customers may force the firm to enter new product-markets, sometimes reluctantly. Many companies will then take appropriate action, assuming that the opportunity fits the present business mission and adequate resources are available.
- Proactiveness is the fourth stage and implies corporate entrepreneurism has surfaced in the organization. This means that larger companies simulate the innovation, flexibility, creativity, and speed-to-market of their smaller counterparts.
- Anticipatory marketing is the aspirational level and attained by relatively few firms (and then only infrequently). At this point, companies understand virtually all of the market nuances and treat their customers as business allies and partners. Kinko's Copy Centers have done a good job in this area by offering around-the-clock service and anticipating customer base desires in new product offerings.

An effective market definition and strong customer orientation can guide organizations through the continuum to, ultimately, the proactive and anticipatory stages.

MARKETING APPROACHES TO ACHIEVE A CUSTOMER FOCUS

Customer-oriented organizations

- Build on the marketing concept (market orientation is the firm's implementation of the marketing concept)
- Design customer-driven processes and programs
- Establish a strong marketing information system
- Segment and target markets
- Hire the best talent
- Stress operational efficiency
- Continually measure and fine-tune their customer focus

ComUnity Lending is a medium-sized regional lender in San Jose, California. A three-part company credo helps them achieve their customer-driven focus. This action agenda is: (1) think like the customer — comprehend his needs; (2) focus on the customer — anticipate his needs; and 3) work for the customer — exceed his needs.[18] Figure 2.4 and

- Create customer focus throughout the business.
- Listen to the customer.
- Define and nurture your distinctive competence.
- Define marketing as market intelligence.
- Target customers precisely.
- Manage for profitability, not sales volume.
- Make customer value the guiding star.
- Let the customer define quality.
- Measure and manage customer expectations.
- Build customer relationships and loyalty.
- Define the business as a service business.
- Commit to continuous improvement.
- Manage culture along with strategy.
- Grow with partners and alliances.
- Destroy marketing bureaucracy.

Figure 2.4 Guidelines for the Market-Driven Manager (Adapted from Webster, F.E., Jr. [1994] *Mark. Manage.*, 3(1), 8–16.)

customer value checklist 2.1 provide important planning and evaluative guidelines for market/customer-driven managers.

As Figure 2.5 shows, customer value can be created at three trigger points: (1) company/customers (marketing mix/program); (2) employees/customers (service providers); and (3) technology/customers (e-marketing mix). Traditionally, external marketing (the marketing mix or program) was the focus for the majority of customer-directed activities. Here, the four Ps — product, price, promotion, and place — take center stage. In today's services-dominated economy, this view is limiting; a fifth P — people — becomes paramount.

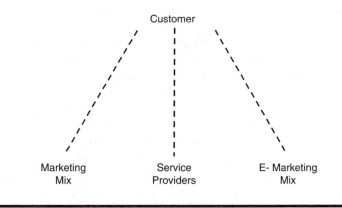

Figure 2.5 Customer-Oriented Marketing Approaches

---------- ▼▲▼ ----------

CUSTOMER VALUE CHECKLIST 2.1: CUSTOMER ORIENTATION GUIDELINES

Do you know your customers' (and their customers') objectives?

Is your service offer designed with the customer in mind?

Are your internal systems (i.e., e-business, ordering, billing, shipping, computers, financial, etc.) geared toward how customers prefer doing business with you?

Do you constantly measure customer satisfaction?

Do you continually meet with your customers to determine their needs today and tomorrow?

How is value created, delivered, monitored, and maximized in your organization?

---------- ▲▼▲ ----------

Customer-oriented service organizations employ personnel that are value adders. Internal marketing is used to develop customer-focused employees. Basic human resource management activities, such as recruitment, training, motivating, compensating, and evaluation, come into play in this area. Don Schultz, a leading thinker on integrated marketing, believes that if chief marketing officers would shift just 5% of their external customer research budgets to study internal customers (those within the organization who are supposed to deliver the corporate promises), dramatic increases in marketing productivity of 50% or more would result.[19]

Two key dimensions for good service providers are the ability to satisfy customer needs and the degree to which interacting with customers is an enjoyable experience. In addition, three personality traits — agreeability, emotional stability, and the need for activity — were found to explain about 40% of the variance in the customer orientation of food service employees.[20] Once people are adequately prepared for their respective business challenges, interactive marketing (face-to-face and other customer contacts) takes over.

Exceptional customer service differentiates market leaders from average companies. Home Depot is known for its careful screening and selection process to find job applicants with a high social orientation (strong people skills). The company's market leadership comes from the price and product mix expected of home improvement superstores coupled with the useful advice and service provided by neighborhood hardware stores.[21] Inspired by a strong competitive threat from Lowes and the need to be more customer focused, the company recently banned forklifts on the sales floor during peak buying hours. Management also directed Home Depot associates to spend more "face" time helping customers with their home repair/remodeling projects and with finding their needed merchandise.

Table 2.3   The e-Marketing Mix Taxonomy

e-Marketing Functions	e-Marketing Tools/Terms
Product	Assortment, configuration engine, planning and layout tools
Price	Dynamic pricing, forward and reverse auctions, name your price
Place	Affiliates, remote hosting
Promotion	Online ads, sponsored links, outbound e-mail, viral marketing, recommendations
Sales promotion	e-Coupons
Personalization	Customization, individualization, rules-based system, collaborative filtering
Privacy	Privacy policy
Customer service	FAQs and help desk, e-mail response management, chat
Community	Chat rooms, user ratings and reviews, registries and wish lists, reputation scoring
Site	Home page, navigation and search, page design and layout
Security	Security policy

Source: Adapted from Kalyanam, K. and McIntyre, S. (2002) *J. Acad. Mark. Sci.*, 30(4), 487–499.

A 21st century marketing weapon that should be added to an organization's arsenal is e-marketing. For the most part, these Internet-based marketing techniques originated from e-tailers during the 5-year dot.com boom of the late 1990s. (The evolution of the new service and information economy is examined in Chapter 4). According to Kalyanam and McIntyre, the e-marketing mix consists of 11 e-marketing functions and more than 30 e-marketing tools; these are explicated in Table 2.3.[22] To be competitive, value-creating organizations must incorporate the latest relevant marketing techniques and technologies into their business plans.

SUMMARY

A firm that has a strong customer orientation fares well on the purpose dimension of the value matrix (introduced in Chapter 1). A market orientation builds the necessary business culture and customer-focused framework to enable service providers to deliver superior value to their target markets.

Chapter 3 will discuss how business processes can be used effectively by service organizations to create enhanced value for customers.

CUSTOMER VALUE ACTION ITEMS

1. How customer oriented is Marriott? Comment on each of the following attributes:
   a. Customer focus — who are its customers and what do they value?
   b. Competitive focus — who are its competitors and what are their strengths and weaknesses?
   c. Interfunctional coordination — how is the company organized and how do the various departments interact?
   d. Market-driven objectives
   e. Market intelligence utilization
   f. Target marketing
   g. Performance measures

2. How market oriented is your neighborhood shopping center? What changes should be made for it to become more customer driven?

3. How market oriented is eBay? How does its market orientation assist the company in delivering superior customer value? What role do its business model; culture (business philosophy); electronic community; and marketing strategies play in getting, keeping, and growing customers?

4. Cite an example of a high-tech company and a service firm that practice market-driving behavior. How can a steel producer or an online matchmaking service utilize the market-driving philosophy?

5. Within the automobile industry, identify manufacturers or products that are or were: nonresponsive; reactive; responsive; proactive; or anticipatory. Consider marketing programs and processes and provide anecdotal support for your view.

6. How well does your organization create value for your customers based on the marketing mix, service providers, and the e-marketing mix? How can these areas be improved? What role should internal marketing play in this process?

7. Based on *Fortune* 500 rankings, the U.S. Post Office, an independent government agency, is the 12th largest organization in America, with revenues of more than $66 billion. As the nation's second largest employer (750,000 employees), it delivers more than 200 billion pieces of mail annually, which is double the amount of 30 years ago. The Post Office's objectives are to evolve into the premier provider of 21st century postal communications products and services and be recognized as the best value in America. (Visit www.usps.gov for further details on this organization.)
   a. How does the U.S. Post Office create value for its customers?

b. Analyze the components of market orientation — customer orientation, competitive advantage, and interfunctional coordination — and their impact on this organization.

c. Discuss how product mix, new product development, and perceived quality affect the market orientation of the U.S. Post Office.

d. What changes should this organization implement to improve its market/customer orientation?

REFERENCES

1. Deshpande, R. and Farley, J.U. (1998) Measuring market orientation: generalization and synthesis, *J. Mark. Focused Manage.*, 2, 213–232.
2. Reichheld, F.F. (1996) *The Loyalty Effect*, Cambridge, MA: Harvard Business School Press.
3. Slater, S.F. and Narver, J.C. (1994) Market orientation, customer value, and superior performance, *Bus. Horizons*, March/April, 22–28.
4. Jaworski, B., Kohli, A.K., and Sahay, A. (2000) Market-driven versus driving markets, *J. Acad. Mark. Sci.* 28(1), 45–54.
5. Kumar, N., Scheer, L., and Kotler P. (2000) From market driven to market driving, *Eur. Manage. J.*, 18(2), 129–142.
6. Dawes, J. (1999) The relationship between subjective and objective company performance measures in market orientation research: further empirical evidence, *Mark. Bull.*, 10, 65–75.
7. Barrett, H. and Weinstein, A. (1998) The effect of market orientation and flexibility on corporate entrepreneurship, *Entrepreneurship Theory Pract.*, 23 (1), 57–70.
8. Narver, J.C. and Slater, S.F. (1990) The effect of a market orientation on business profitability, *J. Mark.*, 54 (Oct.), 20–35.
9. Kohli, A.K. and Jaworski, B.J. (1990) Market orientation: the construct, research propositions, and managerial implications, *J. Mark.*, 54 (April), 1–18.
10. Nwankwo, S. (1995) Developing a customer orientation, *J. Consumer Mark.*, 12(5), 5–15.
11. Wong, V. and Saunders, S. (1993) Business orientations and corporate success, *J. Strategic Mark.*, 1, 20–40.
12. Day, G.S. and Nedungadi, P. (1994) Managerial representations of competitive advantage, *J. Mark.*, 58 (April), 31–44.
13. Raju, P.S., Lonial, S.C., and Gupta, Y.P. (1995) Market orientation and performance in the hospital industry, *J. Health Care Mark.*, 15 (Winter), 34–41.
14. Sheth, J.N., Sisodia, R.S., and Sharma, A. (2000) The antecedents and consequences of customer-centric marketing, *J. Acad. Mark. Sci.,* 28(1), 55–66.
15. Gittel, J. (2003) *The Southwest Airlines Way*, NY: McGraw Hill.
16. Adachi, Y. (1998) The effects of semantic difference on cross-cultural business negotiation: a Japanese and American case study, *J. Language Int. Bus.*, 9(1), 43–52.
17. Barrett, H. (1996) Ultimate goal is to anticipate the needs of market, *Mark. News*, Oct. 7, 4.

18. Fry, W.D. (1995) The holy grail of customer contentment, *Mortgage Banking*, Oct., 167–172.
19. Schultz, D.E. (2002) Study internal marketing for better impact, *Mark. News*, Oct. 14, 8–9.
20. Brown, T.J. et al. (2002) The customer orientation of service workers: personality trait effects on self- and supervisor performance ratings, *J. Mark. Res.*, XXXIX (Feb.), 110–119.
21. Gubman, E.L. (1995) Aligning people strategies with customer value, *Compensation Benefits Rev.*, (Jan.–Feb.), 15–22.
22. Kalyanam, K. and McIntyre, S. (2002) The e-marketing mix: a contribution of the e-tailing wars, *J. Acad. Mark. Sci.*, 30 (4), 487–499.

3

PROCESS AND
CUSTOMER VALUE

If you can't define what you do as a process, you don't know
what your job is.

W. Edwards Deming

Process innovation combines a structure for doing work with
an orientation to visible and dramatic results.

Thomas H. Davenport

INTRODUCTION

As explained in Chapter 2, practicing a market orientation is fundamental
to creating sustainable customer value. Exceeding customer expectations;
knowing the competition's strengths, weaknesses, and strategies; and
encouraging cross-functional sharing and decision-making lead to superior
business performance. This chapter focuses on designing business operations and processes that create value. That is, process design needs to
follow a simple litmus test: does the process create superior customer
value? Moreover, value drives process design as shown in Figure 3.1. Note
that the goal of the organization is to maintain a fit between value and
processes. Successful organizations recognize that value and process are
seamless in the eyes of their customers. Consider the experience of
successful companies that have recognized the link between process and
value.

Before retiring, GE CEO Jack Welch ordered a move to e-processes,
applying business-to-business technology everywhere. For example, at GE

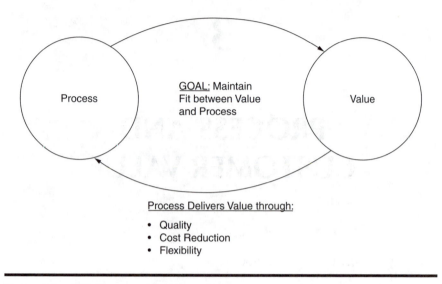

Figure 3.1   Link between Process and Value

Information Services, employees use a system called Trading Partner Network Register to order office supplies from prequalified vendors over the Internet. By GE estimates, making purchases offline can cost $50 to $200 per transaction; online costs amount to only about $1 per transaction.

IBM conducted a wholesale review of its processes a few years ago. Because its large corporate customers were increasingly operating on a global basis, IBM knew it would need to standardize its operations worldwide. It would be necessary to institute a set of common processes for order fulfillment, product development, and so forth to take the place of the diverse processes then used in different parts of the world and in different product groups. IBM even changed its management structure, assigning each major process to a member of its most senior executive body. Furthermore, each process was assigned an owner, referred to as a business process executive, who was given responsibility for designing and deploying the process. Each of IBM's business units is now expected to follow processes designed by its business process executive. Shifting organizational power away from units and toward processes has helped IBM standardize its processes around the world. The benefits have been startling: a 75% reduction in the average time to market for new products; a sharp upswing in on-time deliveries and customer satisfaction; and cost savings in excess of $9 billion.[1]

Giant retail broker firms like Merrill Lynch and PaineWebber have for years excelled at four business processes crucial to overall business success: client management; information delivery; portfolio modeling; and operational statistics. However, with the Internet fast becoming the preferred channel among investors, online trading has emerged as a fifth critical process. PaineWebber and Merrill Lynch, with their fat brokerage fees ranging in the hundreds of dollars per transaction, reluctantly began shifting some of their business to the Internet.

Federal Express Corp. recently announced plans to launch an online service that will let the delivery company's business customers review and pay invoices over the Internet. FedEx, a unit of FDX Corp., said the electronic bill-presentment and bill-payment service, called Invoice Online, will allow customers to schedule payments as many as 15 days in advance. A second, and arguably more ambitious, process improvement effort, involves FDX trying to recast itself as a major provider of supply chain management systems that threaten the company's very existence. FDX plans to design a network that can supplant a company's inefficient stream of faxes and phone calls with digital exchanges of information about demand, factory schedules, and the availability of materials. Such systems would select the most logical, most economical type of transport — air, land, or sea — for delivering packages on time. FDX would then also coordinate customs clearances around the world and minimize the amount of time any item sits in a warehouse along the way (see FedEx case)

Increasingly, evidence from these and other successful companies is that superior customer value results from a combination of the organization's assets (brand image and trademarks) and skills (e.g., innovation, marketing capabilities), when applied advantageously to business processes. According to Mroz, "in the information economy of the twenty-first century, corporate survival will depend on the effectiveness of the corporation's innate business processes ... corporations will be defined not so much by their industry or products, but by the nature of their processes."[2] What prompted these organizations to change their processes? In short, they desired to serve their customers better and, in the process, deliver greater value to enhance their business performance.

In fact, organizations that view themselves as a collection of processes that must be understood, managed, and improved are most likely to achieve this end. Thus, the focus needs to shift from managing departments to managing processes. This chapter will examine key organizational processes and how they relate to the marketing cycle, assessing their effectiveness and achieving a process orientation, and the steps in process improvement and process improvement tools.

Key Organizational Processes

Before discussing key organizational processes, it is necessary to define "process." A process is a specific group of activities and subordinate tasks that results in the performance of a service that is of value. Business

Table 3.1   Process View vs. Traditional Functional View

Process View	Functional View
Emphasis on improving how work is done	Which products or services are delivered
Cross-functional coordination, teamwork stressed	Frequent "hand-offs" among functions that remain largely uncoordinated
Systems view, i.e., entire process is managed	Pieces of the process are managed
Customer orientation	Internal/company orientation

process design involves the identification and sequencing of work activities, tasks, resources, decisions, and responsibilities across time and place, with a beginning and an end, along with clearly identified inputs and outputs. Processes must be able to be tracked as well, using cost, time, output quality, and satisfaction measurements. Businesses need to monitor, review, alter, and streamline processes continually in order to remain competitive. A process view of the organization differs from the traditional functional view, as presented in Table 3.1.

The authors strongly advocate a "process view." Succeeding in the new economy will require companies to weave their key business processes into hard-to-imitate strategic capabilities that distinguish them from their competitors. Corporate survival will depend on the effectiveness of internal processes and their integration with supply chain partners and customers. Competitors can match individual processes or activities but cannot match the integration or fit of these processes between network partners. Building a common process view represents a key component of business process orientation, or BPO, which serves as a building block as firms compete in virtually integrated networks of the new economy (see customer value insight 3.1).

CUSTOMER VALUE INSIGHT 3.1: WHAT IS BPO?[3]

As they enter the new millennium, organizations are undergoing a sea change fueled by ever demanding customers and employees; rapidly shrinking product life cycles and response times; and new global and virtual competitors. A new paradigm is emerging that focuses on the integration of business partners and the alignment of core business processes. Processes are now considered strategic assets. Corporations are extending outside their legal boundaries as a normal way of organizing. Partnering, functional outsourcing, business process outsourcing, alliances, and joint ventures are yesterday's requirements for success. Competition in the future will increasingly occur between networks, rather than stand-alone businesses. Management needs to promote the right conditions not only within the company, but within the organizations that are part of its value-adding and creating network.

A *business process orientation* (BPO) serves as a useful tool to promote such conditions within the firm. A BPO is not simply a new business operations strategy; rather, it emphasizes process as opposed to hierarchies, with special emphasis on outcomes, particularly customer satisfaction. The key BPO elements are: (1) *process management and measurement*; (2) *process jobs*; and (3) *process view*.

In traditional, functionally oriented organizations job design was often based on how to limit responsibility and focus on a task. Authority typically rested with the boss, not someone who actually served the customer. A business process orientation, on the other hand, assigns authority and responsibility to employees who are actually serving the customer. Process-oriented work involves pleasing internal customers as well as the end customer, representing a dramatic shift for many organizations. A process orientation should result in greater responsiveness, thus improving the value delivered.

Using a BPO questionnaire developed by McCormack and Johnson, research was conducted with over 100 domestic and international manufacturing companies. These firms represented a broad cross section of industries, ranging in size from approximately $100 million to several billion in annual sales. The results of the research showed that BPO is critical in reducing conflict and encouraging greater connectedness within an organization, while improving business performance. BPO also led to a more positive corporate climate, including higher esprit de corps.

Educating employees in the organization to understand the benefits of BPO is also critical. A rationale for introducing changes in workflow or job responsibilities must be clearly communicated. McCormack and Johnson's research showed that most employees value less conflict, improved cross-departmental connectedness, and esprit de corps. Using the BPO instrument can prove fruitful as a discussion and diagnostic tool to supply the momentum and energy for process change.

▲▼▲

Processes are not simply obscure, backroom operations of the service concern, but instead an integral part of delivering the value proposition. Processes and service are inseparable, that is, the process *is the service*. An effective process is driven by results and derives its form from customer requirements (how and when customers want to do business with you). Market-oriented companies ensure that the service encounter is positive by asking "how can we make our customer's life easier?" GE asked that question and came up with the idea of GE's Answer Center, a fully staffed customer call center that operates 24 hours a day, offering repair tips and helping owners of GE appliances with their problems.

Which processes deserve the most attention? Keen recommends assigning importance to various processes by classifying them into four categories[4]:

- *Identity* is a process that defines the company; it differentiates a firm from its competitors (e.g., L.L. Bean's order fulfillment, Amazon's one-click ordering, and UNUM [this industry leader in disability insurance defines itself in terms of its processes for pricing risk]).
- *Priority* processes tend to be invisible to customers yet are the source of organizational effectiveness. For a company like FedEx, which defines itself by speed and reliability of package delivery, its aircraft handling would represent a priority process. Southwest Airlines is known for the quick turnarounds of its aircraft at the gate to minimize the time spent on the ground (less than 20 minutes on average). A priority process is the fueling of the planes (see Southwest Airlines example later in the chapter as part of the discussion of benchmarking) and the high level of coordination required among ticket agents, operations agents, ramp agents, mechanics, aircraft cleaners, and caterers to service the planes.
- *Background* processes are necessary to support daily operations, i.e., administrative and overhead functions.
- *Mandated* processes are carried out only because the company is legally required to do so.

Keen also recommends determining a process's worth by determining whether it returns more money than it costs.

Another approach that can be used for evaluating processes is the *value chain* (also referred to as supply chain). Michael Porter proposed the value chain as a tool for identifying ways to create greater customer value. Porter identified nine interrelated primary and secondary generic processes common to a wide variety of firms (see Table 3.2).[5] According to Porter, an organization achieves a competitive advantage by managing its value chain more efficiently or more effectively than its competitors do. Once the generic value chain is specified, relevant firm-specific activities can be identified. Process flows can then be mapped and used to isolate individual value-creating activities. Linkages among the activities should also be identified. A linkage exists when the performance or cost of one activity affects that of another and a competitive advantage may be realized by optimizing and coordinating these linked activities.

With the emergence of e-commerce, information is being used to extend and enhance a firm's physical value chain. The *virtual value chain* is the digital, networked, virtual world of information, which parallels the tangible world of goods and services or the physical supply chain.[6]

Table 3.2   The Generic Value Chain

Process	Primary	Support
1. Inbound logistics	X	
2. Operations	X	
3. Outbound logistics	X	
4. Marketing and sales	X	
5. Service	X	
6. Firm infrastructure		X
7. Human resource management		X
8. Technology development		X
9. Procurement		X

Source: From Porter, M. (1985) *Competitive Advantage: Creating and Sustaining Superior Performance*, New York: The Free Press.

Herman Miller, the large office furniture manufacturer, has successfully exploited the virtual value chain when it comes to order fulfillment. When an order is received, it is immediately sent via the Web to a factory in Michigan or California. Once the order has been transmitted, a manufacturing date is set and space on a truck is reserved to deliver the order a week or two later. The dealer and customer are notified via an e-mail confirmation within 2 hours of the delivery and installation time.

One of the most visible differences between a process-driven enterprise and a traditional organization is the existence of *process owners*. Managers must be given end-to-end responsibility for individual processes; to succeed, they must have real responsibility for and authority over designing the process, measuring its performance, and training the frontline workers who perform it. Hammer recommends that process ownership be a permanent role in order to evolve as business conditions change, and process owners should guide that evolution.[7]

As an example, a successful Canadian hotel chain significantly improved guest relations by asking managers to take ownership of key processes (see customer value insight 3.2). Canadian Pacific Hotels applied process mapping to the cycle of service to determine ways to add value to their guests' experiences (see customer value action item 8 at the end of this chapter).

──────────────── ▼▲▼ ────────────────

CUSTOMER VALUE INSIGHT 3.2: PROCESS IN FOCUS

When Canadian Pacific Hotels set about to gain a competitive advantage through closer relations with business travelers, it realized that it needed to realign its organization around team-based processes that cut across functions. With 27 hotels in the quality tier across Canada, Canadian Pacific Hotels has been proficient with conventions, corporate meetings, and group travel but wanted to excel with business travelers. This is a notoriously demanding and difficult group to serve but also very lucrative and much coveted by all other hotel chains. When conducting in-depth research on this important market segment, it found that frequent guest programs had little appeal because these road warriors preferred airline mileage. They also appreciated beyond-the-call-of-duty efforts to rectify problems when they happened. What they mostly wanted was recognition of their individual preferences and lots of flexibility on when to arrive and check out.

Canadian Pacific Hotels responded by committing to customers in its frequent-guest club that it would make extraordinary efforts always to satisfy their preferences for type of bed, location in hotel (high or low), and all the other amenities. Delivering on this promise proved remarkably difficult. It began by mapping each step of the guest experience, from check-in and parking valet to check-out, and set a standard of performance for each activity. Then it looked to see what had to be done to deliver on the commitment to personalized service. What services should be offered? What processes were needed? What did staff need to do or learn to make the process work flawlessly?

A major challenge was its historic bias toward handling large tour groups, so the skills and processes at hand were not the ones needed to satisfy individual executives who did not want to be asked about their needs every time they checked in. Even small enhancements such as free local calls or gift shop discounts required significant changes in information systems. The management structure was changed so that each hotel had a champion with broad, cross-functional authority to ensure the hotel lived up to its ambitious commitment. Finally, it put further systems and incentives in place to make sure every property was in compliance and performance was meeting or exceeding the standards. In a business that demands consistent attention to innumerable details, no single factor determines whether a customer will be loyal. It is the sum of many elements that makes the difference and the market rewards the effort. In 1996, Canadian Pacific Hotels' share of Canadian business travel jumped by 16%, although the total market was up just 3% and Canadian Pacific Hotels had added no new properties. By all measures it is winning greater loyalty from its target segment.

▲▼▲

Managers should first take a "big picture" view of the company by looking at key processes in relationship to the marketing cycle. Figure 3.2 shows this cycle and how it relates to business processes and process indicators. Note that various market constituents such as customers, suppliers, and publics determine how and to what extent the marketing cycle

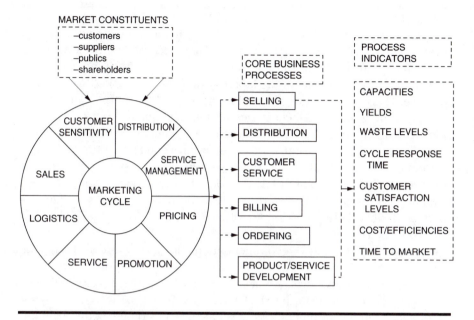

Figure 3.2 The Marketing Cycle and Process Model

elements are performed. Customers, in particular, determine the composition and nature of the marketing cycle and the subsequent core processes required to support these selected marketing cycle functions. For example, the customer service process is performed as part of the service management function of the marketing cycle. Customer service activities would include, but not be limited to, such activities as tracking and trending customer complaints; recovery from customer service failures; and establishing customer service standards.

The process indicators represent the metrics for measuring the core processes. One of the process indicators for the customer service process is gauging customer satisfaction levels. Many banks are now including customer retention as part of their service management process and for good reason. A 5% increase in retention can mean an increase of up to 85% in bank profitability.[8] It should also be pointed out that a synergy exists within the marketing cycle elements. That is, process breakdown in one area, such as logistics, affects other areas such as distribution.

Assessing Process Effectiveness

Dr. W. Edwards Deming pioneered the use of statistical tools and sampling methods for use in product and process quality control. Much of Deming's work in these areas was applied during World War II to improve productivity for the U.S. war effort. Yet, after the war many of his applications never appeared in the American workplace because many companies considered them time consuming and unnecessary. However, Deming's work found wide acceptance in Japan, where he was asked to join the Japanese Union of Scientists and Engineers (JUSE) in the late 1940s. Eventually, he would conduct a series of statistical quality control seminars in Japan, which would later accelerate the movement of Japanese industry into a statistical quality control phase of improvement.

Deming's quality philosophy finally resonated with corporate America in the mid-1980s, as quality of U.S. products and services began to sag. Deming more broadly articulated his views on quality in his now famous Fourteen Points. (Also, see Table 5.1 in Chapter 5 for a more detailed discussion of Deming's 14 points).[9]

One of Dr. Deming's recommendations in his Fourteen Points of Management is for businesses to create a constancy of purpose by continually improving products, services, and processes. *Kaizen,* or continuous improvement, is at the heart of Deming's quality philosophy, relying on innovative and incremental changes to satisfy customers better. Deming argued that products, services, and processes should be continually redesigned and improved for quality. Building on the early work of Shewhart, Deming introduced his PDCA (plan, do, check, act) framework, which helps organizations identify opportunities for process improvement and control.[10] Figure 3.3 illustrates the four separate but linked activities for stabilizing and improving processes.

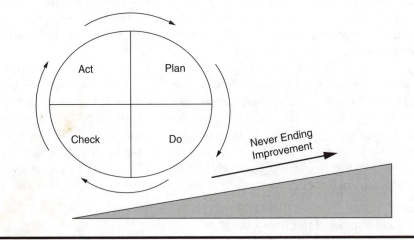

Figure 3.3 The Deming Cycle

The *PDCA* (or Deming) *cycle* is a continuous sequence of activities that, although deceptively simple, represents a powerful decision-making tool for effecting organizational change. Each of these four activities is held in equal balance and is equally important. That is, if you plan but never do, you will not improve. Moreover, the cycle indicates that the task of process improvement is never finished because past results drive future action.

Plan

The first step in the process is *planning*, which involves examining how the type of value firms offer their customers affects their processes. An alignment between the value that customers want and the value the process generates indicates overall effectiveness. A useful tool for representing value attributes and core processes is the value deployment matrix (see Figure 3.4).[11] To ensure that a fit exists between value and process,

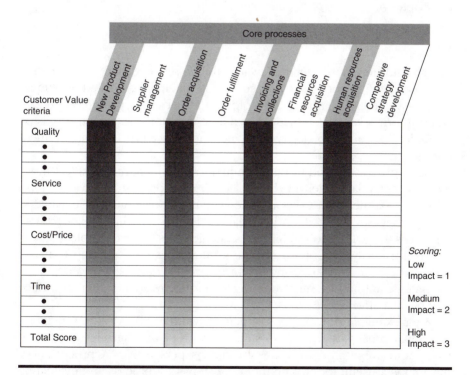

Figure 3.4 Value Deployment Matrix (From Band, W. [1995] *Mark. Manage.*, 4(3), 54. With permission.)

a value statement should be developed that answers the question: "What do we do for our customers and why should they use us instead of our competition?"

A firm's value statement should carry a strong, differentiated appeal to its customers about how its offer differs from its competitors' relative to price/performance characteristics. For example, Southwest Airlines' value statement communicates fun, speed, and economy. Circuit City's value statement suggests not just low prices but also exceptional service ("where service is state of the art"). Simmons College Graduate School of Management's value statement clearly limits what it does and who it serves: a graduate business program exclusively for women. Starbuck's value statement implies reinventing a commodity product as a high-quality, high-price beverage for image-conscious, upscale buyers. Finally, the Charles Schwab & Company value statement consists of delivering low price and convenient investment trading through highly automated systems. Other examples of value statements (also called value propositions) are reviewed in Chapter 4.

Do

The second step in the Deming cycle is the *do* phase, dealing with process design and congruency issues. Once a value statement is created or refined, processes need to be assessed according to their efficacy and congruence with the firm's value statement. A series of questions, such as those listed in Table 3.3, can help determine where to direct process improvement efforts.

Next, processes need to be examined to help identify and select those with the potential to deliver the greatest impact on customer value. John Feather, a partner with Corporate Renaissance, a management consulting group, suggests using a grid similar to Figure 3.5 that isolates those processes that will yield the highest strategic gains.[11] For example, process C, which directly supports the value statement, is ineffective in terms of process performance. Focusing on this process should be a priority, given its strategic importance relative to the value statement and should produce significant performance gains if improved.

After examining processes for their fit with the firm's value statement, individual processes should be studied in order to determine their relevance and importance from the customer's perspective. A process flow diagram is a useful tool for defining the steps of a process and evaluating the importance of those steps in creating customer value. Blueprinting the steps of the process in this fashion helps visualize conceptually not only which steps are performed but also the timing and sequencing of

Table 3.3 Process Assessment

Process Design Issues	Key Management Questions
What?	What are the customer requirements?
Where?	Where do process inefficiencies exist?
When?	When do processes start and end? When is each process activity performed?
Who?	Who is assigned process ownership?
Why?	Why does the process exist? Why organize around the process this way?
Would?	Would the customer be willing to pay for steps performed in the process?
Does?	Does the process (or steps in the process) bring us closer to delivering the service to the customer?
How?	How significant is the process? How does the process support the value?

relationships in the process. A process flow diagram also helps to identify "fail points" or steps in the process likely to go wrong.

Figure 3.5 shows an example of a flow-diagram exercise for a travel services firm. Some other benefits of flowcharting a process include:[13]

- Focusing on the customer and his/her expectations and experiences
- Showing how the technical procedures relate to administrative and relationship building activities of product or service delivery
- Identifying activities that can be proceduralized as well as those that must be individualized and given special attention
- Identifying gaps in the market that need to be addressed
- Showing staff members how their own activities relate to one another

MBNA Corp, the fourth largest credit-card issuer in the U.S., keeps its customers twice as long as the industry average by focusing on critical items that it believes to be break-point issues to its customers, including answering every phone call within two rings and processing every credit-line increase request within an hour.

Finally, process measures need to be developed. Measures are more relevant to management when they are tied to specific processes. The processes selected by a company will vary depending on the type of business; nevertheless, someone in the company needs to take ownership over the results.[14]

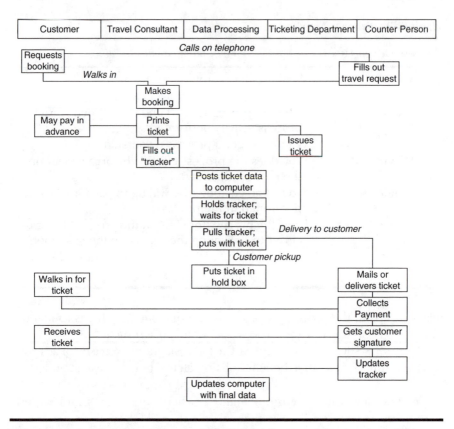

Figure 3.5 Service Flow Diagram (From Albrecht, K. [1990] *Service Within***, Homewood, IL: Irwin. With permission.)**

Figure 3.6 shows business processes linked to customer needs for the General Business Systems Division of AT&T, along with appropriate metrics for each process. Realize that there needs to be a strong linkage between customer needs and the internal metrics developed to assess the underlying process. Tracking these internal metrics is very useful, leading to process improvement and, more importantly, enhanced customer service quality.

Check

The third step in the Deming cycle is *check*. Once processes are evaluated for their value-creating effectiveness and measures are developed, then data-driven tools can be used to monitor, inspect, and improve them on a routine basis. Table 3.4 lists some common tools for measuring, monitoring, controlling, and improving process quality. Benchmarking, which compares a company's own practices (processes or tasks) against similar practices of

Business Process		Customer Need	Internal Metric
Overall Quality	Product (30%)	Reliability (40%)	% Repair Call
		Easy to use (20%)	% Calls for Help
		Features/Functions (40%)	Function/Performance Test
	Sales (30%)	Knowledge (30%)	Supervisor Observations
		Response (25%)	% Proposal Made On Time
		Follow-Up (10%)	% Follow-Up Made
	Installation (10%)	Delivery Interval (30%)	Average Order Interval
		Does Not Break (30%)	% Repair Reports
		Installed When Promised (10%)	% Installed on Due Date
	Repair (15%)	No Repeat Trouble (30%)	% Repeat Reports
		Fixed Fast (25%)	Average Speed of Repair
		Kept Informed (10%)	% Customers Informed
	Billing (15%)	Accuracy, No Surprises (45%)	% Billing Inquires
		Resolve on First Call (35%)	% Resolved First Call
		Easy to Understand (10%)	% Billing Inquiries

Figure 3.6 Strategic Marketing Information Used to Focus Business Processes (Adapted from Kordupleski, R. et al. [1993] *Calif. Manage. Rev.,* **35(3), 89.)**

Table 3.4 Tools of Process Improvement

Process Tool	Purpose
Benchmarking	Measuring and comparing process results to a standard of excellence (see Figure 3.7)
Data collection tools (surveys, sampling, check sheets)	Document internal and external customer assumptions and perceptions about appropriateness and effectiveness of a process and reveal unstable processes
Control chart	Identify stability, capability, and central tendency of a process (see Figure 3.8)
Scatter diagram	Show graphically the relationship between process performance data and some overall performance measure such as customer satisfaction or service quality (see Figure 3.9)
Pareto chart	Separate the "vital few" causes of process failures (see Figure 3.10)
Fishbone diagram	Show possible causes of process shortcomings or weaknesses (see Figure 3.11)

firms recognized as superior in these areas, is the most important tool for evaluating and improving processes. By comparing itself against the best possible practices, the benchmarking firm seeks to identify gaps between its current processes and processes that should be implemented.

According to Camp, benchmarking is a process of consistently researching new ideas for methods, practices, and processes, adopting the practices or adapting their good features, and then implementing them to obtain the "best of the best."[15] When this is done persistently for each company process, management can determine where improvements are possible and then realistically assess how much improvement is possible. Benchmarking does not set hard goals for how much progress is feasible, but it does provide a source of rich ideas for improvement that go beyond internal experience. The upshot is that benchmarking facilitates the search for practices that will lead to superior industry performance.

Besides uncovering industry-best practices, benchmarking offers others advantages. For example, benchmarking may help identify technological breakthroughs that might otherwise have gone unrecognized. Although benchmarking traditionally focuses within an industry, many firms look outside the industry for breakthroughs in process redesign. For example, Xerox gained knowledge of warehousing and materials-handling operations technology by studying L.L. Bean.

Benchmarking also enables companies to meet customer requirements more adequately, leading to higher customer satisfaction. In addition, it helps firms determine true measures of productivity; isolating the factors leading to higher productivity can facilitate process simplification and redesign. Finally, benchmarking helps firms attain a competitive position. Although some organizations view benchmarking as a fad (28%), most companies clearly endorse the benchmarking concept; 79% believe they must benchmark to survive and 95% feel they do not know how to benchmark effectively.[16]

Which companies are worthy of being benchmarked? Of course, that depends on the particular core process. Table 3.5 reveals a list of companies that excel in applying quality practices in selected core processes and thus represent ideal candidates for process benchmarking. Companies considered ideal candidates for benchmarking should also be of similar size or attract similar customers. For example, Northern Telecom, the Canadian telecommunications giant, benchmarked other high-tech companies, not just other telecommunication companies.

How is benchmarking conducted? In *Benchmarking: the Search for Industry Best Practices That Lead to Superior Performance*, Camp describes a benchmarking process, looking at a range of business processes across a range of different industries (see Figure 3.7).[17] The generic benchmarking process is divided into two parts: benchmark metrics and benchmark

Table 3.5   Exemplar Companies in Selected Service Marketing Areas

Core Processes to be Benchmarked	Companies
Customer loyalty management	Starwood Hotels and Resorts, Pizza Hut
Sales and service support	Maytag, IBM
Order fulfillment	L.L. Bean, Dell Computer
Logistics	Ryder, UPS
Transaction processing	Amazon.com, eBay
New service development	Disney, Charles Schwab
Customer database management	Harrah's Entertainment, Inc., American Express
Procurement	Wal-Mart, General Electric
Customer service	Lands' End, Ritz-Carlton

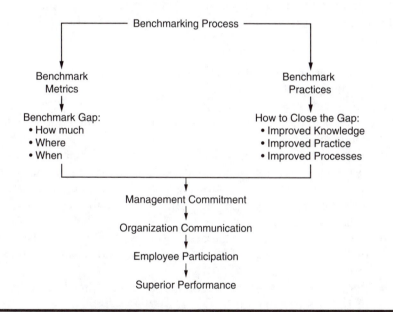

Figure 3.7   Generic Benchmarking Process (Adapted from Camp, R. [1989] *Benchmarking: the Search for Industry Best Practices That Lead to Superior Performance*, **Milwaukee, WI: ASQC Quality Press.)**

practices. Metrics represent the best practices in quantified form and practices are the methods used to perform a process. Benchmarking should begin by investigating industry practices first. Once industry practices are understood, they can be quantified to show their numeric effect. Benchmarking must also be understood by the organization in order to obtain the commitment necessary to take action. Management commits to benchmarking by communicating its importance to employees and securing their participation, leading to the ultimate goal of benchmarking: superior business performance.

Perhaps the most difficult part of benchmarking is to identify the variables/issues to be benchmarked. The key to determining what is to be benchmarked is to identify the *result* of the business process. For example, the marketing cycle function of logistics consists of several strategic deliverables such as the level of customer satisfaction expected; the inventory level to be maintained; and the desired cost level to be achieved. These deliverables serve as a starting point for benchmarking, at which point each of these would need to be broken down further into specific activities to be benchmarked. Customer satisfaction may be benchmarked by investigating factors responsible for customer satisfaction, such as service response time and reliability, as well as professionalism, competence, and empathy of the service worker.

Finally, several common denominators are used in the benchmarking process:

- Know your operations thoroughly, assessing the strengths and weaknesses of your internal processes.
- Know industry leaders or competitors. Why are they better and how much better are they? What do they do that can be adopted by your company?
- Learn from the industry leaders and emulate their strengths. For example, Southwest Airlines looked to Formula One racing when it wanted to improve its refueling process. Adopting Formula One turnaround processes used during pit stops, Southwest can now refuel an airplane in 12 minutes.
- Use benchmarking as a proactive tool by looking not only at competitors, but also at what customers value and how other practices meet those needs.
- Benchmarking needs to be continuous and institutionalized as part of the company culture.

Although benchmarking is an important technique for improving business processes, other tools should also be employed (review Table 3.4). For example,

- *Data collection tools* such as surveys or checklists can be extremely helpful in assessing customers' views of your business processes, especially the importance and relevance of specific activities and tasks. Typical information obtained from surveys or checklists includes: (1) what happens; (2) how it happens; (3) how often it happens; (4) how long it takes; and (5) how important it is.

■ *Control charts* are useful for monitoring the performance of a process by reporting measurements that are predictable within a given process and those that are random in nature. Control charts usually show fluctuations within a process that occur within control limits. Points that fall outside the control limit range should be reported or investigated (see Figure 3.8).

■ A *scatter diagram* examines two variables at one time to determine the relationship existing between them. The graphic display can help to determine possible process fail points or to measure the results of recently changed processes. For example, a direct mail company might want to use a scatter diagram in order to understand better how order fulfillment time is related to customer retention (see Figure 3.9).

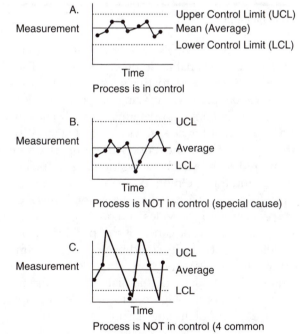

Figure 3.8 Control Chart Example

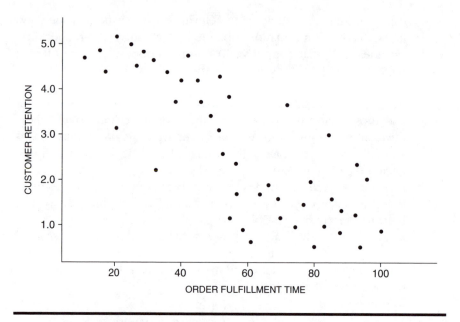

Figure 3.9   Scatter Diagram

- *Pareto charts* are used when it is necessary to determine the relative importance of certain variables in process variation. They help isolate the vital few (as opposed to the trivial many) causes of process variation. For example, by analyzing its online banking customers' deposit activities, a bank can determine which customers represent the greatest potential for new services (see Figure 3.10).
- The *fishbone* (or cause and effect) *diagram* is useful in process analysis and redesign by stimulating thinking about a process under investigation and thus helping to organize thoughts into a rationale whole. The fishbone diagram documents the level of understanding about a process and provides a framework for expanding an understanding of the root cause of the problem. A hospital experiencing delays in lab results could begin by first defining the *effect* (i.e., lab result delays) and then brainstorming the *causes* by diagramming the "bones" of the fish (i.e., equipment, policies, procedures, and people). Figure 3.11 provides a graphic representation between a problem and its potential causes.

Act

The final step in the Deming cycle is *act*. Based on data collected using the process improvement tools described, corrective actions should be

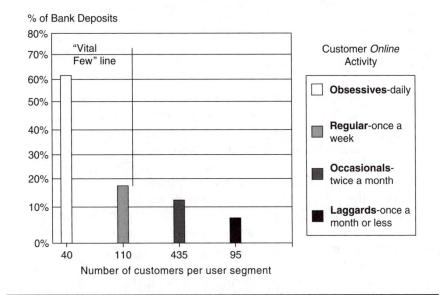

Figure 3.10 Pareto Chart (Online Banking)

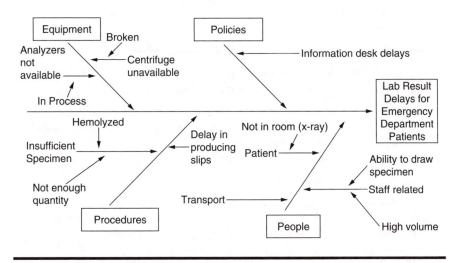

Figure 3.11 Fishbone Diagram

taken to improve processes that fail to add value. Listed below are five ways to improve business processes:[18]

■ Eliminate tasks altogether if it has been determined that they are unnecessary.

- Simplify the work by eliminating all nonproductive elements of a task.
- Combine tasks, where appropriate.
- Change the sequencing to improve the speed and execution.
- Perform activities simultaneously.

Savin Corporation, a large copier company, conducted a careful analysis and found that call backs were related to deficiencies in the training process (call backs are situations in which technicians are sent out on repeated service calls). Pareto diagrams were prepared depicting service engineers responsible for the largest number of call backs. It was determined that training only five engineers reduced call backs by 19%. In most cases, the people who perform the processes are the ones most capable of determining how to improve or simplify them. Management must create a culture that values employee input and rewards people for process innovation.

Once a process improvement has been made, the change must be measured and evaluated for effectiveness. Comparing before and after indicators would be useful here as well as comparing results with the targeted performance. Also, efforts should be made to celebrate and reward those participating in the process improvement activity (see customer value checklist 3.1)

––––––––––––––––––– ▼▲▼ –––––––––––––––––––

CUSTOMER VALUE CHECKLIST 3.1: KEY SUCCESS FACTORS FOR IMPROVING BUSINESS PROCESSES

The following questions represent some key factors in developing processes that are truly value-added. Does a "yes" or "no" response most closely fit your company's situation?

Does your company organize around value-added processes, not tasks?	Y or N
Do those who use the output of the process perform the task (that is, are the people closest to the process the ones who actually perform the activity)?	Y or N
Does your company put the decision point where the work is performed and build control into the process?	Y or N
Does your company capture information once and at the source where it was created?	Y or N
Does your company design processes in cooperation with customers?	Y or N
Does your company "blueprint" the process cycle, defining not only steps performed in the process, but also the timing and sequencing of relationships of those steps?	Y or N
Does your company regularly practice process simplification to remove unnecessary and bureaucratic procedures?	Y or N

Does your company utilize appropriate process measurements
(i.e., cycle response time, customer satisfaction, etc.)?   Y or N
Does your company reward process improvement efforts?   Y or N

▲▼▲

SUMMARY

As organizations enter the 21st century networked economy, dramatic shifts are occurring in information technologies and network capabilities that are transforming how firms connect with their internal as well as external customers. The effective use of process integration is enabling firms to organize in new ways and to manage supply chains and business relationships better. Survivors in the new economy will be companies that can clearly define their processes; organize around those key processes rather than functions; and effectively integrate their processes with their supply chain partners.

Companies today are integrating their processes across the supply chain by using networks, shared databases, intranets, and the Internet in order to share information about customer requirements, delivery schedules, etc. instantly. Where a high level of process integration occurs, information is made available in real time to all members of the supply chain simultaneously. As never before, many companies now consider processes to be strategic assets. Witness how some dot-com firms like Amazon.com have jealously protected their process technology through patents and litigation. Processes represent more than simply the operations of the company, but rather serve as a means to superior performance.[19]

CUSTOMER VALUE ACTION ITEMS

1. Describe the relationship between process and value.
2. How does the process view differ from the functional view?
3. Explain how you would use the marketing cycle and process model to analyze your current business situation.
4. Explain the purpose of the Deming cycle for assessing process effectiveness.
5. What questions would you ask if your company were currently undergoing a review of its processes?
6. A maker of karaoke machines for the commercial and consumer markets, the Singing Machine, is looking for ways to add value to its retail and end-user customers. How can this company exploit the "virtual value" chain to deliver greater value to retailers (e.g., Best Buy, Circuit City) as well as consumers?

7. What is service "blueprinting" and when is it appropriate to use?
8. Suppose you are the manager of a quick serve restaurant and you begin to notice that your lunch business is steadily declining. Moreover, you notice that customers are lining up longer at the drive-through window. Which of the process improvement tools would you consider using and why?
9. The next two applications involve the use of the various process tools:

Application A

The following raw data represent complaints from a recent study conducted among customers of a large car rental firm, based on their most recent car rental experiences. Suppose you are called in as a consultant in order to isolate the most critical factors so as to improve service quality in the future. Construct a Pareto diagram from the raw data and make recommendations based on your analysis.

Long Lines At Counter	Popular Models Unavailable	Priced Too High	Vehicle Cleanliness
_/_/_/_/_/	_/_/_/_/_/	_/_/_/_/_/	_/_/_/_/_/
_/_/_/_/_/	_/_/_/_/_/	_/_/_/_/_/	_/_/_/_/_/
_/_/_/_/_/	_/_/_/_/_/	_/_/_/	_/_/_/_/_/
_/_/_/_/_/	_/_/_/_/_/		_/_/_/_/
_/_/_/_/_/	_/_/_/_/_/		
_/_/_/	_/_/_/_/_/		
	_/_/_/_/_/		

Application B

Naturally Yours, a small health food producer in the Midwest, was facing a severe decline in profits. The company packages and sells wholesome snack foods, such as potato chips, salsa chips, pretzels, crackers, just to name a few. Naturally Yours' two plants are responsible for producing the total product line, consisting of 42 snack-related items, most of which carry a premium price due to the higher quality ingredients used. The company president recently remarked, "Profitability will only result from running our plants at capacity. Adding new products to utilize our excess capacity will allow us to spread our costs over a greater volume."

Most of the company's products are distributed through national and mom-and-pop health food stores. The company has a line-forcing policy, requiring any store wanting to carry its snack foods to be willing to carry the entire Naturally Yours product line. Many of the smaller health food stores refuse to carry the company's line because of this stocking policy.

Average retail inventory turnover for the company's snack line is 22 times, vs. the industry average of 25.

Naturally Yours uses limited trade magazine advertising and attends one trade show annually. The company employs 11 salespeople who call on the national chains, such as GNC, or natural food brokers, who service the smaller health food stores. (Note: many of the large national chains are beginning to stock and promote their own labels.) The company president issued a terse memo concerning inadequate market coverage of their products, blaming this failure on the salespeople. The company has very little leverage with their suppliers, given their relatively low volume of purchases.

You are called in as a consultant to this firm. Your task is to identify the problem and symptoms facing this company. Prepare a Fishbone diagram to guide you in formulating your response.

REFERENCES

1. "Does the e-marketplace fit into your business plan?" (2001) http://www-1.ibm.com/services/feature/emarket.html.
2. Mroz, R. (1998) Unifying marketing: the synchronous marketing process, *Ind. Mark. Manage.*, 27, 259.
3. McCormack, K. and Johnson, W. (2001) *Business Process Orientation: Gaining the E-Business Competitive Advantage*, Boca Raton, FL: CRC/St. Lucie Press.
4. Keen, P. (1997) *The Process Edge*, Boston, MA: Harvard Business School Press.
5. Porter, M. (1985) *Competitive Advantage: Creating and Sustaining Superior Performance*, New York: The Free Press.
6. Rayport, J. and Sviokla, J. (1995) Exploiting the virtual value chain, *Harvard Bus. Rev.*, 73(6), Nov–Dec, 76.
7. Hammer, M. and Stanton, S. (1999) How process enterprises really work, *Harvard Bus. Rev.*, 77(6), Nov–Dec, 109.
8. Zion Boosts Customer Service (2003) *Desert News*, Feb. 20, p. D10.
9. Deming, E. (1986) *Out of Crisis*, Cambridge, MA: MIT Center for Advanced Engineering Study.
10. Shewhart, W.A. (1931) *Economic Control of Quality of Manufactured Product*, New York: Van Nostrand.
11. Band, W. (1995) Customer-accelerated change, *Mark. Manage.*, 4(3), 54.
12. Feather, J. (1998) Using value analysis to target customer service process improvements, *IIE Solutions*, May, 33–39.
13. Congram, C. (1991) Focuses on the customer, in *The Handbook of Services Marketing*, New York: The American Management Association, 479–490.
14. Kordupleski, R., Rust, R., and Zahorik, T. (1993) Why improving quality doesn't improve quality, *Calif. Manage. Rev.*, Spring, 82–95.
15. Camp, R. (1989) *Benchmarking: The Search for Industry Best Practices That Lead to Superior Performance*, Milwaukee, WI: ASQC Quality Press.
16. Sprow, E. (1993) Benchmarking: it's time to stop tinkering with manufacturing and start clocking yourself against the best, *Manuf. Eng.*, 111(3), 58.

17. Camp, R. (1989) *Benchmarking: The Search for Industry Best Practices That Lead to Superior Performance*, Milwaukee, WI: ASQC Quality Press.
18. Johnson, W. and Chvala, R. (1995) *Total Quality in Marketing*, Boca Raton, FL: St. Lucie Press.
19. McCormack, K. and Johnson, W. (2001) *Business Process Orientation: Gaining the E-Business Competitive Advantage*, Boca Raton, FL: CRC/St. Lucie Press.

II

CREATING VALUE THROUGH SERVICES AND E-COMMERCE

4

THE SERVICE SECTOR AND THE NEW ECONOMY

It's no longer about the Information Age. It's about the age of your information.

KPMG advertisement, Wall Street Journal, *November 7, 2000*

Everything we ever said about the Internet is happening.

Andrew S. Grove, Intel Corporation

Service opportunities create value in business and consumer markets. In addition, services affect all aspects of people's lives and drive advanced economies. Many experts feel that the next economic wave is imminent — a transition into an information-led economy. It has been estimated that about 50% of work in industrialized countries is knowledge work.[1]

Nicholas Negroponte, author of *Being Digital*, explains it best by saying that in the future, when people talk about products, they will more likely be talking about bits than atoms.[2] Internet companies such as Ameritrade, DoubleClick, and Earthlink have clearly demonstrated the rewards of competing in marketspace as opposed to the marketplace. Today, a Web site presence is about as commonplace as a listing in the Yellow Pages.

According to Jupiter Research, online retail spending in the U.S. will grow by 28% in 2003 to $52 billion. Furthermore, it is projected to reach $105 billion by 2007, account for 5% of total U.S. retail spending, and influence more than a third of retail sales.[3] Even more significant is the business-to-business arena for e-commerce transactions. Aron Sharma explains that worldwide business-to-business (B2B) transactions are estimated to be about $800 billion for 2003 (five times as much as the business-to-consumer marketspace). Dr. Sharma adds that the establishment of an Internet presence in B2B markets means an evolution through five stages — information, knowledge, conversation, relationship, and e-commerce.[4]

The Progressive Policy Institute (PPI), Washington, D.C., recently completed a major research study that measured the new economy on a statewide basis. The project used 21 weighted indicators in five categories to capture the essence of the economic structure of the U.S. Table 4.1 summarizes these key factors. Based on composite scores of greater than 70, nine states — Massachusetts, Washington, California, Colorado, Maryland, New Jersey, Connecticut, Virginia, and Delaware — can now be considered active participants or progressives in the new economy. Nine other states – West Virginia, Mississippi, Arkansas, Alabama, Wyoming, Louisiana, North Dakota, South Dakota, and Kentucky — have aggregate scores of less than 50; these laggards are still firmly rooted in the old economy. The remaining 32 states score between 50 and 70; these states are taking definite strides toward entering the new economy.[5]

Table 4.1   New Economy Indicators

Knowledge Jobs	Globalization	Dynamism and Competition	Digital Economy	Innovation Infrastructure
IT professionals	Export orientation	"Gazelle" jobs	Online population	High-tech employment
Professional and manufacturing jobs	(FDI) foreign direct investment	Job churning	.com domain names	Scientists and engineers
Manufacturing workforce education		IPOs	Technology in schools	Patents
			Digital government	R & D
			Farms and technology	Venture capital
			Manufacturing and technology	
			Broadband	

Source: Adapted from Atkinson, R.D. (2002) Technology, innovation, and new economy project, www.ppionline.org, June.

Today's new, hybrid economy consists of three major components:

- The traditional economy (agriculture, construction, manufacturing, wholesale and retail trade, etc.)
- A dominant services sector
- A technology-based economy (high-tech firms, information-based businesses, and Web-based companies)

This chapter first addresses the changing economy via a brief look at the North American industrial classification system. Second, it probes further into the expanding services sector and important services marketing issues. Third, it discusses the Internet phenomenon and concludes with guidelines for developing winning CV strategies in the new economy.

RESHAPING THE TRADITIONAL ECONOMY: THE NORTH AMERICAN INDUSTRIAL CLASSIFICATION SYSTEM

Standard industrial classification (SIC) codes that served marketers well for many years, was recently replaced by a more relevant coding system, the North American-industrial-classification-system (NAICS — rhymes with snakes). In existence for more than 60 years, SIC codes transitioned from a U.S. government statistical data facilitator to a customer/supplier tool for business marketing. In its current incarnation, NAICS is an evolving, responsive industry categorization tool that is useful for forecasting, market share analysis, research, segmentation, and strategic planning. Such marketing activities are insightful in analyzing customers and potential opportunities for creating value.

NAICS has several notable improvements over SIC. There are twice as many major industry groups (there are now 20 categories). A much stronger emphasis on the new economy is reflected by the inclusion of many new services and technology sectors. This results in a more detailed directory consisting of 1170 industries — 358 of which are new and 250 of which are services-producing.[6]

For example, the new information sector, which was not represented in the SIC manual, comprises more than 50 subsectors. The resulting six-digit market identifier, the NAICS code, replaces the basic four-digit SIC code (an example is provided in Table 4.2). As an added bonus, the NAICS system is regional in scope; Canadian and Mexican industry analysis is built into the framework. The beauty of the NAICS system should be its widespread acceptance (note, SIC analysis was a staple part of industrial marketers' toolkits for many years). Many public (Census Bureau) and private (Dun & Bradstreet and Information Access Corporation) marketing

Table 4.2   The NAICS Hierarchy

NAICS Level	Industry Description	NAICS Code
Sector	Information	51
Subsector	Broadcasting, telecommunications	513
Industry group	Telecommunications	5133
Industry	Wireless carriers, except satellite	51332
U.S. industry	Paging	513321

Source: From www.census.gov/epcd/www/naics.html.

references use the NAICS code as a basic data-gathering unit. Therefore, market analysis through multiple sources is feasible.

SERVICE FIRMS CREATE VALUE

Service-producing industries now account for the majority of the gross domestic product (GDP) and jobs in the U.S. and in Australia, Canada, the European Union, Japan, and other industrialized nations. According to research by Kenji Suzuki, Luxembourg generates 79% of its economic activity from the service sector. The U.S. is ranked number two at 74%; it is followed by Greece, Belgium, France, Australia, Denmark, Sweden, Netherlands, and the U.K. All of these countries produce more than 70% of their GDP from services.[7]

The U.S. service sector comprises six major subsectors: (1) transportation and utilities; (2) wholesale trade; (3) retail trade; (4) finance, insurance, and real estate (FIRE); (5) other consumer and business services; and (6) government services. In 1950, more than 40% of U.S. payroll was found in goods-producing industries.[8] In the 23 most advanced countries, employment in manufacturing fell from 28% of the workforce in 1970 to 18% by 1995.[9] Strong evidence of the decline of manufacturing and the transition to a new services economy is shown in Table 4.3.

In the U.S., 87% of projected job growth through 2006 will be in the service sector.[10] Table 4.4 shows that 81% of Americans are now employed in the service-producing industries. Some of the fastest growing service employment opportunities today include business, computer, education, engineering, health care, and security services. Table 4.5 forecasts the "hot" U.S. job opportunities for the year 2010 based on growth rates in percentages and projected new job creation.

Table 4.3   U.S. Manufacturing Losses and Service Gains, 1960–2002

Industrial Sector	Number Employed 1960	Number Employed 2002
(–) Textiles	924,000	433,000
(–) Apparel	1,200,000	522,000
(–) Metal industries	1,200,000	593,000
(+) Education	616,000	2,500,000
(+) Business	656,000	9,300,000
(+) Health	1,500,000	10,700,000

Source: Adapted from Hagenbaugh, B. (2002) *USA Today*, Dec. 13, 1B–2B.

Table 4.4   U.S. Employment Data, 2001

Industrial Sector	Employment (millions)	Employment (percent)
Services, other	41.0	31.0
Retail trade	23.5	17.8
Government	20.9	15.8
Manufacturing	17.7	13.4
Finance, insurance, real estate	7.7	5.8
Transportation and utilities	7.1	5.4
Wholesale trade	6.8	5.2
Construction	6.8	5.2
Mining	.6	.4
Total U.S. employment	132.1	100.0

Note: sectors in italics produce goods; nonitalicized sectors produce service.

Source: Adapted from U.S. Department of Labor, Bureau of Labor Statistics (2002) Industry at a glance, www.dol.gov, August 20.

What Is a Service?

Products can be defined as goods, services, and ideas. Today, there are very few pure goods. Almost all consumer and business products (for example, cars, cell phones, computers, etc.) are packaged with strong service components. This can include a service warranty, monthly rate plan, 24-hour access to technical support, and other service options. In the majority of cases, companies market blended products. A fast food meal is the classic example: although the burger, fries, and Coke are the

Table 4.5   U.S. Job Outlook, 2010

Fastest Growing Careers[a]	Largest Number of Openings
Computer-support specialist	Cashier
Systems analyst	Managers and top executives
Database administrator	Office clerk
Desktop-publishing specialist	Personal care aides
Paralegal and legal assistants	Registered nurse
Personal and home health aide	Retail salesperson
Medical assistant	Teacher's assistant
Social and human health assistants	Truck driver
Physician assistant	

[a] Based on percentage growth.

Source: Adapted from *Chicago Tribune* (2003) www.ajc.com (*Atlanta Journal–Constitution*), January 5.

goods, the service experience (speed, brand image, atmospherics, etc.) is often more highly valued by consumers.

Pure services such as insurance are highly intangible and present unique challenges to marketers. Management consulting is an example of an idea (selling a client a feasibility study or reengineering plan). As Figure 4.1 illustrates, a continuum exists based on the degree of product tangibility. Effective service marketers must be able to make the intangible tangible (this service quality issue is discussed in Chapter 5).

To shed further light on business opportunities in the service sector, a 2 × 2 services classification matrix consisting of four cells and four examples of organizations in each category is presented in Figure 4.2. Two caveats are necessary. First, some companies compete in more than one cell (banks, CPAs, insurance agents, etc.). Second, the term *professional* used in the context of the matrix is to describe firms that have specialized knowledge and advanced education or training. In contrast, professionalism is a critical success factor for all organizations. The automotive detailer who takes 2 days to return telephone calls; shows up an hour late for scheduled appointments; or fails to make a car shine appropriately will not stay in business for long.

Figure 4.1   Three Types of Products

Type of service	Business	Consumer
Professional	Accounting, legal, marketing research, and management consulting	Attorneys, dentists, financial planners, and physicians
Other	Logistics, janitorial, printers, and security	Fast food, hair stylists, lawn care, and pest control

Figure 4.2   Service Classification Matrix (Adapted and expanded from Gronroos, C. [1979] *Ind. Mark. Manage.*, 8, 45–50.)

Service marketers must change in response to changing environmental forces (e.g., societal trends, economic conditions, new technologies, etc.) and market forces such as competition, collaboration, and regulation (see the Chapter 1 appendix on the the customer value funnel). As an example, global leaders such as American Express, Dow Jones, Lufthansa, Nortel, Royal Caribbean Cruises, and United Parcel Service are obsessed with using information to improve customer service. Eight value-adding practices were identified in a recent study[11]:

- Personalization
- Offering tiered service levels
- Collecting information to enhance customer experiences
- Keeping it simple
- Responding to what customers do not like doing
- Providing one-stop shopping
- Balancing customer self-service with support
- Getting to know the customer best

THE EMERGENCE OF THE NEW ECONOMY

According to Michael Dell, there are only two types of companies: the quick and the dead. The Internet has been the major change agent of the new economy during the past decade. In the late 1990s, the Net experienced astronomical growth on several fronts — online users and usage; promotion; public awareness; billions of dollars in venture capital infusion; and Web business start-ups. During this period of *explosive growth* (1995 to 2000), business was typified by excesses that greatly affected profitability: new dot.coms were running $2 million Super Bowl commercials; companies were overinvesting in CRM (customer relationship management) systems, computer technology, and office furniture/furnishings; executives were regularly flying first class; and stock options were liberally dispensed.

From the latter part of 2000 through 2002 (*rapid descent*), it became evident that the much-hyped virtual marketspace (dubbed by some the dot.bomb, dot.con, or dot.gone economy) failed to achieve many of its lofty ambitions. Thousands of online businesses and supporting companies failed; hundreds of thousands of highly educated technology managers were laid off; inflated Internet stocks crashed; and local economies in tech-friendly cities like San Francisco were negatively affected.

By 2003, the dot.com shakeout led to a *re-energization* — a stabilized and growing Web sector that was a part of, but not, the new economy. Online sales are expected to grow 26% to $96 billion in 2003 (representing 4.5% of total retail sales vs. 3.6% in 2002). Currently, about a third of computer hardware and software is sold online, followed by tickets for events (17%), and books (12%). Perhaps more significantly, it took online retailers only 6 years to match the sales level of the catalog industry in 100 years.[12] Eight perceptions and realities about e-business today are summarized in Figure 4.3.

In addition to technology, globalization, and market deregulation, Kotler explains that the major drivers of the new economy include customization; digitalization and connectivity; industry convergence; and new types of intermediaries.[13] CV insight 4.1 explains how Yahoo! successfully evolved and repositioned itself in the new economy.

—————————————▼▲▼—————————————

Customer Value Insight 4.1: Yahoo!'s Shift into Fee-Based Services[14]

Although the dot-com implosion negatively affected many Internet service providers (e.g., in the fourth quarter of 2002, AOL's revenue dropped 50% compared to the earlier year), Yahoo! has successfully reinvented itself in a most challenging economic environment. The company's fourth-quarter revenues were up 51% from a year ago to $286 million. The company's net income was $46 million, beating analyst expectations for three straight quarters.

A major part of Yahoo!'s revitalization has been its foray into paid Web-based services. More than 2.2 million consumers have signed up for online personals; larger e-mail boxes; high-speed Internet access; and more than a dozen other new fee-based services. Recent industry studies indicate that about a third of online users would be willing to pay for content. Yahoo! has capitalized on this finding and built its paid offerings from less than 10% of annual revenues in 2000 to 32% of revenues by the end of 2002. Fee-based revenue in the fourth quarter alone was $89 million — up from $55 million in the first quarter of 2002 — and represents a 120% increase from a year ago.

—————————————▲▼▲—————————————

Perception	Reality
Profitable Internet companies are rare.	About 40% of 200+ public Net companies made a 4th quarter profit in 2002.
IPO investors in e-tailers lost gobs of money.	If you invested $1,000 in every e-tail IPO (including dogs), you would be up about 35%.
Online advertising died.	It is just changing. Banner ads have given way to search-oriented advertising, boosting online advertising to $6.6 billion annually.
Broadband has not gained traction.	U.S. subscriptions are growing 56% and should reach 29 million households by the end of 2003.
B2B e-commerce never really happened.	Although hundreds of business exchanges failed, $3.9 trillion worth of e-commerce will be transacted in 2003 worldwide.
Companies ditched Web efforts amid the tech recession.	Spending on e-business projects has risen every year since the bust and now comprises 27% of all tech spending.
The productivity gain from e-business turned out to be modest.	Productivity growth doubled as the Net proliferated. Most of the acceleration was in industries that use technology, such as automotive.
Web-era productivity gains are confined to tech companies.	More than 80% of post-1995 acceleration is in non-tech industries.

Figure 4.3   Perceptions and Realities of the New Economy (From Mullaney, T.J. et al. [2003] *Bus. Week*, May 12, 60–67.)

In the revamped Internet sector, only companies that provide needed products, services, and technologies and truly deliver superior customer value (given competitive options) will survive in the short term and thrive over the long term. Market leaders in 12 key sectors that have emerged from Net 2.0 include:[15]

- Automotive — CarsDirect.com (new cars), eBay Motors (used cars)
- Banking — Wells Fargo, E-trade Bank
- Business-to-business — Cisco Systems
- Computers — Dell
- Education — University of Phoenix (Apollo Group)
- Entertainment — Real Networks
- Financial services — Lending Tree
- Health — Web MD

- Media — Yahoo! and Google
- Real estate — Realtor.com
- Retail — Amazon.com, eBay
- Travel — Expedia

KEYS TO COMPETING SUCCESSFULLY IN THE NEW ECONOMY

Many of the critical success factors for 21st century organizations are emphasized in this book. For example, 10 imperatives are to:

- Be customer oriented
- Excel in process management
- Design winning value propositions
- Provide outstanding customer service
- Offer innovative and high quality products
- Forge strong relationships with collaborators and customers
- Stress retention marketing (keeping and growing accounts)
- Seek ways to add value for customers continually
- Understand the changing nature of the global business environment
- Have a long-term management perspective

Taken in combination, these marketing initiatives represent the building blocks for developing and implementing an effective, efficient, and adaptable program for customer value management.

A second set of strategic guidelines for management aspiring to become CV market leaders in 2004 and beyond include:

- Differentiate via unique business models
- Hire and retain great employees
- Balance marketing and technology in the organization
- Maximize the usage of the customer database
- Be super-responsive to customers
- Develop an outstanding Internet strategy
- Create a "buzz" for the business

Research by Dutta and Segev found that about two thirds of companies treat the Internet as a publishing medium (corporate Web sites) and another third are content transporting their existing models into cyberspace (engage in e-commerce). They add that few firms have used the Internet effectively to launch new business models; some exceptions have included Amazon, Dell, eBay, and Yahoo!.[16]

Too often, top executives promote weak managers to important positions. They prefer to have "yes-men" that will not question any of their moves even if they are not in the best interest of the organization. These insecure leaders feel threatened by knowledgeable and highly competent free thinkers who may have the guts to question the status quo. Top companies do not fall victim to this trap. As an example, Andy Grove, Chairman of Intel, actively recruits engineers and other corporate managers who are smarter than he is (no small feat) and have new ideas for this semiconductor powerhouse. In addition to finding the talent, the best people need to be properly rewarded via salary, bonus, stock options, stature, or other perks commensurate with their value to the organization.

As Amazon.com has learned, technology can invent or redefine markets in our electronic era. Amazon is generating expanding sales from large retail partners who sell via Amazon's mega Web site such as Babies-"R"Us.com, Marshall Field's, Office Depot, Target, and Toys"R"Us.com.

Many high-tech companies are headed by engineers and scientists; too often these firms place marketing activities on the side burner. Other firms are led by salespeople or entrepreneurs; they know how to generate new business but lack the supporting technological infrastructure to service clients effectively. Hewlett-Packard is a company able to maintain a strong focus on technology, while simultaneously executing its sharp marketing edge. This twofold approach is critical for creating a winning business strategy in the highly competitive and turbulent marketplace/space.

Customers are the most important asset to an organization. Recent customer equity and relationship marketing emphases demonstrate that the value of a firm lies in the long-term value of its customers rather than its brands.[17] Also, the customer database is the rich Swiss bank in which information resources about customers are stored, analyzed, and managed. Amazon, General Electric, and Lands' End are examples of companies that have done an excellent job of utilizing customer data to find new sales opportunities.

Customers want to do business with organizations when and how it is convenient for them to do so. This means any day, any time. The Web naturally lends itself to a 24 hour/7 days a week/365 days a year model and many traditional retailers such as Wal-Mart, McDonald's, and supermarkets are now extending their hours to satisfy changing lifestyles. Service firms are also operating on nights and weekends to better meet customer needs. Bank Atlantic, dubbed "Florida's most convenient bank," is an innovative regional bank based in Ft. Lauderdale, Florida; in addition to 7-day branch banking, the bank offers extended weekday branch hours and 24/7 live customer service. Responsiveness is also evaluated by customers or potential customers as to promptness in returning phone calls; e-mail messages; scheduling appointments; user-friendly Web sites;

personalization; time savings; and product mix. These initiatives offer a major source of competitive advantage (or disadvantage) for organizations.

The Web must be an integral part of every organization's business strategy in the 21st century. The Internet can be used as a sales channel; promotional vehicle; customer service center; market research tool; and community builder. In addition, business marketers can use the Net to connect with remote customers and suppliers; reduce sales and travel expenses; minimize inventory levels; be more productive; and add value (see Chapter 9).

Undoubtedly, the most successful Internet pure play is the online auction company, eBay. This virtual firm has gone from selling Beanie Babies to building billion dollar markets such as used cars and its business and industrial sites. eBay has no real costs of goods — customers hold the inventory, ship the products, and do the marketing — and it is growing exponentially, largely due to the "buzz factor" (see next paragraph). By 2005, this company projects $3 billion in revenues and an astounding $1 billion in profits.[18]

Finally, successful new economy firms provide interesting experiences for their customers. Long-term relationships with these companies are due to very high customer loyalty and retention rates. Valued parts of individuals' lives now might include

- Amazon's personalized mega-retailing site
- eBay's online auction (with its strong focus on community)
- Southwest Airlines' fun flights
- Starbucks' atmospherics and plans to go wireless
- Ben & Jerry's indulgent ice cream
- Harley-Davidson's motorcycle counterculture

These admired or "cool, hip, and happening" companies generate a tremendous amount of positive word-of-mouth promotion and favorable publicity and this creates the buzz that others want to enjoy.

SUMMARY

The new millennium has brought a changing and challenging business environment. E-business, global business, technology companies, and information providers will play a major role in creating value for customers in this service-dominant economy. This chapter provided a wealth of data about the new economy, such as key sectors, indicators, and output measures. The services and Internet components of the new economy were carefully examined and two sets of success factors were offered for 21st century CV managers. In addition, the chapter briefly reviewed important service classification concepts. The next two chapters will extend this discussion by exploring service quality and e-service quality ideas.

CUSTOMER VALUE ACTION ITEMS

1. How does your company's current service mix create value for customers?
   a. What new service products should be introduced that your firm does not offer?
   b. Are there new types of value providers (adders) that your organization should employ to do a better job of serving customers?
   c. Which existing management or staff positions should be restructured or eliminated because they add little or no value to customers?
2. How important is an MBA degree in the new economy? What are some specialty areas that today's/tomorrow's executives will need to master?
3. Across the Web, companies are seeking revenue-generating services/strategies from information. How do you feel about paying for online services that were once free? What are the CV implications of this trend?
4. It has been estimated that Expedia, now the number one leisure travel agency, was responsible for almost 15% of traditional travel agency closings in the year 2002. Is this good or bad for society? Why or why not?
5. Based on the trends discussed in this chapter, how would you envision the U.S. and world economy of 2020? Assume you had to prepare a talk to executives in the pharmaceutical industry.
6. Write an executive summary of a business plan (one to two pages) sketching out your thoughts on a viable online marketing niche opportunity that would create or maximize value for 21st century customers.

REFERENCES

1. Kaplan, R.S. and Norton, D.P. (2001) Building a strategy-focused organization, *Ivey Bus. J.*, May/June, 12–19.
2. Negroponte, N. (1995) *Being Digital*, New York: Alfred A. Knopf.
3. Jupiter Research (2003) Online retail spending to soar in the U.S., www.jupiterresearch.com, January 10.
4. Sharma, A. (2002) Trends in Internet-based business-to-business marketing, *Ind. Mark. Manage.*, 31, 77–84.

5. Atkinson, R.D. (2002) Technology, innovation, and new economy project, www.ppionline.org, June.
6. NAICS Association Newsletter (2002) What are the main differences between NAICS and SIC?, www.naics.com, February.
7. Suzuki, K. (2002) OECD: service sector, share of gross domestic product (GDP [2000]), www.hhs.se/personal/suzuki/default.htm, November 21.
8. Meisenheimer, J.R. (1998) Nonagricultural payroll and employment by industry, annual averages, 1939–97, U.S. Department of Labor, Current Employment Statistics Survey, June 8, Washington, D.C.: Bureau of Labor Statistics.
9. Rowthorn, R. and Ramaswamy, R. (1997) Deindustrialization — its causes and implications, Econ. Issues, 10, Washington, D.C.: International Monetary Fund, 1–8.
10. Franklin, J.C. (1997) Industry output and employment projections to 2006, *Monthly Labor Rev.*, November, 39–57.
11. Willcocks, L.P. and Plant, R. (2001) Pathways to e-business leadership: getting from bricks to clicks, *MIT Sloan Manage. Rev.*, Spring, 50–59.
12. Shop.org/Forrester Research Study (2003) Online sales soar 48 percent in 2002, www.shp.org/press/03051503.html, .
13. Kotler, P. (2003) *Marketing Management*, Upper Saddle River, NJ: Prentice-Hall, 34–38.
14. Swartz, J. (2003) Yahoo soars as rivals fight for balance, *USA Today* January 16, 1B.
15. Kessler, M. et al. (2003) Successful Internet titans set pace for future financial win, *USA Today*, June 23, 3B.
16. Dutta, S. and Segev, A. (1999) Business transformation on the Internet, *Eur. Manage. J.*, 17(5), 466–476.
17. Rust, R.T., Zeithaml, V. and Lemon, K.N. (2000) *Driving Customer Equity: How Customer Lifetime Value Is Reshaping Corporate Strategy*, New York: The Free Press.
18. Schonfeld, E. (2002) eBay's secret ingredient, *Bus. 2.0*, March, 52–58.

5

DEFINING AND MANAGING
SERVICE QUALITY

Quality is a journey, not a destination.

Danielle Clermont

Quality in a service or product is not what you put into it. It is what the customer gets out of it.

Peter Drucker

As shown in Chapter 1, quality is one of the core components of value. Along with price, product and service quality serve as foundations for the value triad. Today, many feel that quality is still a powerful competitive force facing U.S. companies. In a recent American Management Association survey of North American, Western European, and Japanese managers, 78% indicated that improving quality and service to customers is the key to competitive success. Kenneth Case, president of the American Society for Quality (ASQ), identified seven key forces that will influence quality in the future[1]:

- Quality must deliver bottom-line results.
- Management systems will increasingly absorb the quality function.
- Quality will be everyone's job.
- The economic case for a broader application of quality will need to be proved.
- Global demand for products and services will create a global work-force.

- Trust and confidence in business leaders and organizations will decline.
- Customer expectations will rise.

The search for quality is arguably the most important business trend of the past two decades because demanding customers have come to expect fast, reliable and friendly service. Disney Chairman Michael Eisner established the Disney Vision of Excellence — Quality, Service and Smiles, a value proposition that inspires service personnel to deliver a memorable customer experience. This chapter explains what quality is (and what it is not); the essentials of service quality; why quality is important; and how to improve service quality. Although quality is examined here in a "generic" fashion, the emphasis in the discussion will clearly be on *service quality*.

WHAT IS QUALITY?

Today, many products and services have become standardized; even private label brands meet or exceed minimum standards. Modern communications permit and, in some cases, encourage customers to shift their patronage from one producer to another. Global competition has resulted in increased choice and has raised customer expectations of what constitutes acceptable quality. Marketing is a contest for the consumer's attention and the Internet is now competing for that attention as the number of Internet users worldwide continues to rise — by 48% in 2000 and 27% in 2001 to more than 10% in 2002. According to researcher IDC, Internet trade between companies and online retail spending also rose 73% (to $496 billion) and 56% (to $112 billion), respectively, from 2000 to 2001.[2]

The Internet has shifted power away from businesses to consumers, who can quickly compare products and prices from a range of suppliers. Now competition is "just a click away." All these developments point to the need for companies to offer customer-defined quality that differentiates them in the global and digital marketplaces — but what is meant by "quality"?

Quality is one of those elusive concepts that are easy to visualize but difficult to define. The term has many definitions, ranging from specific to general, and varies by functional area. For example, Philip Kotler, a leading marketing guru, defines quality as "the totality of features and characteristics of a product or service that bear on its ability to satisfy stated or implied needs."[3] To expand on this definition, it should be added that quality must provide goods and services that completely satisfy the needs of *internal* and *external* customers. Moreover, quality serves as the bridge between the producer of goods or services and the customer.

Quality gurus such as Deming view quality as reducing variation. Table 5.1 presents Deming's quality philosophy, which is summarized in his 14 points and aims at changing cultural and organizational systems of a company.

Along the same lines, customers prefer to conduct business with companies whose quality levels are consistent, i.e., with little or no variation. Six sigma is a methodology consisting of analytically based practices and procedures aimed at eliminating variation in any process. A six sigma process — producing only 3.4 defects per 1 million opportunities — was pioneered by Motorola and made famous by GE. According to Gregory Watson, a consultant and past president of the ASQ, "Six sigma might be the maturation of everything we learned over the last 100 years about quality." Six sigma involves a five-step approach:

- *Define* the process.
- *Measure* it to obtain a performance baseline.
- *Analyze* the data to determine where errors are occurring.
- *Improve* the process.
- *Control* it to ensure that errors do not recur.

Many six sigma efforts are too internally focused, when improvements internally will never positively affect the customer.[4]

The concept that the six sigma process is important in quality improvement is not limited to manufacturing, however. Services and transactions can also benefit from these principles. For example, Starwood Hotels & Resorts recently introduced a comprehensive six sigma program for all of its hotel properties. The focus of the program is to deliver consistent and exemplary service to its guests worldwide. From the reservation and check-in process to room standards and cleanliness, Starwood's goal in implementing Six Sigma is to provide each guest with a flawless experience during every visit. Wellmark Inc., a Des Moines managed care company, significantly reduced the time it took to add a new doctor to Blue Cross and Blue Shield medical plans, slashing the time to 30 days from 65 days or more. When Wellmark applied the six sigma analytical tools, it found that half the processes performed were redundant.

Other gurus, such as Juran, define quality as "fitness for use" in which products possess customer-desired product features and are free from deficiencies. The Juran philosophy of quality centers around three basic quality processes: planning, improvement, and control. Juran believed that a continual striving toward quality must take place, consisting of a number of steps from research; development; design; specification; planning; process control; etc. and then back to research again.[5]

Table 5.1 Summary of Deming's Fourteen Points

Principle	Explanation
1. Constancy of purpose	Continuation of business requires a core set of values and a purpose that is stable over time.
2. Adopt the new philosophy	Learn new responsibilities and take on leadership of change.
3. Cease dependence on mass inspection	Quality does not come from inspection, but rather from improvements in the process.
4. End the practice of awarding business on the basis of price alone	Price has no meaning apart from perceived quality; work on minimizing total costs.
5. Improve constantly and forever the system of production and service	Build quality into the product in the first place; systems should be redesigned continually for improved quality.
6. Institute training	Equip managers and workers with tools they need to evaluate and improve systems, including basic statistical methods.
7. Institute leadership	Leaders should know the work they supervise; the aim of leadership should be to help workers do their jobs better.
8. Drive out fear	Deming claimed that workers perform best when they feel secure. Fear breeds hidden agendas and padded numbers and may cause workers to satisfy a rule or quota at the expense of the company.
9. Break down barriers among staff	Workers in various functional areas need to work together as a team.
10. Eliminate slogans, exhortations, and targets	Such exhortations only create adversarial relationships; the real cause of low quality is in the system.
11. Eliminate work quotas	Emphasis on extrinsic motivators, such as quotas or other numerical goals, works against quality and productivity improvements.
12. Remove barriers to pride of workmanship	Remove any bureaucratic hindrances that rob workers' pride of workmanship. Listen and follow up on worker suggestions and requests.
13. Institute a vigorous program of education and self-improvement	Deming advocated lifelong learning — formal or informal.
14. Put everyone to work on the transformation	Everyone needs to be involved if business systems are to be improved.

Source: From Deming, E. (1986) *Out of Crisis*, Cambridge, MA: MIT Center for Advanced Engineering.

Crosby, another leading quality guru, defines quality as "conformance to requirements, not as goodness." Crosby believes that quality is created by a system of prevention, not appraisal (doing it right the first time or DIRFT), where the performance standard is "zero defects — meeting specifications 100% of the time." Crosby also believes it is necessary to build a quality-driven corporate culture.[6]

Garvin takes a more aggressive and strategic approach to defining quality. He views quality as a means of pleasing customers, not simply protecting annoyances. He eschews the defensive quality posture practiced by many U.S. companies in favor of a more strategic approach based on a combination of eight quality dimensions, including a product's:

- Performance
- Features
- Reliability
- Conformity
- Durability
- Serviceability
- Aesthetics
- Perceived quality

Implied in Garvin's eight quality dimensions are five overall categories of quality, including[7]:

- Transcendent — some form of innate excellence
- Product based — measurable, based on attributes of the product
- Manufacturing based — conformance to requirements
- User based — quality is "in the eyes of the beholder"
- Value based — defined in terms of price/cost tradeoffs

Sparks and Legault take Garvin's eight dimensions of quality and apply them to the firm's business cycle. Figure 5.1 illustrates the elements of the quality process as viewed by the customer, as well as those that the customer never sees but that help define quality from the producer's viewpoint.[8]

Integrating the voice of the customer ensures a practice known as *quality function deployment* (QFD). This process needs to precede new product or service introductions in order to ensure design quality. QFD enables companies to identify and prioritize customer needs and respond to them effectively. Motorola was one of the pioneers in applying "design for quality" in manufacturing to ensure that initial engineering specifications reflected customer requirements. Ford Motor Company determined that fewer than 15% of its quality problems could be traced to shoddy

Design —— Production ———	Sales Process — Delivery ———	After the Sale

Performance		Facilities	Quantity			
Features	Conformance	Communication process	On-time	service	service	Anticipated
Aesthetics			Place	Unanticipated	Unanticipated	service
Reliability		Transaction system		service		
Durability						
Safety/Security						

Overall Impression

Perceived Quality

Figure 5.1 Quality and the Business Cycle (Adapted from Sparks, R. and Legault, R. [1993], *SAM Adv. Manage. J.*, 58 (1), Winter, 17.)

workmanship or other factory errors. The real source of quality problems could be traced to the front-end development process — how the product was designed; who designed it; and what processes and materials were used.[9]

Toyota improved its rust prevention record from one of the worst to one of the best in the world by coordinating design and production decisions to focus on this key customer concern. Using the "house of quality" model (see Figure 5.2), designers were able to break down "body durability" into 53 items covering everything from climate to modes of operation.

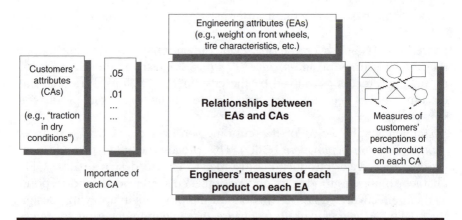

Figure 5.2 House of Quality (Adapted from Hauser, J. and Klein, R. [1988], *Mark. News*, 22, January, 1–2.)

The importance of each design dimension in Figure 5.1 also varies by product (or service). For example, aesthetics would be less important for Dell Computer, which sells direct via the phone or Internet. The goal of QFD is to determine not only *what* customers want, but which product or service attributes are most important to them.

SERVICE QUALITY GUIDELINES

Until recently, most managers associated quality with manufactured goods and production. However, during the 1980s, a broadened definition of quality to include services, as well as goods, emerged. Defining quality for services is more difficult than for products, due to the intangible, variable nature of service characteristics. A recent study of U.S. consumers by the Yankelovich Monitor confirms this phenomenon; 72% of those surveyed said they needed a better way to evaluate the quality and value of what they buy.[10]

Furthermore, unlike product quality, consumers frequently lack the necessary information to evaluate service quality. For example, consumers of durable goods such as cars or major appliances often conduct research before making a purchase, allowing use of *search quality* prior to the purchase. Moreover, consumers can also use *experience quality* based on postpurchase evaluation of the product to determine whether their expectations were met.

With services, however, consumers are usually limited to using *credence quality* to evaluate the experience, relying solely on the overall credibility of the service provider. A consumer receiving legal services or medical treatments has little basis from which to judge the quality, other than the reputation of the law firm or medical facility. Here, consumers are not always sure what to expect and may not know for some time, if ever, whether the outcome was performed satisfactorily. These factors make it more difficult for consumers to evaluate services in advance while at the same time creating greater risk. Managers can help reduce this risk by providing information that helps customers evaluate alternatives before the purchase as well as providing documentation of the firm's service reputation.

Another challenge presented in assessing service quality arises when viewing services along a continuum ranging from presale to postsale activities. Figure 5.3 shows the progression of these activities and where the potential for service failures may occur in the process. For example, a brokerage house might offer free seminars on estate planning as part of presale services, providing valuable information that participants can later use when choosing a particular investment plan. Lincoln Suites Hotel proactively manages presale services by calling its guests several days

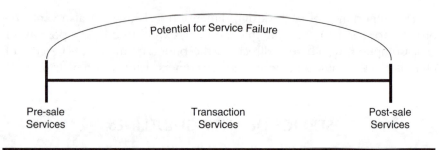

Potential for Service Failure

Pre-sale
Services

Transaction
Services

Post-sale
Services

Figure 5.3   Continuum of Services

before their scheduled arrival date, and confirming arrival and departure dates; the number of people in the party; smoking/nonsmoking preferences; directions to the hotel, etc. This attention to detail prior to check-in minimizes hassles later and eases travel anxiety by addressing last-minute concerns. By the same token, firms risk alienating prospects by poorly handling presale services. Most people have experienced the frustration of calling a firm's toll-free line only to be placed on "endless hold" or to get trapped in the "voicemail maze."

Customers also form perceptions of quality during the *service transaction* — how effectively and efficiently the service was delivered and the speed and convenience of completing the transaction. Anyone who has purchased a product over the phone has experienced the frustration when the "computers go down" and processing the order and payment grinds to a halt. Amazon.com, the online retailing pioneer, has revolutionized book buying and flawlessly handles customer purchase transactions. For starters, it builds customer profiles by preference with each visit, recommending titles within categories and sending e-mails to prompt browsing. Most importantly, it gives the customer a sense of power over the entire retail transaction, from initial entry to random search to final selection and ordering. It is not necessary for a customer to supply name, address, and credit card number each time he or she shops because Amazon.com creates a user profile from the initial visit.

Finally, customers evaluate support activities that occur after the transaction, that is, *postsale services*. Joe Girard, who holds the Guinness record for most retail automobile sales, believes that when a customer returns with a complaint or needs service, he drops everything and makes sure the customer gets the best service available. He maintains that "the sale begins after the sale." He is also known for sending out birthday cards to his customers every year. Sales follow-up in the form of phone calls, letters, or cards shows a genuine concern for the customer and leads to repeat business and business loyalty. Phil Breslin, a Domino's Pizza franchisee in Baltimore, requires his store managers to make customer calls at the end of each business day, even if that means letting close-outs wait until the next business day. These examples demonstrate a commitment to building repeat business through effective postsale follow-up.

Generally, a user of services has a set of attributes or characteristics in mind when judging service quality. Using extensive, in-depth interviews with 12 consumer focus group interviews, Parasuraman et al. found that customers assess service quality using 10 dimensions[11]:

- *Reliability* — perform promised service dependably and accurately
- *Responsiveness* — willingness/readiness to provide prompt service
- *Competence* — possess knowledge and skill to perform the service
- *Access* — approachability and ease of contact of service personnel
- *Courtesy* — politeness, consideration, and friendliness of service personnel
- *Communication* — keeping customers informed; listening to customers
- *Credibility* — trustworthiness, believability, honesty
- *Security* — freedom from danger, risk, or doubt
- *Understanding/knowing the customer* — knowing customers' needs
- *Tangibles* — physical evidence of service

These 10 service quality dimensions were further summarized into five broad service quality dimensions:

- *Reliability* — ability to perform the promised service dependably and accurately
- *Responsiveness* — willingness to help customers and provide prompt service
- *Assurance* — knowledge and courtesy of employees and ability to inspire trust and confidence
- *Tangibles* — physical facilities, equipment, and appearance of personnel
- *Empathy* — caring, individualized attention that the firm provides to customers

Research on the relative importance of these dimensions found that reliability was consistently the most critical dimension, followed by responsiveness; empathy was the least important.[12]

Parasuraman and his colleagues found that service quality is a measure between service *perceptions* as well as *expectations*. Service quality stems from a comparison of what a consumer feels a service firm *should* offer (desires or wants) vs. his perception of what the service firm actually *does* offer. Thus, ensuring good service quality involves meeting or exceeding

Table 5.2 Service Quality Gaps

Service Quality Gap	Definition
1. Research gap	Managers have difficulty in translating customer requirements into service quality specifications or precise performance standards
2. Planning and design gap	Performance standards and specifications (as well as systems) do not always measure up to what customer expects
3. Implementation gap	Discrepancy between service quality specifications and the delivery of service performance in accordance with those specifications; affected by job design; employee selection/development; perceived control by the employee; low role ambiguity; and role conflict[29]
4. External communications gap	Discrepancy between the level of service quality delivered and the communication of that delivery to the customer (i.e., overpromising and underdelivering)

Source: From Parasuraman, A. et al., *J. Mark.*, 49, Fall, 41–50.

consumers' expectations. The authors attended a workshop at which it was reported that hotel patrons, when asked to indicate what they consider most essential in choosing a hotel, revealed five factors that indicate their likelihood of a return visit: cleanliness; breakfast; friendliness of the personnel; value; and check-in speed.

These researchers further determined that customer perceptions are influenced by a series of gaps, which are presented in Table 5.2. The task of managers is to close the gaps using the following recommended strategies:

- Gap 1 — learn what the customer values, and values most, using such tools as benchmarking, quality function deployment, and competitive analysis
- Gap 2 — design a proper system using blueprinting and other quality tools such as fishbone diagrams
- Gap 3 — ensure good employee job fit; foster teamwork; provide employees with appropriate tools or technology to do the job; create a work environment in which employees feel in control; and introduce good supervisory control systems (i.e., appraisal and formal/informal feedback procedures)

- Gap 4 — provide accurate information by informing customers of the true level of service that they can expect and holding to those pledges

Parasuraman et al. later operationalized these gaps in the form of SERVQUAL, a 21-item instrument that measures expectations and customer perceptions of the service encounter (see Figure 5.4).[13] Their revised scale also reflected the respondent's "zone of tolerance" or the range of the company's performance between "acceptable" and "desired" service levels.

SERVQUAL can serve as an effective diagnostic tool for uncovering broad areas of a company's service quality shortfalls and strengths.[14] The SERVQUAL scale also offers the potential to determine the relative importance of the five major service quality dimensions and to track service quality performance over time. The scale serves as a suitable generic measure of service quality, transcending specific functions, companies, and industries. Service quality ratings are obtained when consumers compare their service expectations with actual service performance on distinct service dimensions: reliability, responsiveness, assurance, empathy, and tangibles. Poor service quality results when perceived performance ratings are lower than expectations, whereas the reverse indicates good service quality.

Managers of service organizations should pay close attention to the "cardinal principles of service quality" as well (see customer value insight 5.1). These insights can be used to make service quality a winning value-added strategy.

CUSTOMER VALUE INSIGHT 5.1:
CARDINAL PRINCIPLES OF SERVICE QUALITY[30]

√ Listening precedes **action** — integrating the voice of the customer in designing processes and establishing service standards. Chat rooms and e-mail are excellent listening posts for responding to customer concerns and complaints.

√ Reliability is **key** — a huge factor in service quality; without reliability, customers lose confidence in the service provider's ability to deliver on its promises.

√ Flawless execution of the **basics** — mastering competencies that you, as a service provider, are expected to perform well, i.e., Domino's delivering food that is hot and what the customer ordered.

√ Pay attention to service **design** — service design, not people, is often responsible for inconsistent and unreliable service delivery. Service systems that are not properly designed or maintained hinder service personnel from performing their jobs and satisfying customer needs. Furthermore, without process consistency, quality is impossible.

Directions: Based on your experiences with ABC, please think about the quality of service ABC offers compared to two different levels of service defined below: For each of the following statements, please indicate: (a) how ABC's performance compares with your *minimum service level* by circling one of the numbers in the first column; and (b) how ABC's performance compares with your *desired service level* by circling one of the numbers in the second column. There are no right or wrong answers — all we are interested in are two ratings on each feature that best represent your perception of ABC's performance compared to your *minimum service level* and your *desired service level.*

	Compared to my minimum service level, ABC's service performance is:	Compared to my desired service level, ABC's service performance is:
		Lower Same Higher No Opinion
ABC provides services as promised.	1 2 3 4 5 6 7 8 9 N	1 2 3 4 5 6 7 8 9 N
ABC demonstrates dependability in handling customers' service problems.	1 2 3 4 5 6 7 8 9 N	1 2 3 4 5 6 7 8 9 N
ABC performs services right the first time.	1 2 3 4 5 6 7 8 9 N	1 2 3 4 5 6 7 8 9 N
ABC provides services at the promised time.	1 2 3 4 5 6 7 8 9 N	1 2 3 4 5 6 7 8 9 N
ABC keeps customers informed about when services will be performed.	1 2 3 4 5 6 7 8 9 N	1 2 3 4 5 6 7 8 9 N
ABC's employees offer prompt service to customers.	1 2 3 4 5 6 7 8 9 N	1 2 3 4 5 6 7 8 9 N
ABC's employees are willing to help customers.	1 2 3 4 5 6 7 8 9 N	1 2 3 4 5 6 7 8 9 N
ABC's employees are ready to respond to customers' requests.	1 2 3 4 5 6 7 8 9 N	1 2 3 4 5 6 7 8 9 N
ABC's employees instill confidence in their customers.	1 2 3 4 5 6 7 8 9 N	1 2 3 4 5 6 7 8 9 N
ABC's employees make customers feel safe in their transactions.	1 2 3 4 5 6 7 8 9 N	1 2 3 4 5 6 7 8 9 N

(continued)

		Lower	Same	Higher	No Opinion
ABC employees are consistently courteous.	1 2 3 4 5 6 7 8 9	N	1 2 3 4 5 6 7 8 9	N	
ABC employees have the knowledge to answer customer questions.	1 2 3 4 5 6 7 8 9	N	1 2 3 4 5 6 7 8 9	N	
ABC gives customers individual attention.	1 2 3 4 5 6 7 8 9	N	1 2 3 4 5 6 7 8 9	N	
ABC's employees deal with customers in a caring fashion.	1 2 3 4 5 6 7 8 9	N	1 2 3 4 5 6 7 8 9	N	
ABC has the customers' best interests at heart.	1 2 3 4 5 6 7 8 9	N	1 2 3 4 5 6 7 8 9	N	
ABC employees understand the needs of their customers.	1 2 3 4 5 6 7 8 9	N	1 2 3 4 5 6 7 8 9	N	
ABC has modern equipment.	1 2 3 4 5 6 7 8 9	N	1 2 3 4 5 6 7 8 9	N	
ABC's physical facilities are visually appealing.	1 2 3 4 5 6 7 8 9	N	1 2 3 4 5 6 7 8 9	N	
ABC's employees have a neat, professional appearance.	1 2 3 4 5 6 7 8 9	N	1 2 3 4 5 6 7 8 9	N	
ABC has visually appealing materials associated with the service.	1 2 3 4 5 6 7 8 9	N	1 2 3 4 5 6 7 8 9	N	
ABC has convenient operating hours to customers.	1 2 3 4 5 6 7 8 9	N	1 2 3 4 5 6 7 8 9	N	

Notes: Captures three pieces of information: (1) how perceptions compare with minimal service expectations (measure of service adequacy, or MSA); (2) how perceptions compare with desired service expectations (measure of service superiority or MSS); (3) how wide a "gap" exists between these two.

MSS score > 5 = "above tolerance zone"; MSA score < 5 = "below tolerance zone"; MSS score ≤ 5, MSA score ≥ 5 = "within tolerance zone".

Figure 5.4   SERVQUAL — Two-Column Format (From Parasuraman, A. et al. [1994], *J. Retailing*, Fall, 70(3), 207.)

✓ Perform **service recovery** well — service failures are almost inevitable, so a well-managed recovery from a service failure can create levels of loyalty from a customer greater than before the failure occurred, assuming the problem is handled promptly and favorably resolved.

✓ Surprise **customers** — discover the "wow" factor by seeking excellence in the service process and outcome. Meeting customer expectations is simply the admission price to compete; customers will shift their loyalty to service providers that can perform the unexpected.

✓ Practice **fair play** — customers expect equitable treatment and become distrustful when they perceive otherwise. They expect two types of justice: *distributive justice* refers to the perceived fairness of the actual outcome or consequence of a decision, e.g., the level of refund or exchange offered; *procedural justice* refers to whether the procedures or criteria used in making the decision are perceived as fair, e.g., how quickly a problem was resolved and when presented information is given attention and consideration.

✓ Promote **teamwork** — when service workers help one another and are invested in one another's success, service tends to improve. Smooth "hand-offs" among service workers are also critical for a satisfying customer experience.

✓ Internal service begets external **service** — employees are customers of internal service; internal service quality is improved to the extent to which tools; policies and procedures; teamwork; management support; goal alignment; effective training; communication; and rewards and recognition are properly introduced.[15]

————————————▲▼▲————————————

Service quality can also be defined according to *what* and *how* product or service is delivered. Gronroos distinguishes between technical quality and functional quality.[16] Technical quality is concerned with the outcome of the delivered product or service, such as a well-prepared restaurant meal or an acceptable haircut or styling. Customers use service quality attributes such as reliability, competence, performance, durability, etc. to evaluate technical quality. For example, when bringing a videocassette recorder (VCR) in for repair, the customer would expect it to be properly serviced, thus eliminating the problem and preventing it from occurring again. Functional quality has more to do with how the technical quality is transferred to the consumer. In the VCR example, the customer would expect not only competence and accuracy in the repair, but also that the service personnel were helpful and courteous. Service quality attributes such as responsiveness and access would be important in helping the customer judge the functional quality of the service encounter.

Service quality can also be judged by considering the various "spheres," or thresholds, of the service offering as presented in Figure 5.5. The *core benefit* is the most fundamental level for which the service offering stands, that is, what the consumer is actually seeking. The core benefit represents

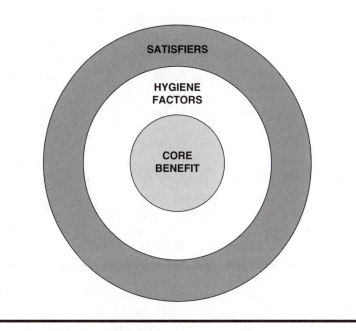

Figure 5.5   The Three Levels of Service

basic reasons why people buy, such as hunger; safety; convenience; confidence; status; self-esteem; and so on. Gonroos uses the term "service concept" to indicate the core of a service offering, such as offering a car rental as a solution to a short-term transportation need.[17]

The *hygiene factors* constitute the minimally acceptable level of service attributes that customers would expect to be present in the service offering. For example, a mid-priced hotel catering to business travelers would be expected to offer such services as express check-out, fitness room, high-speed Internet connections, a restaurant, and a lounge. Failure to offer these services or performing or delivering them poorly will likely lead to dissatisfaction. In contrast, simply offering these services and performing them adequately will not delight the customer, who expects them as part of doing business.

Truly delighting customers requires service providers carefully to consider *satisfiers*. Satisfiers are those service attributes that differentiate the service firm from its competitors, while at the same time exceeding customer expectations in one or more areas of service by delivering above what is expected. According to Naumann, hygiene factors need to be delivered at an acceptable level before satisfiers become important.[18] Satisfiers have the potential to create high customer satisfaction levels once expectations on hygiene factors have been met. Firms that would offer satisfiers need to consider the value-added services that would delight and surprise the customer. Consider some of the following examples in the effective use of satisfiers.

- Before a guest ever sets foot in Le Parker Meridian Hotel in New York, he can use the hotel's quicktime virtual reality (QTVR), which enables potential guests to "walk" through the lobby and rooms. In addition to virtual reality tours, the site offers in-depth, timely information about room rates, events, and points of interest for the business and pleasure traveler. The hotel also welcomes repeat guests with amenity baskets accompanied by handwritten notes.
- Ritz-Carlton works hard at learning its customers' preferences to better serve them in the future. From the moment guests book a room for the first time at a Ritz-Carlton hotel, their guest-history profiles begin. Every preference they have is recorded, and all 30 Ritz-Carlton hotels and resorts have access to the information. Ritz-Carlton employees take every opportunity to note guest preferences; in fact, employees carry guest-preference pads to note comments, which are later recorded in the guest-history files. For example, if a guest likes an iron in the room, prefers not to have turn-down service, or requests a Cadillac instead of a Lincoln when needing car service to the airport, the information will be recorded and will follow the guest to every subsequent stay.

Finally, it should be emphasized that quality is more than simply meeting specifications and that the customer's point of view on quality is key. That is, *quality is what the customer says it is*. Remember, it is the customer, not the company, that sets the quality and value agenda. A study recently found that consumers consider reliability; durability; easy maintenance; ease of use; trusted brand name; and low price with a high value as indicators of quality dimensions for consumer durable goods.[19] The losers in the quality battle will be those who attempt to "do things right," while the winners will be the organizations that learn to "do the right things."[20] The next section discusses the importance of quality and the payoffs that a quality-oriented culture produces.

WHY QUALITY MATTERS

Xerox enjoyed a near stranglehold on the copier market until the late 1970s, when it saw its near 100% market share devoured almost entirely by more cost-efficient Japanese producers. In the late 1970s, Fuji Xerox, its Japanese subsidiary at the time, launched a total quality process under the name New Xerox Movement with the goal of better satisfying customer requirements and bringing costs under control. Quality circles were introduced and quality tools became the norm. The turnaround was nothing short of spectacular. The prestigious Deming Quality Award was bestowed on Fuji Xerox, while revenues and profits soared. Xerox learned firsthand that quality works.

The global market is becoming more competitive every day as companies continually search for new ways to gain an edge over their competitors around the globe. Global competition and deregulation in a number of industries are forcing companies to turn to quality in order to survive. GE's former CEO Jack Welch recently commented, "Quality is our best assurance of customer allegiance, our strongest defense against foreign competition, and the only path to sustained growth and earnings."[21'] The Council on Competitiveness conducted a study examining the competitiveness of the U.S. economy since 1985 and found that factors accounting for the largest gains in U.S. competitiveness included: (1) product, process, and management of innovation; and (2) the focus on quality and customer needs. Although U.S. companies have made great strides in improving quality during that time, their products still lag behind those of Japan and Germany, according to a Bozell–Gallup worldwide quality poll.[22] The study found that consumers around the world rated Japanese products "excellent" or "very good" 41.2% of the time and American goods "excellent" or "very good" 34.9% of the time (see Figure 5.6).

Perhaps the most important reason for pursuing quality is that *quality pays*. W. Edwards Deming stressed the favorable economic outcomes that result from a strategy of offering high quality. In Walton's book *The Deming Management Method*,[23] Deming is quoted as saying,

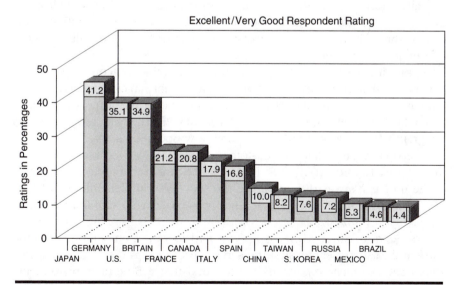

Figure 5.6　Global Quality Leaders

I want to make it clear that as you improve quality, your costs go down. Continual reduction in mistakes, continual improvement in quality, mean lower costs...less waste of materials, machine time, human effort...As costs go down, through less rework, the result is fewer mistakes, less waste, while productivity goes up.

Research has been conducted that also shows a relationship among quality, market share, and return on investment. The exhaustive database from the profit impact of market strategy (PIMS) clearly documents these relationships. Higher quality yields a higher return on investment (ROI) for any given market share. For example, among businesses with less than 12% of the market, those with inferior quality averaged an ROI of 4.5%; those with average product quality an ROI of 10.4%; and those with superior product quality had an ROI of 17.4%.[24] Quality also pays in the form of customer retention. Considering that the average business today loses 10 to 30% of its customers each year, customer defections represent a significant cost to companies. In a study by Michaelson and Associates, 69% of customers indicated "poor service" as the reason for leaving the company.[25]

Finally, adopting quality principles strongly correlates to corporate stock and earnings appreciation. A study conducted over a 5-year period assessed the performances of some 600 publicly traded winners of 140 annual quality awards given by state or private agencies. The study found that the award winners did about 50% better in stock appreciation, and two to three times as well in growth of operating income, sales, assets, and employment (see Figure 5.7).[26]

Improving quality also leads to other desirable outcomes, such as customer satisfaction. In fact, several researchers have proposed a link among employee satisfaction, customer satisfaction, and firm profitability, better known as the *service–profit chain* (SPC).[27] The SPC represents an integrative framework for understanding how operational investments into service quality are related to customer satisfaction perceptions and how these translate into profits (see Figure 5.8). Sears' remarkable turnaround in the mid 1990s was due in part to the successful implementation of the SPC. Using the SPC model, Sears' vision was based on a simple algorithm: *work × shop = invest.*

For Sears to succeed *financially*, it had to be a compelling place to *work* and to *shop*. Sears tested the service–profit chain (Sears called it the *employee–customer profit model*) and found that a 5-point improvement in employee attitudes resulted in a 1.3-point improvement in customer satisfaction; this resulted in a 0.5% improvement in revenue growth. Sears also tied manager compensation to these results.[28] A Swedish quality index

Stock Price Change Over Five Years

Figure 5.7   How Winners Win on Wall Street

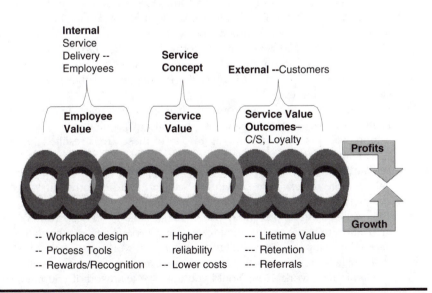

Figure 5.8   The Service Profit Chain (Adapted from Heskett, J., Sasser, J., and Schledinger, L. [1997]. *The Service Profit Chain*, The Free Press, New York, p. 19.)

has also shown a strong relationship between quality practices and performance. Companies in their study capable of increasing their quality index by one point every year for 5 years improved their average return on assets during that period by almost 12%.[29]

HOW TO IMPROVE QUALITY

Improving quality is a lot like taking vitamins, eating healthy, and exercising regularly. Although the results may not be immediate, long-term benefits are significant. Quality is not a quick fix or the program of the month, but rather a *way of life* for companies serious about improvement (see customer value checklist 5.1 for help in diagnosing service quality problems).

▼▲▼

CUSTOMER VALUE CHECKLIST 5.1:
PROBING FOR SERVICE QUALITY IMPROVEMENT

1. Does your company do a good job of *listening* to its customers? Give a specific example of how listening resulted in improved service quality to your customers.
2. *Reliability* is the ability of the company to perform the promised services dependably and accurately. On a 10-point scale, where 1 is unreliable and 10 perfectly reliable, at what point along this scale would you place your company and why?
3. How well does your company perform the "*service basics*," that is, knowing and responding to the fundamental service expectations in your industry? (e.g., an automobile service department that fixes the car right the first time).
4. How effectively does your company manage the *service design* elements — systems, people, and the physical environment? Provide an example of how lack of planning in one of these areas resulted in a "fail point" during a customer encounter.
5. *Service recovery* refers to how effectively companies respond to service failures. Cite an example of when a service failure occurred in your company and how it was handled.
6. *Teamwork* is an important dynamic in sustaining service workers' motivation to serve and in minimizing service performance shortfalls. Rate your company on its ability to foster teamwork on a scale of 1 to 10, where 1 indicates the absence of teamwork and 10 indicates maximum teamwork. How would you improve teamwork if you rated your company low on this attribute?
7. *Internal service* is crucial to service improvement because customer satisfaction often mirrors employee satisfaction. To what extent does your company assess internal service quality, i.e., asking employees

about the adequacy of systems to support the service; how they interact and serve one another; and where service failures occur. Give examples of how internal service might be measured in your company.

————————————▲▼▲————————————

Quality is fundamental to creating value, yet it is a moving target and must meet the customer's current definition of quality. Thus, the following recommendations are offered as ways for improving service quality and ultimately delivering superior customer value:

- Design services in cooperation with customers. Learn what customers truly value by incorporating the "voice of the customer" earlier in the service development process. Also, it is important to determine not only customers' service attributes but also their *relative importance.*
- Focus your improvement programs outward, on market "breakpoints." Only by defining episodes in which the customer comes in contact with the organization and focusing on the most critical ones can you see things as the customer sees them. Also, visualize the complete sequence of moments of truth that a customer experiences in getting a need met. Remember, the customer sees service in terms of a total experience, not an isolated set of activities. Mapping the service cycle helps companies see these activities as the customer sees them.
- Create a tangible representation of service quality. Hotels and restaurants often advertise and display on their properties ratings by one of the major motor clubs, such as AAA or Mobil Oil. Hertz #1 Club Gold service communicates a premium, value-added bundle of services to business travelers seeking a hassle-free car rental experience.
- Use teamwork to promote service excellence; service workers who support one another and achieve together can avoid service burnout. As the preacher in Ecclesiastes said, "Two are better than one, because they have a good reward for their labor. For if they fall, one will lift up his companion" (Ecclesiastes 4:9–10).
- Create a "service bias" based on each of the following service quality determinants: professionalism; attitudes/behaviors; accessibility and flexibility; reliability/trustworthiness; service recovery; and reputation/credibility. These criteria can be used as guidelines for influencing positive service quality perceptions.
- Develop proper measurements. Use metrics that are specific in nature, such as a 95% on-time delivery, customer wait time, or order processing time. Benchmark the best practices for each service area measured, such as wait time or order delivery.

■ Employee selection, job design, and training are absolutely crucial to building customer satisfaction and service quality. Structure the jobs of service workers so that their ability to respond quickly and competently to customer needs is maximized. Also, train service personnel in areas of service delivery and attitude. Role play different service scenarios, showing various service recovery strategies. Provide service workers with some basic tools, such as those discussed in Chapter 3, to help control service quality variation and uncover service problems.

■ Reward total quality efforts in marketing. Look for opportunities to reinforce quality behaviors when they occur. Employees should be rewarded on the basis of these behaviors (commitment, effort) rather than strictly on outcomes, such as sales quotas. Rewarding a salesperson for meeting or exceeding quota with a bonus, while giving a nominal award such as a pin or plaque to the person who fixes the product or process, sends a clear message about the importance of quality.

■ Think of service as a process, not a series of functions. Service quality occurs when the entire service experience is managed and the organization is aligned to respond accordingly.

■ Integrate customer information across sales channels. Regardless of which channel a customer uses to contact the firm, the information made available to online and offline customer service representatives should be consistent.

SUMMARY

The modern quality revolution that began in Japan in the early 1950s and was exported to the U.S. during the 1980s has forever changed how corporations and institutions are managed. The sheer size of the service economy, competing demands on scarce resources, and more demanding customers force management to place greater emphasis on creating high-quality customer experiences. Competing in a global economy requires firms to understand what "world-class" quality really means. The challenge facing firms today is to know their customer's definition of service quality and how to deliver that at a reasonable cost — in short, how to create superior customer value.

This chapter discussed various definitions of quality and the use of quality function deployment in determining service quality dimensions and their importance, as well as consumers' difficulty in assessing service quality. The Gap Model was presented along with some major service quality dimensions and how internal and external service quality are related and influence company performance. The importance of service quality and its relationship to competitiveness, customer retention, and firm performance was explained further, using the service–profit chain concept. Finally, some practical strategies were offered for improving service quality by focusing on how services are designed, measured, and delivered. The next chapter extends the discussion of service quality to the electronic arena.

CUSTOMER VALUE ACTION ITEMS

1. Why has quality become such a priority today?
2. What are some of the common denominators in the definition of quality?
3. How does quality function deployment bridge customer requirements with product/service features?
4. Determine the extent of search quality, experience quality, and credence quality for each of the following situations:
   a. Buying a personal computer
   b. Applying to graduate school
   c. Setting up a retirement program
   d. Dining at a local restaurant
   e. Visiting a theme park
5. Suppose you were interested in purchasing personal tax preparation software. Give examples of how service failures could occur during presale, transaction, and postsale phases of the buying process.
6. Suppose you were managing a mid-priced hotel catering to business travelers. Determine the key factors for assessing service quality; also, suppose you were a customer of that same hotel, what factors would you use to judge service quality? Rank your choices for each situation and then compare the two lists.
7. List evidence that quality and improving quality are important to a business's success.
8. Service encounters are the means that customers use to assess the functional quality of a firm's value offering. Every service encounter consists of a repeatable sequence of events in which the firm's service personnel attempt to meet the customer's needs and expectations at every potential point of contact. The cycle of service begins with the very first point of contact between the customer and the firm. Furthermore, each point of contact between the customer and the company has the potential to leave a positive or negative impression. According to Albrecht and Zemke, when these *moments of truth* go unmanaged, "the quality of service regresses to mediocrity."[30] The metaphor of the moment of truth

is a very powerful idea for helping service businesses shift their points of view and think like customers. These moments of truth represent the times and places where service firms evidence their service competency or lack of it.

Consider the cycle of service for a drug store visit, which might include the following episodes: (1) parking the car; (2) entering the store; (3) getting a shopping basket; (4) selecting a few over-the-counter remedies; (5) requesting help from a clerk; (6) waiting in line at the pharmacy; (7) talking to the pharmacist about a medication; and (8) paying for the items selected. Think about a typical service experience (i.e., dry cleaner, movies, QSR, haircut, airline) and diagram the cycle of service. Also, give examples of potential moments of truth and the potential effect on service quality perceptions. Finally, recommend strategies to manage those moments of truth effectively.

9. Choose one of these service quality situations: (a) auto repair; (b) hospital visit; (c) theme park; (d) haircut; (e) supermarket; (f) QSR; or (g) air travel. Then answer the following questions:
   a. How unique/standardized is the product and/or service?
   b. What is the type of service, i.e., experience, search, credence?
   c. Is this pure service or a product–service blend?
   d. What factor most affects service quality?
   e. After service is delivered, is corrective action possible?

REFERENCES

1. Case, K. (2002) Coming soon: the future, *Qual. Prog.*, 35(11), 27.
2. Hof, R. and Hamm, S.T. (2002) How e-biz rose, fell, and will rise anew, *Bus. Week*, May 13, 65.
3. Kotler, P. (1997) *Marketing Management*, 9th ed., Upper Saddle River, NJ: Prentice–Hall.
4. Velocci, A. (2002) Full potential of six sigma eludes most companies, *Aviation Week Space Technol.*, September, 58.
5. Juran, J.M. (1986) The quality trilogy, *Qual. Prog.*, August, 25.
6. Crosby, P. (1979) *Quality Is Free*, New York: The Free Press.
7. Garvin, D. (1988) *Managing Quality*, New York: The Free Press.
8. Sparks, R. and Legault, R. (1993) A definition of quality for total customer satisfaction: the bridge between manufacturer and customer, *SAM Adv. Manage. J.*, 58(1), Winter, 17.
9. Muller, J. and Kerwin, K. (2001) Cruising for quality, *Bus. Week*, September 3, 74.
10. Duckler, M. (2001) Price, quality only part of value, *Mark. News*, 35(10), May 7, 17.
11. Parasuraman, A., Zeithaml, V., and Berry, L. (1985) A conceptual model of service quality and implications for future research, *J. Mark.*, 49, Fall, 41–50.

12. Parasuraman, A., Berry, L., and Zeithaml, V. (1991) Refinement and reassessment of the SERVQUAL scale, *J. Retailing*, 67(4), Winter, 423.

13. Parasuraman, A., Zeithaml, V., and Berry, L. (1994) Alternative scales for measuring service quality: a comparative assessment based on psychometric and diagnostic criteria, *J. Retailing*, 70(3), 206.

14. Parasuraman, A., Zeithaml, V., and Berry, L. (1988) SERVQUAL: a multiple-item scale for measuring consumer perceptions of service quality, *J. Retailing*, 64(1), 35–36.

15. Hallowell, R., Schlesinger, L., and Zornitsky, J. (1996) Internal service quality, customer and job satisfaction: linkages and implications for management, *Hum. Resour. Plann.*, 19(2), 23.

16. Gronroos, C. (1990) *Service Management and Marketing*, Lexington, MA: Lexington Books.

17. Gronroos, C. (1984) A service quality model and its marketing implications, *Eur. J. Mark.*, 18, 36–43.

18. Naumann, E. (1995) *Creating Customer Value*. Cincinnati, OH: Thomson Executive Press.

19. Brucks, V., Zeithaml, V., and Naylor, G. (2000) Price and brand name as indicators of quality dimensions for consumer durables, *J. Acad. Mark. Sci.*, 28(3), 364.

20. Johnson, W. and Chvala, R. (1995) *Total Quality in Marketing*. Boca Raton, FL: St. Lucie Press, 106.

21. Cycles of learning: observations of Jack Welch, (2001) *Six Sigma Forum Magazine*: 1, Nov. 2.

22. Bozell–Gallup Second Annual Worldwide Quality Poll, 1994–1995.

23. Walton, M. (1990) *The Deming Management Method*, New York: Putnam, 26.

24. Buzell, R. and Gale, B. (1987) *The PIMS Principles*, New York: The Free Press, 44.

25. "80 things every manager should know" (1998). *Sales and Marketing Management*: October, 150(11), 157.

26. Anon. (1998) The rewards of quality, *Bus. Week*, September 21, 26.

27. Heskett, J., Jones, T., Loveman, G., Sasser, E., and Schlesinger, L. (1994). Putting the service–profit chain to work, *Harvard Bus. Rev.*, 72(2), 174.

28. Rucci, A., Kirn, S., and Quinn, R. (1998) The employee–customer-profit chain at Sears, *Harvard Bus. Rev.*, 76(1), Jan./Feb., 91.

29. Grant, L. (1998) Your customers are telling the truth, *Fortune*, February 16, 166.

30. Albrecht, K. and Zemke, R. (1985) *Service America*, Homewood, IL: Dow Jones–Irwin, 31.

31. Chenet, P., Tynan, C., and Money, A. (2000) The service performance gap: testing the redeveloped causal model, *Eur. J. Mark.*, 34,(3/4), 488.

6

MANAGING E-SERVICE QUALITY

Organizations that have survived [the industry] meltdown have one thing in common — they learned quickly to embrace the e-service paradigm.

Roland Rust and P. K. Kannan

My definition of perfection in service is customers serving themselves so effortlessly — through "transparent" technological intermediaries — that they are hardly aware of doing so.

Regis McKenna, from Real Time

A major change in 21st century marketing involves a shift in emphasis from products and transactions to service and relationships. Advanced technologies and ever-expanding electronic networks (i.e., the Internet, wireless technologies, kiosks) are shaping customer expectations on where, when, and how to choose a service provider. e-Service quality is defined as the extent to which e-commerce providers effectively and efficiently manage customer interactions involving searching, shopping, purchasing, and order fulfillment. This chapter provides an overview of some key research findings involving online customer service and offers guidelines for firms to improve their customers' online experiences.

E-SERVICE AND CUSTOMER SATISFACTION: RESEARCH INSIGHTS

Service providers have come to realize that the Internet presents great opportunities as well as challenges in serving customer needs. The new e-consumer is more informed and expects more from his service provider — traditional or online.

According to a Jupiter consumer survey, only 41% of respondents were satisfied with the state of online customer service.[1] In another study involving B2B customers, Jupiter revealed that poor customer service presents a serious threat to e-commerce. The study reported that B2B customers are unhappy with the expediency of online channels, specifically when it comes to processing inquiries, i.e., customers who expect rapid responses to their e-mail inquiries were frequently disappointed.[2] Poor service translates into lost revenues as well. Datamonitor indicates that e-businesses will lose $3.2 billion in sales because of inadequate customer service on their Web sites.[3]

Companies doing business online need to see the link between customer service and repeat visits. According to Forrester Research, 42% of shoppers who use online customer service have stopped shopping at a particular Web site because they were unhappy with the service they received.[4] Some evidence indicates that Web customers tend to consolidate their purchases with one primary supplier when purchasing from that supplier becomes part of their regular routine.[5] Moreover, loyal customers frequently refer new customers to suppliers. eBay, one of the e-commerce leaders, gets more than half of its customers from referrals.

In the early days of consumer e-commerce, the problems experienced by many Web shoppers involved Internet orders that were never fulfilled or were incorrectly fulfilled. The problem was further compounded when consumers were unable to contact customer service agents or find any kind of resolution. In fact, many of the early dot.com failures can be traced to order fulfillment foul-ups. According to a recent study, one of the main reasons for dot.com failures was a lack of service management processes to support the back-end technology.[6] This finding supports the assertion in Chapter 3 that a *business process orientation* is fundamental to service quality. Companies need to integrate front-office applications like order generation and customer support with back-office processes such as logistics and order fulfillment.

Service has become even more important when doing business online. Research conducted by the management consultant firm Accenture reports that 80% of nearly 1000 corporate buyers rate a *strong brand* and *reliable customer service* ahead of low prices when deciding companies with which to do business online.[7] Research for luxury purchases online confirms the

Table 6.1 Online Service Quality for Luxury Purchases

Service	Rating[a]
Good customer service	4.55
Money-back guarantee	4.48
Easy return or exchange of merchandise	4.46
Control over use of personal data	4.43
Site reliability	4.42
Ease of use	4.33
Wide product selection	3.99
Fast site	3.97
Information related to products/services sold	3.93
Wide range of shipping/delivery options	3.88
Brand name	3.65
Site personalization	3.55
Physical presence	3.49
Discounts or coupons	3.24
Personalized product recommendations	3.12
Recommendations to complement previous purchases	2.95

[a] Ratings ranged from 1 (very unimportant) to 5 (very important).

Source: From Forrester Research Inc., 2001.

importance of good customer service. A survey of consumers rated what was important to them when deciding to buy online from a luxury store. Table 6.1 provides the responses, with answers ranging from 1 (very unimportant) to 5 (very important).[8]

Forrester Research found that online customer satisfaction is most affected by a business that is well staffed and responsive; offers simple and easy returns; and provides order tracking capabilities. In another study, subjects from an NPO panel of Internet users found that the following factors most significantly influenced e-satisfaction levels (in descending order): convenience, site design, financial security, and product information.[9]

Generally speaking, online customer service has failed to live up to customers' rising expectations, especially regarding *responsiveness*. Online customers' patience is short lived; in fact, the "15-second rule" usually applies. Customers will quickly abort online activity if they become frustrated while navigating a site or attempting to place an order.

Customers also expect timely responses to their e-mail inquiries. More than half of all consumers expect online retailers to respond to e-mail inquiries within 6 hours, according to Jupiter Research; yet only 29% actually meet those expectations.[10] When consulting firm CustomerRespect.com spent 4 months e-mailing the 100 largest corporations, the results were quite startling: 37% did not respond at all — not even with automated form letters; it took 3 days or more for an additional 22% to answer.[11] According to Jupiter Media Metrix, only 30% of retailers answered customer service e-mail messages within 6 hours. Jupiter also found that 40% of 250 online retailers whom they investigated took at least 3 days to respond. A study of 50 retail companies by Giga Information Group found that the average response time to e-mail inquiries was 12 hours.[12] It is fairly obvious that lack of online responsiveness is widespread and needs to improve.

The previous chapter examined the key determinants of service quality. Zeithaml and colleagues conducted research examining whether traditional service quality dimensions differ from e-service quality determinants. Based on a series of focus groups concerning e-service quality, they proposed a model and 11 major dimensions of perceived e-service quality including the original dimensions of reliability; responsiveness; access; assurance; and empathy are still relevant in e-commerce. However, several new dimensions of e-service quality emerged from their research including ease of navigation; flexibility; efficiency; site aesthetics; price knowledge; and customization/personalization. Price knowledge refers to the ability of online shoppers to determine shipping price, total price, and comparison prices. In fact, an interesting finding of Zeithaml et al. was that, contrary to conventional wisdom of how value is framed, price and quality were more strongly intertwined in online shopping.[13] Data collected from 271 subscribers to a regional Internet service provider revealed that six e-service quality indicators (reliability; access; ease of use; personalization; credibility; and security) follow closely to the original service quality indicators developed by Zeithaml et al. Reliability was the strongest predictor for Internet purchasers' perceived service quality, followed by personalization, ease of use, and access.[14]

Online consumers are pretty clear about what they expect online. A recent study conducted by Mercer Management Consulting confirms the importance of *information* and *convenience* as reasons why consumers value using the Internet medium. According to a study of online consumers, the information gathered in making purchase decisions offered the greatest value to online shoppers (see Figure 6.1).

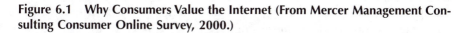

- Provides Information to Inform Decisions — 82%
- Saves Me Lots of Time — 75%
- Become Part of "Community of Interest" — 57%
- Saves Me Money — 49%
- Helps Me Better Manage My Life — 45%

Figure 6.1   Why Consumers Value the Internet (From Mercer Management Consulting Consumer Online Survey, 2000.)

E-SERVICE QUALITY AND CUSTOMER LOYALTY

e-Service quality is essential in creating customer satisfaction with e-commerce transactions, but what about in building loyalty in the online environment? It has been estimated that it costs an Internet site anywhere from $30 to $90 to attract an online shopper to visit its site and buy something. Customers must continue doing business with most online firms for at least 2 to 3 years for them simply to recover their initial acquisition costs.[15] Somewhat surprisingly, at the beginning of a relationship, the outlays needed to acquire a customer are considerably higher in e-commerce than in traditional retail channels. Customer acquisition costs for pure-play online apparel retailers are 20 to 40% higher than for traditional brick and mortar apparel retailers with physical and online channels. Yet, in future years, profit growth accelerates at a faster rate; in apparel e-tailing, repeat customers spend more than twice as much in months 24 to 30 of their relationships than they do in the first 6 months.[16]

SurveySite conducted a study among American and Canadian Web sites (Web magazines; software/Internet firms; entertainment; retail; travel; and health related) and found that the most important variable for predicting repeat visits to the Web site was the site's *content*. Respondents cited "frivolous content" as a primary reason for not planning a return to the Web site. The second most important factor in determining repeat visits was whether the respondent found the visit enjoyable. Respondents enjoyed their visits when they were able to find the specific content or information for which they were looking or if the site provided a novel experience, was entertaining, and had an interesting interface. Finally, site layout was cited as the third most important factor in influencing the rate of repeat visits.[17]

Another study among Webmasters from Fortune 1000 companies identified information quality; system use; system design quality; and playfulness as four major determinants for future visits to company Web sites. Company Webmasters can improve service quality by focusing on the way in which customers use their Web site. It is the customers rather than business organizations who should control the online transaction process.[18]

Dell Computer, currently the leading personal computer company, has been extraordinary in creating a loyal customer base. Dell has determined that its major loyalty drivers are: order fulfillment; product performance; and postsales service and support. Dell then determines the optimal measure of each one of these drivers. Success in order fulfillment, for example, is measured according to "ship to target" — a measure of the percentage of orders delivered accurately and on time.

HOW TO IMPROVE E-SERVICE QUALITY

Given the dismal record of many e-commerce providers, what should firms do to improve customer service? The fundamentals of customer service for e-marketing are the same as in traditional marketing. Most consumers today are looking for ways to streamline their shopping — to get it done quickly without compromising price or quality. The online shopping experience needs to be simple and efficient or shoppers will "click and move." Many companies mistakenly view technology as a cure-all to customer service problems. However, no amount of sophisticated technology can make up for lack of a customer-centric culture.

Research has proposed that the five following components be considered in delivering e-service quality:[19]

- The *core service* represents the "reason for being" and is designed to meet the primary demand need of a specifically described target market. Using the example of online book retailers, a core service would be displaying information on new products and offering recommendations.
- *Facilitating services* make it possible to use the core service and, without them, the core service collapses. In the case of online book retailers, a facilitating service might be archiving and searching capabilities.
- *Supporting services* do not facilitate using the core services but rather add value to them; support services might include the availability of useful links or "virtual book clubs."
- *Complementary services* accompany the core service and support their acquisition and use or disposition. For online booksellers, a

complementary service might represent book reviews or their shipping capabilities.

- The *user interface*, through which the customer accesses the services, is a means of communication between the e-service marketer and the potential customer. What information appears on screen, how it is organized, and how users access the information define the user interface. Limited menus, poorly designed navigation systems, and difficulty comparing multiple products on different screens have adverse effects on electronic shopping.[20]

Even with the shift of business activity to the Web, the fundamentals of marketing exchange remain the same: to create enduring and profitable customer relationships. A key factor in establishing and maintaining profitable customer relationships is *trust*. One study of eBay buyers found that, to a considerable extent, price premiums were based on the buyer's trust of the seller's credibility (see customer value insight 6.1).[21]

----------------- ▼▲▼ -----------------

CUSTOMER VALUE INSIGHT 6.1: EBAY BUILDS TRUST ONLINE

eBay, which is arguably the Web's most successful pure play, has gone from a funky online garage full of Beanie Babies and collectible Elvis prints to a powerful global marketplace in slightly over 8 years. With its 50 million registered users, eBay is now five times larger than its nearest competitor, Yahoo!. eBay primarily earns its revenue (nearly $2 billion in 2003) by charging a commission on every trade on its electronic exchange; the rest of its revenue comes from listing fees and other charges. eBay is also spectacularly profitable because it has no real cost of goods and customer acquisition is largely driven by word of mouth. The company has created a powerful value proposition by creating a fun, fast, efficient trading environment where buyer-seller risks are kept to a minimum.

The real genius of eBay is that it has figured out how to tap into the social capital created on its site by the millions of people who trade there daily. A primary source of its social capital is its feedback system, which indicates whether users are legitimate sellers or if a user has had a bad experience with an online seller or buyer. Buyers can enter feedback (positive, negative, or neutral ratings) about sellers and vice versa. Sellers also achieve star ratings based on the number of positive votes (yellow for 10 to 99 votes; gold for over 10,000), and the stars appear next to their sale items.

On eBay, sellers are forced to wear their reputations on their sleeves. Sellers go to great lengths to avoid negative comments because negative feedback causes sales to go down. In fact, sellers are often brutally honest about their wares in order to avoid negative feedback. eBay also features community-related tools that create a self-governing and self-policing body of customers Sellers who have built solid reputations with buyers are rewarded by higher than average prices for their auctioned goods. A research study conducted on eBay found that buyers bid 7.6% more for goods listed by repeat sellers with high reputations.[25] eBay's feedback system creates tremendous transparency, allowing buyers to "price" a seller's reputation. This degree of transparency and accountability has generated tremendous trust that allows eBay to continue to grow and support millions of buyer–seller transactions.

--------------------------------▲▼▲--------------------------------

Yet, trust online seems to be scarce. According to Consumer WebWatch, only 29% of online users trust Web sites that sell products and services, a far lower percentage than for traditional, offline institutions.[22] According to a survey by Jupiter Media Metrix, 45% of U.S. companies said that lack of trust prevented them from conducting more business online.[23] Some of the keys for building Web site trust:[24]

- Maximize cues that build trust on your Web site.
- Use virtual-advisor technology to gain customer confidence and belief.
- Provide unbiased and complete information.
- Include competitive products.
- Provide open and transparent organizational communication.
- Keep your promises.

Finally, e-service quality mirrors many of the service quality dimensions discussed in Chapter 5. Consumers may use their brick and mortar service quality experiences to form expectations when shopping online; however, their zone of tolerance may be considerably narrower. e-Shoppers tend to be less patient and competitors' Web sites are only "one click away."[26] Figure 6.2 provides a broad framework for understanding the major dimensions of e-service quality.

"Incubative" dimensions would be considered before a Web site is launched and are largely related to site design issues, such as layout, content, ease of use, and general appearance. Recall from earlier discussion that site layout was highly correlated to repeat visits. On the other hand, certain factors (active dimensions) need to be considered throughout the period in which a company's Web site remains active, such as reliability, efficiency, support communication, security, and incentives. These factors are responsible for increasing customer retention and for encouraging positive word-of-mouth referrals.

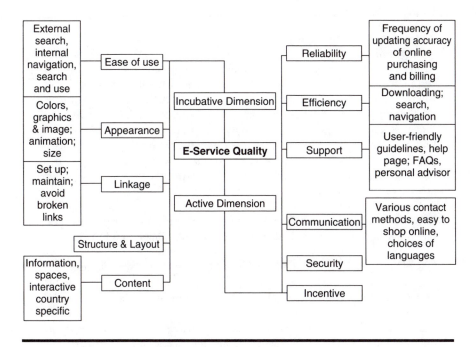

Figure 6.2 A Model of e-Service Quality (Adapted from Santos, J. [2000]. Managing Service Quality, Emerald Publishing, 13(3).)

Finally, as with service quality in general, the challenge for e-service marketers is to determine the relative performance and valence on each of these various service quality attributes and devise strategies to improve in these areas. Customer value checklist 6.1 lists some of the major e-service quality dimensions and suggestions on how to improve in these areas.

CUSTOMER VALUE CHECKLIST 6.1: KEYS FOR IMPROVING E-SERVICE QUALITY

Access — give customers access to their accounts, to check their profiles or track recent orders; also give them numerous ways to contact you. Do not bury the telephone numbers somewhere deep in the Web site.

Personalization — when the prospect (or customer) grants permission to be contacted, e.g., "opt-in," thank him for the visit; subsequent visits should present information based on the customer's earlier preferences, i.e., using "rules engines." Customers also want the opportunity for detailed shipping, billing, and credit card information as well. Many Web sites today offer a section called Your Account, which offers such information. The Lands' End (now owned by Sears) Web site offers a feature called My Virtual Model — a mannequin that users can set to their own measurements to see how the clothing items might fit. Sites should consider using online live chat; however, sites that offer this should make sure to give visitors who select this option an expected wait time for an agent.

Responsiveness — customers expect a prompt response to their inquiries. At the very least, visitors should immediately receive an automated e-mail response and a more detailed response to the customer's inquiry should follow. More than half of all consumers expect retailers to respond to e-mail inquires within 6 hours, but only 29% of online retailers actually meet those expectations, according to Jupiter Research. Customers also want to find information and access it quickly, which would suggest offering faster page loading. Finally, keep customers informed when the status of their orders change because today's e-consumer expects to be updated when changes to their orders occur.

Navigation — main links should be clearly visible on the tops of all pages, as well as on the sides or bottoms of pages. Once the prospect has navigated each individual page, second-level links should be visible under the main links. Access to "home" should always be present, regardless of tier level. Your site navigation scheme must be intuitive and easy to follow. By the time your visitors get to the second page, they must understand how your site is set up; key pages must be clearly labeled in the main menu; and the submenus must be very obvious. If a visitor gets lost in your site, he is much more likely to leave it than to try to figure out a confusing navigation scheme. Finally, according to research by Kearney, shoppers want to get in and out, quickly and efficiently.[27] Thus, online retailers should limit requests for information; never ask for the same information twice; and state the return policy clearly.

Assurance — involves confidence that service providers will keep their promises and that the information presented is clear, truthful, and secure. A study conducted by Consumer WebWatch, a nonprofit research project organized by Consumers Union and funded by several nonprofit foundations, recommends that in order to improve credibility with consumers online merchants should:

1. Disclose the physical location at which they are produced, including an address, telephone number, or e-mail address. Ownership, purpose and mission should also be clearly disclosed.
2. Clearly distinguish news and information from advertising. Web sites should also clearly disclose sponsorships and relevant business relationships, including links to other sites.
3. Disclose financial relations, particularly when the relationships affect the cost to a consumer. Fees for service, transactions, shipping, and handling should be clearly stated.
4. Any posted incorrect information should be immediately corrected, and policies on consumers' rights if a purchase is made based on incorrect information should be clearly stated.
5. Privacy policies should be easy to find and clearly and simply stated. Web sites should clearly disclose how a customer's personal information will be used.[28]

e-Sellers should also be able to offer assurances about delivery. One of the major reasons many dot.com businesses collapsed was due to problems with order fulfillment. Customers never gave these e-tailers a second chance when their orders arrived 3 weeks after Christmas.

Price clarity — extent to which the seller makes clear the final price to be paid. Prices should be clearly displayed alongside the items and a running total of purchases and shipping costs should be shown as the order progresses. Foreign consumers in particular have been hesitant to buy U.S. goods online when they did not know what the final cost would be after adding in customs and other fees. Comerxia, a Hallandale, FL-based company, uses their Web site, DoUWantIt.com, to arrive at a guaranteed price for products ordered online. Comerxia gets raw data on customs duties and taxes from UPS and their sources and applies its proprietary technology to come up with guaranteed prices. Before buying the product, the customer can see the price of the product, customs duties, and taxes. The products are then delivered from the retailer (such as Amazon.com) to a Mail Boxes Etc. or UPS center for pick-up by the customer.

▲▼▲

SUMMARY

Service quality is an important aspect of electronic commerce. Online customer service expectations such as reliability and responsiveness often mirror offline service expectations. Given online clutter and the myriad sites vying for the consumer's attention and loyalty, establishing online trust will become critical. e-Commerce marketers who regularly assess the performance and relative importance of these dimensions should be rewarded with loyal customers. This chapter has proposed that an opportunity exists to use online service quality to create high levels of satisfaction and repeat visits. Also, a framework of some of the key service quality dimensions controlled and managed by the e-marketers has been provided. The next chapter will discuss how value is conceived and communicated through the value proposition.

CUSTOMER VALUE ACTION ITEMS

1. For each of the following businesses, identify **core**, **facilitating**, **support**, and **complementary** services: (a) portal (e.g., AOL, Yahoo); (b) university; (c) large public library; and (d) large brokerage (e.g., Merrill Lynch, Charles Schwab).
2. Visit the Web sites of three major airlines comparing each of them using the incubative dimensions in the E-Service Quality Model (see Figure 6.2).

3. Suppose as a consultant you are asked to advise a client in setting up a food catering and delivery business in a large metropolitan area. The client anticipates that 70 to 85% of the orders will be placed online. Thus, your client is interested in learning the following: (a) which service dimensions will be most critical in creating ongoing customer value; (b) how to design the business and, in particular the Web site, to maximize customer service; and (c) how to assess service quality once the business is operational. Write a one-page plan for the client that addresses these needs.

4. Simplicity marketing gives consumers choices but in new ways that reduce the stress associated with making purchases. Leaders in this area include Amazon.com, Honda, Southwest Airlines, and Target Corp. For example, SWA mastered low-cost production of quality air transport and its Web site now accounts for more than half of its volume. Given what you know about CV and e-service quality, identify an Internet company (exclusive of Amazon) that practices simplicity marketing and briefly describe how it implements this strategy successfully.

5. A recent survey found that a third of Web users would pay for content. Yahoo! has capitalized on this finding and rolled out 17 paid consumer services last year. During the past year, Yahoo!'s paid services increased from 21 to 37% of revenues. How do you feel about paying for online services that were formerly free? Across the Web, companies are seeking revenue-producing strategies from information. What are the CV implications of this trend?

6. Exercise: a retail or virtual shopping experience?[26]
Situation: Customer A has an urgent need to buy an all-in-one printer that copies, scans, faxes, and prints. He drives to the electronics superstore where he has bought products previously. Nobody helps him, but he finds a model that may suit him. He asks a question about a feature and is told it is not available and "that's just the way it is." He still wants to buy, but it is out of stock and he is told to try the next week.
Discuss:
   a) How did the store lose its three possible competitive advantages — press its buttons (product); press his buttons (immediate customer gratification); or press the flesh (customer service)?
   b) What should have happened to create superior customer value?
   c) How could an e-tailer overcome these potential competitive disadvantages/advantages — press its buttons (product); press his buttons (immediate customer gratification); or press the flesh (customer service)?

d) What additional advantages and disadvantages occur in the e-commerce arena? How do these factors affect the creation of customer value.

e) Comment on customer retention/relationship marketing threats and opportunities.

REFERENCES

1. Anon. (2001) 74 % of companies to increase spending on customer service, *Direct Mark.* 64(6), October, 7.
2. Jupiter Research (2001). www.ecrmguide.com/insights/article.php/770721, May 22.
3. Freeman, L. (2000) Keeping 'em happy, *Mark. News,* May 8, 21.
4. Houck, J.B. (2001) The E-service emergency, www.CRMDaily.com, January 16.
5. Reichheld, F.F. and Schefter, P. (2000) e-Loyalty: your secret weapon on the Web, 78(4), July–August, 107.
6. Anon. (2001) The dog-com dilemma (2001). *Logistics Transp.t Focus,* 3(1), Jan/Feb, 6.
7. Clark, P. (2001) Online service flunks, *B to B,* May 28, 1.
8. Zimmerman, A (2002) e-Commerce (a special report): selling strategies — Web design: keep it simple — luxury retailers still haven't learned an important lesson for their Web sites: glitz is great, but not online. *WSJ,* April 15, R10.
9. Szymanski, D. and Hise, R. (2000) e-Satisfaction: an initial study, *J. Retailing,* 76(3), 317.
10. Houck, J. (2001). "The E-Service Emergency," www.CRMDaily.com, Jan. 16.
11. Weintraub, A. (2002) e-Mail: signed, sealed, deleted, *Bus. Week,* November 11, 14.
12. Hirsh, L. (2002) e-Tail customer service: finally working?, *E-Commerce Times,* Sept, 1.
13. Zeithaml, V., Parasuraman, A. and Malhotra, A. (2000) A conceptual framework for understanding e-service quality: implications for future research and managerial practice, MSI Working Paper, Report No. 00-115, 24.
14. Yang, Z. and Jun, M. (2002) Consumer perception of e-service quality: from Internet purchaser and nonpurchaser perspectives, *J. Bus. Strategy,* 19(1), Spring, 33.
15. Reichheld, F. and Schefter, P. (2000) e-Loyalty: your secret weapon on the Web, *Harvard Bus. Rev.,* 78(4), July–Aug, 106–110.
16. Ibid. p. 110.
17. Rice, M. (1997) What makes users revisit a Web site, *Mark. News,* 31(6) March 17, 12.
18. Liu, C. and Arnett, K. (2000) Exploring the factors associated with Web site success in the context of electronic commerce, *Inform. Manage.,* 38, October, 27.
19. Allard, C.R., van Riel, A., Liljander, V., and Jurriens, P. (2001) Exploring consumer evaluations of e-services: a portal site, *Int. J. Service Ind. Manage.,* 12(4), 362.
20. Lohse, G. and Spiller, P. (1998) Electronic shopping, *Assoc. Computing Machinery, Commun. ACM,* 41(7), July, 86.

21. Sulin, B. and Pavlou, P. (2002) Evidence of the effect of trust building technology in electronic markets: price premiums and buyer behavior, *MIS Q.*, 26(3), 265.

22. Consumer WebWatch Research (2003) http://www.radionewssource.com/Scripts/consumerWebwatch.htm.

23. Stein, T. (2003) Lack of trust threatens online commerce success, http://optimizemag.com/issue/017/trust.htm, March, issue 17.

24. Urban, G., Sultan, F., and Qualls, W. (2000) Placing trust at the center of your Internet strategy, *Sloan Manage. Rev.*, Fall, 40.

25. Resnick, P., Zeckhauser, R., Swanson, J., and Lockwood, K. (2002) The value of reputation on ebay: a controlled experiment, Working Paper RWPO3-007, (John F. Kennedy School of Government), July 6.

26. Allard, C.R., Semeijn, J., and Janssen, W. (2003) e-Service quality expectations: a case study, *Total Qual. Manage. Bus. Excellence*, 14(4), June, 437.

27. Sean Carton, (2000) "What Do Online Shoppers Want," November 29, http://www.clickz.com/tech/lead_edge/print.php/833091.

28. Wingfield, N. (2002) e-Commerce cover story — a question of trust: online consumers are buying — but warily; here's how you can minimize the risk, *WSJ*, Sept. 16, R6.

III

PLANNING AND IMPLEMENTING A WINNING VALUE PROPOSITION

7

DEFINING AND REFINING THE VALUE PROPOSITION

It ain't that hard to be different.

Tom Peters

Understand what we mean by *best value*. It isn't always the lowest price. It's the best combination of price, quality, features, service, training, and that confident feeling you have when you're getting a great deal.

Gateway Country circular

One of the most critical challenges for service firms is to differentiate themselves from competitors. It is relatively easy to be like everyone else; great companies have their own unique identities and carefully conceived value propositions. Realize that different is not always better, but *better is always different*. This chapter explores what is meant by a value proposition (VP); examines value disciplines; explains how organizations must constantly work on getting better through rethinking and redesigning their value propositions; and discusses the strategic implications of VPs for customer value managers.

THE VALUE PROPOSITION AS BASIS FOR COMPETITIVE STRATEGY

According to Frederick Webster, the value proposition is a "verbal statement that matches up the firm's distinctive competencies with the needs and preferences of a carefully designed set of potential customers." He adds that the VP helps firms as a communications device and is a basis for creating a shared understanding between the company and its customers.[1] Boyd et al., however, view value propositions and positioning statements as almost synonymous: both reflect customer benefits rather than features, relevant product categories, and target market. They add, however, that the VP typically includes information about pricing relative to competitors.[2]

The perspective here is somewhat different. The value proposition should be developed first because this is the company's promise to the customer. A well-designed VP is a strategic business tool that includes but goes beyond product mix, pricing, and promotion (marketing communications) to define the organization's competitive advantage through offerings, people, processes, and technology. For example, the "passionate pursuit of perfection" is the Lexus value proposition. This value statement encapsulates the essence of this upscale Japanese automobile manufacturer's worldwide marketing commitment to customer delight and retention with respect to product line quality; sales philosophy; dealership atmospherics; customer service; image; distribution; and logistics. A positioning strategy that supports the VP is how the organization delivers and differentiates value to its customers (discussed further in Chapter 9).

Value propositions should be clear, concise, credible, and consistent over time. For example, the "Intel inside" personal computer campaign demonstrated that an industrial part (computer chips) could be differentiated in a similar manner to consumer products (potato chips). The overwhelming success of this program demonstrated that users valued Intel as a trusted component, the heart of the PC. In fact, to many computer buyers, the so-called "Wintel" standard (Microsoft Windows software, Intel microprocessors) has become more valued than the hardware manufacturer/assembler.

IBM's "global solutions for a small planet" was another highly effective VP. This strategic thrust illustrated that this business giant was fully prepared to deliver e-business solutions to companies, large and small, across the globe. It reflected the new reality that IBM was no longer just a hardware company and generated a majority of its revenues from the new economy — services such as consulting, software, service contracts, etc. Realize that a good value proposition is more than just a cute slogan or a short-term positioning effort; it is a corporate commitment to pursue a specific strategic direction. Figure 7.1 lists nine great examples of value propositions (note that these are simple yet powerful messages).

VALUE DISCIPLINES AND MARKET LEADERSHIP

In Treacy and Wiersema's 1995 best-selling and influential book, *The Discipline of Market Leaders*, they argue that companies can excel by

Company	Value Proposition
FedEx	When it absolutely, positively has to get there overnight
IBM	Global solutions for a small planet
Intel	Intel inside
Lexus	Passionate pursuit of perfection
Motorola University	Right knowledge, right now
Nordstrom	Shopping humanized
Publix Super Markets	Where shopping is a pleasure
Snapple	Natural beverages, made from the best stuff on Earth
Visa	It's everywhere you want to be

Figure 7.1   Examples of Value Propositions

practicing one of three principal business strategies — product leadership, operational excellence, or customer intimacy. Let us examine some examples of how firms successfully execute the value discipline idea as the basis of their VPs and business models. Product leaders such as Johnson & Johnson, Nike, and Nokia strive for the best quality goods and services. Operational excellence is delivered by Dell Computer, Southwest Airlines, and Target stores. The best total solution (customer intimacy/service) is provided by Airborne Express, Frito-Lay, and Nordstrom. The core capabilities required to implement these strategies successfully are innovation (product leadership); process efficiency and low cost (operational excellence); and relationship building (customer intimacy).[3]

Waggoner extends the value disciplines concept by adding four additional approaches to market: (1) organizational flexibility (Nucor); (2) speed to market (Intel); (3) time manager (DuPont); and (4) value chain player (Amazon.com).[4] A summary of the three core value approaches that includes image factors is presented in Table 7.1.

Table 7.1   Value Disciplines

Value Disciplines	Value Focus	Image Driver	Image
Customer intimacy	Service	Create relationship	Best friend
Product leadership	Quality	Unique attribute	Best product/ service
Operational excellence	Cost	Low cost	Best deal

Source: Adapted from Scholey, C. (2002) *CMA Manage.*, October, 14.

In the financial services arena, the Morgan Stanley Group emphasizes innovation and new product offerings (world-class products), while Charles Schwab competes via low price and convenient automated systems (lowest cost) and J. P. Morgan stresses hiring the best bankers to build flexibility and customer intimacy (best total solution).[5] Additional research of the online brokerage industry found that E*Trade is a contender in the product leadership area; Ameritrade and Scottrade have a clear emphasis on cost value and practicing operational excellence; and Fidelity and Schwab emphasize service value and would be classified as using a customer intimacy strategy.[6]

THE VALUE PROPOSITION: SOME APPLICATIONS AND GUIDELINES

Because all organizations are separate entities, ideally each should have its own identity. This requires a careful analysis of all potential value proposition ingredients — service, quality, image, and price. The more unique the articulation of the core and augmented VP elements is, the more memorable the message and more likely the success.

A good value proposition is difficult to imitate. Although many online companies or pure plays exist, there is only one eBay — dubbed the Internet's most successful venture. eBay gets nearly 50,000 new "try-ers" a day and has captured nearly 50 million customers so fiercely loyal that 90% of them would not consider doing business on other Web-based auction sites. In this virtual global marketplace where innovation and community collide, devotees can buy ("win") or sell almost anything. Mom-and-pop sellers, who market antiques, baseball cards, computer equipment, and a cornucopia of miscellaneous treasure/stuff, account for more than 90% of the company's revenues. eBay users exchanged 170 million items worth $9.3 billion in 2001. First-quarter 2002 revenues surged 59% and profits doubled.[7]

According to Amit and Zott, e-business has four sources of value creation: efficiency, complementarities, lock-in, and novelty.[8] Clearly, these apply to eBay, where trading is characterized by low transaction costs; vast selection; motivation to engage in repeated transactions; and technological empowerment.

A value proposition can be defined as benefits less costs. Summarized next is a value equation from a health care provider. This example clarifies how consumers measure value in this context[9]:

VP = (quality + service + intangibles) − (price + nonmonetary costs)
Quality or outcomes = correct diagnosis and treatment, prevention of illness, etc.

Does it take the customer's perspective?

Is it easy to understand?

Does it encapsulate the value you offer to: your people, the sales channel, the press, and your customers?

Is it strategically compatible with your business?

Is it acceptable given your organizational culture?

Is it honest?

Is it promotable? (i.e., is logical; is easily communicated; is solutions oriented; has a headline or graphic with stopping power; has different benefits for different buying influences; and is original)

Figure 7.2 Critiquing Your Value Proposition (From Dovel, G.P. [1990] *Bus. Mark.*, July, 43–51.)

Service = accessibility, compassion, dependability, employee knowledge, etc.

Intangibles = reputation of the provider, special services, long-term outcomes and the relationship, use of latest technology, etc.

Price = consumer's expenditure for the service

Nonmonetary costs = time, energy, and psychological stress

Because customers, rather than management, set the true value agenda, organizations must carefully assess customers' interpretation of value. How does one know if the value proposition or value statement is effective? Figure 7.2 lists several questions for management to address.

BUILDING YOUR VALUE PROPOSITION: THE S-Q-I-P APPROACH

As noted in Chapter 1, customer value consists of four major components: service, quality, image, and price (see Figure 7.3). Extracting key differentiators from one or more of these core elements provides the basis of an organization's value proposition. The vertical axis on the diamond (service and quality) represents the backbone of the firm's offerings, while the horizontal axis (image and price) provides signaling cues to the target market. The *S-Q-I-P* elements create value for customers; establish a solid business philosophy for the organization; guide all strategic decisions; and, ultimately, affect business performance.

Many companies compete successfully on service dimensions. For example, service can be operationalized based on speed or time. Today, 1-hour photo finishing shops, 24-hour dry cleaners, and drive-through

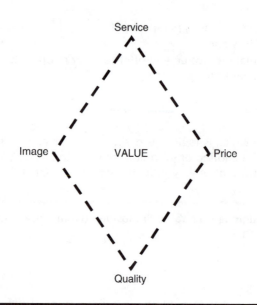

Figure 7.3   Designing a Value Proposition — the S-Q-I-P Diamond

wedding chapels all respond to the customer need for convenience or immediate gratification.

FedEx built its reputation based on a strong value proposition that guarantees package delivery by 10:30 a.m. the next morning. In contrast, the U.S. Post Office's priority mail service suffers some because of a much weaker value statement. Although the flat-rate, 1-pound envelope is a good deal at $3.85, the relatively slow 2- or 3-day delivery is a serious drawback. Many customers often send items priority mail because of image rather than speed — the red, white, and blue package looks more important than regular mail when it arrives on a client's desk. A 30% price increase (to $5.00) to ensure 2-day delivery would greatly strengthen this product — it would still be about a third of competitive offerings.

Broderbund Software knows that quality products are essential to its business success. It has used innovative offerings and niche marketing to compete effectively in the educational and gaming software markets. Value innovation can be fostered in companies by reducing investment in business units that are *settlers* (offer me-too products and services); increasing investment in *migrators* (businesses with value improvements); and using corporate entrepreneurship initiatives to create *pioneers* (businesses that represent value innovations). Research on the source of high growth in diverse organizations found that only 14% of new business initiatives were true value innovations; yet, these breakthrough concepts yielded 38% of total revenues and an impressive 61% of total profits.[10]

The American Productivity & Quality Center (APQC) has studied more than 100 companies and found that learning how to tap into and use knowledge can be an important source for creating customer value and obtaining a competitive advantage in the marketplace. Specifically, five knowledge-based routes to designing successful value propositions have been identified[11]:

- *Knowledge as product* — selling consulting services, databases, etc.
- *Knowledge transfer* — adapting best practices from high-performing units of an organization
- *Customer-focused knowledge* — data mining, using database information, customized responses to customer concerns, etc.
- *Personal responsibility for knowledge* — empowering front-line service employees to have the necessary information and ability to act to solve customer problems
- *Intellectual-asset management* — use patents, licensing, and technology to generate value for the customer and the company

Virgin Enterprises uses a strong brand name and a unique global image to create value for customers. Richard Branson's business empire now extends into an airline; cell phones/service; music production business; music retail stores; soft drinks; and other youth-oriented products. In business, names matter; the success of the Virgin idea has been demonstrated — Slipped Disc was rejected because it was not as catchy and lacked wide appeal for other product lines.[12] Developing a new and improved image can also have dramatic impact on the success of a professional sports franchise (see customer value insight 7.1). Price can play a major or support role in the value proposition. Companies such as Best Buy, Costco, Discount Auto Parts, Nobody Beats the Wiz, and Priceline.com communicate to the marketplace that they are price leaders. Readers are highly encouraged to review the pricing chapter (Chapter 8) for an in-depth review of this strategic marketing variable and how it affects customer value management.

The customer value assessment tool (CVAT) assesses 42 measures of customer value in the four major VP areas — service, quality, image, and price (see the appendix at the end of this chapter). CVAT is a diagnostic instrument that is most valuable for capturing information on how CV thinking is practiced within the organization.

DEVELOPING UNIQUE VALUE PROPOSITIONS

A major challenge for firms is to be seen as different by the market; this requires the development of a unique value proposition. The S-Q-I-P idea

Shop the way customers shop.	Schwab pioneered "around the clock" service; this included automated phone trading for securities as well as PC-based electronic trading.
Pay careful attention to how customers really use the product or service.	By really listening to its customers, Schwab eliminated the need for follow-up confirmation calls.
Explore customers' latent dissatisfactions.	Schwab's One Source created a single point of purchase and account statement for hundreds of mutual funds.
Look for uncommon denominators.	Schwab separates high-volume equity traders from ordinary investors with simpler financial management needs.
Pay careful attention to anomalies.	Schwab's concept of retail sales offices ran contrary to the prevailing mindset in the industry (i.e., discount brokers do not need costly overhead). However, the retail network generated substantial walk-in traffic and provided reassuring sites for current clients to transact business.
Look for diseconomies in the industry's value chain.	Schwab became a financial intermediary via One Source in the mutual fund sector rather than create its own product line of funds.
Look for analogous solutions to the industry's compromises.	Schwab demonstrated that firms could break the industry compromise between low price and reliable service (similar to Southwest Airlines).

Figure 7.4   How Charles Schwab Redefined the Brokerage Market (Adapted from Stalk, G. et al. [1996] *Harvard Bus. Rev.,* **September/October, 131–139.)**

discussed earlier in this chapter may be sufficient; however, many 21st century companies find that the best path to creating value and setting them apart from the rest of the field is to change the rules of the game.

Smart companies recognize compromises that their business/industry imposes on their customers and seek to break these compromises, thus releasing tremendous value. Customer-focused companies can exploit these unnecessary concessions to find a competitive advantage. Figure 7.4 lists seven ways that Charles Schwab has revolutionized the discount brokerage industry and prospered by breaking industry compromises for nearly a quarter of a century.[13]

Airlines and hotels are two service industries (among many) that have created "artificial" resistance barriers for customers. For airlines, it is the

Saturday night stay-over requirement, which can double or triple round-trip fares. Southwest Airlines does not force its customers to spend a Saturday evening somewhere they choose not to be and still get low fares.

————————————————▼▲▼————————————————

CUSTOMER VALUE INSIGHT 7.1 — PEWTER POWER: HOW A NEW IMAGE HELPS TRANSFORM PERENNIAL LOSERS INTO SUPER BOWL CHAMPIONS*

How much does an image matter to an organization? In outstanding companies such as Southwest Airlines or Virgin Enterprises, market perception or image defines their essence. Although strong leadership and quality products and services are a given, customers often choose to patronize certain businesses because of who they are and what they stand for. Typically, image is a part of the customer value proposition along with product quality, service, and price. In many situations, organizations must proactively change an image that is unfavorable or weak to its target market. This is particularly true in professional sports where image is elevated to an even higher plane. A sports team's image can favorably or unfavorably affect fan support, marketing/merchandising opportunities, and even performance on the playing field.

On January 26, 2003, the Tampa Bay Buccaneers stunned the favored Oakland Raiders 48 to 21 in Super Bowl XXXVII. As hundreds of millions of people watched, a long-suffering football franchise finally won the ultimate game and was now champion of the world. An evolving, changed image played a key part in the Bucs rise from worst to first to become the National Football League's most dominant team.

Tampa Bay entered the NFL in 1976. As expected of expansion teams, the team immediately struggled. However, it brought the meaning of losing to depths never previously witnessed; the Buccaneers did not win a single game in their inaugural season and went 26 games before finally winning (nearly two full seasons). When their coach, John McKay, was asked about his team's execution, he said he was in favor of it.

A talented defense led by Lee Roy Selmon and a serviceable offense featuring Doug Williams' arm, Jimmie Giles' hands, and Ricky Bell's legs shocked the football world by making the NFL playoffs three times from 1979 to 1982. Unfortunately, questionable personnel moves, poor decisions in the annual NFL drafts, and misguided ownership quickly led to the team's downfall. By late 1983, they were the "old Bucs" again. Some shouted for McKay to be thrown into Tampa Bay; however, his departure following the 1984 season did little to shift the team's misfortunes. A series of unsuccessful coaches (and players) just brought more losing to the Buccaneers and more heartbreak for their fans. Incredibly, the team managed to reel off 14 straight losing seasons. The team labeled by some as the Yucks or Yuckaneers provided endless comedic value for late-night talk show hosts. Some Bucs

————————————

* Prepared by Art Weinstein, Ph.D.

fans went to games with paper bags over their heads. Forget about the playoffs — Buccaneer fans had more modest goals for their team, such as not losing 10 games during a 16-game season. By the end of 1996, Tampa Bay had lost almost 70% of the football games it had ever played. Based on winning percentage, this was the most unsuccessful franchise in American professional sports history.

During this era of great ineptness, the Buccaneers sported unattractive orange and white uniforms and helmets featuring a logo of a winking, friendly pirate. The team's mascot at the time was Bucco Bruce and it played its games in Tampa Stadium, a facility rapidly on the decline.

The mid-1990s brought a new ownership group (Malcolm Glazer and family); a new defensive-minded head coach (Tony Dungy); excellent Pro Bowl players (Mike Alstott, Derrick Brooks, John Lynch, and Warren Sapp); and a positive, winning attitude toward the team. Rich McKay, the knowledgeable general manager and the original coach's son, was retained in the transition. One of management's great early ideas was to decimate the old losing apparel, dubbed the "creamsicle" look. The revamped, late 1990s Bucs gear was designed in stylish red and pewter colors. The pewter power image features a menacing-looking pirate/theme on the team's helmets, uniforms, and merchandising. The phrase "feel the power" featuring a pirate's flag and dagger was used to promote this incarnation of Buccaneer players.

Although Dungy's gang lost their first five games in 1996, the team finished strongly, winning five of their last seven games (Bucs fans now had a reason to believe that the team would soon succeed). Following a 15-year hiatus, by 1997 the winning ways returned. The team went 10 and 6 and earned a home field, wild-card playoff appearance. The 20 to 10 win over the Detroit Lions, which was the last game ever played at Tampa/Houlihan's Stadium, showed how far the team had come.

In 1998, the team moved into the brand-new Raymond James stadium. "Ray/Jay" is a state-of-the-art facility featuring a multimillion dollar replica of a pirate ship that explodes booming cannons when the Buccaneers score touchdowns. Unlike the game days of yesteryear in which thousands of empty seats were found in Tampa Stadium, today's Bucs rule Tampa town and a waiting list for season tickets numbers in the tens of thousands.

From 1997 to 2001, Tampa Bay was one of the most successful NFL franchises, winning one division title and making the playoffs four out of five years. The former laughingstock "Yucks" aura was now eradicated. Although the new-found success was exciting, the team was unable to advance in the playoffs under the laid-back coaching style of Tony Dungy. Following a third straight playoff appearance in which the team failed to score a TD, Dungy was fired; the fiery Jon "Chucky" Gruden (formerly of the Oakland Raiders) was brought in to replace him.

Gruden's widely praised, high-powered offense failed to materialize at times throughout the regular season; nevertheless, he inspired the Bucs to win 12 games (a team record) and another division title, as well as to reach new heights throughout the season. Gruden built on the team's defensive dominance established during Dungy's reign and instilled an increased confidence level that helped it slay dragons such as not winning in temperatures under 40°; not winning a playoff game on the road, a four-game losing streak against the Philadelphia Eagles; and, of course, not getting to and winning the Super Bowl. Postseason, Gruden's team really shone, outscoring three excellent opponents 106 to 37 and culminating in their superb Super Bowl effort.

It has not hurt that Gruden has inherited outstanding players like Ronde Barber, Keyshawn Johnson, and Sapp, who share his passion for winning and being spotlighted in the media. Although Barber has already established himself as a television personality in the Visa check card ad with his twin brother Tiki (the New York Giants' star running back), the commercialization of the victorious, post-Super Bowl Bucs is ready to begin. Because about a dozen Bucs players are already well exposed in the Tampa radio and TV market, the national spotlight may be a natural progression for many of them.

In addition, the marketing possibilities for Buccaneer merchandising in the year 2003 and beyond are huge. Pre-Super Bowl Bucs gear currently ranks as one of the top selling of NFL teams. A huge, upward spike in sales will now occur due to the team's increased national exposure.

As this minicase illustrates, image is not everything (first-rate leadership and high-quality products are required), but it does play a major role in the marketing of an organization. This is true in analyzing an image-based company such as Ben & Jerry's Ice Cream or Harley-Davidson, or a company or football team that can benefit from repositioning such as the Tampa Bay Buccaneers. An improved image can help attract more customers, increase revenues, and build organizational performance.

■▼▲

Hotel check-in times are often imposed through standard operating procedures that are unquestioned. Inconvenient hotel check-in (for example, by 4:00 p.m.) and check-out (for example, by 10:00 a.m.) policies mean that a day is not really a day. Although the folly (or short-term profitability) of these unnecessary requirements is readily apparent, great companies do not take these industry "rules" as given; these companies design their own rules for the game. Crowne Plaza and Sheraton are some hotel chains that have experimented with more equitable day rates for their valued guests.

Value Rental Car's now defunct $0.99 per hour pricing plan was widely embraced by customers as an innovative marketing strategy. Unfortunately, the accountants had more work to do and the profitability of this tactic was not demonstrated. Regardless, as these travel industry examples illustrate, companies do not need to succumb to questionable industry trade practices or standard operating procedures — they must constantly search for better ways of doing business in a time-conscious society.

THE VALUE PROPOSITION: STRATEGIC IMPLICATIONS

As markets change, so must firms' value propositions. Consider the approaches used by two of the office superstores, Staples and Office Depot (note that they sell essentially the same products and have similar service and pricing strategies). Staples uses its extensive database for target marketing, promotional activity, and product enhancements. This office supply store chain learned that, as many of their small business customers grew larger, they defected to competitors with delivery services. Staples recently introduced this value-added option to do a better job retaining customers.[14]

Office Depot's current value proposition is "what you need, what you need to know." This replaced "business is crazy, Office Depot makes sense," which featured Dilbert, Scott Adams' cartoon character, as spokesperson. In response, Office Max, the third giant in this market, removed all Dilbert products from its store. The competitive situation and potential niche opportunities should guide management's thinking about the appropriate value proposition to employ. The convergence and deregulation of the financial services industry means that everyone is entering each other's business. One industry expert noted that retail insurance services could evolve into one of a bank's top three businesses. To accomplish this, five new value propositions might be provided[15]:

- Instant insurance
- Deep discount insurance
- Transformational insurance (to deal with life changes)
- Indexed insurance (automatically adjusts to income levels)
- Solutions-based insurance (e.g.,, a single policy for a homebuyer's financial risk protection rather than mortgage insurance, title insurance, homeowner's insurance, disaster insurance, etc.)

It is interesting to note that none of these products is offered to bank customers at this time.

After years of tremendous success, Toys"R"Us has recently struggled due to complacency and lack of innovation; competition from Wal-Mart, Target, and other discount giants and membership warehouse chains; and new/creative competitors in the educational toy market. As part of the business renewal process, organizations should use cost/benefit analysis periodically to assess how their value proposition compares to competitive options.

As Figure 7.5 shows, companies may occupy one of five positions — best value, discount value, expensive value, fair value, or poor value —

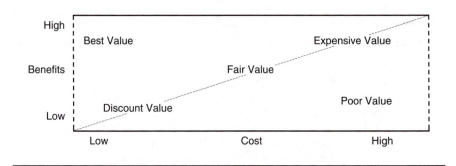

Figure 7.5 Assessing a Company's Value Position

in the mind of the customer (note, the diagonal is the fair-value [FV] line). Bradley Gale, a leading thinker on customer value, explains that the fair-value line is the line of points at which competitors would neither gain nor lose market share with respect to price–quality tradeoffs.[16] Discount, fair, and expensive values have benefits consistent with their costs. Best value (above the FV line) represents a strong competitive advantage, while poor value (below the FV line) is a prescription for failure for an organization.

In the case of Toys"R"Us, the company lost ground in the marketplace, moving from the "best value" to "fair value" position. Their toy registry initiative is a relatively new strategy aimed at winning back some of the lost market share. The registry acts as a "wish list" to let family and friends know the toys that children want for birthdays, holidays, or special occasions.

Finally, review the 10 questions in customer value checklist 7.1 to explore the key customer value concepts discussed in this chapter.

SUMMARY

The value proposition establishes the basis for developing a unique position in the marketplace. Service, quality, image, and value-based pricing are the core elements of the VP. Companies that are value winners also innovate, strengthen their value statements, and are not afraid to break industry rules occasionally. Rather than viewing the VPs as separate elements, good managers try to create synergy among all of the components to achieve differentiation and secure competitive advantage. Furthermore, the value proposition should be reshaped when changing market conditions call for adoption of a revised business strategy.

▼▲▼

CUSTOMER VALUE CHECKLIST 7.1: 10 BASICS OF CUSTOMER VALUE[17,18]

Who is your customer?

How does your customer experience value?

What is unique about your value proposition?

Are you competing primarily on price or value?

Do you design products and services that deliver the desired value?

Do you design effective sales and service channels?

Do you recruit and equip employees to deliver and increase customer value?

What are you willing to do to deliver better value?

How have you added value to customers of late?

Do you refine and measure the value proposition to ensure customer loyalty and retention?

▲▼▲

CUSTOMER VALUE ACTION ITEMS

1. Your chief marketing officer (CMO) has given you a high-profile, make-or-break assignment at work: develop a customer value plan for your firm. Consider the following seven questions in your two-page executive summary for this report.

   a. Which core aspect of the value proposition (VP) does your company emphasize — service, quality, image, or price?

   b. Which value discipline does your organization emphasize (product leadership, operational excellence, or customer intimacy)?

   c. Define your company's value proposition. What is unique about your VP?

   d. How does your company work on a daily basis at being different and better than the competition? Consider purpose and process issues in your response.

   e. Has your company broken any industry "rules" lately? If so, explain.

   f. Does your firm offer a *best value, discount value, expensive value, fair value,* or *poor value*?

   g. What can your organization do to truly deliver superior customer value?

2. You were hired as a management consultant by one of the leading dot.com's in the *USA Today* top 25 consumer firms index and asked to design/refine the value proposition for this company. How would you proceed in this project? Provide a draft of the working VP for this company to assess.

3. Compare and contrast how any two of these companies — British Airways, Microsoft, Nokia, Sony, and Target — create value for their customers.

4. Assume you are thinking about purchasing a new car. Go to the manufacturer's or auto dealer's Web site and KelleyBluebook.com to obtain product and pricing information about your vehicle. Based on this research, discuss the value-based pricing, quality, service, and brand-identification (image) strategies used to market this automobile.

5. Using a company to which you are highly loyal (e.g., favorite restaurant or small business, bookmarked Web site, etc.), use the CVAT (see appendix) to conduct a mini value audit of this organization. Based on this informal analysis, identify three to five potential problems and possible strategies to overcome these shortcomings.

APPENDIX
CUSTOMER VALUE ASSESSMENT TOOL (CVAT™)*

Overview

In today's competitive business environment, offering superior customer service is no longer the exception; it is the rule. Customers expect it, and businesses are relentlessly trying to provide it. Unfortunately, relatively few organizations are able to provide truly memorable service to their customers. Two words seem to capture exceptional service: "customer value." It is easy to interpret a successful response to the moments of truth. Such companies "go the extra mile" and add value in order to delight their customers. The bottom line is that you know customer value when you see or experience it.

Purpose

The CVAT has been created as an instrument to help product and service providers evaluate and improve their value delivery to their customers. Supplying outstanding service and value must be a dynamic process; therefore, this tool has been designed to be utilized on a regular basis. This helps to evaluate the extent of any changes and improvements that may need to be initiated. The four S-Q-I-P components used to appraise customer value in this tool are perceived as: service quality, product quality, image, and value-based price. The survey focuses on each component as an individual indicator of customer service and value.

---

* Developed by Brett A. Gordon and Pamela Gordon. ©June 1998 Brett A. Gordon and Pamela A. Gordon. All rights reserved.

Collectively, these components will help companies achieve excellence in managing customer value.

Guidelines for Using the Customer Value Assessment Tool

The purpose of the CVAT is to rate your current employer based on the four components used to appraise customer value. Rank how well your company matches each statement in the survey, using the following criteria:

1 = happens all of the time
2 = happens most of the time
3 = happens some of the time
4 = never happens

The results obtained via the CVAT can be organized into a report that will help identify strengths as well as opportunities for improving customer value in your organization.

Perceived Service Quality

Definition: *the service given is viewed to be timely and appropriate by the customer. This service may also anticipate future needs or wants of the customer.*

1. The company conducts focus groups with customers to determine what they view as strengths and weaknesses about the customer service provided.

    1   2   3   4

2. The company continually conducts customer satisfaction surveys and utilizes the results in order to improve services provided.

    1   2   3   4

3. The company provides special training for all employees on customer service, including ways to handle difficult customers.

    1   2   3   4

4. The company has a monthly "best practices" newsletter that details innovative ways to provide customer service.

    1   2   3   4

5. The company provides its customers with a range of professional and technical assistance.

   1   **2**   **3**   **4**

6. The company commits to and exhibits empathy when dealing with customers.

   1   **2**   **3**   **4**

7. The company constantly seeks ways to enhance its relationships with customers.

   1   **2**   **3**   **4**

8. The company provides a means for customers who wish to comment or complain.

   1   **2**   **3**   **4**

9. The company provides its customers with complete, easy-to-understand information concerning products or services.

   1   **2**   **3**   **4**

10. The company ensures that complaints and problems are resolved to the complete satisfaction of the customer.

   1   **2**   **3**   **4**

11. The company regularly compares its customer satisfaction levels with those of the competition.

   1   **2**   **3**   **4**

12. The company rewards employees for innovative actions/ideas concerning customer service, irrespective of sales outcome.

   1   **2**   **3**   **4**

13. The company regularly reviews progress on customer service goals and objectives.

   1   **2**   **3**   **4**

14. Policies and procedures for serving customers are consistent across departments.

   1   **2**   **3**   **4**

Be sure to note any comments you have about issues covered in this section.

Perceived Product Quality

Definition: *the product is viewed as dependable (zero defects) and meets or exceeds the consumer's expectations.*

1. The company conducts focus groups with customers to determine what they view as strengths and weaknesses about the company's products.

    1   2   3   4

2. The company forms strategic alliances with vendors, suppliers, and distributors.

    1   2   3   4

3. The company selects vendors on the basis of quality, not just price.

    1   2   3   4

4. The company uses quality function deployment (i.e., builds customer expectations into the product).

    1   2   3   4

5. The company is committed to design quality: "do it right the first time."

    1   2   3   4

6. The company uses external benchmarking to determine the strengths and weaknesses of its products.

    1   2   3   4

7. The company has a system for analyzing product performance data (i.e., quality control data) and translating the results into continuous product improvements.

    1   2   3   4

8. The company monitors supplier/vendor performance to ensure that the company's quality requirements are met.

    1   2   3   4

9. The company views corporate setbacks as an opportunity to develop a new approach to solving the problem.

    1   2   3   4

10. The company's marketing programs, methods, and strategies add value to the firm's offerings.

    1   2   3   4

11. The company demonstrates through thought, word, and deed that low quality is expensive and that high quality has a high return on investment.

    1   2   3   4

12. The company is viewed as having a commitment to continuous improvement: *kaizen*.

    1   2   3   4

Be sure to note any comments you have about issues covered in this section.

Perceived Image

Definition: *the company is viewed as having a commitment to the customer, top management, continuous improvement, and the firm as a whole.*

1. The company treats its internal customers with the same care and respect with which it treats its external customers.

   1   2   3   4

2. The company conducts focus groups with customers to determine what they view as strengths and weaknesses about the company's image.

   1   2   3   4

3. The management style exhibited by the leaders of the company reflects that of a facilitator, coach, and enabler.

   1   2   3   4

4. Employees are viewed as positive representatives of the company's ideals.

   1   2   3   4

5. The company uses "systems thinking" to solve its internal and external challenges (e.g., the company understands that all events within the corporation are interrelated and each has an influence on the other).

   1   2   3   4

6. The company encourages its employees to seek a good balance between their work and family lives.

   1   2   3   4

7. The company eliminates obvious examples of excess.

   1   2   3   4

Be sure to note any comments you have about issues covered in this section.

Perceived Value-Based Price

Definition: *the price level that a customer is willing to pay to receive a given level of product and/or service performance.*

1. When establishing a price for a product or service, the company starts with the customer first; considers the competition; and then determines the appropriate price, as opposed to setting price only according to costs.

   1   2   3   4

2. The company's product or service is viewed by the customer as exceeding the expected benefits of a competitive product.

   1   2   3   4

3. The company meets customer expectations without hindering financial performance.

   1   2   3   4

4. The company offers as many convenient payment methods and terms as possible in order to satisfy its customers better.

   1   2   3   4

5. The company looks for ways to cut back on costs and still deliver products or services that meet customer expectations.

   1   2   3   4

6. The company utilizes new technologies that allow it to lower prices and increase profits.

   1   2   3   4

7. The company creates innovations that allow it to offer more for less than the competition.

   1   2   3   4

8. The company raises quality and service to new levels.

   1   2   3   4

9. The company is viewed as value adding with respect to the price it charges for its product or service.

   1   2   3   4

Be sure to note any comments you have about issues covered in this section.

REFERENCES

1. Webster, F.E., Jr. (1994) Defining the new marketing concept (part 1), *Mark. Manage.*, 2(4), 22–31.
2. Boyd, H.W., Jr. et al. (2002) *Marketing Management*, 4th ed. New York: McGraw-Hill.
3. Treacy, M. and Wiersema, F. (1995) *The Discipline of Market Leaders*, Reading, MA: Addison–Wesley.
4. Waggoner, R. (1999) Have you made a wrong turn in your approach to market? *J. Bus. Strategy*, Nov./Dec., 17–21.
5. Callan, C. and Mara, J. (1997) Living the value proposition, *Banking Strategies*, Nov./Dec., 16–20.
6. Dewan, S. (2002) Value disciplines and returns on IT investments, IAB discussion paper, www.crito.uci.edu/events/iab2002-02/.
7. Swartz, J. (2002) eBay faithful expect loyalty in return, *USA Today*, June 30, www.usatoday.com/life/cyber/2002/07/01ebay.htm,
8. Amit, R. and Zott, C. (2001) Value creation in e-business, *Strategic Manage. J.*, 22, 493–520.
9. Ettinger, W.H., Jr. (1998) Consumer-perceived value: the key to a successful business strategy in the health care marketplace, *J. Am. Geriatr. Soc.*, 46, 111–113.
10. Kim, W.C. and Mauborgne, R. (1997) Value innovation: the strategic logic of high growth, *Harvard Bus. Rev.*, Jan./Feb., 102–12.
11. Grayson, C.J., Jr. and O'Dell, C.S. (1998) Mining your hidden resources, *Across Board*, April, 23–28.
12. Crainer, S. (1999) *The 75 Greatest Management Decisions Ever Made ... and Some of the Worst*, New York: MJF Books.
13. Stalk, G., Jr., Pecaut, D.K., and Burnett, B. (1996) Breaking compromises, breakaway growth, *Harvard Bus. Rev.*, 74, Sept./Oct., 131–139.
14. Reichheld, F.F. (1994) Loyalty and the renaissance of marketing, *Mark. Manage.*, 2(4), 10–21.
15. Kaytes, D.G. (1997) Jump starting insurance sales, *Banking Strategies*, 73, Nov./Dec., 104–108.
16. Gale, B.T. (1994) *Managing Customer Value: Creating Quality and Service That Customers Can See*, New York: The Free Press.
17. Tucker, R.B. (1997) *Customer Service for the New Millennium: Winning and Keeping Value-Driven Buyers*, Franklin Hills, NJ: Career Press.
18. Larrew, T. (1998) The six steps of convergent marketing: putting customers at the center of business decisions, *Credit World*, Jan./Feb., 18–19.

BIBLIOGRAPHY

Anderson, K. and Zemke, R. (1991) *Delivering Knock Your Socks Off Service*, New York: AMACOM.

Bateman, T.S. and Snell, S.A. (1996) *Management: Building Competitive Advantage*, Chicago: Irwin.

Davis, B.L., Hellervik, L.W., Skube, C.J., Gebelein, S.H., and Sheard, J.L. (Eds.) (1992) *Successful Manager's Handbook: Development Suggestions for Today's Managers*, New York: Personnel Decisions International.

Gables, W. and Ellig, J. (1993) *Introduction to Market-Based Management*, Center for Market Processes, Fairfax, VA.

Gibson, J.L., Ivancevich, J.M., and Donnelly, J.H., Jr. (1994) *Organizations*, Burr Ridge, IL: Irwin.

Melnyk, S.A. and Denzler, D.R. (1996) *Operations Management: a Value-Driven Approach*, Boston: Irwin.

Naumann, E. (1995) *Creating Customer Value: The Path to Sustainable Competitive Advantage*, Cincinnati: Thomson Executive Press.

Noe, R.A., Hollenback, J.R., Gerhart, B., and Wright, P.M. (1997) *Human Resource Management*, Chicago: Irwin.

Tucker, R.B. (1997) *Customer Service for the New Millennium: Winning and Keeping Value-Driven Buyers*, Franklin Lakes, NJ: Career Press.

Zeithaml, V.A., Parasuraman, A., and Berry, L.L. (1990) *Delivering Quality Service: Balancing Customer Perceptions and Expectations*, New York: The Free Press.

8

COMMUNICATING VALUE THROUGH PRICE

Price is what you pay. Value is what you get.

Warren Buffett, CEO, Berkshire Hathway

The key to profitable marketing is setting a price commensurate with the value the customer actually receives.

Bob Donath, CEO, Donath and Co. Inc.

INTRODUCTION

Price communicates value by serving as a signal. Just as a traffic signal communicates "go," "slow," or "stop," price signals "higher quality" or "economy class." Marketers use price to signal value for their products or services, differentiate their offering from competitors, or shift customer demand. In the new economy, especially in reverse auctions, price functions as part of a "demand collection system." Customers bid on a unit of demand and sellers than decide whether or not to fill that demand. Priceline has revolutionized the pricing of airline tickets and hotel rooms by allowing prospective customers to announce what they are willing to pay and then alerting them whether or not their bid was accepted.

Customers consider price a cue of how much they must "give up" in order to acquire the possession or use the service. Competitors view price as a signal to match, beat, or use as a weapon to block another company's entry. A pricing strategy can help penetrate an existing market, such as the approach AT&T took to entering the credit card market by initially offering their card at no annual fee for life.

Prices are often determined based on the type and location of the purchase. During a recent trip to Thailand, one of the authors shopped in a bazaar in the southern part of the country and found that the price of everything was negotiable. Even in more industrialized countries, prices for big ticket items such as televisions, stereos, furniture, and automobiles are often subject to some price flexibility. Negotiated prices are even more common in business-to-business settings: for example, advertising media, telecommunications and consulting services

Today, managers set prices for goods and services before consumers and businesses ever meet. Managers often consider costs, demand, and competition, the hallmarks of value pricing, before arriving at a final price. This does not imply that pricing has become an exact science. Price is often set based on convention or rules of thumb, or even intuition about what the customer will (or should) pay. Regardless of whether price is viewed as an art or science, the price set is only as good as the value delivered to the customer. In today's competitive markets, companies cannot afford to neglect sound pricing policies. In a study conducted by *Purchasing* magazine, 62% of buyers indicated that price is "extremely important" and 65% rated price and quality as the most important factors in making purchase decisions.[1]

Setting the right price can often make or break the bottom line, especially for new products and services. Although most companies view price decisions as important, prices are often set on purely tactical grounds or in response to a competitor's move. Instead of simply a knee-jerk response to market conditions, pricing decisions should be made based on segmentation analysis, cost analysis, demand elasticities, and the firm's value proposition (see Chapter 7).

The quality components of customer value have already been discussed. Product and service quality influence a consumer's perception of value, although price also serves as a major signal for quality. However, innovative companies recognize that value for their customers is more than simply low price. This chapter examines how customers view price — the "give" component of the value equation — as an indicator of value. Next, how customers evaluate price is considered, as well as price in the context of a company's overall marketing strategy. The different approaches to pricing and principles that lead to better pricing decisions are then discussed. Finally, the chapter concludes with a brief overview of some future pricing issues.

RELATING PRICE TO VALUE

Today, value is often misunderstood to mean low price or bundled price. However, the essence of value revolves around the trade-off between

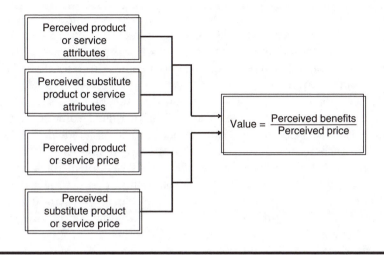

Figure 8.1   Price, Benefits, and Value

the benefits customers receive from a product or service and the price that they pay for the offering (see Figure 8.1). From a customer's standpoint, price only has meaning when paired with the tangible and psychic benefits delivered. For a given price, value increases when product or service benefits increase. For example, Men's Warehouse, a retailer of men's suits based in Fremont, California, offers low prices on brand-name men's suits, but also offers free pressing for as long as its customers own the suit, sport coat, or trousers. Taco Bell, a value-pricing innovator, knows that for every dollar spent at Taco Bell, customers get back $0.27 for food, $0.08 for advertising, $0.13 worth of overhead, and $0.12 for rent. They reasoned that rather than giving the customer $0.27 worth of food, give them $0.40 worth of food and find ways to reduce costs in the other areas.[2]

By the same token, value decreases when perceived benefits go down relative to price. Many companies were initially attracted to managed health care because of its ability to control skyrocketing health care costs. Yet, despite the cost savings, employees of these companies became frustrated by the loss of control over their medical destiny, i.e., reduced choice of physicians and reductions in certain types of care normally available under traditional fee-for-service coverage. These managed care companies were shortsighted by equating price to value.

Moreover, consumer value assessments are often comparative. Value judgments by consumers as to the worth and desirability of the product or service are made relative to competitive substitutes that satisfy the same need. Hewlett-Packard Co., one of the world's largest high-tech companies, has successfully introduced a line of Photosmart digital photography gear that has pitted it against Kodak, Canon, Fuji, and other industry leaders. HP has been a pioneer in the digital imaging technology market, turning its gear into a "home digital darkroom" comprising printers, scanners, cameras, and papers that enable users to produce true-to-life prints to rival anything from a photo lab.

The price of perceived product or service substitutes also goes into consumers' evaluation of value. The advent of digital cameras notwithstanding, Kodak continues to battle it out with its chief rival Fuji in the film market, where an all-out price war has erupted since mid-1997 at the low end of the film market. By bundling rolls of film in packs of four and five, Fuji has forced the price per roll of film down to just over $1, recalibrating the value equation in this market. Small, freestanding kiosks that can make fast prints from digital photos now sit in drugstores, supermarkets, and even hotels, further eroding the price for conventional camera film. Thus, consumers determine a product or service's value based on a company's perceived benefits and price as well as those from a competitor's offer.

HOW BUYERS EVALUATE PRICE

Buyers often use price as a perceptual cue to indicate the product or service quality. That is, all things being equal, the higher the price, the higher the perceived quality. Historically, product quality has been treated as the mirror image of price. This is still particularly the case when the brand is relatively unfamiliar to the buyer, such as medical-related products. The quality–price link also tends to be stronger for durable goods than for nondurable goods, such as major appliances or furniture.[3]

Buyers also use "frames of reference" to evaluate prices. Consumers evaluate purchases in terms of gains or losses relative to a referent point. The referent point is the consumer's state of well-being at the time of the purchase. According to prospect theory, buyers are influenced by anticipated changes in well-being.[4] For example, suppose two companies sell long-distance calling plans. Company A advertises its plan for $25 per month, with a $12 rebate for continuing the contract for at least 1 year. Company B advertises its plan for $24 per month, with a $12 surcharge for dropping out of the program before a year is up. Which is the better deal after 1 year's worth of calls? The answer, of course, is that the economic costs are identical here, yet most consumers would be more psychologically influenced to buy the call plan from Company A. Consumers would prefer the offer from Company A because of the way it has framed the price, leading to a perceived "gain."

Framing affects how consumers evaluate price, as do price "benchmarks" or *reference prices*. Reference prices are any price set against which other observed prices are evaluated.[5] These prices may be internal (stored in the consumer's memory) and serve as a basis for judging or comparing actual prices. Consumers store, retrieve, and use a rich array of price information in making price judgments. These internal benchmark prices are influenced by the product's perceived quality and by previously acquired information based on prior purchasing situations or on advertising cues. Consumers approach purchase situations with a target price (usually a price range) in mind and react positively or negatively when price deviations fall within the zone of acceptance. Thus, the challenge for marketing managers is to determine what that acceptable range is and set prices accordingly. Sellers can enhance buyers' value perceptions by comparing a lower selling price to a higher advertised reference price.

Reference prices may also be external, determined in the presence of marketing stimuli, such as point-of-purchase shelf tags indicating suggested retail price or the price of another product against which price is compared. For example, it is not uncommon for stores selling private label brands to encourage shoppers to compare the house brand with the "nationally advertised brand." Sellers can also create value for their customers by showing the suggested retail price alongside the sale price. Buyers respond favorably to this approach as long as the suggested retail price is not inflated. Furniture retailers have been attacked for misleading and deceptive advertising practices in advertising furniture at bogus discount prices. Burdines, a Florida-based department store, was investigated by the Attorney General's office for advertising a dining room set at a sale price that ran for 8 consecutive months, effectively making it the regular price.

STRATEGIC PRICING

Today, intelligent pricing (or the lack thereof) is determining winners and losers in a host of competitive markets such as airlines, fast food, and telecommunications. Price is a critical element of a company's marketing mix and is the only one that directly generates revenue. It seems that most companies react, rather than proactively manage their businesses, which would necessarily lead to more profitable pricing. Strategic pricing involves managing customers' expectations in order to encourage them to pay for the value they receive.[6] Yet, price cannot be considered apart from the other marketing mix variables, given their interdependence; thus, it must be viewed in the context of the overall marketing strategy. Too often, pricing is treated as a tactical response in the marketplace instead of as part of a well-integrated marketing strategy. Pricing messages, like all others, need to be strategically integrated with brand messages in order to send customers and potential customers a coherent, meaningful statement.[7]

Moreover, the price established needs to be consistent with the company's overall value proposition. Target Stores is a good example of pricing that aligns with the company's value proposition. Target's typical customers are slightly more upscale than those of Wal-Mart and K-mart, so it offers exclusive products like housewares designed by architect Michael Graves and apparel by California sportswear company Mossimo. Target recently began selling mid-market varietals from many of the world's leading wineries, even featuring its own sommelier. These wines, priced between $7 and $12 are in keeping with Target's "cheap chic" image.

Price also tends to be managed by functions within organizations, such as finance or sales, that frequently have their own agendas and conflicting views with marketing. Because of these competing agendas, companies end up with a pricing policy that bears little or no connection to marketing. For example, the sales staff may want authority to cut special deals, while marketing wants to retain a high-price, high-quality image. Surprisingly, most companies do not manage pricing cross functionally even though pricing can have a much greater bottom-line impact than other marketing initiatives. Firms can become more strategic in their pricing decisions by considering the following four points:

- *Prepare a value map.* A value map shows the value position of each competitor in a market by comparing relative price to relative quality (see Figure 8.2a through Figure 8.2d). A value map represents a powerful tool for comparing value positions within an industry, suggesting strategic shifts in either price or quality depending on the company's perceived location on the map. The "market wants" line (or fair value line) represents a trade-off between quality and price that customers are prepared to accept. Note that as long as congruence exists between each competitor's price and relative quality, the position (on the market wants line) and market share will be unchanged. Price and quality are the factors that can be leveraged, depending on the market wants. For example, a competitor can shift its relative position in an innovation-driven market, i.e., moving to the right of the market wants line, by building a strategy to increase relative quality (see Figure 8.2b).[8]
- *Relate pricing to the target market's demand elasticity.* A given industry such as airlines or hotels comprises customer segments with varying degrees of price sensitivity. The challenge for management is to determine the price floor and the price ceiling of the offering along with the price–value segments in the middle. For example, airlines use very sophisticated yield-management systems that not only manage seat inventory but also customize prices to match demand. This use of revenue management assures that companies

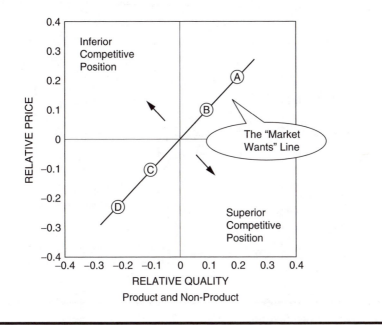

Figure 8.2a   Customer Value Map

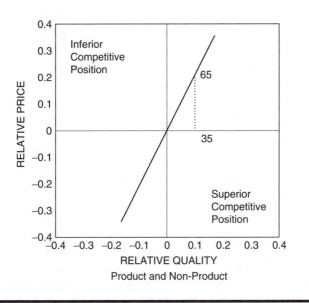

Figure 8.2b   Innovation-Sensitive Market

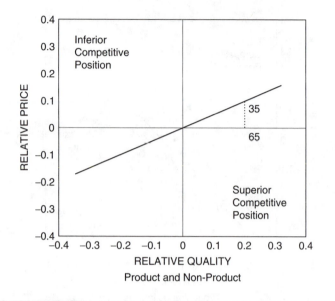

Figure 8.2c Price-Sensitive Market

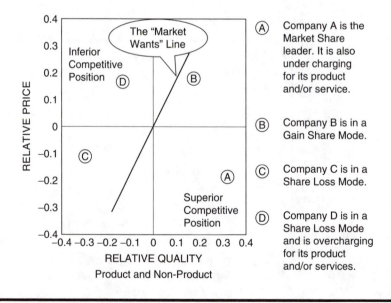

Figure 8.2d Strategy Implications

will sell the right product to the right consumer at the right time for the right price. The premise here is that no two customers value the product or service in exactly the same way. For example, leisure travelers and business travelers may be buying a ticket on the same flight, but they pay widely different fares. Leisure travelers are willing to book well in advance and are flexible on schedule, but are not willing to pay as much as business travelers, who book on short notice with little flexibility in scheduling, yet are less price sensitive.

■ *Make your pricing strategy reflect the perceived value of the service, not simply delivered value.* For example, Bugs Burger Bugs Killer (BBBK), a pest control company, is able to charge 10 times the price of other firms serving the commercial property industry by focusing on a segment of the market that is not price sensitive, i.e., hotels and restaurants. BBBK meets a critical need of these establishments: pest elimination rather than simply pest control. This segment will assign such a high importance to the guarantee that price becomes almost irrelevant when it assesses value of the offering

■ *Assign price-setting responsibility to a dedicated staff function.* Choose someone with a "blended" background in marketing/sales, finance, and economics to head up the department. Give this person the latitude to coordinate *with* other departments in aligning price with the overall business strategy. Continental Airlines assigns a high priority to pricing; it has created a position called senior vice-president of pricing and revenue management. Other industries, such as telecommunications, services, and pharmaceuticals, are already experimenting with this approach.[9]

PRICING METHODS

The purpose of this section is not to review all the possible pricing methods, but to discuss those that are truly customer oriented. Many traditional pricing methods are driven by cost or profit. Cost-driven methods seek to recover a reasonable return over the product's full cost. Profit-driven pricing attempts to maximize profitability by making trade-offs between price changes and changes in sales volume.

Value-driven companies may use any of the following five market-based pricing approaches:

■ *Price-driven costing* involves setting a price by starting with the estimated price customers are willing to pay and working backwards from this price specification. This requires the firm to figure out how to get the costs down in order to sell the product or service at the price indicated by customers while allowing for a reasonable profit. Kodak followed this approach when pricing its instant camera in the mid-1970s. Before introducing the camera, Kodak conducted concept tests for the proposed product, in which participants were shown descriptions of different versions of the camera, each with a different price. Respondents were then asked to indicate their purchase intentions for each version, ranging from "definitely would not buy" to "definitely would buy." Kodak introduced an instant camera based on these data, arriving at an introductory price of $39.95.

■ *Demand-based pricing* requires that price be set based on an estimate of volume that can be sold at different prices, based on market conditions, purchase situation, and price sensitivity. In certain situations, customers are sensitive to price increases, especially when their purchasing power has eroded. A local hotel in Jakarta, Indonesia, seized the opportunity when the Rupiah, the Indonesian currency, plunged in value against the dollar by setting the price of hotel rooms at a "fixed" exchange rate (see Figure 8.3). The price for Super Bowl tickets or a heavyweight boxing pay-per-view fight will often vary based on the teams and the fighters, respectively. Airline pricing is often subject to the "Southwest effect" or the change in fares that occurs when Southwest enters a new market. According to the U.S. Department of Transportation, fares drop by an average of 65% when Southwest enters a new market. Each of these examples demonstrates that price is often set based on what the market will bear.

Figure 8.3 Value Pricing Example

■ *Price customization* (also known as discriminatory pricing), which may be a form of price discrimination, occurs when the company seeks to modify its price to accommodate differences in customers, locations, and the manner or time in which the product or service is used. As indicated earlier, the airline companies are masters at price customization, using data-driven tools to wring out as much revenue as possible from each flight.

Price customization — selling the same products to different buyers at different prices — is a legal practice as long as it does not have a negative effect on competition (price is set in "good faith" to meet the competition; price reflects different uses of the product, distribution in different markets, or sales at different points in time). Price customization is often based on the type of customer served. For example, seniors or children frequently receive discounts at restaurants and entertainment activities. Business travelers pay higher airfares than leisure travelers when taking the same flight. Prices may also be customized based on the channel of delivery. For example, staples such as soft drinks or milk are often priced higher in convenience stores than in supermarkets. Customers sometimes pay higher prices depending on the "urgency" of the purchase, such as when placing rush or custom orders with the seller. Finally, a seller's price may also be determined by time and place. For example, rates for hotel rooms, car rentals, and long-distance telephone vary depending on the time the service is used. By customizing price, marketers can recognize the convenience that customers incorporate into the value ratio.

The Web is now making the practice of price customization and price discrimination much easier. Computers can now collect and analyze highly detailed data on individual customers as they make their purchases over the Internet or at the cash register. New software will distinguish the thrifty from the spendthrifts and price accordingly. Bill Gates predicts that Web sites will soon recognize individual consumers, remember what they paid for items in the past, and charge them a customized price based on that history. "Sellers will use technology to extract the highest price they can from a particular shopper," Gates wrote recently.

Amazon.com discovered, much to its chagrin, that charging different prices for the same item left customers feeling duped. It occurred when some shoppers in the DVD section of Amazon noticed that prices were not always the same; they soon discovered that, indeed, some shoppers were getting "test" prices. When customers discovered the differential pricing, they flooded chat boards with complaints against the company. Amazon quickly dropped its differential pricing and refunded the difference to customers who paid the higher price. Amazon was trying to gauge what impact price variations have on buying habits, a practice CEO Jeff Bezos referred to as "random pricing."

■ *Price differentiation* is a pricing approach taken in response to competitive forces. Often the competitive strategy chosen to compete in a given market determines how prices will be established. For example, Wal-Mart has chosen a strategy of "beat their price" in competing in the mass merchandising industry. Other companies such as Circuit City offer a low-price guarantee boasting in their ads, "You can't get a lower price. We guarantee it!" as well as "We'll beat any legitimate price from a local store stocking the same new item in a factory-sealed box and we'll refund 110% of the difference."

Companies may also resort to meeting the price of their competitors. Airlines typically match a competitor's move to lower fares to selected destinations. For example, several years ago Southwest Airlines offered a round-trip fare from Baltimore, Maryland to Los Angeles for $209, compared with a ticket on American Airlines priced at $418. American quickly dropped its price to match Southwest's discounted fare.

Some companies choose the "not to compete (on price) approach," preferring to compete on nonprice factors such as service, instead. Nordstrom and Tupperware are two well-known retailers who compete primarily based on their high levels of customer care. Customers appreciate and are willing to pay for the "extra" services they enjoy while patronizing these companies (see Figure 8.4). Sometimes it does not make sense to compete, because of lack of resources or scale economies, and thus firms should retreat on price. Xerox stopped competing in the financial services market when it was no longer profitable by cutting its losses and exiting the market.

■ *Value-based pricing* — Firms that pursue value-based pricing are committed to the belief that pricing should be set to reflect and capture customer value. Today, value pricing is often associated with low prices, such as McDonald's "extra value meals." Managers using value pricing need to educate the customer to redefine value from its current perception of "inexpensive." For IKEA, the Swedish furniture retailer, the goal is to make furniture less expensive without ever making customers feel cheap. In fact, Ikea's corporate mantra is "low price with meaning."

Value pricing involves adjusting the value equation by lowering prices or raising quality, or both. Consider Xerox color laser

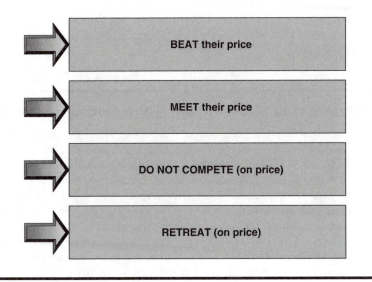

Figure 8.4   Price Differentiation Strategies

printers. Six years ago, a typical color laser workgroup printer from Xerox that produced output of two pages per minute (ppm) cost approximately $10,000. Today, that same printer, infused with newer technologies, can produce 16 ppm at a price of $2,200. Also, air time charges for digital wireless communications have dropped by half in the past year, while transmission quality has increased with the advent of digital networks and handsets. One of the keys to profitable marketing is setting a price commensurate to the value the customer actually receives.

Berry and Yadav recommend that companies pursuing value pricing consider using service guarantees to reinforce this approach. For example, Hampton Inn will refund a guest's money if for any reason he is unhappy with his or her hotel room.[10] They also recommend using relationship pricing, such as offering price bundling by selling two or more services together at a cost lower than if the individual services were purchased separately. Some telecommunication firms are now offering bundled offerings consisting of long-distance telephone service; paging; video conferencing; Internet access; and even cable TV for a set price.

A useful tool for guiding value pricing is the price-value grid, which helps firms determine the efficacy of their value pricing. As shown in Figure 8.5, this grid is defined along the price/quality dimensions, the cornerstones of value creation. A firm offering a high-quality offering at low prices would possess a strong value proposition, e.g., Wal-Mart selling well-known brands at everyday low prices or Southwest Airlines offering reliable and enjoyable air travel at extremely affordable prices (see customer value insight 8.1)

CUSTOMER VALUE INSIGHT 8.1: WHY LESS IS MORE AT WAL-MART

You might say that Wal-Mart is concerned with *value*. A quote from a recent annual report sums it up quite well: "At Wal-Mart, everything we do is about value: finding it, making it, and sharing it with our customers. Our job is to see how little we can charge for a product, not how much — how easy we can make it to shop with us, not how difficult." An illustration of how Wal-Mart puts this philosophy into practice is their highly successful "rollback program." Wal-Mart introduced this program in 1992 as a way of reminding customers that it was committed to its slogan "Always Low Prices." Wal-Mart loyal customers quickly discovered that the rollbacks were not a gimmick or a sale because, once the price of an item is rolled back, it tends to stay that way for a while. Wal-Mart's rollbacks are highlighted using a sunny yellow smiley face simply known as Smiley.

Wal-Mart gains credibility with its customers by staying true to its value foundation. For example, its opening price point is the lowest price available for an item of its kind. Another way in which Wal-Mart creates value for its customers is through its private label brands, providing brand quality but at a lower cost. Some of those brands, such as Ol' Roy dog food and Equate vitamins, quickly became the top sellers in their categories. Wal-Mart never cuts corners when selling its private label brands. Consumer testing laboratories ensure that these products meet recognized industry standards or government regulations, regardless of the price. Wal-Mart's cheerful exchange policy further enhances value, leading to a satisfying customer experience.

CUSTOMER VALUE CHECKLIST 8.1: DISCOVERING OPPORTUNITIES FOR VALUE-BASED PRICING

1. Using the price–value grid in Figure 8.5, choose four firms in a given market and locate and then discuss their relative positions on the grid.
2. What is the real difference between competing on price and competing on value? Explain.
3. Provide specific examples of companies adapting the following approaches in an attempt to change and improve their value pricing.
   a) Selling less for less (no frills)
   b) Selling more for more
   c) Selling the same for less

d) Selling more for less
e) Selling more for same
4. How might introducing value pricing be different for services rather than goods?
5. Where on the grid does the opportunity for a competitive advantage exist and why?

▲▼▲

Firms whose offerings have low-perceived quality at high prices would represent a poor or troubled value proposition. People in many local communities view cable service as a "poor value" due to regular price increases with limited measurable improvement in programming quality. This value proposition puts firms at a major competitive disadvantage if reasonable substitutes are available. The point here is that value pricing will be effective to the extent that price and quality are considered in tandem. Customer value checklist 8.1 provides guidance to firms considering value pricing.

HOW TO MAKE GOOD PRICING DECISIONS

Pricing decisions draw on many areas of marketing expertise. The pricing decision requires a comprehensive understanding of the forces that shape the market, including competitive interactions, technology, and consumer psychology. Sometimes these forces interact. For instance, customers have

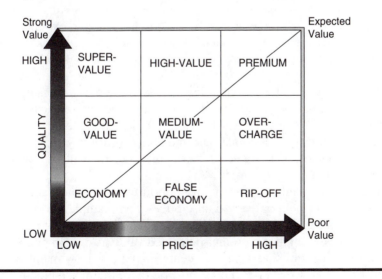

Figure 8.5 Price/Quality Strategies

learned to anticipate the price reductions that often accompany technological innovation. Yet, it seems that few companies conduct serious pricing research to support an effective pricing strategy. A 1997 Cooper & Lybrand study found that 87% of the companies surveyed had changed prices; however, only 13% of the price changes came as a result of a scheduled review of pricing strategy.[11]

A shift is occurring in how price is determined. The trend is to move away from the traditional "cost-plus" heuristic (compute costs and add desired mark-up) and toward "smart" pricing, For example, Ford Motor Company's effort to better formulate its pricing began in 1995, when the company experimented with using margins and value-added rather than strictly unit sales as metrics in assessing the effectiveness of its pricing. In addition, research was conducted to identify "features that the customer was willing to pay for but the industry was slow to deliver."

This research helped Ford's decision makers to understand demand at different price points and consumer perception of value-added features better. As a result, the company slightly reduced prices on higher margin cars (e.g., Crown Victorias and Explorers) producing an increase in unit sales of 600,000. Ford also raised prices on lower-end cars (e.g., Escorts and Aspires), increasing margins although selling 420,000 fewer units. Although Ford lost nearly 2 percentage points of market share between 1995 and 1999, earnings during 1999 were $7.2 billion, a new auto industry record. The five regions in which its new pricing strategy was tested beat profit targets by a collective $1 billion.[12]

As Figure 8.6 shows, some of these factors, such as substitutes; technological advances; price-driven competition; customer experience; and changes in internal forces, such as sales forecasts, are likely to put downward pressure on prices. Customer experience makes it difficult to raise prices because repeat customers' ability to perceive incremental value of a company's product/service diminishes over time, especially as substitute or competitive products emerge. Increased internal expectations, in the form of expected sales increases or new budgets, can also send prices on a downward spiral. Customer price sensitivity may also serve to keep prices in check, especially in the presence of available competitive substitutes or among a company's marginal customers.

Even in a deflationary economy, opportunities are available to keep prices from dropping or even to raise prices. For example, product/service enhancements or improvements often warrant maintaining, if not increasing, price due to higher customer-perceived value. A case in point: a hotel that offers a new business services center may be able to maintain above market rates. However, customers must perceive that these enhancements deliver a genuine, meaningful benefit or they will continue to seek lower-cost alternatives. Price deflectors, such as loyalty or frequency programs,

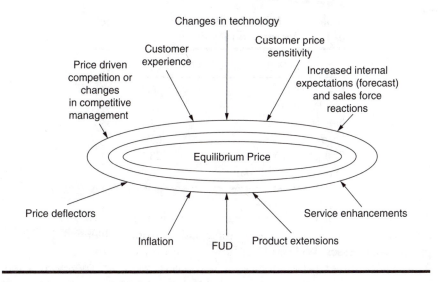

Changes in technology

Customer experience

Customer price sensitivity

Price driven competition or changes in competitive management

Increased internal expectations (forecast) and sales force reactions

Equilibrium Price

Price deflectors

Service enhancements

Inflation

FUD

Product extensions

Figure 8.6   Sources of Pricing Pressures

may effectively insulate a company from destructive price competition. Many airline travelers, especially business travelers, will not select an airline based solely on price, but rather on the mileage program in which they are members.

Finally, business customers who are motivated to reduce risk will not be overly concerned with price as they evaluate value of a product or service. As discussed earlier, hotels feel that high-priced BBBK offers considerable value. The sight of an undesirable pest can drive away many profitable guests. Risks may be internal as well as external. In the early days of the PC industry, IT managers often reminded, "No one ever got fired for buying an IBM," suggesting the importance of FUD (fear, uncertainty, doubt) in buying decisions.

Firms should be motivated to avoid price decreases that can erode margins and chip away brand equity. In contrast, price increases can have a dramatic impact on the bottom line. Michael Marn of McKinsey and Company found that a 1% increase in price can boost a firm's profits by an average of 11.1%; a 1% increase in volume, on the other hand, produces only a 3.3% increase in operating profits.[13] Table 8.1 shows some estimates of the impact of a 1% price increase on profits, assuming volume remains constant.[14] General Motors recently announced that it will charge extra for antilock brakes on some of its newer models, instead of including them at no charge.

It is quite easy to become seduced by the quick results produced by price discounting and fail to recognize the long-term consequences. Sometimes a firm will try to gain an advantage from being the lowest-price competitor. This advantage disappears if competitors follow with price

Table 8.1 Price–Profit Elasticity (1% Impact of Price Increase on Profits)

Company	Increase in Profits (%)
Coca-Cola	6.4
Fuji Photo	16.7
Nestlé	17.5
Ford	26.0
Philips	28.7
Typical U.S. company	12.0

reductions of their own. Some marketers view this pattern as a form of the "prisoner's dilemma" game. In the classic prisoner's dilemma, if neither prisoner confesses, both go free; however, if only one confesses, he goes free but the other prisoner faces severe consequences. Therefore, each prisoner must guess what the other will do.

Similarly, in a market with a small number of competitors, each firm must guess how others will respond to price reductions. If everybody drops the price, all will lose profits. Consider the example of Phillip Morris, which discovered this when it dropped the price on its leading Marlboro brand. In a sequence of events begun on Marlboro Friday, other cigarette brands also dropped their prices and some discount brands were introduced. As a result, PM's net operating profits dropped by $2.3 billion, in spite of the increase in the brand's market share by seven points.

Discounting as a regular practice is perilous for other reasons as well. Brand loyalty usually suffers when firms engage in regular discounting. Price-seeking customers are rarely loyal, pitting one seller against another. They will maintain repeat patronage only until the next deal is presented. The company unwittingly "prostitutes" the brand to a point at which it eventually assumes a commodity status. Perpetual discounting also produces undesirable effects on the brand's image, often cheapening it. Izod Lacoste all but destroyed the brand's cache in the late 1970s by repeatedly discounting the brand. Low prices ultimately made their crocodile become an "endangered species."

Finally, repeated discounting also conditions customers to seek price, rather than the *value* of the firm's offer. For example, owners of finicky cats have been conditioned to watch for sales of premium Fancy Feast cat food, at which point they stock up on the brand. Firms can avoid the pitfalls associated with price discounting by better understanding how their customers' value different product/service and company attributes. The objective here is to find segments of customers who have problems for which unique and cost-effective solutions can be developed.

FUTURE PRICING ISSUES

As Woody Allen once said, "The future isn't what it used to be." Well, neither is pricing in today's marketplace. The electronic marketplace is ushering in an era of sweeping changes that will leave no business untouched. A senior retail analyst for Forrester, an Internet research firm, forecasted that 2002 e-commerce sales would total nearly $80 billion — a 54% increase over the $52 billion spent in 2001. Also, according to the U.S. Department of Commerce, 39% of Internet users now make purchases via the Internet and half of the U.S. population is online, even though online retail sales accounted for a mere 1.7% of total retail sales during 2001. However, the Commerce Department projects online sales as a percentage of total retail sales to grow to 2.3% for 2002, a growth rate for online sales of 41%, far outpacing regular retail growth.

One of the major results of the digital era will be fluid pricing as never seen before because prospective buyers can now easily compare products and prices, putting them in a much better bargaining position. The more price information diffused across the Internet, the more skillful customers will become at haggling, and the less sellers can defend posted list prices. Today, online auctions let consumers bid on everything from antiques to treadmills. The Internet has made interaction costs so cheap that competitive bidding for everything is now possible.

So, what does this mean for marketers doing business in the 21st century? Clearly, the balance of market power has shifted from the marketer to the customer. Customers now have access to information that once was the exclusive purview of marketers. Customers using the Internet can now call up intelligent agents or "bots" such as pricescan.com; shopper.cnet.com; CNET Shopper.com; and mysimon.com to search the Web, ruthlessly seeking the product or service at the best price according to specifications set by the user (see Figure 8.7). Imagine the effect of these intelligent agents that work 24 hours a day constantly searching for the lowest prices on branded products and services.

However, companies are not powerless when competing in the digital arena. A few companies, such as Long's Drugs as well as supermarket chains D'Agnostino's, Winn Dixie, and Safeway, are using powerful price-optimization software designed to generate an ideal price for each item sold at the individual store level. These programs are based on sophisticated algorithms that compute individual demand curves for each product in each store. A host of other companies (besides the airlines, which helped pioneer this type of pricing) such as Best Buy, DHL, Ford Motor Co., Home Depot, JC Penney, Saks, Staples, UPS, and General Electric are adopting scientific or "smart" pricing, using sophisticated computer programs to set prices.

List price: **$199.00**

Lowest price: **$113.00**

Palm i705

Manufacturer: **Palm Inc.**

Part number: **P80503US**

Product Tour

CNET product briefs *beta*   What is a product brief?

Description	Pros	Cons	Suitability	Value	Suggestions

The Palm i705 is a Palm OS-based, business handheld device. Relative to other business handhelds on the market, it is very low priced at around $194. It accepts Secure Digital/MutiMediaCard media, for adding memory or expansion devices.

Reseller	Rating	Description	Pros	Cons	Suitability	Value	Suggestions
Gateway — Trusted since 1985 — Company info I Buy now	★★★	$193.95 as of 5/26/2003	Yes	CA	Free Shipping	Yes	1-800... Buy info
buydig.com 800-617-4686 — Your Trusted Source since 1983 — Company info I Buy now	★★★	$149.00 Brand New/ Fast Service as of 5/26/2003	No	NJ	19.95	Yes	1-800... Buy info
PC Mall — Company info I Buy now	★★★	$198.00 as of 5/27/2003	Yes	CA	FREE!	Yes	1-800... Buy info
Beach Camera — Company info I Buy now	★★★	$199.00 Brand New/Fast Service as of 5/27/2003	Yes	NJ	19.95	Yes	1-800... Buy info
eCOST.com — Company info I Buy now	★★★	$198.00 See Cart Special! as of 5/27/2003	Yes	CA	FREE!	Yes	1-877... Buy info
State Street Direct — Company info I Buy now	★★★	$198.00 as of 5/24/2003	Yes	NH	$7.91	Yes	1-800... Buy info
pcRUSH — Company info I Buy now	★★★	$186.65 as of 5/16/2003	No	CA	$8.99-$13.15	Yes	1-888... Buy info
Harmony Computers — Company info I Buy now	★★★	$349.00 as of 5/26/2003	No	NY	19.99	backorder	1-800... Buy info
MPSuperstore.com — Company info I Buy now	★★★	$114.95 as of 5/26/2003	No	NY	15.95	Yes	1-800... Buy info
Kaanza.com — Company info I Buy now	★★★	$113.00 as of 5/27/2003	No	VA	$15.00	Yes	1-877... Buy info
Global Computer — Company info I Buy now	★★★	$129.00 as of 5/27/2003	No	NY	Starting at $7.95	Yes	1-800... Buy info
Compu America — Company info I Buy now	★★★	$114.00 as of 5/24/2003	No	CA	15	Yes	1-800... Buy info
California Computer Center — Company info I Buy now	★★★	$269.00 as of 5/27/2003	No	CA	$18.00	Yes	

Figure 8.7   Price Comparison Using CNET Shopper.com (From http://shopper.cnet.com/shopping/resellers/0-205442-311-8602250-0.html?tag=prices.)

Systems produced by SAP and start-ups DemandTec and ProfitLogic sift through massive databases crammed with up-to-date information about orders, promotions, product revenues, and stock levels in warehouses and stores; among other things, they reveal to companies when to start discounting. The Casual Male Retail Group used a system developed by ProfitLogic to give it guidance on what to discount and by how much. The software led the Casual Male to discount less, but a lot sooner.

Granted, the transparency of the Web will certainly expose price differentials; companies can and should respond by personalizing their products and services. Dell is probably the best example of how to avoid "commodity" selling on the Web. Dell largely achieves its differentiation by maintaining direct contact with its accounts, allowing its salespeople to customize solutions to match its clients' particular needs. "Dell's helping to define what customers are buying," says Jeff Gans of Easton Consultants in Stamford, Connecticut.[14]

Dell also sets up customized intranet sites for its large customers. Shell Oil, for example, has been using such a site, otherwise known as a premier page, to purchase computers from Dell. The site keeps purchasing managers up to date on product and pricing changes, while also tracking the order status of Dell computers purchased on the Web. If Shell needs personal assistance, it can access the pager number of any marketing or technology employee that services its account.

SUMMARY

This chapter discussed the importance of price as a key strategic element and value driver. Price does not communicate value by itself, but only in the presence of perceived product and/or service quality. That is, price only has meaning when it is paired with benefits delivered. How buyers typically evaluate price was considered. Buyers will use price as a cue, especially in the absence of other marketing cues such as a well-known brand name. Buyers also will evaluate products or services based on how marketers "frame" the price, either as a perceived gain or loss. Marketers need to understand price benchmarks or reference prices in each of their product or service categories. Consumers often use these reference points in determining an offer's value.

The importance of viewing pricing in the context of the firm's overall marketing strategy was also stressed. Firms can become more strategic in their pricing by creating a price position in the company; using value maps; relating price to elasticity of demand; and ensuring that price reflects perceived, not simply delivered, value. A number of different market-based pricing methods were introduced, including price-driven costing;

demand-based pricing; price customization; price differentiation; and value-based pricing.

A discussion of how to make good pricing decisions concluded the chapter. It was recommended to consider various industry forces such as competition, technology, substitutes, and buyer experience to make more informed pricing decisions. Finally, caution should be exercised against the overuse of discounting due to its "narcotic" effect on buyers and its adverse impact on brand loyalty.

CUSTOMER VALUE ACTION ITEMS

1. How well understood is the pricing function in your company? Discuss.
2. Discuss the relative importance of price in each of the following purchase situations:
   a. Automobile
   b. Life insurance
   c. Graduate education
   d. Haircut/style
   e. Symphony tickets
   f. Health care
3. How much does price contribute to an offering's perceived value?
4. Select an industry and create a value map that shows individual brands and how they compare to one another on price and performance (follow the example given in Figure 8.2a).
5. Price customization involves setting prices based on differences in customers and how they use the product/service and when and where the offering is used. Give several examples of how price could be customized in each of the following situations:
   a. Concert tickets
   b. Car rental
   c. Management consulting services
   d. Restaurant meal
   e. Airline travel
   f. Internet service provider
6. Suppose a local used car dealer was faced with the threat of AutoNation opening up a dealership a few miles away. Which price differentiation strategy would you recommend and why?
7. Determine your reference price for each of the following products/services:
   a. 2-Liter bottle of soda
   b. Best seller book

     c. Oil change for your car

     d. 1-Hour massage

8. Value pricing exercise — American Airlines NetSAAver fares: In addition to providing information about its services, routes, and fares, American Airlines is also using its Web page to sell unsold seats on flights throughout its system. Through its NetSAAver program, American sells seats as much as 70% below the lowest fares that would be quoted if a consumer called a travel agent or American's 800 number. The only way to find NetSAAver fares is by accessing American's Web page and subscribing to an electronic mailing list. Each Wednesday, American e-mails the week's NetSAAver fares; interested fliers book the fares by calling an 800 number.

     a. Go to the American Airlines Web site and sign up to receive this week's NetSAAver fares by e-mail. When you receive them, describe how AA adds value through its various partnerships.

     b. How is American Airlines using price differentiation to segment markets based on type of customer, occasion/use, or time of purchase?

     c. Based on what you observe from the American Airline's Web page and your general understanding of the airline industry, which of the four price differentiation strategies (refer to Figure 8.4 in text) does AA appear to be practicing and why?

REFERENCES

1. Anon. (1996) Price still gets their attention, but … . *Purchasing*, March 21, 24.
2. Berry, L. (1996) Retailers with a future, *Mark. Manage.*, 5(5), 42.
3. Peterson, R. and Wilson, W. (1985) The perceived risk and price-reliance schema and price-perceived-quality mediators, in *Perceived Quality*, Jacoby, J. and Olson, J., Eds., Lexington, MA: Lexington Books, 247–268.
4. Smith, G. and Nagle, T. (1995) Frames of reference and buyer's perception of price and value, *Calif. Manage. Rev.*, 38(1), Fall, 98–116.
5. Biswas, A. and Blair, E. (1991) The effects of reference prices in retail advertisements, *J. Mark.* (55), July, 1–12.
6. Nagle, T. and Cressman, G. (2002) Don't just set prices, manage them, *Mark. Manage.*, November/December, (11)6, 27–33.
7. Duncan, T. and Moriarty, S. (1997) *Driving Brand Value*, New York: McGraw–Hill.
8. Cleland, A. and Bruno, A. (1996) *The Market Value Process*, San Francisco, Jossey–Bass, 19.
9. Dolan, R. and Simon, H. (1996) *Power Pricing*, New York: The Free Press, 312.
10. Berry, L. and Yadav, M. (1996) Capture and communicate value in the pricing of services, *Sloan Manage. Rev.*, Summer, 45–47.

11. Monroe, K. and Cox, J. (2001) Pricing practices that endanger profits, *Marketing Management*, October, 43.
12. Coy, P. (2000) The power of smart pricing, *Bus. Week*, April 10, 160.
13. Stern, A. (1997) The pricing quandary, *Across Board*, May, 17–18.
14. Dolan, R. (1997) Power pricing policies, lecture, Harvard Business School, June 17, 1997.
15. Marchetti, M. (1997) Dell Computer, *Sales Mark. Manage.*, 49(11), 51.

9

STRATEGIES FOR ADDING AND PROMOTING VALUE

The whole value-added thing is in some ways like a new medium. It reminds me of the early days of cable: how do we know what we're getting?

Stacey Lippman, Chiat/Day/Mojo

Things only have the value that we give them.

Moliere

An advertisement for SAS software proclaimed that "you can delight your customers or your customers will be delighted to leave." The customer value approach advocated in this text stresses the need to go the "extra mile" because customer satisfaction and retention are keys to business success. In addition to having a solid value proposition, firms can differentiate themselves from the competition by adding value to their goods and services and promoting the organization's uniqueness to its target markets. Building on the value proposition idea introduced in Chapter 7, this chapter also emphasizes how marketing communications add value to customers. Specifically, it explores the unique selling proposition (USP); positioning; value-added marketing strategies; and integrated marketing communications (IMC).

THE USP AND DIFFERENTIATION

Advertising executives know that having a strong unique selling proposition is critical to support the firm's value proposition (VP) (note that the VP goes beyond communications issues and includes how management relates to the customer; defines the business model and market; and designs business processes to deliver superior value). Recently, some marketing professionals have begun to call USP the unique "service" proposition. The authors prefer this latter term because it demonstrates that companies must distinguish themselves with respect to offerings as well as message.

Over the years, Avis did a fine job using marketing communications to differentiate itself from Hertz, the market leader in the car rental business. Promotional themes regularly depicted the underdog position to win the hearts of its target markets. Some of the advertising concepts Avis used included: "We're number two, we try harder!"; "Rent from us, our lines are shorter"; and "Rent from the employee–owners of Avis." As these slogans show, a strong attention-grabbing promotional sound bite is often simple, basic, and powerful. How many firms can articulate their promotional message in 10 words or less?

An USP creates and communicates value. Once it is finalized, all components in the company's value proposition (service, product quality, image, and price) must work in harmony to support the firm's promise to its customers. Whole Foods, Inc. sells natural groceries to nutritious-conscious Americans. Using a multipronged strategy of offering healthy foods; large selection; reasonable prices (possibly due to national purchasing power); product tasting/sampling; and knowledgeable and caring employees, this retailer has carved a solid niche in the marketplace that has been noticed by traditional supermarket chains.

To maximize value, organizations must stand out from the pack and differ from their competitors. If the firm is essentially the same as everyone else, it will not be perceived as better than its rivals (in fact, the market may view it as not even necessary). The firm that is different may not be better, but it has a good chance to be seen as innovative and superior. Amazon.com's Internet-based, virtual bookstore redefined the industry. Barnes and Noble and Borders were forced to compete online and play "catch-up" to maintain their market leadership positions. Amazon's recent product line expansion has transformed the company into an online retail giant (the Wal-Mart of cyberspace?). Customer value insight 9.1 takes a closer look at Amazon's amazing growth strategy.

▼▲▼

CUSTOMER VALUE INSIGHT 9.1: AMAZON.COM COMPANY PROFILE

Overview. Founded in a Seattle garage in July, 1995, by Jeffrey P. Bezos, a former whiz-kid hedge-fund manager on Wall Street, Amazon.com (named after the world's largest river) is the top online bookstore, the Web's biggest retailer, and a *Fortune* 500 company. Bezos, a Princeton graduate, was 31 years old at the time and realized the tremendous potential of the Internet as a sales and distribution channel. In April 2001, Amazon served its 30 millionth customer.

Amazon offers millions of book titles for sale (new and used), many times more than available in the largest bookstores in the physical world. However, it keeps relatively few in stock; distribution centers quickly ship books to customers. In June, 1998, Amazon.com launched an online music store with more than 150,000 CD titles and added video sales to form its big-three product lines of books, music, and video/DVD. Recently, the company has become a diversified online department store adding apparel and accessories; computers; electronics; hardware and tools; home and garden products; kids and baby products; office products; professional supplies; software; toys; and other product categories to its merchandise mix. The company even offers services such as corporate accounts; credit cards; gift registries; and travel to its customers in cyberspace.

Revenues for the second quarter ended June 30, 2003, were $1.1 billion, a 36% net sales increase over last year's figures. Projected revenues for 2003 are $5.1 billion. International sales were up 81% from a year ago. In spite of this impressive sales gain, the company reported a $43 million loss for the quarter.[1] In fact, the company has generated quarterly profits only twice. The bulk of the company's capital goes to visibility enhancement with ads on popular Web sites as well as some traditional media such as the *New York Times Book Review*.

Customer value strategy. Amazon's value proposition stresses service and selection, and to a lesser extent, price. Other online bookstores operate in a similar way, but none is as successful as Amazon. The business model is simple: comprehensive selection (if it is in print, it is available); delivering first-rate customer experiences; brand promotion; and discounted prices. Amazon knows that in today's chaotic lifestyles, time saving and great service are highly valued.

Standard shipping for regular orders is 3 to 7 days and 1- or 2-day priority service is available. Amazon maintains records of customer preferences and then acts on that information, e.g., offering recommended items based on customer purchase histories, sending e-mail notifications when a new book by a favorite author has arrived, etc. Customized book selections create "bookworm" forum communities that provide interactivity between readers and authors.

Millions of dollars have been invested in the company's Web site and brand-building strategy, taking precedence over generating short-term profits. The site is rich and resourceful. It emphasizes information over graphics and includes separate pages for each book, featuring brief descriptions, author and customer reviews, and sample content. The site is easy to use, fun, and colorful; it loads quickly and is browser friendly. Visitors are prompted for ways to make the service even better. Online contests, announcements, and promotions encourage customers to return to see what is new at Amazon. Personalization, multiple electronic order confirmations, and its patented one-click ordering technology are features valued by its worldwide customers.

Promotional deals with leading Internet search engines such as America Online, Netscape, and Yahoo!; joint ventures with Borders and Waldenbooks; and national partners such as Office Depot and Toys R Us extend Amazon's reach. Over 900,000 "associates" have links to Amazon, which yields them commissions of 2.5 to 15% for every order generated.

─────────────────────────────── ▲▼▲ ───────────────────────────────

Rory Sutherland, executive creative director of London-based Ogilvy-One, says that a USP should give way to a more personalized approach called the ISP, or individualized selling proposition. Because mass marketing has been replaced by customized marketing, firms must tailor their offerings and promotions to relationship-seeking customers. Apartment complexes, health clubs, Internet service providers (ISPs), and preschools are paying loyal customers with cash (e.g., $50 referral fee) or services (e.g., 1 month free rent) for referring friends or family members to patronize their businesses.

Differentiation means having an advantage over the competition. This advantage can be real (a more durable product, better service, or lower price) or perceived (based on the image component of the S-Q-I-P framework). Air Around the Clock's (a South Florida-based air conditioning and appliance service contractor) differentiation is based on outstanding service, which includes emergency night and weekend repairs; a preferred customer program; a fleet of more than 40 trucks; and a "fix it right the first time" philosophy executed by knowledgeable technicians. Guardian Swimming Pool's trucks advertise next-day service and the fact that it "shows up." This sends a clear signal to the company's target market that its competitors are likely to be weak in customer service; thus, Guardian gains an important competitive advantage.

Although companies can actively reposition themselves via changing the product or service mix, image-based positioning is more often the approach through which unique market identities are created. Thus, as Ries and Trout note, positioning is often done in the minds of the customers.[2] In this over-communicated society, companies that can best break through the "noise clutter" with clearly focused promotional campaigns will strike responsive chords with their target markets and succeed in the marketplace. Miller Lite's controversial ad featuring the "Miller Lite girls," which included a "cat-fight," mud-wrestling, and suggestive language (for the cable TV version), generated accolades and criticism from advertising experts and consumers.

THREE LEVELS OF POSITIONING

Apple Computer is a good example of a firm that was a market leader in the 1980s, fell on very hard times in the 1990s, and is trying to find

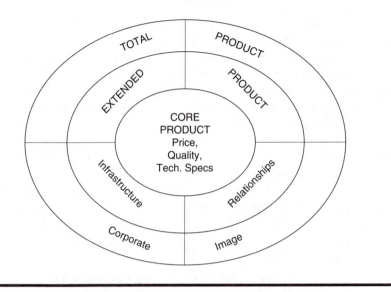

Figure 9.1   Three Levels of Product Positioning

its way in the new millennium. Steve Jobs, architect of the firm's successes in the glory days, is making nice progress in getting Apple on track after being essentially banished from the company for many years. Because value creation is a dynamic process, repositioning must be ongoing.

As Figure 9.1 illustrates, the three levels of product positioning are: the core, extended, and total product.[3] The core product is short-term positioning and typically works for a year or less. In this phase, companies focus on the tangibles — price, quality, and technical specifications. Packard Bell used its borrowed name recognition (from Hewlett-Packard and the Bell phone system) and price leadership philosophy to become a dominant force in the low end of the retail personal computer market. Acer's inspired idea of colored computers as decorative furniture briefly catapulted the firm into the top 10 in the U.S. home user and SOHO (small office, home office) market segments in the mid-1990s. Although the core product variables are relatively easy to adjust, it is difficult to "own" such market positions. Competitors can quickly emulate a low price or comparable quality strategy.

A more effective approach is to build the extended product. In this phase, firms create the necessary infrastructure to develop strong marketing relationships with channel members, suppliers, and, of course, customers. This strategy tends to last in the intermediate term — 1 to 5 years. Compaq's (now part of Hewlett-Packard) diverse product line can be found in computer stores, office supply superstores, department stores, and other retail outlets. Dell's direct marketing machine enables it to serve

Fortune 500 firms and other business users effectively. Extended product positioning takes time, money, and process innovations.

Companies that position themselves at the total product level have clearly identified who they are and what they stand for. Firms that have garnered a long-term position (more than 5 years) have clearly won the market's respect. Hewlett-Packard's reputation for high-quality products and IBM's computer know-how and excellent service have been established over the decades. These companies have well-earned reputations that stress positioning on the intangibles. A total product image gives these companies the benefit of the doubt if they occasionally stumble. Remember IBM's PC Jr. fiasco? The "halo effect" enabled the company to recover quickly from this misguided marketing move. A less respected firm may have found it difficult or impossible to recover from such a market blunder.

HOW TO ADD VALUE TO PRODUCTS

As differentiation implies, companies must constantly search for new ways to add value to their goods and services to distance themselves from their rivals. Here are 13+ ways to accomplish this vital strategic objective (note: a baker's dozen adds value).

- *Additional features and benefits.* Cellular phone companies such as Cingular and Verizon do a great job of adding special services for their customers. Voice mail, directories, Internet access, family plans, free long distance for nights and weekends, and three-way calling are some options that create satisfied customers. Hotels are responding to customer desires by adding business amenities, exercise centers, free breakfast buffets, and social hours. Many credit unions now offer specialized loan programs as part of their business strategy to provide home banking services to their members.
- *Affordability.* Price is closely related to value. Customers will pay more for a product that is highly valued. Nevertheless, the marketing challenge is to provide offerings that are affordable to the masses. Although PC sales in the U.S. leveled off in 1997, the industry was reinvigorated when computers broke the $1000 price point. Today, a decent basic computer can be had for less than $500. The automobile industry experienced dramatic growth in the recessionary period of 2001 to 2002 largely due to 0% financing for new vehicles.
- *Branding.* The power of brand building is unquestioned. In the hypercompetitive environment of the 21st century, the brand name and the equity that it generates create lasting value for organizations

and their customers.[4] The brand creates an image and identity to distinguish it from competitive offerings. Brands such as Budweiser, Coca-Cola, Disney, Harley-Davidson, IBM, Levi's, Microsoft, Mercedes, McDonald's, Nike, Sony, Virgin, and others have become ingrained into pop culture. For example, Harley-Davidson knows how to develop and exploit a "brand community." Over the 2003 Labor Day weekend, more than 250,000 Harley owners (even some from Europe) converged in Milwaukee, Wisconsin, for the company's 100th anniversary celebration. Realize that commodities and business products as well as consumer goods and services can be successfully branded.

■ *Customer involvement.* Successful companies know how to add value and establish strong bonds with their customers. Country and rock music stations attempt to get close to their radio listeners through concert and music request phone lines; community-based special events; contests; informative/interactive Web sites; sponsorship of concerts; and other promotional strategies. These marketing activities build customer loyalty and attract national as well as local advertisers.

■ *Customization and choice.* Twenty-first century companies are moving from segmented to one-on-one marketing. The *Farm Journal* has a circulation of more than half a million readers and publishes more than 1000 different versions of each issue to readers whose interests vary widely by acreage, crops, livestock raised, geography, and even farm practices.

■ *Enhanced quality.* Motorola and General Electric are companies renowned for outstanding products and their pursuit of six sigma (and beyond) quality. Whether manufacturing digital pagers or locomotives, being the "best in the class" is not just a management goal; rather it is an intrinsic part of the corporate business culture. In-N-Out Burger shuns chemical processing and frozen, microwaveable, and prepackaged fast food. This California-based chain has provided "make to order" high-quality burgers (100% pure beef, real American cheese, fresh lettuce and tomatoes); French fries (made from the highest grade whole potatoes); and drinks (shakes made from ice cream) for more than 55 years.

■ *Exceptional service.* The Ritz-Carlton hotel chain, a Malcolm Baldridge National Quality Award winner, is known for unparalleled customer service that is highly personalized, genuinely caring, and super-attentive to detail. Management empowers its employees to "move heaven and earth" to satisfy customer needs. Using a master database of customer profiles, employees track customer desires in amenities, room features, and other facets of guests' stay patterns and preferences. Requests for hypoallergenic pillows and peanut butter (rather than chocolate chip) cookies will be noted in computerized files for repeat customers.

■ *Frequency marketing incentives.* In today's highly competitive environment, customers seek reasons to remain loyal to firms. It seems as if everyone is building on the frequent-flyer concept developed by American Airlines and jumping on the frequency marketing program bandwagon. Car rental firms, car washes, coffee bars, hotels, restaurants, and small businesses now offer frequency-based clubs to encourage continued patronage by their valued customers.

■ *Internet as a value adder.* The Web is the driving engine of the new economy and can have a favorable impact on all facets of a company's marketing plan — e.g., online product catalogs with pricing information; electronic communications with customers about new offerings; market research/customer feedback; customer service programs; etc. David Aaker, a leading scholar on brand management, explains that the Internet is excellent for integrating multichannel marketing programs. His examples of stellar use of the Net include FedEx tracking; Procter & Gamble's Pampers Perks (a customer loyalty program in which diaper purchases are redeemed for toys) and Tide's "Stain Detective" Web sites; and Nick.com (Nickelodeon TV's online presence for children under 12).[5]

■ *Simplify or bundle the offering.* Microsoft has greatly profited from this adaptable and practical business strategy. Case in point: its Word (word processing) application is available as a freestanding unit, upgradeable product, or in a variety of integrated suite packages with multiple other software products such as Access, Excel, Outlook, PowerPoint, etc. Microsoft also offers flexible service packages for which customers can pay by the minute or incident, buy annual contracts, and/or select from other fee-based programs.

■ *Solve customer problems.* The old sales adage that customers do not buy drill bits but buy round holes is sounder today than ever before. Customers want answers to their questions, and they will do business with companies that best know how to provide realistic solutions to important problems. Radio Shack says, "You got questions, we got answers." GE does not want to be simply a solutions provider but rather the "essential" solutions provider. eBay's explosive growth is largely due to its unique ability to provide virtual exchange forums for almost any kind of product. One of its fastest-growing areas is its business-to-business marketspace in which manufacturers and wholesalers can dispose of excess inventory at bargain-basement prices.

■ *Technological leadership.* State-of-the-art technology can be a great source of differentiation (and competitive advantage) for businesses.

Customer databases; electronic promotional techniques (brochures, catalogs, and Web sites); inventory control systems; sales automation equipment/procedures; and "the latest and greatest" technologies in industry are approaches likely to be valued by customers. Consider three examples of superior technology:

1. Click Camera and Video's investment in expensive digital technology and one-stop service for all photographic needs set the company apart from drugstores and supermarket competitors in the film processing and photofinishing business.
2. Malden Mills (Lawrence, Massachusetts) developed a new generation of high-tech jackets that create their own warmth, powered by lightweight lithium batteries.
3. Weathernews (a service based in Japan) provides content for approximately 130 U.S. Web sites combining weather forecasting with sophisticated data analysis (i.e., tailoring weather data to clients' needs — whether certain events will spur or dampen demand).

■ *Warranties.* Service marketers know that a sale does not end when the purchase is made. Postsale servicing differentiates excellent companies from average enterprises. Case in point: Kensington stands behind its product line. If a computer/cable lock combination fails, it cheerfully and expeditiously replaces this item, no questions asked. When customers have a need for another Kensington product, they will be confident of buying from a company that cares not only about its products, but also about its customers. Also, Hyundai's 5-year–60,000 mile, bumper-to-bumper warranty got this South Korean manufacturer's vehicles noticed in the crowded U.S. automotive marketplace.

Some Additional Value-Added Approaches

Companies should not limit themselves to the aforementioned 13 value-adding strategies. The use of ambiance and atmospherics (Lexus automobile dealerships); dominant merchandise assortments (Bass Pro Outdoor World); hassle reduction (Take-out Taxi); one-stop shopping (Wal-Mart and Sam's Club); segmented marketing (utilities providing specialized market knowledge and energy management information to their small commercial customers); speed (FedEx); supply chain management (Motorola's relationships with its suppliers); or other sound and creative customer value strategies can provide a sharp competitive edge in the marketplace.

Effective value-based marketing creates interest for customers. New restaurant concepts such as California Pizza Kitchen, Cheesecake Factory, and Outback Steakhouse have succeeded recently, largely because their value propositions are different from mainstream dining establishments. Chili's is one of a number of casual restaurants that has added a curbside delivery option to its menu; Chili's-To-Go appeals to consumers seeking convenience.

IMPLEMENTING A VALUE-ADDED SERVICES PROGRAM

Clean Rite Centers is a chain of progressive self-service laundromats in the New York City area. Superstores five times the size of typical mom-and-pop laundromats offer a multitude of value-added features. These include children's play areas; clean bathrooms; on-site parking; smart card-operated machines; televisions featuring the latest movies; security systems; and, most importantly, customer-friendly help (realize that many customers visit weekly for 2-hour periods).[6]

A process for adding value in a retail context follows (note that this approach is readily adaptable to e-tailers and service firms). The six steps are[7]:

- Specifying business objectives, e.g., increasing traffic, increasing sales, targeting best customers, etc.
- Designing a program to accomplish these objectives
- Being sure that the value offered really includes an added value
- Determining whether the program is sustainable financially and in terms of consumer interest
- Explaining and executing the program (sales associates must be involved and motivated)
- Measuring and fine-tuning the program to maximize long-term results.

Customer value checklist 9.1 identifies seven issues that customer value managers must consider in developing a value-added program.

━━━━━━━━━━━━━━━━ ▼▲▼ ━━━━━━━━━━━━━━━━

CUSTOMER VALUE CHECKLIST 9.1 DESIGNING A VALUE-ADDED PROGRAM

How do you define your business?

Do you know your customers' definitions of value: the basics; what is expected; what is desired; and how you can provide unanticipated customer value?

Do you know your competitors' definitions of value?

Have you recently carefully assessed your current product/service offerings (including value-added benefits)?

Have you reconfigured your product/service mix to mesh with customer desires and stay ahead of the competition?

Do you continually seek new opportunities for adding and delivering superior customer value?

Does your management team take a long-term view of the organization's value-added strategy/program?

▲▼▲

COMMUNICATING VALUE THROUGH AN IMC PROGRAM

Integrated marketing communications means coordinating all promotional activities — advertising; databases; direct marketing; Internet; personal selling; sales promotion; and public relations. As an example, Johnson & Johnson launched the Campaign for Nursing's Future in 2002 to deal with a projected nursing shortage (currently 126,000 in hospitals and estimated at 400,000 nurses in all health care facilities by 2020). J & J is investing more than $20 million over a 2-year period to attract people to the nursing profession via television advertising celebrating nurses' contributions; scholarship funds and national fundraising events; a Web site (www.discovernursing.com) with career and educational opportunities including searchable databases; and recruitment brochures, posters, and videos.[8]

The objective of IMC programs is to provide a synergistic and consistent message (one look, one voice) that communicates value to targeted audiences. Don E. Schultz, a professor at Northwestern University, has researched and written extensively about IMC over the past decade. Some of this guru's major thoughts on this strategic marketing area are summarized in Table 9.1.

Although companies are doing an adequate job of utilizing IMC principles, clearly room for improvement exists. Research has found that about 75% of companies now coordinate all or most of their promotional activities. Retailers do it best (85%) while service organizations are least successful in their IMC endeavors (55%). Service firms tend to farm out a lot of promotional work to different vendors in the areas of direct response, public relations, and sales promotion, which partly accounts for this discrepancy from the norm.[9] Standardizing promotional campaigns becomes a much greater challenge to marketing managers in service businesses.

Recent evidence of practitioners' satisfaction with IMC is disappointing. In a study of marketing communication professionals at *Fortune* 500 companies, only 8% were very satisfied with campaign results (92% were only somewhat satisfied).[10] In an online survey of marketing managers, only 11% stated that integrated marketing delivered significant success (79% reported some success and 10% said that IMC was not successful at all).[11]

Table 9.1 Forces Affecting Integrated Marketing Communications (IMC)

IMC Drivers	IMC Restraints
Small organizations	Large organizations
Business marketers with a strong sales force — marketing communications is a support technique	Consumer marketers with a brand management system
Single brand or line of products under one brand name	Multibrand packaged goods companies
A database of customers/prospects and their purchase histories	Limited usage of databases
View marketing communications as an entity	View marketing communications as a segmented process
Accept risk-taking	Unwilling to take a risk
Willing to rethink the system of promotional incentives	Locked into traditional rewards for promotional activities
Strong top-down management	Bottom-up management
Less formal marketing structures, limited marketing history	Formal marketing structures, sophisticated marketing organization
Realization that IMC is a major creator of value for the organization	Promotional strategies are just another part of the marketing mix

Source: Adapted from ideas offered by Schultz, D. E. (1991), *J. Promotion Manage.*, 1(1), 99–104.

Although the integrated marketing communications idea is intriguing, implementation is a major problem for most organizations. The corporate database (marketing information system) is the key to success for IMC. Only 15% of companies take database marketing to a higher level than mailing lists (which 70% of the firms maintain). The failure to implement an IMC program is due to lack of expertise, budget, and/or management approval.[12]

CREATING AN IMC PROGRAM

Here is an eight-point plan for initiating an IMC program in an organization:

■ *Use zero-based budgets.* Most companies use incremental approaches in allocating promotional budgets. For example, if they spent $10 million last year, they may "tack on" another 5% to get this year's figure. Other companies base their decisions on competitive spending, industry averages, or a percentage of sales. A preferred approach is the objective and task approach. Start with a zero budget and force all promotional managers to justify their investment. This might result in a $9 million or $12 million (or many other possibilities) budget for IMC activities.

■ *Primarily focus on current customers.* Many organizations direct 80% or more of their advertising and selling efforts activities to trying to win new business (conquest marketing). An IMC program recognizes the importance of retention marketing (see Chapter 10) and inverts that ratio so that a majority of the promotional activity is earmarked for relationship building with existing customers. This reduces customer defection, upgrades business relationships, and creates advocates for the firm's services.

■ *Use highly targeted mass promotion.* Direct mail, specialized lists, trade publications, and the Internet can be used effectively to reach prospects rather than suspects. Business-to-business interactive direct marketing sales were projected to be about $20 billion by 2002. For every dollar direct marketers invest in Internet advertising, seven dollars in sales are generated.[13] A Web site has become an indispensable marketing technology for 21st century companies. It has evolved into a one-stop, online corporate information source; customer support tool; distribution channel; order taker; product catalog; price list; promotional vehicle; research technique; segmentation source; and a strategic and tactical marketing differentiator.

■ *Build marketing relationships.* Strategic partnering is a major part of a good IMC program. In addition to the Internet (discussed in number 3) and intranets (protected corporate information resource centers), progressive companies are creating extranets that link an enterprise's extended family of suppliers, distributors, retailers, and partners.[14] Thus, customer, channel, referral, and stakeholder relationships can be nurtured through carefully conceived promotional efforts.

■ *Note that everything an organization does sends a message.* Image and atmospherics are very important in communicating value to customers. "Little things" like stationery, signage, telephone greetings, Web site design, etc. should reflect professionalism and a consistent message to the marketplace.

■ *Two-way dialogue is key.* In an overcommunicated society, the marketing challenge is to establish a meaningful dialogue with customers as to how the firm's service mix can provide maximum benefits/value. Interactivity and involvement on the part of the customer are important for sharing information and creating firmer bonds. The Web is an ideal medium to accomplish this objective. Its selectivity and flexibility create a customized business experience for each user.

- *Use 21st century communication technologies.* In today's changing marketplace, companies must seek new and better ways to stay in touch with their target markets. Appropriate communication options include e-mail, electronic commerce, fax on demand, telemarketing, point-of-sale promotion, special events, multimedia, etc.
- *Measure promotional effectiveness.* Traditionally, advertising executives competed with sales managers for their "fair share" of the corporate promotional budget. Today, management requires accountability and demands to know and justify the return on investment of limited resources — it will no longer accept the nonmeasurable communications methods used by marketers in the past.[15] A marketing information system/database is the key tool for effectively monitoring and measuring the success of an IMC program. As part of this process, job descriptions and reward systems are likely to be redesigned. In a strong IMC-centered environment, in-house competition is replaced with cooperation/teamwork. Joint rewards help the organization do what is best, rather than just protect individual turf. Perhaps, the sales manager will accept a 5% cut in new hires and the advertising manager will agree to a 10% reduction in advertising expenditures to redirect dollars to needed sales promotion or public relations activities if it is for the good of the organization. Under this scenario, if the overall net effect of the promotional strategy improves through an IMC plan, all key players share in the rewards of their efforts.

SUMMARY

Service organizations must rethink the way that they compete from a strategic perspective. This requires a two-pronged attack: (1) add value to offerings; and (2) use integrated marketing communications (IMC) to promote a value edge. First, this chapter reviewed the importance of creating a strong USP (unique selling proposition), competitive differentiation, and basic positioning techniques. Second, it explored 13+ strategies for adding value to goods and services. Companies can use this foundation set as the marketing "toolbox" to enhance their current offerings. Third, the chapter explicated the IMC philosophy and presented an eight-step plan for implementing this approach. The next chapter explains how service companies can keep customers over time by using retention marketing strategies.

CUSTOMER VALUE ACTION ITEMS

1. How does your firm differentiate itself from its rivals?
    a. Describe your real and perceived competitive advantages.
    b. Discuss your current USP (unique selling proposition).
    c. Can you develop an even stronger USP that simply but elegantly communicates maximum value to your target market(s)?
2. Given the following value-added strategies, identify which techniques you: (1) currently use; (2) should use; and (3) could use more effectively.

	Using	Should Use	Can Use Better
Additional features/benefits			
Affordability			
Branding			
Customer involvement			
Customization/choice			
Enhanced quality			
Exceptional service			
Frequency marketing incentives			
Internet			
Simplify or bundle the offering			
Solve customer problems			
Technological leadership			
Warranties			
Other value-added strategies (describe)			

3. Identify three retailers that use a positioning strategy based on the core, extended, or total product, respectively. What can the first two companies do to position themselves via a longer-term time horizon?
4. Assume you are a consultant brought in to advise a local, alternative/pop-culture newspaper on how to design and deliver superior customer value. What would be some of your recommendations on how this newspaper publisher could add value and communicate more effectively with its readers and information seekers?
5. Explain how an e-tailer or service firm can use the six-step value-adding process to attract new business as well as do a better job satisfying and retaining existing customers.
6. On a five-point scale where 1 is "not very successfully" and 5 is "very successfully," how good a job does Disney do with respect to practicing integrated marketing communications (IMC)? Provide a rationale for your response.

7. IMC can be used as a foundation for communicating customer value and strategic promotional planning. Select a "basic" product in one of five product categories: consumer goods; consumer service; industrial goods; industrial service; or Internet service. How can you differentiate your basic product (e.g., notebook computer, overnight delivery service, travel Web site, etc.) to gain a moderate or strong competitive advantage.

   a. Based on the S-Q-I-P model and value-added strategies discussed in this chapter, how will you create value for customers?

   b. Devise an ad theme (USP), list key selling points, and outline a media plan (including the Web) to market the differentiated product/service.

   c. How can you apply IMC concepts to your promotional campaign?

REFERENCES

1. Anon. (2003) Amazon lifted by international sales, *Reuters*, http://news.com.com/2100-1021-998280.html?tag=sas_email, April 24.
2. Ries, A. and Trout, J. (1982) *Positioning: The Battle for Your Mind*, New York: Warner Books.
3. Nesbit, M. and Weinstein, A. (1989) Positioning the high-tech product, in *Handbook of Business Strategy 1989/1990 Yearbook*, Glass, H.E., Ed., Boston: Warren, Gorham & Lamont, 30-1–30-8.
4. Schultz, D. (1998) What's in a name? Your brand can be your most valuable long-term asset, *Ind. Week*, March 16, 20.
5. Aaker, D. (2002) The Internet as integrator: Fast brand building in slow-growth markets, *strategy+business*, 28(3), 48–57.
6. Anon. (1998) Service-centered innovation comes out of the wash, *Nation's Bus.*, Aug., 12.
7. Gill, P. (1991) Added value: relationship marketing is one way for retailers to build loyalty, *Stores*, Oct., 39–40.
8. Anon. (2002) The Campaign for Nursing's Future awards first scholarships to encourage new nurses, *SSM Online*, http://www.ssmonline.org/News/ViewRelease.asp?ReleaseID=1940, April 4.
9. McArthur, D.N. and Griffin, T. (1997) A marketing management view of integrated marketing communications, *J. Advertising Res.*, Sept./Oct., 19–26.
10. Roznowski, J.L., Reece, B.B., and Daugherty, T. (2002) An exploratory study of marketing communication practitioners' embracement of and satisfaction with IMC, in *Am. Mark. Assoc. Proc.*, Kehoe, W.J. and Lindgren, J.H., Jr., Eds., Summer, San Diego, 367–373.
11. Berlin, C. (2003) How's it integrating? http://www.reveries.com/reverb/research/integrated_marketing/, February 20.
12. Cleland, K. (1995) Few wed marketing, communications, *Advertising Age*, Feb. 27, 10.

13. Berger, M. (1998) It's your move, *Sales Mark. Manage.*, March, 45–53.
14. McKenna, R. (1998) Marketing in real time, *Executive Excellence*, April, 3–4.
15. Schultz, D.E. (1997) Integration is critical for success in 21st century, *Mark. News*, Sept. 15, 26.

IV

DELIVERING LONG-TERM SUPERIOR VALUE TO CUSTOMERS

10

MAXIMIZING VALUE THROUGH RETENTION MARKETING

Most companies are a lot better at prospecting for new customers than maintaining their customer list... I behaved as if every IBM customer were on the verge of leaving and that I'd do anything to keep them from bolting.

Buck Rodgers, former CEO of IBM

A good customer should not change his shop, nor a good shop change its customers.

Chinese proverb

Operating 26 casinos in 13 states, Harrah's Entertainment has branded itself as the only nationwide consumer gaming business and has the most loyal customers in the industry. The key to its customer retention success is mining the company's database to understand its customer base; developing compelling promotional incentives; and delivering outstanding service. The company found that 26% of its patrons generated 82% of revenues. Contrary to industry perceptions, the best customers were not stereotypical high-rollers but rather middle-aged bankers, doctors, teachers, and even machinists who enjoyed playing slot machines on a regular basis. Customers who were very satisfied with their casino experiences increased their spending on gambling at Harrah's by 24% annually (see the Harrah's Entertainment case).[1]

Custom Research, Inc. (CRI), a Minneapolis-based marketing research firm, was able to cut its customer base in half yet triple its revenues and double its profits over a 10-year period ending in 1998. This was accomplished by practicing individualized "surprise and delight" marketing for three dozen high-volume/high-margin clients (CRI's core partners); hand-picking and growing profitable new accounts (averaging $200,000 annually); and systematically eliminating more than a hundred low-volume/low-margin customers.[2]

This chapter explains how companies must develop customer retention (CR) strategies to maximize long-term customer and shareholder value. The following will be specifically examined:

- Importance of customer retention
- Integrated customer retention model
- How usage segmentation can assist in CR planning
- A five-step process for designing a CR program
- Customer retention approaches

WHY FOCUS ON CUSTOMER RETENTION?

Most companies spend a majority of their time, energy, and resources chasing new business. Although it is important to find new customers to replace lost business, grow the enterprise, and expand into new markets, this goal should be secondary to the main objective — keep customers and enhance customer relationships. According to Keveaney, customers leave service organizations due to *service reasons* in about two-thirds of the cases. Realize that these issues (core service problems, service encounter failures, inconvenience, and response to failed service) are largely controllable from the firm's perspective. Pricing, competition, ethics, involuntary switching, and other factors account for the balance of the switching motives.[3]

Frederick Reichheld, of Bain & Company, is a leading consultant on loyalty management. In his fine book, *The Loyalty Effect*, he builds a strong case for emphasizing employee retention and customer retention in business. Service companies must retain the best personnel to win and keep good customers (the average company loses about half of its employees in 4 years). He notes that "it's impossible to build a loyal bank of customers without a loyal employee base." Reichheld also shares these important statistics on the significance of customer retention[4]:

- On average, U.S. corporations lose half of their customers in 5 years.
- A typical company has a customer defection rate of 10 to 30% per year.

- Raising the customer retention rate by 5% can increase the value of an average customer (lifetime profits) by 25 to 100%.
- Lexus has repurchase rates more than 20% higher than Infiniti. Although Lexus only accounts for 3% of Toyota's sales, it contributes 30% toward its profits.
- State Farm determined that a 1% increase in customer retention will increase its capital surplus by more than $1 billion over time.

Later, Reichheld advised firms to "be picky" because a "truly humble company knows it can satisfy only certain customers, and it goes all out to keep them happy." Vanguard was cited as an exemplary organization in this regard. Targeting long-term investors rather than day traders, Vanguard's service/expense ratio (0.3%) was a quarter of the industry average (1.2%).[5]

A study by Marketing Metrics, a New Jersey firm, found that corporations spend 53% of their budgets on customer retention; nevertheless, concern remains that most effort is spent wooing new customers or the great "one-night stand." A vice president at that firm urged managers to look at this figure with skepticism. He noted that the definition of retention marketing is so broad that databases, satisfaction surveys, and couponing can qualify as retention activities (often such initiatives do not target existing high-value customers); compensation and promotions are generally based on demonstrating short-term profits (transaction business) at the expense of longer-term paybacks; and retention is viewed by many companies as the "fad of the week."[6] In reality, 80% or more of marketing budgets are often earmarked for getting new business (or less than 20% for keeping customers). At least 75% of your marketing budget should be invested in customer retention and relationship marketing activities. Conventional wisdom suggests that it costs at least five times more to get a new customer than to keep an existing one. Three other well-accepted beliefs about customer relationship management are[7]:

- Treat individual customers as assets (portfolio models can be useful)
- Create valid estimates of customer lifetime value
- Be willing to *fire* unprofitable customers

Philip Kotler, the internationally renowned professor at Northwestern University, states that "the key to customer retention is customer satisfaction." He notes that satisfied customers stay loyal longer; talk favorably about the organization; pay less attention to the competition; are less price sensitive; offer service ideas to the organization; and cost less to serve than new customers.[8]

CUSTOMER VALUE/RETENTION MODEL

Marketing managers know that it is critical to deliver superior value to their customers — this ensures business profitability. The customer value/retention model offers a good way of explaining key relationships among the core elements that create value in an organization (see Figure 10.1). As discussed earlier in the book, customer value is built through the proper mix of S-Q-I-P (service, quality, image, and price) — elements that attract customers to the organization. Companies should segment markets via demographic, psychographic, and usage approaches to locate new customers that find the firm's value propostion appealing.

Business and technology firms typically use account size and industry as a basis for identifying and targeting markets. These data are readily accessible, but often provide little insight about how specific goods and services are actually used by the customer. Therefore, product application segmentation can be used as a value analysis tool. Novartis Generics classifies physicians based on customer attractiveness and relative competitive position. The latter dimension is self-explanatory and the former consists of the number of prescriptions written; whether they prescribe generics; interest in the product line; and company loyalty. Based on their potential, doctors are placed into four groups: A = top clients (stress

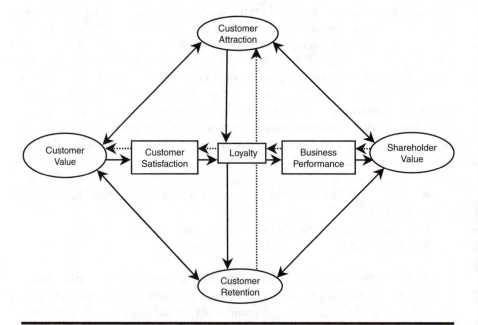

Figure 10.1   Customer Value/Retention Model

customer service); B = high potentials (marketing and promotion are important); C = low potentials (serve cost effectively); and D = unsatisfactory.

Realize that a one-time *buyer* is really a *try-er*, rather than a customer. To move beyond the transaction stage, organizational experiences must meet or (preferably) exceed the buyer's expectations. Repeated incidents of high satisfaction are sought through the effective utilization of relationship marketing strategies, leading to higher customer loyalty. Satisfaction may be viewed as largely a passive customer condition; however, loyalty requires an active or proactive relationship.[9]

Simon Knox notes three guiding principles to loyalty management:

■ Most customers buy on a portfolio basis.
■ All customers are not created equally.
■ Loyalty is retention with attitude.

He adds that *loyals* (involved) and *habituals* (indifferent) are usually the most profitable customers, while *variety seekers* (proactive searchers) and *switchers* (price shoppers) are generally less profitable.[10] Factoring time into the equation results in four customer loyal segments (note that only one of these segments is highly desirable). *Strangers* are short-term, low-profit customers while *butterflies* have high-profit potential but tend to be short term and disloyal. *Barnacles* stay around for the long term, but generate relatively low profits. Finally, *true friends* are highly profitable and are long-term customers.[11]

Loyalty (which results from the quality of the customer–company relationship) in turn leads to improved business performance/shareholder value and increased customer retention rates. Furthermore, the ability to retain customers successfully results in increased market values. The vertical customer retention chain shown in Figure 10.1 indicates that, ideally, loyal new customers are retained for many years. Research has shown that companies may expect loyal customers to range from about 40 to 75%, depending on the sector; loyalty, however, does not equate with exclusivity.[12] The business model of Amazon.com is based on retaining customers for a considerable number of years — 12 years by some analysts' forecasts — in order to develop deep, continuing relationships that will justify the company's heavy investment in its site.

Ralston's *SURe* model states that as satisfaction (S) increases, the likelihood that customers will continue to use (U) a service increases, as does the likelihood of the customer recommending (Re) the service provider to another potential customer. Multi-industry research using regression techniques in the service sector found that a 5% increase in satisfaction produces a 3% increase in continued use (0.6) and a 2.5% increase in recommending (0.5); a 5% increase in use results in a 2% increase in recommending (0.4).[13] Feedback loops are also depicted in the customer value/retention model. Good value secures customers over the long term. Similarly, customers (new and existing) want to maintain relationships with well-respected organizations that have high market values.

The customer value/marketing implications of the model are readily apparent. First, the key variables and their relationships to one another are clarified. This provides strategic guidance to management. Second, it stresses long-term relationships (retention) but still realizes that some customer defection and attrition will occur, so customer attraction must remain a priority. Third, the model is interfunctional and systematic — it ties marketing objectives to the big picture and the financial situation. Consider these three telling examples of the impact of CR on business performance:

- A mere 0.1% of the U.S. automobile industry is worth $2.5 billion.[14]
- A 2% increase in customer retention yields the same profit as a 10% reduction in overhead.[15]
- At Harrah's, a 1% increase in retention is worth $2 million in net profit annually.[16]

USAGE ANALYSIS AND CUSTOMER RETENTION

Segmenting markets by consumption patterns can be quite insightful for understanding a customer mix. Lands' End and L.L. Bean use "customer purchase patterns to compute the probability of purchase for each of the merchandise lines. Armed with this information, these firms send the customer only those catalogs for which the calculated purchase probability exceeds a threshold value."[17]

Differentiated marketing strategies are needed for the various user groups: first-time users, repeat customers, heavy users, and former users. By classifying customer accounts based on usage frequency and variety, companies can develop effective strategies to retain and upgrade customers. Many highly informative, low-cost applications of usage analysis should be considered by management. Examples include assessing:

- Heavy, medium, light, former, and nonusers (A, B, C, D, X)
- Heavy half segmentation (80/20 rule)
- Users vs. nonusers
- Competitive users
- Loyal (degree) vs. nonloyal customers
- Product/service applications by user group
- Adopter categories — innovators, followers, laggards
- Geographic comparisons (customer penetration indices, growth)

For example, a hotel grades customers based on the number of rooms booked annually. The key accounts are A1 users — large organizations that reserve thousands of room nights and conference facilities. A2 customers also book a high volume of rooms without the conference arrangements. A third category of heavy users is the A3 account that is a solid, loyal customer generating hundreds of room nights annually. Four descending usage levels of B customers (B1 to B4) are considered medium users. Finally, five types of C accounts (C1 to C5) represent light users. The C5 guest may only visit the hotel once a year.

By classifying customers into usage categories, management can design appropriate strategies to create value for each market segment. The objective is to move customers up the ladder, where possible. The implication of usage analysis is that all customers are not equal; some (heavy users) are clearly more important than others. For example, McDonald's Corporation actively targets "super-heavy" users. These customers are typically male, aged 18 to 34, and eat there several times a week, accounting for a majority of its sales.

In business and professional service markets, the best customers may be identified as key accounts based on customer ranking (e.g., the 100 most important customers); minimum sales volume level (e.g., $1 million in annual business); or market share (e.g., an annual account exceeds 1% of total business). The Pareto principle or 80/20 rule is insightful in this context. Realize that, in a typical business, approximately 80% of sales come from about 20% of customers and, generally, about 80% of sales come from 20% of the goods or services offered. It is essential to defend this core business because heavy users (A accounts) are primary targets for key competitors. These highly profitable customers require frequent advertising, promotions, sales calls, and ongoing communication efforts. Customer value insight 10.1 shows how Fast Industries applied 80/20 analysis to improve operations and increase business performance.

Strategy Consulting Inc.'s usage analysis revealed that 26% of its business (long-term clients) accounted for 84% of its profits. In addition, 22% of its revenues (mergers and acquisitions) yielded 87% of its profits. Operational projects (33% of its revenues) were found to be a losing proposition for the company; and subsequent inquiries in this area were farmed out to specialty consultancies.[18] Medium users (B customers) form the solid base of a business. Revenue enhancement strategies such as cross-selling or value-added services can be used to keep these customers satisfied and grow their business. Telephone calls, e-mail, and occasional sales calls are suggested to stay in touch with this group. By knowing the better customers (the As and Bs) through geographic, demographic, psychographic, and benefit research, a profile of typical users is established. This information is very helpful in planning subsequent customer attraction/conquest marketing efforts. Realize that the marketing information system, the database, plays a key role in customer analysis and decision making.

For unprofitable customers (many C accounts), the company often needs to find new ways to serve them more effectively. Technology such as ATM machines can be used in this regard. Quarterly contact through newsletters and direct mail or access options such as toll-free telephone numbers and Web sites maintains adequate communication with low-volume users. In some cases, it may even be desirable to sever the relationship with certain unprofitable customers.

An understanding of customers' purchasing patterns helps companies hold on to their key customers and gain a larger share of their business. Share of customer (customer retention focus) has supplanted market share (customer attraction focus) as a relevant business performance dimension in many markets. Share of customer is adapted by industry and goes by such names, among others, as share of care (health care); share of stomach (fast food); and share of wallet (financial services). If a company can increase a customer's share of business from 20 to 30%, this will have a dramatic impact on market share and profitability. A case in point: Harrah's increased its customer share from 36% ($0.36) of every dollar that their customers spent in casinos) to 42%. The financial implications for Harrah's were enormous; a one percentage point increase in share of its customers' overall gambling budgets coincided with an additional $125 million in shareholder value.[16]

Recency, frequency, and monetary value (RFM) analysis is a helpful tool in evaluating customer usage and loyalty patterns. Recency refers to the last service encounter/transaction; frequency assesses how often these customer–company experiences occur; and monetary value probes the amount spent, invested, or committed by customers for the firm's products and services (see Figure 10.2).

A few years ago, one of the authors purchased about $75 worth of brochure materials from a direct marketer for a one-time consulting project. This eager vendor immediately placed this purchaser into the preferred customer category and began sending him expensive catalogs about every 3 weeks without any follow-up orders. RFM analysis indicates that this is not a sound marketing practice because this company essentially treated all one-time "try-ers" as "best" customers. Note that this transaction fared poorly on all critical RFM dimensions: recency — 5+ years ago; frequency — a single purchase; and monetary value — relatively low.

Several online retailers have applied RFM analysis with surprising results. For example, for apparel e-tailers, new customers cost 20 to 40% more to acquire when compared to their brick-and-mortar counterparts. However, online repeat customers spend more than twice as

Access a summary of each customer's RFM transaction history; this includes
most recent purchase, frequency of purchases, and monetary value spent
per order.

Sort customers by purchase dates in reverse chronological order. Divide
the customer list into five equal segments. Tag the most recent customer
purchase quintile as "1"; the least recent purchases are quintile "5."

Sort customers by frequency (number of orders) and apply the same
methodology and tagging process as in the preceding step.

Sort customers by monetary value (average dollar amount of each order)
and apply the same methodology and tagging process as in step 2.

You now have created RFM scores for each of your customers, from your
best customer segment (111) to your worst (555).

Notes: It is likely that the best segment(s) can be substantiated by Pareto's
80/20 rule. The goal is to acquire "look-a-likes" of best customers and
improve marketing effectiveness with the other "good" RFM segments.

**Figure 10.2   How to Perform an RFM Analysis (Adapted from Kahan, R. [1998]
J. Consumer Mark., 15(5), 491–493.)**

much in months 24 to 30 of their relationships as they do in the first
6 months.[19]

A more effective strategy is to classify customers via usage analysis (as
previously described) and design differentiated marketing approaches for
each target market. According to Rust et al., FedEx categorized its customers internally as the good, the bad, and the ugly based on profitability.
These marketing scholars propose a generalized, four-tier usage segmentation system[20]:

- *Platinum tier* — the company's most profitable customers, typically
  heavy users, not overly price sensitive, willing to invest in and try
  new offerings, and committed customers of the firm
- *Gold tier* — profitability levels not as high as platinums, seek price
  discounts, less loyal, and use multiple vendors
- *Iron tier* — essential customers who provide the volume needed to
  utilize the firm's capacity, but their spending levels, loyalty, and
  profitability are not substantial enough for special treatment
- *Lead tier* — customers who cost the company money, demanding
  more attention than they are due, given their spending and profitability, and sometimes problem customers, complaining about the
  firm and tying up resources

In sum, usage analysis can greatly assist in customer retention activities.
Think about how to:

- "Hold" heavy users and key accounts
- Upgrade light and medium users
- Build customer loyalty
- Understand buying motives to meet/exceed expectations
- Use appropriate selling strategies for each targeted usage group
- Win back "lost" customers
- Learn why nonusers are not responding to the value proposition

Note that customer relationship management (CRM), an expensive information technology, is also frequently used by large companies for business usage analyses. Unfortunately, this much-hyped alternative has been criticized recently for unfulfilled promises, i.e., not being an effective and profitable communications system with customers. As a result, the CRM business has experienced declining sales, ongoing consolidation, and unhappy end users.[21] (CRM will be discussed in greater detail in Chapter 11.)

CUSTOMER VALUE INSIGHT 10.1 — FAST INDUSTRIES*

Fast Industries is a plastics manufacturing company located in Ft. Lauderdale, Florida. The company is the world's largest producer of label holders and serves leading retail store chains including Wal-Mart, Target, CVS Drugs, and Michael's Crafts.

Fast Industries is undergoing a transformation from a smaller, family-run manufacturing company to a more professionally structured, staffed, and managed organization. Because of the recognition that customer retention is more important than customer attraction, much effort was spent ensuring that Fast's most valuable customers perceived this change as positive and were more likely to remain customers. Two strategic initiatives that played a central role in the new marketing strategy were the 80/20 principle and the value proposition.

The 80/20 principle was integral in determining the focus and location of Fast's most important customers. Although over 2000 retail chains are in the U.S., due to variations in the number of stores and size of stores per chain, it was estimated that about 90 of them would purchase 90% of the store fixture components that Fast can offer. Currently, Fast does business with 30 of these retailers; for each of these key accounts delivering superior customer value is a top management priority.

Next, the value proposition was utilized to determine the exact nature of each customer's relationship with Fast. Because there are four basic

---

* Prepared by Robert Fast, vice president of Fast Industries. This example originally appeared in Weinstein, A. (2002) Customer retention: a usage segmentation and customer value approach, *J. Targeting, Meas. Anal. Mark.*, 10(3), 265.

providers of value to a customer (price, service, quality, and image), each customer was surveyed by its respective sales representative on exactly why it did business with Fast and what aspects of value were derived from doing business with the company. Using an internally designed strategic assessment form based on the value proposition, it was found that no relationships with Fast were based on image or price alone, but that service and quality were laden with further nuances. To one customer, service might mean high levels of in-stock orders; to another, it might mean ease in placing an order. To yet a third it might be constant attention from a sales representative. Quality as a criterion can be broken down into components as varied as the product's engineering and design, on-time delivery, and/or whether the product was packed and billed correctly.

A second assessment tool was a SWOT analysis conducted at individualized and aggregate levels. Strengths, weaknesses, opportunities, and threats information was gathered from each strategic customer. An assessment of Fast's overall relationship with all accounts plus a future forecast and recommended strategy was developed. What was perhaps most unique about this analysis was that it sought to describe the strategic position of business relationships in terms of the value proposition.

Through the sound application of strategic marketing principles rooted in segmentation and customer value, Fast Industries is now designing and delivering superior products/services to its most important customers — and it is working in a big way. Management projects that this customer retention strategy will have a significant impact on profitability for the year 2001 with revenues increasing by 20% and profits increasing by 25%.

──────────▲▼▲──────────

DESIGNING A CUSTOMER RETENTION PROGRAM

To develop an effective customer retention (CR) program, organizations can follow this five-step process:

1. *Determine your current CR rate.* It is surprising how few companies know the percentage of customers that leave (the defection rate) or the percentage of customers that they are able to retain annually (the retention rate). Customer retention can be measured in many ways, including:
   - Annual and targeted customer retention rates
   - Weighted customer retention rates (accounts for usage differences)
   - Segmented retention indicators (subgroup analysis based on geographic, demographic, lifestyle, product preferences, or other categories)
   - Share of customer
   - Customer lifetime value (CLTV)

- Recency, frequency, and monetary value (RFM)

   Choosing an appropriate measure provides a starting point for assessing a firm's success in keeping customers.

2. *Analyze the defection problem.* Step two is a three-pronged attack. First, identify disloyal customers. Second, understand why they left. According to DeSouza, six types of defectors exist. Customers go elsewhere because of lower price; superior products; better service; alternative technologies; market changes (e.g., they move or go bankrupt); and "political" considerations.[22] An analysis of switching motives can also provide insight here. Third, strategies need to be developed to overcome nonloyal purchasing behavior (discussed later in the chapter).

3. *Establish a new CR objective.* Assume that your company is currently retaining 75% of its customers. A realistic goal may be to increase client retention by 3% to 78%, annually, and to keep 85% of your clients within 5 years. Customer retention objectives should be based on organizational capabilities (strengths, weaknesses, resources, etc.); customer and competitive analyses; and benchmarking with the industry/sector, comparable firms, and high-performing units in your company.

4. *Invest in a targeted CR plan to enhance customer loyalty.* The cost (potential lifetime value) of a single lost customer can be substantial. This is magnified exponentially when you realize the overall annual cost of lost business. Consider the impact of a 25% defect rate for a hospital. As Figure 10.3 demonstrates, a $9.375 million loss in revenues results in a $703,125 dive on the bottom line. The hospital that invests even $100,000 in patient retention training and CR program initiatives can dramatically improve its profitability. Targeted retention planning means that organizations should segment customers by relevant dimensions such as geography, demographic and socioeconomic variables, and other criteria in order to understand customer profiles and purchasing patterns. Cole Taylor is a Chicago-based bank holding company that ascribes to the "first dollar" principle. If the bank only has $1 to spend on

15,000 = patients annually
3750 = defections annually (25% defection rate; 75% retention rate)
$2500 = average per patient revenue, annually
$9.375 million = annual lost revenues
$703,125 = annual lost profits (7.5% profit margin)

Figure 10.3   The Cost of Lost Business for a Hospital

marketing (generally, not a problem for a $2 billion organization), it will invest it on existing customers rather than using it to attract new business.[23]

5. *Evaluate the success of the CR program.* As an iterative process, the final phase in designing a solid customer retention plan is to ensure that it is working. Careful scrutiny is required to assess the program's impact on keeping existing customers (see customer value checklist 10.1 for further guidance in this area). Upgrading current customer relationships may be a secondary business objective. At this point, gather new information to learn to what extent the CR rate has improved. It may be necessary to revisit benchmarks and further probe isolated causes of defection. CR strategies and tactics will be closely analyzed to determine the methods that worked best and those that had little or no impact on keeping customers.

―――――――――――― ▼▲▼ ――――――――――――

CUSTOMER VALUE CHECKLIST 10.1: GATHERING CUSTOMER RETENTION DATA

What are your current and targeted CR rates?

Given your current defection rate, how often must you replenish your customer pool?

Has your CR rate increased during the past 3 years?

What is the lifetime value of a customer (CLTV)?

What is the cost of a lost customer?

What percentage of your marketing budget is spent on customer retention activities?

On average, how much do you spend on current customers annually?

What criteria do your company use for developing targeted retention programs by market segment?

Do you invest more on high-value (A) customers?

How does your firm use RFM analysis?

―――――――――――― ▲▼▲ ――――――――――――

CUSTOMER RETENTION APPROACHES

Literally dozens of methods can be used to keep customers. Customer retention tactics (for example, promotional incentives) are short term in nature while CR strategies create lasting value for customers. Customer retention efforts should begin as soon as the firm acquires a customer and should include[24]

■ Learning as much as possible about customer needs

- Responding promptly to any indications of disinterest
- Making customers feel truly cared for
- Resolving complaints quickly and efficiently
- Being willing to negotiate with high-value customers who show signs of inactivity

As the customer value/retention model explained, companies must create loyalty from new customers in order to retain them. Some of the most common and effective approaches for enhancing retention include

- Building a customer database/marketing information system
- Designing ongoing customer programs (continuity and loyalty-based initiatives such as frequent-flyer miles)
- Offering long-term services (membership/subscription programs)
- Customizing promotion (using reminder advertising and press releases)
- Focusing on key accounts and heavy users
- Using newsletters/informational materials to stay in touch with infrequent customers
- Attending trade shows
- Researching customers' needs and wants
- Welcoming suggestions and complaints

As other innovative loyalty-building strategies, you can[25]

- Send salespeople to work at the offices of your best customers
- Participate in customers' events
- Interview your customers' customers
- Hold a retreat with a major customer to share best practices
- Invite customers to participate in training seminars
- Set up a customer advisory council
- Develop a preferred-customer pricing strategy
- Reward customers for referring new business
- Develop 3- to 5-year business plans with customers
- Partner with key accounts on industry research projects

Hospitals are turning to customer retention ideas to keep patients in highly competitive environments. A list of 30 patient retention ideas in five key areas is summarized in Figure 10.4.

As the preceding shows, a multitude of potential customer retention ideas, tactics, and strategies can be utilized successfully by value-creating managers. How do you know which approaches should be employed by

Tactic	Examples
Image/promotion	Community service; direct mail; educational offerings; health fairs; integrated marketing communications; newsletters; regular contact with patient; useful informational materials; Web site
Service quality	Continuous quality initiatives; convenience; customer service training; demonstrate that patients are highly valued; mystery shopping; patient representatives/ombudsmen; service failure training; smile; treat patients as family
Research	Analyze defection rates/reasons; classify customers by usage/satisfaction/loyalty; develop targeted retention programs; "inside-out" (patient-focused) health care model
Internal marketing	Loyalty task force; prepare "solutions" to recurring problems; share appropriate patient data with staff; reward and publicize customer care patient of the month
Patient centered	"Dialogue" marketing; patient bill of rights; patient care councils; understand patient expectations

Figure 10.4   Patient Retention Tactics

your company? The following seven criteria provide a useful point of reference:

- Efficiency (low cost)
- Effectiveness (likelihood to succeed)
- Adaptability (strategic fit with your organizational culture)
- Consistency (works well with your current marketing plan)
- Competitive advantage
- Ease of implementation
- Projected profitability

Marketers generally examine past and current purchase patterns in analyzing customer retention. An often overlooked measure is customers' future orientation. Recent research initiatives have identified several useful metrics for evaluation: expected future use; anticipated regret; intent to switch; and intent to remain loyal (return to provider and recommend provider).[26,27] Innovative customer value managers should consider these measures to gain additional insight on retention and a potential edge over their competition.

SUMMARY

Companies that deliver superior value to customers on an ongoing basis are able to keep them over the long term. This chapter reviewed the essentials for establishing a customer retention focus. By maintaining consistently high levels of customer satisfaction and loyalty, customer defection becomes less likely. This results in enhanced business performance and increases shareholder value. Relationship marketing is the key strategy to obtain the desired results of retaining more customers; getting better customers; upgrading customer relationships; and using existing customers as advocates for acquiring new customers. This issue is discussed in the final chapter of the book.

CUSTOMER VALUE ACTION ITEMS

1. Identify three companies that do a good job in retaining customers and upgrading customer relationships.
2. What is the relationship among customer value, customer satisfaction, loyalty, customer retention, and business performance? How can an advertising agency or accounting firm use the customer value/retention model to do a better job getting and keeping customers?
3. Clarify the distinction between a company that focuses on product management vs. one that focuses on customer retention.
4. In today's fast changing and highly competitive market environment, customer retention is more important than customer attraction. Do you agree or disagree with this statement? Why or why not?
5. Should companies develop a separate marketing plan for keeping customers? Why or why not?
6. Identify five product or service categories (and organizations, as applicable) which exhibit varying customer loyalty patterns:
   a. Complete loyalty
   b. Situational loyalty
   c. Multiple loyalty — a high degree of loyalty to two or more organizations in a category
   d. Limited loyalty
   e. No loyalty
7. What are the top three reasons that customers leave your company? How can these switching motives be overcome?
8. List some of the customer retention strategies and tactics that your organization uses. What are some additional CR approaches that it should think about using?

9. Does your firm segment its market through usage analysis? Describe your usage segments and explain how you would implement a targeted customer value/marketing program for each key market segment.

10. (a) Identify approaches that companies can use to retain customers and build long-term relationships for a:

1. Business service provider
2. High-tech firm
3. Industrial goods distributor
4. Web-based company

(b) Rank your top three strategies for each of the four businesses listed in part a.

(c) Estimate the lifetime value of an average customer for these companies.

(d) How should these organizations measure long-term customer satisfaction, loyalty, and retention?

REFERENCES

1. Loveman, G. (2003) Diamonds in the data mine, *Harvard Bus. Rev.*, May, 109–113.
2. Greco, S. (1998) Choose or lose, *Inc.*, December, 57–66.
3. Keveaney, S.M. (1995) Customer switching behavior in service industries: an exploratory study, *J. Mark.*, April, 71–82.
4. Reichheld, F.F. (1996) *The Loyalty Effect: The Hidden Force Behind Growth, Profits, and Lasting Value*, Boston: Harvard Business School Press.
5. Reichheld, F.F. (2001) Lead for loyalty, *Harvard Bus. Rev.*, July–August, 76–84.
6. Pruden, D. (1995) Retention marketing gains spotlight, but does reality match philosophy? *Brandweek*, February, 15.
7. Fader, P. (2001) Request — CRM conventional wisdom, http://www.columbia.edu/~pbp1/elmar/, July 10.
8. Kotler, P. (1994) *Marketing Management: Analysis, Planning, Implementation, and Control*, 8th ed., Englewood Cliffs, NJ: Prentice–Hall.
9. Fredericks, J.O., Hurd, R.R. and Salter II, J.M. (2001) Connecting customer loyalty to financial results, *Mark. Manage.*, Spring, 26–32.
10. Knox, S. (1998) Loyalty-based segmentation and the customer development process, *Eur. Manage. J.*, December, 729–737.
11. Reinartz, W. and Kumar, V. (2002) The mismanagement of customer loyalty, *Harvard Bus. Rev.*, July, 86–94.
12. Odell, S.M. and Pajunen, J.A. (2000) *The Butterfly Customer: Capturing the Loyalty of Today's Elusive Consumer*, Toronto: John Wiley & Sons.
13. Ralston, R.W. (1996) Model maps out a sure path to growth in the marketplace, *Mark. News*, May 20, 12.
14. Waldrop, J. (1994) How to succeed despite slow growth, *Am. Demogr.*, April, 52–56.

15. Marchetti, M. (1996) How the CEO of Unisys creates customer value, *Sales Mark. Manage.*, October, 45.
16. Nickell, J. (2002) Welcome to Harrah's, *Bus. 2.0*, April, 51–52.
17. Shaw, M.J. et al. (2001) Knowledge management and data mining for marketing, *Decision Support Syst.*, 31(1), 127–137.
18. Koch, R. (1998) *The 80/20 Principle: The Secret of Achieving More with Less*, New York: Currency Doubleday, 65–68.
19. Reichheld, F. and Schefter, P. (2000) E-loyalty: your secret weapon, *Harvard Bus. Rev.*, July–August, 106.
20. Rust, R.T., Zeithaml, V.A., and Lemon, K.N. (2000) *Driving Customer Equity: How Customer Value is Reshaping Corporate Strategy*, New York: The Free Press, 191.
21. Pockard, D. (2003) Why CRM is at a fateful crossroads, *CNET News.com*, March 13.
22. DeSouza, G. (1992) Designing a customer retention plan, *J. Bus. Strategy*, March/April, 24–28.
23. Taylor, B. (1996) The relationship builders: organizing around the customer, *Bank Manage.*, January/February, 30–34.
24. Passavant, P. (1995) Retention marketing needs a new vision, *J. Direct Mark.*, Spring, 2–4.
25. Brewer, G. (1998) The customer stops here, *Sales Mark. Manage.*, March, 31–36.
26. Lemon, K.N., White, T.B., and Winer, R.S. (2002) Dynamic customer relationship management: incorporating future considerations into the service retention decision, *J. Mark.*, January, 1–14.
27. McDougall, G.H.G. and Levesque, T. (2000) Customer satisfaction with services: putting perceived value into the equation, *J. Serv. Mark.*, 14(5), 392–410.

11

CREATING VALUE THROUGH CUSTOMER AND SUPPLIER RELATIONSHIPS

If you're selling a service, you're selling a relationship.

Harry Beckwith, founder of Beckwith Advertising and Marketing

In the new economy, the sturdiest barrier to competition is customer allegiance — building the strongest relationships with the most profitable customers…building marketing and operations network that offers exceptional convenience, reliability, speed and customization.

Adrian Slywotzky, vice-president, Mercer Management Consulting, Inc.

Think for a minute about the purpose of a business. Ask most business people and they might reply, "to make a profit" or "to grow shareholder value." As commendable as these goals are, should they be the primary focus of an enterprise? Harvard business professor Theodore Levitt once remarked, "The purpose of a business is to create and keep a customer."[1] The sale merely consummates the courtship according to Levitt, at which point the relationship begins. Peter Drucker, a leading management theorist, puts it this way: "There will always, one can assume, be a need for some selling. But the aim of marketing is to make selling superfluous. The aim of marketing is to know and understand the customer so well that the product or service fits him and sells itself."[2]

The traditional marketing paradigm consisting of the four Ps of marketing is beginning to lose some of its influence among marketers. This approach focuses on the transaction and the core product, taking a short-term perspective; customer attraction (conquest marketing) is the overriding goal This perspective is no longer sufficient because the powerful forces of industry globalization; the "value" movement; rapid advances in technology; and a shift in the balance of power toward customers have coalesced to change the rules for business success. Marketing guru Regis McKenna places "relationships," which he believes represent the true marketing ideal, at the center of this shift[3]:

> Marketing really only became a term about a hundred years ago. The concept of marketing prior to its first common usage in the third quarter of the last century was that it was everything that you do prior to the promotion of the product, whereas now we think of it as everything you do after. It really has flipped itself almost 180°. If you look at what in my mind marketing is, it is this ideal of having a consumer–producer relationship based upon providing value and an exchange of value, and that means proximities between the buyer and seller, or producer and consumer.

Relationship marketing represents a fundamental transformation from traditional marketing in that relationships shift from adversarial to cooperative and the goals shift from market share to share of customers. Philip Kotler concurs, saying that "companies must move from a short-term *transaction-orientation* to a long-term *relationship-building* goal."[4] In the new economy, products will not matter as much as the relationship between company and customer.[5]

The complicated nature of buyer–supplier interactions today makes repeated negotiations too much of a hassle and too costly, leaving success in marketing more dependent on creating and maintaining the relationship. A recent study by Net Future Institute, a New Hampshire-based new economy think tank, confirmed this situation. In a 2001 study, the institute found that 91% of the respondents indicated that the most important factor to their customers 2 years from then would be "quick response to inquiries and complaints." The second most important factor reported was "ease of interaction with their company," followed by "quick turnaround for orders." These findings suggest that relationships are going to be more, not less, crucial to responding to customers and creating effective value-added exchanges.

Chapter 10 examined retention marketing, looking at ways to create a loyal customer base. This chapter examines how to preserve the customer base following the principles of relationship marketing. It begins by defining relationship marketing as well as considering the rationale for following such an approach. It then contrasts traditional vs. relationship marketing. The requirements for building healthy and lasting relationships are also explored. Finally, some of the keys for successfully practicing relationship marketing strategies are presented.

WHAT IS RELATIONSHIP MARKETING?

The cornerstone of marketing is getting close to customers in order to identify and satisfy their needs better. Realize that marketing is responsible for more than just the sale. The way in which business is conducted has changed significantly, with the focus shifting from the transaction to the relationship. This is particularly true for services marketing because it is difficult to separate service operations and delivery from relationship building. Marketing departments in today's organizations are now responsible for becoming experts on the customer, while keeping the rest of the company informed about customer activities.[6] Managing customer relationships continues to be paramount, yet so is the growing importance of managing relationships with suppliers and resellers as well.

Due to the strong interest in relationship marketing, a number of useful definitions have been offered. Len Berry, first credited with using the term *relationship marketing* in the services literature, says that "relationship marketing is attracting, maintaining, and enhancing customer relationships."[7] A more expansive definition is proposed by Parvatiyar and Sheth: "Relationship marketing refers to all marketing activities directed toward establishing, developing, and maintaining successful relational exchanges."[8] Although both of these definitions help in understanding the nature and purpose of relationship marketing, the authors tend to endorse Gordon's view of relationship marketing in which he explains that "relationship marketing is the ongoing process of identifying and creating new value with individual customers and then sharing the benefits from this over a lifetime of association."[9]

Notice that relationship marketing is ongoing. A business relationship is like a marriage: success is achieved not just through good intentions but also through hard work and close attention to the other party's needs. Further, the goal is to identify and create *new value* with individual customers. Amazon.com achieves this via a personalization technology known as *collaborative filtering*. Once a customer makes a purchase from the company, Amazon.com recommends a new book by comparing his tastes with those of fellow book buyers who have reported liking the same kinds of books.

Not only should new value be created, but the resulting benefits also need to be shared over the lifetime of the relationship. Revenue sharing is a marketing strategy used by new economy companies to share value with their partners. A revenue sharing agreement formed between Kodak and AOL called "You've Got Pictures!" allows AOL subscribers to store photos in a private, online photo album. Customers, who would get a free allotment of storage space, can also purchase additional space and buy mugs, T-shirts, and calendars embossed with personal snapshots. They also can order reprints online and have them developed at Kodak film processors located near their homes.

Another successful example of revenue sharing is Apple Computer's online service called "iTunes," a service that offers more than 200,000 songs at $0.99 a download and has the support of all five major record labels, with whom Apple splits the revenue. Consumers have been drawn to the service because there is no copy-protection and Apple's offering lets them keep songs indefinitely; share them on as many as three Macintosh computers; and transfer them to any number of iPod portable music players. Moreover, no subscriptions are necessary and buyers can burn unlimited copies of the songs onto CDs, which can also be copied without restrictions. When Apple launched its online music store in May, 2003, it hoped to sell 1 million songs by the end of that month. Instead it sold 1 million songs in its first week and 3 million in its first month.

American Airlines created a program called "Airpass" for one of its large corporate customers, Perot Systems. When Perot employees book flights, they do not need to wait for tickets; they just simply present a card at the ticket counter or gate. Miles are automatically credited to the employee's American frequent-flyer account. Upgrades are readily available and American allows Perot employees to use its Ambassadors Clubs for business and leisure travel.

TRADITIONAL VS. RELATIONSHIP MARKETING

In the frenzied 1980s, companies focused most of their marketing efforts on acquiring new customers. Little attention was given to existing customers. With the cost of customer attraction continually going up, companies are giving much more serious attention to holding on to their existing customers. For example, for cellular phone companies, the cost of acquiring a new subscriber is now about $400 with an average payback period for the operator of 3 years.[10] According to a study by the Boston Consulting Group and Shop.org, dot-coms that did not have stores or catalogs spent an average of $82 to acquire each new customer in 2000; catalog and store retailers spent $12 to acquire each new customer in 2000.[11] Furthermore, online customer acquisition costs have been

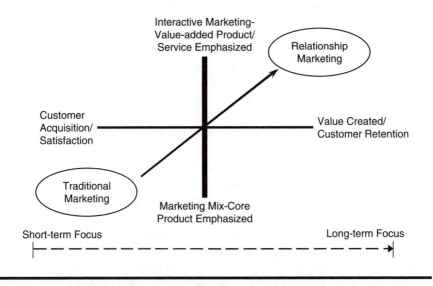

Figure 11.1   Traditional vs. Relationship Marketing (Adapted from Sheth, J., AMA Strategic Marketing Faculty Consortium, Scottsdale, AZ, 1996.)

steadily falling. Boston Consulting Group and Shop.org report that all online retailers spent an average of $20 to acquire a customer in the last quarter of 2000, down from $71 during the same quarter in 1999.

Long-standing customers are less expensive to reach and less expensive to serve. Moreover, taking into account the lifetime value of a customer, the financial toll of losing customers is staggering. Customer relationships are assets that should be evaluated and managed as rigorously as any financial or physical assets (see customer value insight 11.1). Figure 11.1 presents an overview of how traditional marketing differs from relationship marketing.

As this figure shows, relationship marketing not only focuses on customer retention, but also takes a long-term perspective. Companies that exploit their customers for short-term advantage will "win the battle, but ultimately lose the war." In the mid-1980s Ryder System Inc. began a relationship with one of the large Bell operating companies via a short-term truck rental. Over time, Ryder has provided more value to the customer, including full-service equipment leases; drivers; a full outbound delivery network; and logistic solutions. Ryder also assumed operation of all inbound transportation and distributor center packaging/shipping/cross docking and storeroom operations, all staffed and operated by Ryder personnel. In 2000, Ryder introduced *e-Channel Solutions*, which offered a global network of e-commerce capabilities for on-demand delivery to consumers that facilitates online replenishment from distribution centers to a network of neighborhood depots, then unattended or attended delivery to a consumer's home. Ryder will manage the entire fulfillment channel for its clients — operating the distribution centers; managing the transportation of goods to the neighborhood depots; coordinating the "last mile" delivery through Ryder's network of couriers; and leveraging the infrastructure to facilitate returns.

Traditional marketing also differs from relationship marketing based on how the firm's marketing mix is treated. For example, packaged-good producers serving mostly consumer markets attempt to blend the marketing mix elements, although not always in an integrative sense. Furthermore, the number of points of contact with the customer is limited under traditional marketing. In relationship marketing, value is created in the relationships that companies have with their customers. Companies' interactions with buyers (or prospective buyers) are not limited to or always initiated by the marketing function or department. In fact, many of the contacts with the buyer are "nonmarketing" or what Gummesson refers to as *part-time marketers*.[12] Although these employees' primary responsibilities may be nonmarketing, i.e., technical support, back-office, or frontline workers, they also perform crucial marketing tasks because of their vital customer contacts. Remember that customers evaluate value at *every point of contact* in the organization to determine if they received what was expected or promised.

The goals and outcomes of relationship marketing also differ from traditional marketing. Whereas the goal under traditional marketing is customer acquisition, under relationship marketing the focus shifts to creating value. Case in point: Nabisco created the account-specific sales expanding techniques (ASSET) program — a menu of tactics that can be executed at the store level for mass, club, and grocery chains in conjunction with Nabisco's national efforts. For example, around the national Cool School Bus promotion (Nabisco will give away buses full of Tiger Toys and Nabisco snacks to one winner per state), Nabisco has developed two major account-specific overlays: a store-by-store sweepstakes offering Thermos lunch totes filled with Tiger Toys and Nabisco snacks ($100 value overall) and customized TV spots. Kraft/General Foods has also been effective in creating value for its retail customers. Working with one retailer in upstate New York and using a merged database consisting of the retailer's frequent-shopper program members and Kraft's proprietary household database, Kraft prepared a customized mailing to households in the retailer's area.

If the goal is to create more value through interdependent, collaborative relationships with customers, the outcome is customer retention. As was emphasized earlier, relationship marketing is ongoing — constantly looking for opportunities to generate new value. Thus, customer retention is not a given, especially when new value is not created. BellSouth trains its service representatives to act as consultants for its small business customers in order to work with them in addressing their communications as well as business–marketing needs. Many small business clients have limited marketing budgets and appreciate the "bundled" solutions offered by BellSouth, such as local and long-distance, as well as Web services.

Retaining customers requires marketers to exhibit care and concern *after* they have made a purchase.[13] In fact, the sale often represents just the beginning of the relationship between the buyer and seller. Dick Berry suggested modifying the original marketing mix, adding three new elements that focus more on after-marketing elements. Based on a study with marketing managers, he added an S and two Cs to the traditional four Ps. Table 11.1 describes the revised marketing mix, along with a ranking of importance to management.[14] The greatest opportunity for achieving high customer retention lies with these three newer items: customer sensitivity, customer convenience, and service.

QVC's online shopping service is a great example here. Web shoppers can visit the iQVC site, then click on "My iQVC." Customers are then informed, "We'll ask you a few questions, you'll give us a few answers, and we'll deliver custom content right to your desktop." Shoppers who click on "My Mailing List" can choose from several categories, such as cookware, jewelry, toys, and collectibles. Once the customer has chosen, iQVC will e-mail the shopper with relevant news on the subject he or she has chosen. The site also offers "My Style Advisor," where customers complete an online questionnaire and receive a style advisor profile, personalized for body line, face shape, and coloring. QVC then makes

Table 11.1 The Relationship Marketing Mix

Marketing Element	Rank
Customer sensitivity — employee attitude, customer treatment, and response to customers	1
Product quality — features and reliability	2
Customer convenience — availability to the customer, customer convenience, easy to do business with	3
Service — postsale and presale	4
Price — price charged, pricing terms, and pricing offers	5
Place — provider accessibility, provider facilities, and availability to customer	6
Promotion — advertising, publicity, selling	7

Source: Adapted from Berry, D. (1990) *Mark. News*, Dec. 24, 10.

appropriate fashion and jewelry recommendations. QVC creates loyalty by being open 24 hours and offering efficient and helpful service before, during, and after the sale.

Evidence is growing that something is unique about the online shopping experience, especially as it relates to the exchange process. For example, in traditional marketing, the seller's actions (i.e., communication activities) tend to be unidirectional and largely influence the exchange process. However, in the new economy, the communication activities are often bidirectional, and not always between the buyer and seller. For example, many online communities serve as forums for consumer-to-consumer exchange of common interests, i.e., evaluating past service experiences. Furthermore, consumers often initiate the communication with the seller rather than passively attending to the seller's messages. For example, in reverse auctions such as Priceline.com, the prospect initiates the exchange process by submitting a bid on a flight or hotel room; Priceline then tries to locate sellers interested in accepting the bid.

This section looked at how relationship marketing and traditional marketing differ; the next section will discuss the determinants of building strong customer relationships.

BUILDING LASTING CUSTOMER RELATIONSHIPS

Relationships, whether business or marriage, seem to be subject to the second law of thermodynamics: unless maintained, they gradually deteriorate and wear down. Apart from sound management, the relationship erodes because both parties' focus turns inward and moves toward insensitivity and inattentiveness.[15] Recall an American Airlines commercial a few years back in which a senior-level manager is gathered with his subordinates, lamenting that "we just got fired by our best customer." He reminds them that they used to conduct business with a visit and handshake — now it is by fax or voice mail. He proceeds to hand out airline tickets to each person present in the meeting, instructing them to pay a personal visit to each of their key customers. He, of course, is going to visit the customer who "fired" them. The message is: never take customer relationships for granted.

Sellers can resist this natural tendency toward decline and complacency by developing what is referred to as "relationship enablers." It is the seller's responsibility to nurture the relationship beyond its simple dollar value. Using the relationship enablers shown in Figure 11.2, sellers can minimize relationship decay and strengthen the bonds that lead to long-term, perhaps even lifetime, associations:

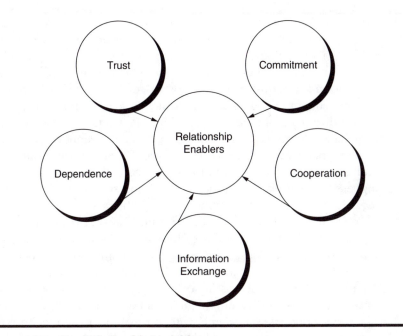

Figure 11.2 Key Relationship Variables

■ *Trust* — the effect of trust is an important factor to consider in the development of marketing relationships that exists when there is confidence in an exchange partner's reliability and integrity. A seller can create confidence in the eyes of the buyer by being credible and following through on what it promises. FedEx dominates the market for overnight delivery because it promises to have the customer's package there "absolutely, positively, overnight." FedEx's customers rest easy at night knowing that this statement is not simply an advertising slogan, but a pledge to deliver on what it promises (see the FedEx case).

One of the best tools for establishing trust is effective communications. It is important to be open and honest, as well as clear and thorough. Establishing a good channel of communication can help avoid countless potential disasters and loss of customer trust down the road. Remember also that trust is a "bank account" in which deposits and withdrawals are made over time. The trust account accumulates interest only when the seller's messages and actions are clear, consistent, and reliable. The evidence is that trust plays a critical role in building durable online relationships as well.[16] Some experts believe that trust is the "single most important factor for customers choosing an online supplier."[17]

- *Commitment* is another important relationship enabler. While trust involves reliance on the seller, commitment is an implicit or explicit pledge of maintaining and supporting the relationship. Although a distinction is made here between trust and commitment, a recent study found that trust actually leads to commitment.[18] A high level of commitment encourages both parties in a relationship to pursue their individual and joint goals. UPS and JC Penney recently formed a $1 billion partnership in which UPS becomes Penney's sole mail-order carrier, as well as its logistics carrier; UPS brings its equipment and expertise to the partnership. Such a commitment signals a willingness by each player to modify its existing systems to fit the other, inextricably binding these companies together.

  Trust and commitment are the two most crucial relationship enablers. Finding a successful relationship without trust and commitment is rare. Moreover, trust and commitment seem to be strongly associated with satisfaction with how complaints are handled. That is, successful customer complaint resolution leads to greater trust and commitment in marketing relationships.[19] The authors conducted research with three global high-technology firms, obtaining rankings of these relationship enablers from key marketing informants, and found that earlier thinking on the relative importance of these relationship factors was in fact supported. That is, trust and commitment were consistently ranked higher when marketing personnel from these hi-tech companies were asked to consider the factors most important in maintaining strong business relationships. Rankings for all five relationship enablers are shown in Table 11.2.[20]

- *Cooperation*, another relationship enabler, involves coordinated activities between buyer and seller aimed at producing desirable results for both firms. The gains experienced by cooperating can more than offset the loss of autonomy in a relationship. Furthermore, cooperation frequently involves a willingness to develop joint goals and even

Table 11.2   Rankings of Relationship Enablers among Global Hi-Tech Firms

Relationship Enabler	Ranking
Trust	1
Commitment	2
Dependence	3
Information exchange	4
Cooperation	5

share resources. Consider Procter & Gamble for instance. P & G actually manages Wal-Mart's inventory, and it is that company's responsibility to decide when Wal-Mart needs shipments. To do this, P & G has complete access to Wal-Mart's inventory. It manages everything and makes decisions on its own shipments. This arrangement is beneficial for both parties: Wal-Mart can charge less because it does not have the cost of tracking or storing inventory, while P & G has a much bigger share of business and does not need to compete with other suppliers.

Even competitors can benefit from cooperation. For example, a recent alliance was formed among Delta, Northwest, and Continental to connect their frequent flier programs and to sell seats on each other's domestic and international flights. This practice, known as code sharing, would allow members of each airlines' respective frequent-flier programs to earn miles on domestic and international flights operated by any of the three carriers as well as offer reciprocal access to the airport lounges worldwide.

- *Dependence* — willingness to invest time and dedicate resources for the purpose of establishing and strengthening a business relationship — serves as another relationship enabler. In business-to-business marketing, resource-specific investments increase the dependence of retailers and vendors on each other.[21] Gillette's relationship with ADC, a promotional materials supplier, serves as a good example. ADC's partner relationship with Gillette initially started when ADC was chosen to help develop a display program for Gillette's new men's toiletry line, the Gillette Series, consisting of shaving preparation products, deodorants, antiperspirants, and after-shave products. ADC's involvement began with the initial display concept, followed by prototyping, engineering, and assembling prepacked displays that were shipped to Gillette's major distribution centers. ADC acted as an extension of Gillette's manufacturing and marketing by providing coordinated logistics; display development; pack-out; and distribution. ADC committed 54,000 square feet of manufacturing space and over 100 employees to this product launch.
- *Information exchange* is the lubricant that keeps the other relationship enablers from corroding. If price attracts a relationship, information sustains it. In fact, as Figure 11.3 shows, when buyers offer more information, sellers in turn are willing to provide more services, creating a win–win situation. McKesson Corporation, a major drug wholesaler representing thousands of independent pharmacies, helps them set up accounting and inventory systems, as well as computer ordering systems (i.e., electronic data interchange or EDI). The

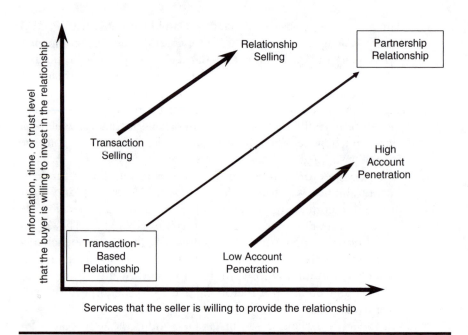

Figure 11.3   Information Sustains a Relationship

retailers gain value from improved stock planning, resulting in fewer stock-outs and more satisfied customers. McKesson benefits by creating "captive" retail accounts that grant McKesson unprecedented access to their sales and financial data.

Active information exchange between buyers and sellers can also result in product and process innovation. Von Hippel found that in some industries more than two thirds of the innovations he studied could be traced back to a customer's initial suggestions.[22] In the fragrance industry, suppliers are much more involved in new product planning than in the past. One case is Vanilla Fields, the blockbuster mass-market scent from Coty. Coty presented Fragrance Resources, one of its suppliers, with a challenge to find "the musk of the nineties." Fragrance Resources came up with vanilla, but also gave Coty a lot of other marketing information, such as ways to position a vanilla fragrance.

In many cases knowledge exchange between buyers and sellers develops informally over time through interfirm interactions. The key is to use the information obtained to create value for the exchange partners. For example, Fuji and Xerox have attempted to codify this knowledge by creating a communications matrix, which identifies a set of relevant issues (e.g., products, technologies, markets, etc.) and then identifies the individuals (by function) within Fuji–Xerox, Fuji, and Xerox who have relevant expertise on that particular issue. This matrix provides valuable information regarding where relevant expertise resides within the partnering firms.

In summary, each of the relationship enablers will be evident to some degree in most successful buyer–seller relationships. Clearly, some of these factors will become more important over the life of the business relationship. Trust and cooperation, for example, are critical during the initial stages of relationship building; commitment, dependence, and information exchange become more important later in the relationship. Using customer value checklist 11.1, evaluate your customer relationships based on the preceding relationship enablers and determine how closely your relationships lead to long-term business goals. The discussion of relationship marketing up to this point has been limited to buyer–seller relationships. Just as the opportunity to work with customers in creating new value is important, so is working with supply chain partners to accomplish the same purpose. Creating new value through improved supply chain relationships is discussed next.

▼▲▼

CUSTOMER VALUE CHECKLIST 11.1: DIAGNOSING THE HEALTH OF BUYER–SELLER RELATIONSHIPS

Using the relationship enablers in Figure 11.2, choose a key customer (or supplier) and rank the relative importance of each relationship enabler in building the business relationship. Provide a rationale for your rankings.

Using the same customer or supplier from the previous example, rate how it performs on each relationship enabler on a scale of:

	Excellent	Good	Needs Improvement	Unacceptable
	4	3	2	1
Trust				
Commitment				
Dependence				
Cooperation				
Info Exchange				

The goal of relationship marketing is to achieve some long-term business goal leading to a sustainable competitive advantage. Using the same customer or supplier as before, what is the likelihood that improvements in the business relationship will produce positive business outcomes, i.e., a sustainable competitive advantage? Using a 7-point scale, where 1 indicates "no chance" and 7 indicates "complete certainty," assess the likelihood of improvements in your relationship with your buyer(supplier) leading to positive business outcomes.

	Probability						
	No Chance					*Complete Certainty*	
	1	2	3	4	5	6	7
What is the probability that improvements in this relationship will substantially reduce costs or lead to better asset utilization?	1	2	3	4	5	6	7
What is the probability that improvements in this relationship will improve customer service as indicated by the customer?	1	2	3	4	5	6	7
What is the probability that improvements in this relationship will result in higher profitability for both partners?	1	2	3	4	5	6	7

───────────────────────▲▼▲───────────────────────

IMPROVING SUPPLY CHAIN RELATIONSHIPS

So far discussion has been focused mainly on promoting and improving relationships between firms and their customers. Firms increasingly recognize that the value added through the supply chain contributes to overall end-customer value. For example, downstream intermediaries (distributors, wholesalers, retailers) add value to the offering that the producer cannot easily or economically do. Furthermore, an intermediary can be an enduring source for creating new value with end customers by maximizing speed and minimizing costs and investment.

In the early days, supply chain management centered on the management of supply within a single company; however, today the focus is on cross-company planning and implementation, or *integrated supply chain management* (ISCM). An integrated supply chain is a connected set of interorganizational resources and activities involved in the creation and delivery of value. The goals of an integrated supply chain strategy are to speed up product development (including time to market); minimize finished goods inventory; minimize investment in resources (e.g., use "cross-docking"); improve quality; and reduce response/cycle times.

As such, true integration is emerging in industries such as automotive; telecommunication equipment; retailing; and computers in the form of information sharing; product planning; joint problem-solving/strategic planning; and shared benefits. The effective use of innovative, value-creating distribution options such as Amazon.com's virtual bookstore;

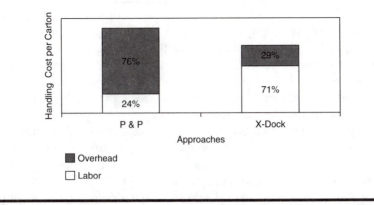

Figure 11.4 Cross-Docking vs. Pick 'n' Pack (From Kurnia, S. and Johnston, R. [2001], *Supply Chain Manage.*, 5(5), 235. With permission.)

Dell's build-to-order direct strategy; the airlines' SkyMall program; and grocery industry use of cross-docking (see Figure 11.4) are examples of ISCM practices that can provide a strong competitive edge to firms. According to consulting firm Accenture, successful supply chain integration can deliver powerful results. Companies often reduce inventories by more than 40% and lower logistics costs by as much as 20%. In addition to Dell and Amazon, leaders in ISCM include Ford Motor Company; Hallmark; Intel; Pharmacia; Raytheon; Cisco; and Whirlpool.[23]

Supply chain management revamps channel strategy from a relatively neglected area to an actively managed marketing/logistics function. According to a recent study, about 50% of companies worldwide and 42% in North America have maintained key supplier relationships for 6 or more years. Yet, less than 25% of global organizations and only 20% of North American companies involve their suppliers in key business processes.[24] A central tenet of the ISCM philosophy is to encourage greater supplier–customer integration, although progress in this area has been slow. A rationale for investing in ISCM projects is that companies want to see improved supply chain performance.[25] Management consulting firm Booz Allen Hamilton surveyed over 200 global companies and found that despite sizable IT investments ($19 billion) made annually by these companies to improve supply chain performance, nearly half were disappointed with the results.[26] Thus, a major opportunity exists to leverage ongoing supply chain relationships further.

In the new economy, competition is shifting to networks of companies cooperating across boundaries in order to achieve market goals. Firms are increasingly competing as a constellation of collaborating partners, each contributing value in the network. A key factor in making the networked business model work is investing in and coordinating cross-company processes. To succeed in the future, corporations will need to weave their key business processes into inimitable strategic capabilities that distinguish them from their competitors in the eyes of customers. Further, the competitive landscape is shifting from competition among companies themselves to competition among trading partner networks.

Competitors can match individual processes or activities but cannot match the integration or "fit" of these processes between network partners.[27] Supply chain management means that collaboration rather than competition becomes the modus operandi as disparate organizations now jointly focus on satisfying customers by aligning and integrating business processes. All participants in the extended supply chain network work in harmony to find new ways to add value at varying points in the distribution cycle. Furthermore, costs may be cut; product/service quality enhanced; delivery time reduced; and overall business performance improved through an effective ISCM system.

Suppliers play a key role in the relationship between seller and buyer. Twelve criteria (in six areas) contribute to being perceived as a world-class supplier[28]:

- Product — features and quality
- Service — features and quality
- Overall cost — level and stability
- Responsiveness — lead time and due date performance
- Organizational capability — resources and stability
- Corporate responsibilities — social and environmental

Each customer will value a different set of criteria; thus, each will have its own view of whether it is working with a world-class vendor.

Li & Fung is Hong Kong's largest export trading company and a leader in SCM practices. On behalf of American and European customers, Li & Fung adds value through design, engineering, and production planning in raw material and component sourcing (front-end activities) and via quality control, testing, and logistics in managing production (back-end activities).[29]

According to Mary Lou Fox, senior vice president of Manugistics (Rockville, Maryland), a supply chain management software and services firm, SCM has five evolutionary stages[30]:

- Emphasis on quality and cost control
- Customer service
- Coordinating supply chain processes across the enterprise
- Looking for ways to provide profitable customized products via the extended supply chain
- Forming tightly knit supply chain communities

As companies move toward level-five integration, many are seeking to implement customer relationship management (CRM). A discussion of the promises and shortcomings of CRM follows.

CUSTOMER RELATIONSHIP MANAGEMENT

What is customer relationship management (CRM)? CRM is a business strategy that involves selecting and managing customer relationships in order to optimize the long-term value of a company. The goal of CRM, according to CRM guru and founder of CRMGuru.com Bob Thompson, is to acquire, grow, and retain the right customer relationships — those with the best long-term profit potential.[31] When stated in these terms, CRM is not new; rather, it is about collaboration with customers and partners in such a way that they receive superior *value*.

Interactions with customers, regardless of the sales channel (i.e., direct sales, call centers, Web site) should be constantly managed to optimize the value of those relationships. Effective CRM systems provide a 360° view of the customer, including frequency; response (i.e., to promotions); and quality (i.e., customer satisfaction) of interactions with the customer. A good CRM system is capable of describing customer relationships in sufficient detail so that management, salespeople, customer service, and even suppliers have direct and real-time access to customer information. The information gathered should help match customer needs with product/service offerings; remind customers of service requirements; predict future purchases; and alert the company when a customer's purchase behavior has changed.

The model proposed in Figure 11.5 should help firms in implementing a customer relationship management program. First, notice the important role that marketing knowledge plays in developing the customer strategy. Recall that a key feature of CRM is sharing the customer experience across the organization and supply chain (360° view). Companies should continuously gather critical customer data known as BADI:

- *Behaviors* (how often and where customers visit)
- *Attitudes* (customer satisfaction, service quality assessments)
- *Demographics*
- *Insights* (share of market, share of wallet)

Proper positioning of the company's offer (and value proposition) necessarily involves an understanding of the competitor's value proposition. Marketing knowledge should also involve evaluating the customer database by performing an RFM analysis (see Chapter 10); determining customer lifetime value (factoring in customer acquisition costs as well as

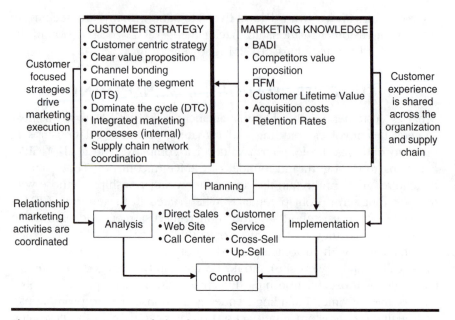

Figure 11.5 Customer Relationship Model (Adapted from Levine, S. [1999], *Am. Network*, Sept. 1, 3.)

costs to serve the existing customer base); and tracking customer retention rates. Marketing knowledge forms the basis of a customer strategy driven by a customer-centric orientation (see Chapter 2); a clearly defined value proposition (see Chapter 7); an aligning with key channel partners; dominating the segment (focused on a particular market segment) or cycle (dominate the evolving value proposition aimed a group of customers); and internal and supply chain process integration. Finally, marketing knowledge and a sound customer strategy guide the coordination and practice of the relationship marketing activities of analysis, planning, implementation, and control.

How successful have CRM initiatives been so far? Thompson estimates that 70% of all CRM initiatives fail? Why? A report by Bain & Company, a leading management consulting firm, contends that CRM efforts do not fail because the technology is flawed, but because it is implemented without a comprehensive strategy. The report advocated that the first step in building a successful CRM program is to develop a robust customer strategy based on sound market segmentation.[32] Similarly, too many CRM projects are purely technology focused instead of customer focused, with little foresight given to how customers, employees and suppliers will be affected. Below is a list of some common reasons why companies' CRM efforts fail:[33]

- *No focus* — companies are not sure what they want from their CRM program.
- *No change management policy* — CRM ultimately involves change: improving the relationship with the customer; altering the way the firm does business; and changing employee behaviors in the process.
- *No buy-in* — a huge barrier to CRM implementation is "cultural" in nature (see Case 8). Without involving and educating employees and supply chain partners, CRM is doomed to fail.
- *Business unit silos* — a lack of cross-functional planning between departments leads to difficulty in setting up CRM projects; cross-discipline teams need to be established that require the functions, particularly IT and sales, to work together.
- *Complicated procedures* — CRM software will not magically automate already inefficient processes; companies should eliminate inefficient business processes before considering any new software solution. Poor training — technology often far outweighs the capabilities of the people using it.

Many of the problems associated with poor CRM implementation can be avoided by careful planning; appropriate involvement of people in the organization and among supply chain members; customer-driven processes; and a sound platform for introducing CRM. Richard Gerson has described these as the four Ps of CRM success (see customer value insight 11.1).

CUSTOMER VALUE INSIGHT 11.1 — FOUR PS OF CRM SUCCESS[34]

Planning — it is important for companies to know exactly what they want to achieve with CRM and how they want to capture and use the data.

People — employees and partners need to be involved and to get on board with the CRM effort. Lack of coordination within the supply chain network can severely hinder CRM implementation (see Case 8). Implementing CRM across the supply chain requires multiple individuals across different organizations to work in unison to support a customer with whom they do not directly interact.

Process — if people and perceptions are effectively managed during process realignment, the process and technology components will be relatively easy to implement. In this phase, service flow diagrams are useful (see Chapter 3) for describing how a customer contacts the company; how to capture and process customer information; and how to consolidate information from all customer touch points. It is important that everyone in the organization and supply chain understands the process from the customer's point of view.

Platform — finally, after clearly defining the CRM program goals; artic-ulating and coordinating these goals with key personnel in the company and across the supply chain; and mapping the processes, a software solution should be selected that optimally answers the company's CRM needs.

▲▼▲

KEYS TO PRACTICING RELATIONSHIP MARKETING IN THE NEW ECONOMY

Relationship marketing represents a shift in thinking about how companies do business. Because relationships are fragile, the attributes of trust, commitment, dependence, cooperation, and information exchange are crucial for enabling and maintaining strong relationships. This section will review the major factors that contribute to success in practicing relationship marketing in the new economy.

First, and most importantly, relationships are strengthened when sellers *create more value* for their customers. Customers are likely to offer their patronage to sellers who supply greater benefits, lower costs, or both. Companies should look for opportunities to offer new features and ser-vices; customize their offering; unbundle or bundle services; enhance product or service quality; and offer guarantees. Zane Cycles, an inde-pendent bicycle retailer in Branford, Connecticut, understands this prin-ciple well. For example, owner Chris Zane offers free lifetime service for each bike purchased at his store. Zane also offers its customers toll-free numbers — voice and fax — as a way of adding value to the customer relationship. Furthermore, if a Zane customer buys something that costs less than a dollar, Zane gives him the item at no charge and thanks him for his business. Adding value does not always require doing something for the customer in a "big" way; sometimes it is the "tiny little touches" that delight customers and intensify their loyalty (see Chapter 9 for more examples of value-added strategies).

Customer relationships are also improved by *responding to customer needs*. Recall that when Chapter 5 discussed the major determinants of service quality, responsiveness was one of the key predictors of service quality perceptions. Consider the case of Hartness International, a pro-ducer of high-speed, case-packing machines that load bottles of soda, syrup, or ketchup into cartons before they get shipped. For Hartness' customers, time is money; a shutdown bottling line can cost the customer as much as $150 per minute. Hartness recognizes the importance of this potential problem and hires only service technicians who are licensed pilots. That way, whenever Hartness needs to fix a machine, technicians are not held hostage to airline schedules because they can fly one of the company's four planes. Hartness has over 7000 customers in more than 100 countries.

Companies that successfully practice relationship marketing have mastered *mass customization*. In many markets it is not only possible, but also imperative, to mass customize for customers. Buyers often have individual problems that require unique solutions. Giving customers what they want how they want it will grow their loyalties. Dell Computers has known this since Michael Dell began custom building PCs in the mid-1980s. Dell is now planning to introduce a new customer service plan that uses the Internet to automate and customize service much the same way in which it has streamlined and customized PC production. By using communications over high-speed private networks and the Internet, Dell plans to provide personalized Web pages to noncorporate customers as well as to answer customers' technical questions with lightning speed. In fact, Dell's message to its employees is: "Dell wants YOU to OWN your relationship with the customer."

New technology enables efficient customization of products and services, even when the customer base is quite large. Technology can also assist companies in differentiating customers as most valuable; maximum growth potential; and not valuable. Several times a year, QUEST sifts through its customer list looking for money losers who have the potential to be more profitable in the future. By looking at demographic profiles, plus the mix of local vs. long-distance calls, or whether a customer has voice mail, the company can estimate a customer's potential telecom spending. Next, QUEST can determine how much of the customer's likely telecom budget is already coming its way, thus learning where to set the cutoff point for how much to invest in marketing to this customer before profitability suffers.

Effective utilization of *customer information* is another major factor in building stronger customer relationships. As discussed earlier, CRM is an invaluable tool for collecting and managing customer information. CRM enables firms to offer better services and enhance sales and marketing efficiency by leveraging customer information. According to Rasika Versleijen-Pradhan, senior analyst for IDC, a leading IT media, research, and exposition company, "A growing proportion of well-known organizations now perceive the intelligent use of customer information and brand to be core."[35] For example, AT&T offers different levels of customer service depending upon a customer's profitability in its long-distance telephone business. Highly profitable customers are offered a high level of personalized service; less profitable customers get automated, menu-driven service. Similarly, golf equipment manufacturer Taylor Made has a database of over 1.5 million golfers containing their names; addresses; e-mail addresses; birthdays; types of courses played; and vacations taken. Taylor

Made sends biweekly e-mails to stay in contact with its customers and to lead them to its Web site, where new products are announced and special offers are made available.

More and more companies are utilizing Web alliances in order to create superior customer value. These *value Webs* now represent the new economy supply chains. The key to creating superior value in the new economy resides in understanding and leveraging the power of supply chain network relationships. Pioneered by McKinsey, traditional value system (also known as supply chain) analysis assumed linear flow of supply chain activity. Every product or service produced represents a chain of value-added activities. Value is created (or captured) by a company moving upstream or downstream in the supply chain. For example, large food retailers such as Publix and Kroger have moved downstream by introducing more private-label products, essentially becoming food marketers.

Value Webs reflect how many of the new economy firms are organized today. A value Web can be described as an inchoate network of customers; suppliers; complementors; allies; and competitors whose services enhance or drain a firm's value. These relationships can be vertical or horizontal (or both) and are less enduring than in traditional supply chains. Unlike conventional supply chains, adding more users to a value Web actually creates more, not less, value. Robert Metcalfe, who founded 3Com Corporation and designed the Ethernet protocol for computer networks, stated that "the usefulness, or utility, of a network equals the square of the number of users" (which has become known as "Metcalfe's law").

Value Webs are optimized to the extent that a firm understands its relationship with other actors in the Web; how its activities will affect the network; and how the other actors will respond. True value creation takes place when several organizations in the value Web share common technologies and/or intellectual capital. A case in point: Cisco has efficiently outsourced much of its manufacturing to suppliers in its network. Cisco's demand forecasts are visible to everyone in the supply network, allowing suppliers and manufacturers to anticipate orders better. Even though Cisco acts as the orchestrator of this value Web, common goals and benefits are shared with members, not just Cisco. Cartwright and Oliver suggest a four-step approach to conducting a value Web analysis, a useful tool for identifying value Web actors and the major value-adding processes (see question 8 at the end of this chapter).[36]

A final key to practicing relationship marketing is to *track each relationship*. The concept of LTV, or lifetime value, of a customer was discussed earlier. LTV is simply a projection of what customers are worth over a lifetime of doing business with them. Calculating LTV is important because of the impact of retention levels on profitability. A hypothetical automobile example helps illustrate this concept.

Table 11.3 What Is a Customer Worth?

Company	Lifetime Value
GM Cadillac	$426,000
Gateway Computers	$ 25,000
Pizza Hut	$ 12,400
Procter & Gamble	$ 10,000
Safeway Supermarkets	$ 4,800

Source: Adapted from Watt Solutions, Inc.
(2002) http://wattsolution.com/content/cr.htm.

Suppose that, over a 50-year purchasing lifetime, a typical customer buys a new car every 4 years, at a purchase price of $25,000 (in constant dollars). Based on this scenario, the lifetime value of this customer exceeds $300,000. Most customer service experts say that, on average, a satisfied customer will tell at least one other person about his experience. Thus, as a result of positive word of mouth, a second loyal customer is created who repeats the cycle; now the customer is worth over $600,000! Of course, it is necessary to factor in the cost of acquiring and servicing this customer when performing this calculation. Nevertheless, calculating these kinds of numbers can be sobering, especially for companies experiencing high customer attrition. Executives at Taco Bell have estimated that a repeat customer is worth as much as $11,000. (For additional examples of selected companies' customer lifetime values, see Table 11.3.) Data such as these need to be shared with employees in order to see the true cost of losing a customer.[37]

However, it would be naïve to assume that all customers are equally valuable. In fact, many companies today selectively weed out their least profitable customers. Although some customers are less attractive from a profitability standpoint, care should be taken when assessing which customers to "fire" (see customer value insight 11.2).

────────── ▼▲▼ ──────────

CUSTOMER VALUE INSIGHT 11.2: FIRE CUSTOMERS?

Is one of marketing's classic mantras for years —"a customer worth acquiring is a customer worth keeping" — still followed today? Consider the following hypothetical example. A customer of a small computer valued-added reseller is habitually late in paying its bills and demands an inordinate amount of computer and software help. Should this customer be fired? Also, what factors should be used to determine whether to keep or fire such a customer?

Many companies today are analyzing their customer base to determine whether the costs (monetary and nonmonetary) to serve a customer justify the current or even future revenue stream. Several factors could be considered when deciding whether to keep or fire customers. Consider some of the following criteria that progressive companies today are using to "strain" their customers:

Deciding on the type of customer you want to attract — set criteria for what determines a good fit. Some of these criteria might be customer size, willingness to coordinate operations, and cultural and strategic congruency. Ask yourself what has made a "good" customer in the past and seek similar types of accounts.

Sort customers according to their value over time — know what it costs to acquire and service a customer relative to the profits it generates over a defined period of time. It helps to be frank with current customers by showing them the areas responsible for "value leakage" and then letting them decide if they want to continue the business relationship. Sometimes a scorecard (usually based on profitability or growth potential) helps in winnowing out "must have" from "must go." Also, using customer lifetime value (CLV) as a tool for sorting customers by value is a good tactic.

Estimate customers' worth — realize that some customers are valuable to the extent that the cost to service them does not increase. Other customers are more valuable based on their willingness to give selected vendors more of their business. The grid in Figure 11.6 helps in evaluating the worth of a customer. RBC Centura, a medium-size bank in the Mid-Atlantic states, takes a slightly different approach. RBC has created three classes of customers: A, B, and C: "A" customers are highly profitable; "B" customers are somewhat profitable; "C" customers are barely profitable or cost the bank money. Benefits extended by RBC (i.e., lower rates on loans, waived fees, etc.) are based on the customer's rating.

Applying the preceding analyses can be quite revealing. For example, Wells Fargo & Co. of San Francisco discovered that it was losing a lot of money on older customers who were on Social Security. To recoup some of it, the bank raised checking and overdraft fees for Social Security recipients.

It would certainly be naïve to suggest that companies simply "dump" their worst customers. A more creative approach may be to reprice or reconfigure transactions with these customers; consider the approach taken by Webster Bank, based in Waterbury, Connecticut. Webster Bank attempts to understand what is driving unprofitable customers and then develops specific strategies to help bring them into profitability. Webster examined its entire customer base to determine whether customers were in the right account to optimize their relationships with the bank. Customers who were not optimizing their relationship with the bank received a repricing notice in the mail with a recommendation that they consider a different account that better fit their needs. Those who had the potential for greater profitability were contacted personally to make sure they understood what the repricing was; how it affected them, and how to get the most out of their relationship with the bank.

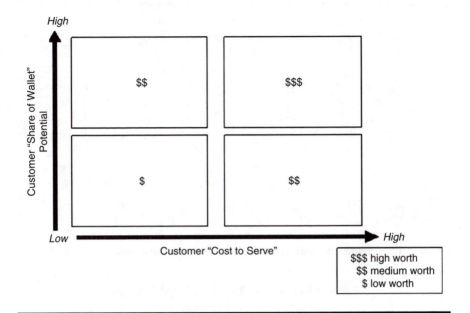

Figure 11.6 Evaluating Customer Worth

Another option to lower costs when serving unprofitable customers is to use technology. For example, staying with the bank example, many banks require their less-profitable customers to bank online or to use their ATMs for many of their transactions. In other circumstances, banks often send unprofitable clients to their competitors; such is the case with mortgage financing.

──────────────── ▲▼▲ ────────────────

SUMMARY

A massive shift has taken place from marketing to an anonymous sea of customers to developing, nurturing, and managing business relationships with individual customers. Just as the marketing concept focused businesses on seeing customers as the center of the universe, relationship marketing takes a quantum leap forward by concentrating on satisfying and keeping each customer over time.

This raises an important question. Based on what has already been learned, how will leading edge service companies successfully compete in the future? Recall that value now represents the key strategic driver, regardless of the scope in which the firm competes. Superior value is most likely to occur in firms that practice a customer orientation. Because customer-oriented firms are more proactive in anticipating their customers' wants, they are better positioned to discover the emerging value drivers.

Process improvement is also crucial to creating superior value. Processes add value when they allow customers control over how and when they buy, while eliminating errors and inconvenience.

Moreover, competing on value requires effectively managing and communicating the value proposition. The value proposition involves the proper blending of price, product, service, innovation and image as a means for establishing a unique position in the market. Finally, strong relationships with end customer and supply chain are necessary for creating and sustaining value. Business relationships are a fundamental asset requiring ongoing investments of time, trust, and commitment. Savvy companies understand that value is created in the relationship they have with their customers — how they connect with them personally and systematically. Companies successful at practicing relationship marketing look for opportunities to add value through their business relationships, offering new features, services, or customized offerings.

CUSTOMER VALUE ACTION ITEMS

1. Compare and contrast traditional and relationship marketing.
2. Why has interest in relationship marketing grown over the past decade?
3. Discuss how to create "win–win" relationships with customers.
4. Are there situations in which relationship marketing is not advisable? If so, why not?
5. Using the following companies, provide examples of how practicing supply chain management would create more value for their end-user customers: (a) Sears; (b) GM; (c) Motorola; and (d) Disney.
6. Discuss how supply chain management enhances each of the following value elements: (a) price; (b) service; (c) quality; and (d) time.
7. A bank customer is angry because of a late fee on his car payment and wants it waived. The customer has an auto loan ($25,000); a checking account balance ($15,000); and mortgage ($75,000); his son has two savings accounts for a total of $100,000 and his wife's business does payroll with the bank. How would the bank benefit from a CRM system? How should the branch manager respond in this situation?
8. Analyze eBay's value Web by going through each of the following steps: (a) collect information on eBay's business model: how and where eBay engages in business; who its customers and competitors are; and the major activities eBay performs in the course of its business (Note: this type of information can be found using such sources as SEC filings and commercial databases such as ABI

Inform.); (b) determine which activities are internal and external to eBay (Note: these are the activities — processes — that are the basis of eBay's business model and contribute to the value that it adds to its customers.); (c) identify eBay's customers, suppliers, competitors, and complementors — these are the key actors that can help create value or, in the case of its competitors, drain value (Note: complementors are firms that supply ancillary services that make the core service more valuable such as Wi-Fi [802.11b] wireless broadband Internet access offered at 2000 Starbuck's locations by the end of 2003.); and (d) diagram a value Web showing the *linkages* between each actor in the Web. (Note: use arrows to show the directions of the resource flows.)

REFERENCES

1. Levitt, T. (1981) The purpose of an enterprise, Harvard Business School Case No. 9-481-146, Boston, MA: HBS Case Service.
2. Drucker, P. (1973) *Management, Tasks, Responsibilities, Practices*, New York: Harper & Row, 64–65.
3. Berkowitz, D. (2003) It's the technology, stupid, *eMarketer*, May 9.
4. Kotler, P. (1991) Phil Kotler explores the new marketing paradigm, *Mark. Sci. Instit. Rev.*, Spring, 4–5.
5. Martin, C. (2001) Relationship revolution, *Advertising Age,* March 5, 22.
6. Webster, F. (1992) The changing role of marketing in the corporation, *J. Mark.*, 56, October, 14.
7. Berry, L. (1983) Relationship marketing, in *Emerging Perspectives on Service Marketing*, Berry, L., Shostack, G.L., and Upah, G., Eds., Chicago, IL: American Marketing Association, 25–28.
8. Parvatiyar, A. and Sheth, J. (1994) Paradigm shift in marketing theory and approach: the emergence of relationship marketing, in *Relationship Marketing: Theory, Methods and Applications*, Sheth, J. and Parvatiyar, A. Eds., Atlanta: Center for Relationship Marketing, Emory University, (1998).
9. Gordon, I. *Relationship Marketing*, Toronto: John Wiley & Sons Canada Ltd, 9.
10. Cane, A. (1997) Churn blightens the development of the telecommunications business, *Financial Times*, November 11, 2.
11. Anon. (2001) Shop.org/BCG Research: retailers competing online this holiday season are scarred but smarter, *PR Newswire*, December 11, 1.
12. Gummesson, E. (1990) *The Part-time Marketer*, Karstad, Sweden: Center for Service Research.
13. Vavra, T. (1992) *Aftermarketing*, Burr Ridge, IL: Business One Irwin, 15.
14. Berry, D. (1990) Marketing mix for the 90s adds an S and 2 Cs to the 4 Ps, *Mark. News*, Dec. 24, 10.
15. Levitt, T. (1983) After the sale is over, *Harvard Bus. Rev.*, Sept–Oct., 90.
16. Ba, S. and Pavlou, P (2002) Evidence of the effect of trust building technology in electronic markets: price premiums and buyer behavior, *MIS Q.*, 26(2), 265.
17. Reichheld, F., Markey, R., and Hopton, C. (2000) e-customer loyalty—applying the traditional rules of business for online success, *Eur. Bus. J.*, 174.

18. Feldman, L., Johnson, W.C., and Weinstein, A. (1998) Trust, commitment, and long-term manufacturer–supplier relationships, 1998 Research Conference on Relationship Marketing, Atlanta, June.

19. DuPont, R. (1998) Relationship marketing: A strategy for consumer-owned utilities in a restructured industry, *Manage. Q.*, Winter 38(4), 11.

20. Johnson, W. and Weinstein, A. (1999) Creating value through customer and supplier relationships, interactions, relationships, and networks: Towards the new millennium (Dublin, Ireland: paper presented at the 15th Annual IMP Conference), September 4.

21. Ganesan, S. (1994) Determinants of long-term orientation in buyer–seller relationships, *J. Mark.*, 58, April, 14.

22. Von Hippel, E. (1988) *The Sources of Innovation*, New York: Oxford University Press, 89.

23. Greengard, S. (2001) The new supply chain, *iQ Mag.*, July/August.

24. Tait, D. (1998) Make strong supplier relationships A PRIORITY, *Can. Manager*, Spring, 21, 28.

25. McCormack, K. and Johnson, W. (2003) *Supply Chain Networks and Business Process Orientation: Advanced Strategies and Best Practices*: Boca Raton, FL: St. Lucie Press, 82.

26. Anon. (2003) Companies often disappointed with supply chain investments, survey finds, Electron. *Commerce News*, May 26, 1, 7.

27. Op. cit., McCormack and Johnson, p. 7.

28. Stevens, K. (1997) World class perceptions, *Supply Manage.*, January 30, 38–39.

29. Magretta, J. (1998) Fast, global, and entrepreneurial: supply chain management, Hong Kong style, *Harvard Bus. Rev.*, September–October, 103–114.

30. Anon. (1998) What customers value most, *Chief Executive*, 8–16.

31. Thompson, B. (2002) Collaboration: the cure for what ails CRM, http://www.crmguru.com/features/2002b/0606bt.html, June 6.

32. Rigby, D., Reichheld, F., and Schefter, P. (2002) Avoid the four perils of CRM, *Harvard Bus. Rev.*, February, 102.

33. Cholewka, K. (2002) CRM: the failures are your fault, *Sales Mark. Manage.*, 154(1), January, 23.

34. Gerson, R. (2001) Secrets of CRM success, http://www.crmguru.com/content/features/gerson/2001_02_08.html, February 8.

35. Anon. (2001) IDC: CRM services continue to experience robust growth, according to IDC; new report looks at whether customer intimacy can drive CRM, *M2 Presswire*, May 29, 1.

36. Cartwright, S. and Oliver, R. (2000) Untangling the value Web, *J. Bus. Strategy*, 21(1), January/February, 25.

37. Kotler, P. (1997) *Marketing Management*, 9th ed., Upper Saddle River, NJ: Prentice Hall.

V

CUSTOMER VALUE CASES: A PRIMER AND QUESTIONS FOR ANALYSIS

The case studies in this section provide in-depth examples of customer value concepts and applications in diverse service-related industries. By reviewing these cases, you can learn more about the types of planning and research that go into customer value thinking; the market factors with which these organizations must contend; marketing and management decisions and strategies; and how market performance may be enhanced through sound business practices.

Think about how the focal organization uses competitive differentiation to take maximum advantage of market opportunities. As a framework for analysis, guiding questions associated with levels of the customer value funnel (review the appendix in Chapter 1 and Exhibit I.1 at the end of this introduction) are listed here to help you assess the relevant customer value issues in each case study. To gain further insight into the business situation, you are also encouraged to review the questions at the end of each customer value case.

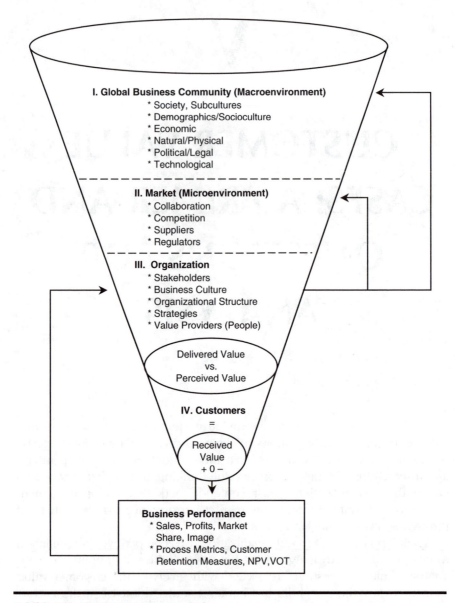

Exhibit I.1   Customer Value Funnel

QUESTIONS

1. Identify the relevant macroenvironmental factors (level 1) in the case study. What impact do these issues have on the focal organization?

2. Discuss the market factors (level 2) in the case study. How do collaboration, competition, supplier, and regulators affect the performance of the focal organization?

3. Explain how the focal organization (level 3) creates value for its customers. What strategic changes are required to deliver outstanding value to its customers?

4. Do customers (level 4) perceive value as unsatisfactory, satisfactory, or superior? Why? Which attributes that customers value are not receiving adequate attention by the organization?

5. Critique the organization's business performance based on traditional (e.g., sales, profits, market share, and image) and value-based (e.g., process metrics, customer retention measures, net present value, value over time) performance criteria. What can the organization do to improve its performance?

CASE 1: BOSTON MARKET — PROCESS FLOW OUTCOMES*

When the clock struck 12 noon, the employees in the JW office building let out a yell. "Lunchtime!" they shouted, "the highlight of the workday." With only half an hour for lunch, their dining choices were limited. Many employees "brown bagged" it; however, just as many wanted to go out for lunch. Fortunately for the workers of the JW office building, a string of fast-food restaurants was across the street.

One of the restaurants was Boston Market. A group of office workers decided to try out the place. They offered to bring back lunch to several of their colleagues. They had been to the McDonald's next door on numerous occasions and had plenty of time to eat lunch and get back to work. The same should hold true for Boston Market. After all, Boston Market considered itself to be a quick service restaurant. This process should not take long. Or should it?

At 12:05 the group arrived at Boston Market. When they got in the line, there were six people ahead of them, not uncommon for that time of the day. Almost 5 minutes elapsed before Sarah, the first member of the group, placed her order. It was now 12:10. After placing her order, Sarah shuffled her way through the L-shaped line. Because all food is made to order, it would take a few minutes to prepare her sandwich. A separate employee took her side dish order while yet another employee served as cashier. Just before she got to the cashier, still another employee grabbed Sarah's completed order from the sandwich window and placed it on her tray. Sarah noticed how all the employees working behind the line kept bumping into each other. The process seemed disjointed and the line moved very slowly.

---

* This case was prepared by Alan Seidman, associate professor of hospitality at Johnson & Wales University, North Miami, Florida.

Sarah was finally able to get to the cashier where she paid her bill and received a paper cup for her drink. She would need to fill her drink order herself. Four minutes had gone by from when she first placed her order until the time she received it. By the time she got her drink and found a table, it was 12:14. Almost half of her lunch period had expired.

One by one her colleagues worked their way through the line and sat with her. It was almost 12:20 before Kenny, the sixth member of the group sat down. This left them 5 minutes to enjoy their lunch. What good was that? Then Sarah remembered that they had neglected to order the food they had promised to bring back to their colleagues. The group turned and looked at the line. It was even longer than when they first got there. "Forget it," Kenny said, "We'll have no time to get their order and get back to work on time."

This case study examines the operational system employed by Boston Market. More specifically, it will look at the history of the company and concept, the queuing system, the production system, and an overview of where the company is today.

COMPANY HISTORY

The first Boston Chicken restaurant opened in 1985 in Newton, Massachusetts. The original concept, a fast-paced operation offering home-style foods, was pioneered by Arthur Cores and Stephen Kolow. Cores had experience working in a gourmet grocery store while Kolow's expertise lay in real estate. Their original menu contained marinated chicken, an array of vegetables and side salads, chicken soup, oatmeal cookies, and sweet corn bread. Their small restaurant was an instant success.

In 1989, George Naddaff, a local venture capitalist, met with Cores and Kolow and successfully convinced them to expand their business. By 1990, they had expanded to 13 restaurants with another 15 slated to open in 1991.

By 1991 the Boston Chicken concept caught the attention of Saad Nadhir and Scott Beck, two former executives of Blockbuster Video. A year later, they purchased a controlling interest in the company. Shortly after, the chain's headquarters was moved from Boston to Chicago (and later to Colorado), and a staff consisting primarily of former Blockbuster executives was assembled. They planned an aggressive growth strategy, changing the names of the individual stores from Boston Chicken to Boston Market, reflecting the broader range of new menu items. Corporately, however, they were still known as Boston Chicken.

In November of 1993 the company went public and made its Wall Street debut, selling for $10 a share. It closed at over $25 a share that day, raising more than $54 million. In 1996, Boston Chicken stock reached a high of over $40 a share and the company was opening the equivalent of one store every day. They finished the year with over 1100 stores, bringing in close to $1.2 billion in annual revenue.

THE QUICK-SERVICE, HOME-COOKING CONCEPT

Boston Market's concept is unique. It involves combining an atmosphere of casual dining and home cooking with the convenience of a quick-service restaurant. The restaurants offer traditional, home-style products such as chicken, turkey, ham, and meatloaf, which can be served as a sandwich or as part of a platter. They also offer a wide variety of accompanying side dishes that include corn, rice and beans, potatoes, spinach, mixed vegetables, green beans, and stuffing. In addition, the menu features chicken pot pies and chicken soup.

The company's biggest success initially was not its restaurants or personnel, but the creation of its own market segment. Almost single-handedly, Boston Market developed the market segment now known as "home meal replacement" (HMR).

HMR has evolved from the changing demographics of today's society. Women have joined men in the workforce in ever-increasing numbers. Gone are the days when the wife stayed home and prepared dinner for the family. Today's consumers do not always want to eat in restaurants nor do they want typical fast food. Neither do they necessarily prefer to cook. Increasingly, demographic studies point to consumers' desire to cocoon, or stay home. Boston Market, the leader in HMR, was clearly in a very desirable position to capitalize on this trend.

SYSTEM

Boston Market's service is built around a single channel, multiple phase queue line (see Exhibit 1.1). As pictured in this exhibit, customers enter the building and get into a line that forms along the side of the building. Once at the front, the queue takes on an "L" shape. It is along this perpendicular crossing that an available service attendant greets the customer and takes his order. This is the first substation (subsystem #1). If a sandwich is ordered, the attendant writes up a ticket and calls it back to the cook.

The second substation (subsystem #2) is where the food is prepared. If the order is a platter or a pot pie, the attendant takes a plate and begins filling it with the customer's choice of side items (about 10 to 12 different side items are available). They are not listed anywhere on the menu but are displayed in the hot food case about halfway down the service line. The chicken, meatloaf, turkey, and ham are kept sliced and under heat

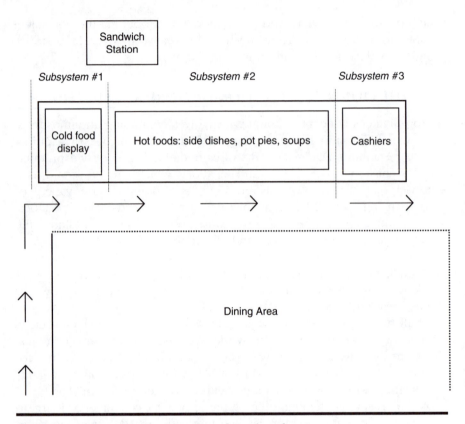

Exhibit 1.1   Boston Market Queue and Service Flow Layout

lamps behind the line next to the sandwich preparation area. To fill these items, the server turns around and places the order on each plate. If the order is not ready, the plate is left under the heat lamp until the cook completes it. A sandwich generally takes a bit more time to prepare. Once prepared, sandwiches are presented to the customer further down the service line. During this time, the tray of food always remains on the service side of the window and not in the customer's possession.

Once the plate is ready, the customer moves to the third substation (subsystem #3). This is at the end of the line where payment is made. Boston Market generally has anywhere from one to three cash registers in operation during peak revenue periods. At this time, the order is finalized. If a drink is ordered, customers are given a cup that they fill themselves at a separate beverage area. Coupons are also presented here.

During peak revenue periods, about five service people and cashiers work the front line. Usually, the cashier's position is designated and he or she remains stationary. The other service personnel tend to float around, randomly assisting customers or performing any tasks that are needed.

Each customer is approached by a different service person to begin the order. Sometimes that person sticks with the customer throughout the duration in the first substation and sometimes the customer is passed on to one or two other employees. The service flow has no continuity.

When the cook finishes preparing a sandwich, he places it on a ledge until an employee picks it up and takes it to the customer. The service time for sandwiches varies tremendously. Sometimes they are presented to the customer shortly after ordering. Other times, the customer has already paid and is waiting at the end of the counter for his sandwich.

During this process, the customer usually receives some degree of personal attention. Unlike other fast-food systems, no number is given to the customer. The service attendants match up each order with each person to the best of their ability. This is in keeping with Boston Market's approach toward maintaining a more upscale position in the quick service industry.

SYSTEM CHALLENGES

During peak revenue periods (i.e., lunchtime) customers can face long waiting times in the queue. When someone first enters the line, the waiting time for a service employee to greet him and take his order can be anywhere from 45 seconds to 1 minute per person. If a customer is the eighth person in line, he can expect a waiting time of 6 to 8 minutes before being approached for service. After he has placed his order, he must wait again until it is completed. Depending upon what he orders, the wait can be anywhere from 3 to 5 minutes (on average). This would bring a total waiting time of 9 to 13 minutes if the customer is the eighth person in the queue. If he has 30 minutes for lunch, the waiting time alone takes up a substantial portion of his time.

Bottlenecks within the queue line at the various substations present another challenge. Production bottlenecks are obstacles to increased output. They can be classified as episodic or periodic. Episodic bottlenecks would include machine breakdowns, material shortages, and/or labor shortages. Chronic bottlenecks result in problems inherent in the process. This includes insufficient capacity, quality problems, poor layout, and/or an inflexible work process. Because of the prominence of labor shortages and equipment failures facing the quick service industry, as well as failure of the system's capacity to meet demand, Boston Market faces both episodic and chronic bottlenecks.

All quick service restaurants suffer from some degree of bottlenecking due to the unpredictable nature of the demand as well as periodic labor shortages. However, Boston Market seems to suffer from a chronic bottlenecking problem. In the Boston Market system, if customers in the rear of the queue get their orders processed first, they move ahead of customers who are in front of them in the queue line. If a question or problem arises during subsystem one, the entire queue is slowed down until the situation is remedied. Likewise, if a problem or question comes up during subsystems two or three, the queue is slowed down and bottlenecking can occur.

Another problem is the lack of sequential consistency; this is not a system of first in, first out. Orders are completed based on the type of order placed, menu availability, prep schedules, etc. Because the service system is unregimented and disjointed, customers often end up "jockeying" for position among each other. This creates an aura of confusion and inequity. Although it is probably not completely avoidable, a system should be in place that would keep this to a minimum.

Lastly, during peak revenue times, a great deal of confusion can occur among the employees. Most peak time periods feature employees bumping into each other, communicating to each other unnecessarily, and mixing up orders. This is largely due to the disruptive nature of the service flow.

COUPONS' UNINTENDED CONSEQUENCES

Because Boston Market started out by concentrating on its dinner business, sandwiches were not part of the original menu. They were added in 1994 as an effort to target more lunch customers. At the same time the company began offering discounts in the form of coupons. Coupons offering discounts on lunch and dinner items began appearing regularly in local newspapers and mailers throughout the country. In 1997, the more elaborate carver sandwiches were introduced and the flow of coupons became even more aggressive.

Although the coupons were successful in increasing lunch traffic, they created other problems for the company. From a strategic point of view, they changed the position of the company from that of a more upscale fast food alternative to an operation appealing to the masses. Before the coupons, Boston Market considered supermarkets and "sit-down" restaurants to be its direct competition; now it aligned itself more closely with McDonald's, Burger King, Taco Bell, and other traditional quick service restaurants.

Another problem brought about by coupons was the logistics involved in collecting them. They were to be collected by the cashier (at the end of the queue) who would apply the discount to the order total. Customers would often forget to present the coupon to the cashier as a result of the confused nature of the queuing system. Customers would often tell the person who took their order about the coupon (who usually expressed little or no interest) and would forget to tell the cashier later on. This presented even more confusion and frustration for the company and the customer.

In an effort to deemphasize the lunch business and reemphasize the more profitable dinner trade, the company stopped issuing coupons in 1999. This strategy was short-lived, however, because coupons were once again introduced a year later.

EPILOGUE

In 1998, with its debt escalating and its profits and stock price plummeting, Boston Chicken, Inc. filed with the U.S. government for Chapter 11 bankruptcy protection. Shortly thereafter the company closed 178 stores. Boston Chicken stock, once as high as $40 a share, dropped to below $0.50 a share. The fledgling company was acquired by McDonald's Corporation for $175 million on May 26, 2000. McDonald's intends to keep the Boston Market concept alive, although it does plan on converting many of the stores to other concepts. The financial failure of the Boston Market concept had many causes. Failure to implement and execute a desirable operational system is one of them. Similar businesses should take note of this and learn from Boston Market's failures (see in-text table and Exhibit 1.2).

**Boston Chicken Inc.: Selected Financial Data
1993–1997**

Year	Net Sales ($000s)	Net Income ($000s)
1993	42,530	1,647
1994	84,519	16,173
1995	126,228	33,559
1996	199,460	66,958
1997	378,934	–223,892

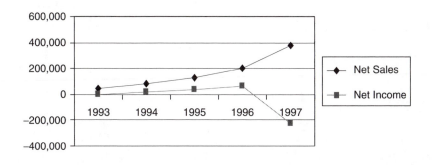

Exhibit 1.2   Net Sales and Net Income

QUESTIONS

1. Compare the queuing system at Boston Market to that of other quick service restaurants. In what ways are they different? In what ways are they similar?
2. How could Boston Market have made its queuing system more equitable and operationally efficient?
3. What were the implications of the aggressive use of coupons on Boston Market's overall strategy? Do you agree with this tactic used by Boston Market? Why or why not?
4. Comment on the importance of defining, measuring, and improving organizational work processes. Approach your response from the company's and the customer's perspective.

CASE 2: DELICATO FAMILY WINERY — BUILDING AND COMMUNICATING VALUE*

We need to change the way that we're doing business here, and this will require a mentality change.

Eric Morham, CEO, Delicato Family Vineyards

INTRODUCTION

In January, 2002, Eric Morham found himself wondering whether he should be congratulating himself on having achieved great success in the past 2 years or questioning why he had not accomplished more. During his brief tenure at Delicato Family Vineyards (DFV), he had made significant strides in increasing the domestic and international brand awareness for the vineyard, as evidenced by a series of medals awarded to Delicato at prestigious wine competitions in 2001 and early 2002. Yet he still faced dilemmas with regard to issues of primary business focus for the company

* This case study was prepared by assistant professor Sally Baack, San Francisco State University; William C. Johnson, professor of marketing, Huizenga School of Business, Nova Southeastern University; associate professor Armand Gilinsky, Jr., Sonoma State University; and Professor Murray Silverman, San Francisco State University. It was designed to be used as a basis for class discussion, not to illustrate effective or ineffective handling of an administrative situation. The authors gratefully acknowledge a business and international education (BIE) grant from the U.S. Department of Education and a matching grant from the College of Business at San Francisco State University in support of this research. Copyright 2003 by Sally Baack, William C. Johnson, Armand Gilinsky, Jr., and Murray Silverman. Dated May 29, 2003. Not for reproduction or distribution without permission of the authors.

and management of company assets and resources, as well as establishing profitability expectations. How far could he take Delicato?

Morham was brought onboard to Delicato by the Indelicato family to head up a major transformation of the company in order to increase the recognition, status, and prestige of DFV. He joined the company in March of 1999 following a 15-year tenure with Heineken N.V. of The Netherlands, where he had served as vice-president of sales and marketing, regional export director, and finally executive vice president for North America.

Morham saw great potential in Delicato. In his view, most companies built their infrastructure after they had built their brand. However, this was not the case with Delicato, which already had a huge infrastructure in place and was now starting to build its own brand name. DFV's business had traditionally focused on bulk wine production for other branded producers in the industry. It built its reputation and position in the industry based on having extensive holdings in vineyards and producing a huge volume of bulk wine for other vineyards to package and sell under their own brands and labels. Morham saw great potential to redeploy Delicato's assets and to focus on its consumer side in a very profitable way. However, redeploying Delicato's assets and shifting its emphasis within its portfolio would create some tensions between its branded B2C (business-to-consumer) and its B2B (business-to-business) business.

Six weeks after he joined the company, Morham pulled all the top management together at a meeting in April. He called it a "fast forward" meeting instead of the usual "retreat." As Morham put it, "Delicato has had too much retreat, it's time to attack." During the meeting, the group did a SWOT analysis of the company and everyone was asked to answer the question "What will Delicato's success look like 5, 7, and 10 years ahead?" This exercise allowed management to think about where the company should head; helped them get a clear picture in their minds; and prepared them to embark on a journey to get there. During the meeting, the participants came up with two broad strategic goals: (1) grow short-term profitability and (2) build long-term brand equity.

WINE INDUSTRY BACKGROUND

Wine consumption has been climbing steadily in the United States from approximately 190 million cases in 1994 to over 235 million cases last year (*Adams Wine Handbook*, 2001). Compared to per capita wine consumption worldwide, the U.S. wine market is still relatively small (see Exhibit 2.1). The market for premium wines in particular is large and growing. Favorable demographics, i.e., aging population of baby boomers; receptivity to favorable health news; and growing disposable income to spend, will power the market during the next decade. Expanded industry advertising and promotion is also attracting new wine drinkers and will

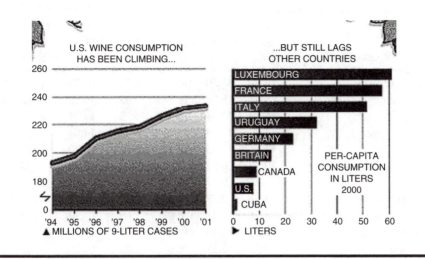

Exhibit 2.1   U.S. Wine Consumption Compared to Other Countries (From *Adams Wine Handbook* [2001], New York: Adams Business Media.)

likely increase the consumption rates of infrequent consumers. Presently, a surplus of high-quality wines from around the world exists that continues to exert downward pressure on retail prices. Typically, strong economic conditions will lift demand, especially for high-end wines.

The U.S. wine industry today is composed of approximately 1500 wineries; however, it was highly concentrated, with the top 10 wineries accounting for 70% (by volume) of U.S. production, according to the 1999 *Adams Wine Handbook*. California dominates the U.S. wine industry with over 800 wineries, accounting for more than 90% of the wine produced in and exported by the U.S. Washington, Oregon, and Idaho account for approximately 200 wineries and are presently developing an export presence and a reputation for quality wines.

Per capita wine consumption was quite low during the late 1950s and early 1960s because wine drinking was perceived as the domain of the wealthy or the poor. Back then, industry structure severely limited wine industry growth. Today, however, the U.S. wine industry continues to evolve from a "cottage industry" in which winemaking had traditionally been viewed more like a hobby than a business. Major advances in viticulture and winemaking methods and the growing sophistication of American winemakers have brought about real improvements in winemaking quality during the past decade. Winemakers have more marketing savvy as well, carefully targeting and positioning their brands. Wine producers have recently responded well to shifting consumer tastes toward higher-priced varietals, a trend likely to accelerate in the future. Overall, per capita wine consumption is projected to increase gradually in future years as premium table wines continue to grow in popularity (see Exhibit 2.2).

1999 Country Rank	1999[a] (gal.)	1998[b] (gal.)	1997[b] (gal.)	1996[b] (gal.)	Average 1991– 1995[c]	Change 1999 vs. 1991–1995
1. Luxembourg	16.07	17.70	18.25	16.61	15.39	4.41%
2. France	15.81	16.28	16.14	15.82	16.96	–6.81%
3. Italy	14.30	14.44	13.99	15.73	15.93	–10.20%
4. Portugal	13.09	12.64	13.06	14.51	14.54	–9.95%
5. Croatia	12.41	12.35	12.49	9.94	10.20	21.60%
6. Switzerland	10.76	10.81	10.81	10.93	11.19	–3.84%
7. Spain	9.91	9.92	9.78	9.69	10.35	–4.28%
8. Argentina	9.12	9.77	10.32	10.30	12.11	–24.68%
9. Uruguay	8.61	9.28	8.87	7.89	7.20	19.67%
10. Slovenia	8.22	10.30	12.88	14.47	10.19	–19.27%
11. Austria	8.12	8.27	8.60	8.42	8.56	–5.15%
12. Denmark	7.73	7.95	7.70	7.18	6.11	26.51%
13. Greece	7.15	7.26	7.20	6.54	7.07	1.10%
14. Romania	6.86	5.04	6.71	8.21	6.24	10.05%
15. Hungary	6.45	7.54	7.54	7.81	8.13	–20.66%
16. Belgium	6.06	6.18	6.43	5.34	5.98	1.28%
17. Germany	6.05	6.16	6.16	6.08	6.05	–0.03%
18. Australia	5.14	5.25	5.01	4.74	4.63	10.90%
19. Chile	4.97	5.06	3.59	4.27	4.38	13.45%
20. Georgia	4.21	3.86	3.86	3.38	4.66	–9.65%
21. Netherlands	4.19	3.76	4.10	3.52	3.67	13.93%
22. United Kingdom	3.89	3.76	3.70	3.40	3.02	28.73%
23. Sweden	3.58	3.30	3.15	3.42	3.17	12.95%
24. Bulgaria	3.05	1.96	2.11	2.53	3.31	–7.91%
25. Moldova	2.98	0.63	0.91	1.82	2.57	16.15%
26. Cyprus	2.93	3.12	3.05	3.01	2.80	4.61%
27. Norway	2.78	2.62	2.54	2.23	1.73	60.63%
28. New Zealand	2.66	2.96	3.01	2.36	2.67	–0.72%
29. Ireland	2.60	1.58	1.39	1.26	0.74	251.11%
30. Lithuania	2.42	2.26	1.91	1.56	0.89	171.88%
31. South Africa	2.38	2.27	2.36	2.38	2.14	11.34%
32. Canada	2.15	2.19	1.95	1.87	1.66	29.86%
33. Slovakia	2.12	1.76	2.05	1.80	2.13	–0.01%
34. United States	2.01	1.95	2.10	1.81	1.82	10.47%
35. Latvia	1.92	1.56	1.47	0.00	0.00	0.00%
36. Finland	1.71	1.62	1.35	1.39	1.27	35.11%
37. Czech Republic	1.68	1.66	1.62	1.62	1.51	11.63%
38. Uzbekistan	1.54	1.79	1.74	1.24	1.49	3.25%

(continued)

39. Estonia	1.42	1.29	1.29	1.30	0.48	193.25%
40. Azerbaijan	1.36	1.29	0.74	0.74	2.13	–35.84%
41. Lebanon	1.20	1.35	2.06	1.36	1.77	–32.18%
42. Macedonia	1.20	1.26	1.25	1.24	1.21	–0.35%
43. Madagascar	1.02	1.28	0.85	0.43	0.62	65.03%
44. Russia	1.00	0.97	1.03	1.04	1.06	–6.26%
45. Paraguay	0.81	0.85	0.85	0.85	0.81	–0.01%
46. Tajikistan	0.72	0.88	0.85	0.85	1.49	–51.93%
47. Turkmenistan	0.70	0.75	0.75	0.82	0.82	–14.66%
48. Japan	0.65	0.67	0.58	0.37	0.28	129.09%
49. Armenia	0.63	0.57	0.46	0.60	2.00	–68.37%
50. Tunisia	0.60	0.73	0.41	0.63	0.44	36.64%
51. Belarus	0.51	0.64	0.90	0.96	0.97	–47.20%
52. Poland	0.46	0.43	0.35	0.24	0.18	162.62%
53. Brazil	0.45	0.42	0.42	0.39	0.48	–5.42%
54. Israel	0.36	0.34	0.36	0.30	0.52	–30.69%
55. Morocco	0.36	0.17	0.33	0.37	0.24	51.74%
56. Kazakhstan	0.35	0.55	0.38	0.25	0.48	–27.38%
57. Kyrgyzstan	0.34	0.36	0.38	0.40	0.37	–6.88%
58. Ukraine	0.32	0.28	0.30	0.32	0.67	–51.78%
59. Bosnia–Herzegovina	0.24	0.37	0.30	1.19	0.99	–75.59%
60. Peru	0.17	0.19	0.19	0.18	0.13	26.14%
61. Algeria	0.17	0.19	0.18	0.23	0.26	–34.65%
62. China	0.12	0.09	0.08	0.07	0.07	73.14%
63. Turkey	0.09	0.10	0.09	0.13	0.10	–6.25%
64. Bolivia	0.08	0.08	0.08	0.08	0.08	–0.14%
65. Mexico	0.04	0.04	0.04	0.04	0.05	–15.88%
66. Egypt	0.01	0.01	0.01	0.01	0.01	–8.37%

[a] Gallons per capita.

[b] Based on total resident population. Per capita consumption will be higher if based on adult population.

[c] Per capita consumption is based on population in 2000 reported by U.S. Bureau of Census *Statistical Fact Book 2000*.

[d] Per capita consumption is based on population in 1995 reported by the Central Intelligence Agency *World Factbook*.

Exhibit 2.2 Per Capita Wine Consumption in Selected Countries[a]: Actual 1996–1999, Average 1991–1995, and Percent Change (From Wine Institute from Ivie International based on data from Office International de la Vigne et du Vin, [O.I.V.]).

During the 1990s a number of major trends emerged in the California wine industry. These trends included: (1) consolidation of the industry's "three-tier" distribution network (winery–wholesaler/distributor–retailer); (2) market segmentation due to consumers' "trading up" from inexpensive jug wines to premium-priced varietals such as chardonnay, merlot, and cabernet sauvignon; and (3) the emergence of global markets for wines (see Exhibit 2.2)

INDELICATO FAMILY AND COMPANY BACKGROUND

As one of California's leading family winegrowers, Delicato Family Vineyards had a history of more than 75 years of growing quality wine grapes. The Indelicato family originally began growing wine grapes and making wines in a small village in Italy. In 1924, Delicato was founded when the Indelicato family immigrated to California from Sicily and purchased a 40-acre dairy farm in Manteca, a dairy community at that time. The family converted the dairy farm into a grape vineyard. Within a very short time, the high quality of Gaspare Indelicato's California grapes became known to home winemakers across the country. Gaspare received more orders than he could fill, even during Prohibition. However, grape prices and sales declined during the Great Depression.

After the repeal of Prohibition, Gaspare decided to try his hand at winemaking, in hopes that selling wine would be more profitable than selling grapes had been. He used the same techniques that his father had used in Sicily. Gaspare, his brother-in-law, and their twin wives began making wines in 1935 by turning a hand-driven press set up in an old hay barn next to the vineyards. The first year they produced a total volume of 3451 gallons of wine. Delicato's reputation for high-quality wine fueled its growth. Producers in the California wine industry began to approach Gaspare and his family for custom-made wines. These producers put their brand names on the label of Delicato wines. Encouraged by the increasing demand for his wines, Gaspare purchased additional vineyards to maintain a consistent supply of grapes. Further acquisitions resulted in the eventual ownership of extensive vineyards.

In the 1970s Delicato developed a number of long-term agreements with a variety of other wineries to produce wine for them. As this number increased, Delicato was able to generate a huge revenue stream, allowing the company to expand its bulk wine production infrastructure significantly. By 2001, Delicato had agreements with 120 growers in California.

In 1988, Delicato became aware of the growth potential of varietal wines; however, the company was concerned about the low quality of the wine that it was producing. Because it could not support the required quality, the company was looking for a new vineyard. In 1988, the Delicato family bought San Bernabé Vineyards — the largest single vineyard property in the world and even more impressive in its diversity. Top California wine-makers turn to the San Bernabé Vineyard for grapes because they know that the world's best wines come from the coolest growing regions. In Monterey, for example, grapes ripen more slowly and stay on the vine longer than grapes in Napa and Sonoma.

MARKET SEGMENTATION IN THE WINE INDUSTRY

Table wines, those with 7 to 14% alcohol content by volume and tradi-tionally consumed with food, are divided into two broad market segments. Table wines that retail for less than $3.00 per 750-ml bottle are generally considered to be generic or "jug" wines, while those selling for more than $3.00 per bottle are considered "premium" wines.

Premium wines generally have a vintage date on their labels. This means that the product was made with at least 95% of grapes harvested, crushed, and fermented in the calendar year shown on the label and used grapes from an appellation of origin (for example, Napa Valley, Sonoma Valley, Central Coast, etc.). Within the premium table wine category, a number of submarket segments have emerged, based on retail price points. For example, "popular premium" wines generally fall into the $3.00 to $8.00 per bottle range, while "super premium wines" retail for $8.00 to $15.00. The "ultra premium" category sells for $15.00 to $30.00 per bottle. Any retail price above $30.00 per bottle is considered "luxury premium."

According to the Wine Institute (2000), 1999 U.S. wine market retail sales were $18 billion, growing from $11.7 billion in 1990. The U.S. wine market ranked third in the world behind France and Italy. However, the U.S. ranked 30th in the world in per capita consumption of wine in 1999 (see Exhibit 2.2). The greatest concentration of table wine consumers was in the 35 to 55 age bracket. About the same proportion of men and women consumed wine. Although all income levels consume wine, greater wine consumption is typically associated with higher-income consumers. In 1998, adults in families earning over $75,000 annually represented 18.7% of the population and 31.4% of the domestic table wine consumption.

WINE INDUSTRY DISTRIBUTION CHANNELS

Wine has traditionally been sold through a three-tier distribution system. Wineries (the first tier) or importers sell wine to wholesalers (the second tier), who provide legal fulfillment of wine products to local retail busi-nesses (the third tier) within a certain state. Wine is a controlled substance, and laws in each state differ regarding how wine can be sold. Typically, wine passes through each tier of the distribution system, making direct shipping to retailers or selling wine through the Internet difficult or impossible in most states. Presently, in 26 states, it is now illegal to ship or receive wine from out of state. In fact, depending on where the consumer lives, he can be charged with a felony for buying a bottle of wine out of state and having it shipped to his home. Furthermore, the winery that sold the wine could lose its license to make wine. The situation may be changing, however. Several grassroots organizations such as American Viticultural Association (representing over 650 wineries) and Free the Grapes (which claims 300,000 members) are trying to get the Supreme Court to repeal these 60 year-old laws that are still on the books.

The third tier of the distribution system consists of retail and nonretail outlets. Supermarkets, convenience stores, club stores, mail-order and Internet retailers, specialty stores, and wine clubs account for 78% of total sales volume. Supermarkets alone account for 52% of retail wine sales and are very influential in wine distribution. Moreover, supermarkets exert considerable bargaining leverage over wholesalers.

The role of specialty stores in wine distribution has diminished due to the increasing power of supermarkets. Specialty stores' share of retail wine sales was about 30% in 1998. Nevertheless, these stores are not likely to disappear soon because they provide superior customer service and their sales staffs have extensive knowledge of wines. Specialty stores also carry specialty brands and limited production labels, attracting wine connoisseurs and enthusiasts. On-premises sales via nonretail outlets such as restaurants, hotels, and airlines account for 22% of wine volume in the U.S., according to *Adams Wine Handbook*, 2001.

GLOBALIZATION OF THE WINE INDUSTRY

By 2000, the U.S. had become the second largest market for exported wine and the fourth leading producer of wine in the world. In 2000, U.S. wine exports to 164 countries totaled $560 million, of which more than 90% came from California. Wine was produced commercially in over 60 countries with 23% (by volume) of the wine produced in the world being exported to international markets, according to *Wines & Vines* (1999). Leading wine producers include the Old World wineries in France, Italy, and Spain, which were also the leading exporters. New World producers, such as the U.S., Australia, Chile, Argentina, and South Africa, have been making production and export inroads globally over the past few decades. For example, France, Italy, and Spain export more than 25% of the wine they produce; Australia exports over 40% and Chile over 80% of its production. Many observers attribute these export numbers to the small size of the home markets.

Until the mid-1990s, the U.S. wine market remained largely a domestic industry, with some imports from France, Italy, and Spain competing with U.S. wineries. By 1999, however, imports had risen to 20% of the U.S. market, seven percentage points above 1995, according to *Wine Business Monthly* (2000). Australian and Chilean wines began making rapid inroads into the U.S. market. For example, from 1995 to 1999, Australia increased the value of its exports to the U.S. by 243% and Chile by 152%. Since 1995, the unfavorable balance of trade for wine in the U.S. had increased by 78%. Tariffs and trade barriers played a pivotal role in obstructing U.S. wineries' access to various countries' markets.

U.S. wine exports nevertheless grew consistently, from a base of $137 million in 1990 to $548 million in 1999, according to the U.S. Department of Commerce (see Exhibit 2.3). Also, in 1998, the U.S. wine industry enjoyed the highest rate of increased wine exports (19.3%) among the major wine-producing countries listed in the *World Vineyard, Grape, and Wine Report* (2000). Although this export growth was impressive, U.S. wineries also faced increasing threats to their domestic market share due to globalization in the wine industry. *Wines & Vines* reported in 1999 that the U.S. had only 4.2% (by volume) of the world export wine market, while producing 8% (by volume) of the wine produced in the world. The U.S. wine industry exported only 13% of the wine it produced, while other countries had more intensely developed their export markets. Ten U.S. wineries accounted for more than 89% of exports. Nearly 50% of U.S. wineries exported their products.

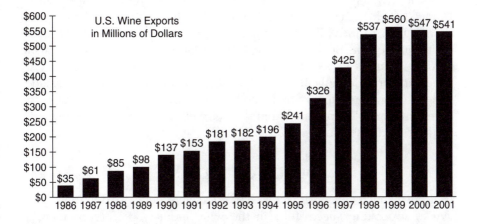

Exhibit 2.3   Growth of U.S. Wine Exports 1986–2001. (From Wine Institute using data from U.S. Dept. of Commerce, National Trade Data Bank.)

The leading U.S. exporter by volume was Ernest and Julio (E&J) Gallo, accounting for about half of U.S. exports and more than four times the volume of its nearest export competitor. E&J Gallo exported approximately 13% of its total production. U.S. wineries typically exported only a small percentage of their production. A notable exception was Wente Vineyards, which had made exports a cornerstone of its long-term strategy; 60% of its annual case sales were from markets in 147 countries.

The super-premium–ultra-premium market was highly fragmented, composed of hundreds of individual, small to large wine-producing operations that were all competing to produce the most acclaimed wines each year. Although larger producers held advantages in scale and capital, the smaller wineries were able to compete by consistently producing-high quality wines in limited quantities that gained critical acclaim by wine enthusiasts. Smaller wine producers, however, were at a disadvantage when trying to compete for grape sources against larger, better-financed competitors such as Beringer; RMC; Kendall-Jackson; Sebastiani Vineyards; Diageo PLC's United Distillers and Vintners' North America (UDV NA) wines division; Gallo; and Constellation Brands' Canandaigua division. Many of these rival firms owned portfolios of brands; invested in wine-making facilities and vineyards across California and abroad; and produced wines across the price spectrum of the premium, super-premium, and ultra-premium market segments.

Due to the globalization of markets and creation of the European Union, trade barriers were falling worldwide. The worldwide consolidation trend accelerated among wineries and distributors. For example, Allied Domecq (U.K.); Diageo PLC (U.K.); BRL Hardy (Australia); Constellation Brands (U.S.); and BFC courted larger premium wineries in Northern California, such as Buena Vista and Kendall-Jackson, for acquisitions. Wine industry analysts expected further consolidation in the wine industry as large wine and alcoholic beverage companies continued to acquire smaller winery operations across national borders, in order to gain access to premium and ultra-premium brands, as well as access to the growing markets for those brands.

DELICATO'S DILEMMA

Delicato Family Vineyards (DFV) had effectively developed its own strategy for operating successfully in the wine industry. Before bringing in Morham, DFV had built its reputation on quality and reliability and had secured an integral position in the region. Since the 1970s, DFV had established itself as the key supplier of quality grapes and bulk wine to various varietal producers in the entire industry. Beginning with its relationship with Almaden Vineyards to produce wine for them, DFV gradually expanded its growing, producing, and distributing capacities to enter into long-term agreements with many vineyards. Additionally, DFV developed agreements with grape growers, specifying the requirements for quality and quantity.

During that time, Delicato winemaking was focused on understanding the vineyard. The company was interested in finding the best combinations of varieties with soil types and vineyard locations. Its research lots were of commercial size, usually producing 25,000 gallons of wine on which to perform experiments; the vineyard had a state-of-the-art winery. The close proximity of this winery to the vineyard helped to preserve the intense flavors of the grapes during transportation. Delicato annually harvested more premium grapes from the Monterey growing region than any other winery. Depending on vintage, the winery crushed between 16 to 20% of all grapes grown in the region, including grapes grown on the San Bernabé vineyards as well as grapes grown by independent growers.

In addition to San Bernabé vineyards, DFV also relied heavily on the Clay Station Vineyard — a 1250-acre vineyard in the Sacramento River delta. This area (the Lodi region) had been ranked as one of the best in California. Although it did not have the cachet that the North coast or Monterey had, a lot of grapes were sold to well-known wineries in Napa and Sonoma. Grapes grown on the Clay Station Vineyard were used to supply the six wines in the DFV line: cabernet sauvignon; chardonnay; merlot; Shiraz; white zinfandel; and zinfandel. As a large-scale, high-intensity, and low-margin grape producer and bulk wine supplier, Delicato facilitated other larger players in the wine industry. Through various B2B arrangements, the company was able to supply the required wine while the industry was growing. However, when the industry growth slowed, Delicato was the first to feel the pain because it facilitated about 1500 wineries in the area.

Delicato embarked on a major strategic shift during the late 1990s when it decided to enter the consumer market — a market of which the company had little understanding. Prior to this, it used a supermarket distribution channel, bottled low-quality wine, and sold it for large quantities. All the company cared about was selling its wine by volume; the goal was to sell a million cases. In doing so, Delicato did not build up its own brand equity; in fact, it had little, if any.

The company did not have the concept of building brand equity and concentrated only on large scale and low pricing. Because it was more concerned about quantity than profitability, to consumers, the name of Delicato was only associated with low-quality wine. Delicato had been going in the direction of creating its own premium brand in the marketplace for years but had not been successful. The company felt that an opportunity existed to build a strong brand image but was not clear about how to achieve it.

TRANSFORMATION OF DELICATO

With a new management team in place, Delicato began developing its own branded wines. In order to change consumers' perceptions, the company needed to change its marketing approach in order to support the images it wanted to build. Part of this strategy involved getting its branded wines "close to the customers' lips" or simply encouraging sampling of its wines. By redirecting and redeploying current facilities and resources to a higher-margin business, Delicato was able to build a broader customer base (B2B and consumer) as well as to diversify its portfolio risk.

According to Morham, business is a game with rules, players, winners, and losers. As he set out to transform the organization, he understood that he needed to change the rules of the game. The transformation project initiated by Morham was a significant work in progress with many unanswered questions, such as

- How fast does the company want to go?
- Where are the current top-notch players going to be in the near future?
- How should the company optimally redeploy its assets?
- Should Delicato continue to be in the bulk wine business in which margins are low?
- Should the company concentrate more on its branded case business because most of its profits come from building its own brand name?
- Should the company sell its facility in Manteca?

These questions were just the beginning of the critical issues Morham needed to tackle in order to achieve a successful transformation of DFV.

DELICATO'S CURRENT MARKETING PROGRAM

DFV now competes in three primary business domains:

- Agriculture business — large-scale vineyard
- Bulk wine business — custom crushing and bulk winemaking
- Branded wine business — Delicato brand names

The agriculture and bulk wine/business-to-business (B2B) segments are the original businesses of Delicato and contribute about two thirds of the company's total sales revenues. Delicato's agriculture segment is mainly on its San Bernabé Vineyard, where the heart of the company's capabilities lies. As far as its B2B segment is concerned, Delicato does large-scale barreling of its bulk wines and selling to other wineries. Not much bottling is done in this segment.

Although Delicato's branded case business only contributes to the remaining one third of the company's total sales revenue, this segment is very profitable with consistently high profit margins. In less than 2 years, Delicato's branded case business was completely turned around from losing millions of dollars to a profit maker. Prior to the turning point, Delicato had not raised the price of its bottled wine for 5 years. The company has been able to turn its branded case business around by repackaging its wine and raising the price. Ideally, Delicato wants two thirds of its total sales revenues to come from its branded business segment and the remaining one third from its agricultural and B2B businesses.

Morham expressed an interest in restructuring the company's B2B business segment as its contracts with its current customers expired. Delicato wanted to restructure its B2B business portfolio to make it smaller and more profitable by dropping the low-margin businesses and holding on to the more profitable ones.

The strategic shift from a bulk wine producer to a branded wine producer was not without risks. For example, Delicato's B2B customers, who were used to the subsidized treatment from Delicato, might become unsatisfied and cut their ties with the company. However, Morham was convinced that this issue would settle on its own. As he said, "They'll get over it." During the transitional period of the transformation, Morham was aware that Delicato needed to put extra efforts into coordinating its business segments. The agricultural and B2B businesses were needed to fuel the branded business until it could fly on its own.

The Indelicatos use only about 15% of the grapes grown on the San Bernabé Vineyard to make their own wines under the Delicato Family Vineyards* and Delicato Monterra† brands (see Exhibit 2.4). The good tasting ratings of Monterra Syrah have earned Delicato a reputation for quality red wines. The company sells the rest of its grape production to other prestigious California winemakers, including Beringer; Niebaum-Coppola; Robert Mondavi; Bonny Doon; Joseph Phelps; Fetzer; Domaine Chandon; Geyser Peak; Morgan; Sterling Vineyards; Sutter Home; and Wild Horse Winery.

---

* Delicato Family Vineyards brands include Cabernet Sauvignon, Sauvignon Blanc, Chardonnay, Shiraz, Merlot and White Zinfandel.
† Delicato Monterra brands include Cabernet Sauvignon, Sangiovese, Syrah, Merlot, Chardonnay and Zinfandel.

Delicato's uses a price–value positioning for its own branded products, which include the following (also see Exhibit 2.4):

- Delicato Monterey Vine Select brand* — $40
- Delicato Monterra brand — $14.99 (zinfandel); $9.99 (merlot)
- Delicato Family Vineyards brand — $5.99

Because Delicato was portrayed as a jug wine producer in the beginning, this image remained in people's minds for a long time. Even though Delicato moved from large bottles to smaller bottles, the jug wine mentality still existed, if only on a smaller scale. Delicato had not developed the concept of brand equity among its old management team. In fact, the new management realized the need to change people's perceptions and the importance of building Delicato's brand image and developing brand equity.

Delicato was dedicated to building its brands by focusing on a value proposition of creating quality wine at several different price points, each brand attractively packaged and supported by a strong sales organization (see Exhibit 2.5). The Delicato team knew that even the most inexpensive wine must provide a great value to the consumer in quality and flavor. Delicato assembled an internationally trained winemaking team, headed by Tom Smith, vice president of production. The team was committed to quality wines that support Delicato's value equation. Because the company controls its products from the vineyards to the wines in the bottles, it was able to deliver a consistent premium quality wine with every vintage.

An integral component of building DFV's brand equity was the international plan. Until a few years prior to the transformation at Delicato, the U.S. wine industry had been mainly a domestic industry, with some imports from the "Old World" — France, Italy, and Spain competing with the local wineries. However, that changed dramatically in the years of 1995 to 2000. Imports rose to 20% of the U.S. market share, a full 7% above the level of imports in 1995 (Love, 2000). This rapid increase was fueled by the tremendous inroads made by the "New World" wines, from Australia and Chile in particular, into the U.S. market.

In line with this fairly unsophisticated approach to international exports by U.S. wineries, Delicato's international business prior to Morham had not been profitable. The business had no strategy to develop the company's brand internationally. In fact, it had no overall plan for its international business. Delicato would sell 100 cases to one market and another 200 cases to another market arbitrarily, depending on demand and supply conditions. As Dave DeBoer, the vice president of international sales, said,

---

* Delicato only produces a limited quantity, about 1200 cases per year.

DELICATO MONTEREY VINE SELECT WINES

One of the most exciting projects from Delicato is the new Delicato Monterey Vine Select wines. These are handcrafted, artisan wines from specially selected vine rows of the San Bernabé Vineyard. These truly ultra-premium wines will be made only in the best vintages and are available in very limited quantities. Monterey Vine Select wines are made to appeal to the wine devotee who appreciates the best. Priced above the $40 range, the quality in the bottle makes the wines a good value selection in keeping with Delicato's value equation marketing philosophy. Currently, three wines are available: chardonnay, merlot and syrah. All three wines are grown on well-drained Aeolian soils, remnants of what were once ancient, windblown sand dunes.

Fruit for the 1998 chardonnay was selected from vine rows growing on a sandy bluff overlooking the Salinas River. The wine, which was bottled unfined and unfiltered, has a rich, rounded mouthfeel and complex layers of fruit, including pineapple and green apple. It was aged 15 months in French oak.

The 1998 merlot was also made from grapes grown on another well-drained bluff of the San Bernabé. It is 100% merlot and was aged 20 months in a combination of French and American oak and was also bottled unfined and unfiltered. The wine has a supple, silky mouthfeel with deep berry fruit leading to a long and layered finish.

The 1998 syrah, too, was harvested from an ancient Aeolian sandy knoll of the San Bernabé Vineyard. The wine was aged 22 months in all new oak, a combination of French and American. It is a powerful wine, with a lovely ruby red color, dominated by black cherry and raspberry flavors. The texture is smooth and velvety. It is a wine with the potential to improve with aging.

With Delicato Monterey Vine Select wines, Delicato is putting its best foot forward and the wines are showing very well indeed.

DELICATO MONTERRA WINES

Delicato's Monterra wines represent one of the world's great premium wine values. They are made exclusively from grapes grown in Monterey County, including the San Bernabé Vineyard, and are styled to capture the essence of Monterey. The wines are priced in the $10 to $18 range. The Monterra brand competes in the newest and fastest-growing California "coastal" wine category. The wines of this category usually bear a California appellation and are created from fruit influenced by the cooling effect of California's long coastline. By contrast; Monterra wines are created only from the strictly delimited Monterey growing region of coastal California. Unlike most coastal wines, Monterra represents a more focused and defined regional wine style. Monterra graphically affirms Delicato's commitment to added value and reward in each and every brand. These wines represent an incredible bargain when compared to wines of equal quality from anywhere else in the world

(continued)

Monterra wines are crafted in the classic Delicato fruit-forward style. Oak is used to enhance and help shape the character of the wines. Oak never overpowers the marvelous Monterey fruit. Wines are segregated by vineyard block and kept separate while aging. Only the best lots are finally blended, with the goal not only to intense fruit, but also to complex layers of flavor. The Monterra red wines — syrah, merlot, and cabernet sauvignon — undergo labor-intensive extended maceration to enhance the concentrated fruit flavors.

It is hard to pick a favorite among the reds. The 1998 syrah is smooth and rich, with bright jammy fruit. The 1998 merlot is elegant and complex with a hint of spicy berries and a long finish. The cabernet sauvignon features rich cherry and bramble flavors.

The sangiovese and zinfandel are limited production wines; the sangiovese features delightful plum and red cherry fruit with an attractive finish. The zinfandel is a super wine, with rich jammy flavors and a powerful finish.

The Monterra chardonnay is barrel aged for added texture and fruit flavor. It is a lively version of a California classic, with lots of ripe fruit and a toasty center. The 1999 version is a real treat. It captures the very essence of crisp Monterey chardonnay fruit, with layers of pear, apple, and tangy tropical fruit.

Overall, the Monterra wines are an exciting showcase for the marvelous fruit of Monterey County.

▼▲▼

DELICATO FAMILY VINEYARDS WINES

Delicato Family Vineyards wines are as comfortable as a trusted old friend. You know what to expect and Delicato delivers it every time. They are honest California wines, true to their varietal character and always a pleasure to put on the table. Make no mistake, however; priced under $10, the Delicato Family Vineyards wines represent not only good value but also good quality. They deliver quality far beyond their price points.

The grapes come chiefly from the family-owned Clay Station Vineyard in the Sacramento River delta near Lodi. The 1250-acre vineyard was planted to cabernet sauvignon, merlot, syrah, sangiovese, zinfandel, and viognier in 1995. The character of Delicato's Lodi wines makes them perfect for consumers who want a sound, everyday wine at a reasonable price. Delicato Family Vineyards wines have the soft, supple character sought by today's wine consumers around the world. They are ideal wines to match with a wide range of foods as well.

There are six wines in the Family Vineyards line — cabernet sauvignon, chardonnay, merlot, Shiraz, white zinfandel, and zinfandel. The wines have in common lively, forward fruit and good varietal definition. The use of oak is limited, and is used only to add a touch of complexity. This kind of wine styling is uncommon in most wines found at this price point.

The cabernet sauvignon has lively cherry and plum fruit with a smooth and fairly long finish. It is a very nice drink now but should be even better with a few years in the bottle.

(continued)

The chardonnay has welcoming hints of pear and tropical fruit with a long, pleasing finish.

The merlot is a medium-bodied wine with spicy cherry fruit and a hint of coffee — a delicious wine that keeps you reaching for another glass.

Designed for immediate pleasure, the Shiraz is a silky wine made in a soft, lively style.

The white zinfandel is always a popular favorite, offering bright, just off-dry fruit, crisp and cheerful.

The zinfandel is a peppery wine with spicy fruit that brings a smile to the face with every glass.

Exhibit 2.4   Types of Delicato's Branded Wines (From Delicato's supplement published in the *Wine and Spirit International*.)

"Delicato would sell its wine to anyone anywhere at any price — just make us an offer" (DeBoer, 2001)

THE FUTURE OF DELICATO

Delicato has been a hands-on, family-owned winegrower; the third generation is now on track to bring in a new management team to make the company a major player in the world wine market. The company continues to carry on the Indelicato family heritage because members of the family remain involved in supervising daily activities. When asked what Delicato is all about, they simply say, "Just growing good grapes and making good wine." In an era of giant mega-wine corporations, decisions affecting the quality of winegrowing may be made on another continent by someone who has never set foot in the vineyard. Small- and medium-size wineries are mostly owned by families and these family-owned wineries have had problems attracting good management people.

Delicato has a 3-year plan for its business and a 10-year plan for its vineyard. The first year of the 3-year plan is more on the operational side, including details such as expenses, revenues, projections, and forecasts. The game plan is not just about creating a vision, but to see some positive results. Delicato needs to build a new company to run on a completely new strategy. It needs to reinvent itself while buying enough time to solve all the problems left from the previous management. As Eric Morham puts it, "We need to change the engines while the plane is in flight!" The winery only produces wine once a year, so it is very important to have good forecasts and plan on the volume of the wine that it can sell. The metaphor that Morham uses to describe the challenges facing Delicato is "how to enter a revolving door and come out ahead."

──────────── ▼▲▼ ────────────

A MESSAGE FROM ERIC MORHAM

Globalization is a fact of life in today's wine business. Just a short time ago, California wines competed only among themselves and solely in the American market. Today, we are selling our wines throughout the world, and successfully competing against excellent wines from many regions of both the Old World and the New.

To be successful in the highly competitive global marketplace, wineries must have a commitment to the highest quality at every price level. They must strive to create the very best wines their vineyards can produce. This goal demands the utmost concentration and effort.

Delicato Vineyards is one of America's leading family winegrowers. For more than 75 years we have been crafting premium wines while assembling and investing in a remarkable portfolio of world-class California vineyards — including the remarkable San Bernabé Vineyard in Southern Monterey County and Clay Station in the rolling eastern Sierra foothills.

To capture the best qualities of fruit grown on these notable estate properties, we have assembled an international team of experienced and highly creative winemakers who have at their disposal some of the most advanced winemaking tools and facilities. The resultant award-winning premium wines — Delicato Family Vineyards, Delicato Monterra, and Delicato Monterey Vine Select — are marketed by a highly skilled and professional distributor network, and compete with the best wines of their type in the international arena.

At Delicato Family Vineyards, we are committed to the global market-place and to the creation of California wines that compete with the best in the world both in quality and value. And we know that many other wineries hope to compete effectively with us. The result is a dynamic market with great benefits to the consumer. We are delighted to be able to play a role in it.

Exhibit 2.5   A Message from Eric Morham as Appeared in Press

QUESTIONS

1. Which elements among the core value drivers (quality, service, and price) and the value adders (image, innovation, and intangibles) were instrumental in cultivating DFV's value proposition for its B2B customers? for its B2C customers?
2. Assess the DFV value proposition in its B2B and B2C markets. Is its value proposition for each market unique and differentiating? Explain.

3. Value exists in relationships with customers. Explain how this applies to DFV as a business-to-business and business-to-consumer marketer.
4. You are a consultant to DFV and are asked to draft a strategy statement for improving the practice of integrated marketing communications (IMC) at Delicato. Prepare a memo addressed to Eric Morham outlining, among other things, the importance of IMC; how IMC can be used to create and/or communicate greater customer (B2B, B2C) value; and a strategy for how DFV should apply IMC to its operations.
5. Assess the overall efficacy of Delicato's strategic shift from primarily a grower and B2B marketer to a branded consumer marketer. What are the key success factors in making this transition? What are the pitfalls?

REFERENCES

Adams Wine Handbook (1999) Adams Business Media, New York.
Adams Wine Handbook (2001) World drink trends, Adams Business Media, New York.
Anon. (1999) And now the numbers, *Wines Vines*, July.
Boyd, G. (1999) Delicato Family Vineyards, *Vineyard Winery Manage.*, May.
DeBoer, D. (2001) Interview, May 18.
Delicato Family Vineyards, http://www.delicato.com.
Love, J.M. (2000) U.S. wine producers face increasing competition, *Wine Bus. Monthly*, June.
Morham, E. (2001) Interview, May 7.
Walker, L. (2001) The world's biggest vineyard, *Wines Vines*, January.
Wine Institute from Ivie International based on data from Office International de la Vigne et du Vin, (O.I.V.).
Wine Institute. http://www.wineinstitute.org
World Vineyard, Grape and Wine Report (2000) Wine Institute, July.

CASE 3: DOW CORNING — CUSTOMER VALUE AND SEGMENTATION*

In 1930, Corning Glass Works began the development of a new material made from sand that combined some of the best properties of glass and plastics. Over the next decade, Corning scientists worked with the scientists at the Mellon Institute of Research in Pittsburgh to develop the promising innovation. Dow Corning was formed in 1943 as a start-up, 50/50 joint venture between Corning Glass and the Dow Chemical Company to explore and develop the commercial potential of the new technology. Over the following decades, Dow Corning grew to be one of the most successful business joint ventures of all time with $2.5 billion in sales and 7500 employees worldwide.

Throughout its history, Dow Corning has pioneered the development of silicon technology innovations to be used in applications as diverse as sealants and gasket waxes and polishes; textiles and water-repellent treatments; pulp and paper processing; and skin care and antiperspirants. Today, Dow Corning is the largest global producer of silicon-based materials, offering more than 7000 different silicon-based products and services. It competes against some tremendous competitors, including GE and Bayer.

Historically, the company's strategy was focused on innovation and new customer applications. It focused and organized to dominate the segment (DTS) for customer innovation, i.e., the DTS strategy for Dow

* Case prepared by Eric W. Balinski, Philip Allen, and J. Nicholas DeBonis. The case was extracted from their book, *Value-Based Marketing for Bottom-Line Success: 5 Steps to Creating Customer Value*, New York: McGraw–Hill and American Marketing Association, 2003, 147–158, and is reprinted with permission. Mr. Balinski may be contacted at ebalinski@synection.net.

Corning was focused on developing a superior value for one specific customer segment and growing its business by growing within this segment. The company grew through discovering and delivering the most advanced technology for demanding customer applications, achieving 4800 active patents worldwide. As such, the company was customer focused before it was fashionable to be so.

CHANGE IN THE MARKET SITUATION FOR DOW CORNING

All market innovations inevitably mature. For a market innovator like Dow Corning, growth resulted in two businesses within one business model. In addition to business growth achieved through innovation, Dow Corning also grew from maturing innovations that were widely used in the marketplace. The latter matured to become Dow Corning's core business that loaded its sales statements and manufacturing facilities. It also attracted competition that ultimately exerted pressure on its pricing and cost positions.

More insidious were the market forces that created a gap between what its maturing innovations could command in the marketplace and a widespread belief in the Dow Corning culture — their commitment to customers and being "innovative" should always command a higher price. Over time, the company's business model, systems, processes, and organizational management and rewards further evolved to strengthen its innovation focus with its customers and DTS.

Although Dow Corning continued to grow and innovate new products and applications with customers, the reality was that it was creating an ever larger collection of mature businesses. Paralleling its success were customers who were innovating and growing their businesses using Dow Corning materials. Dow Corning and its 25,000 customers worldwide prospered together, but over time as the customers' businesses grew and their markets matured, their value ratio or relationship changed with Dow Corning. Many customers in these maturing markets needed Dow Corning not only to innovate new product technology, but also to help them create new value through lower costs in their mature product lines in order to stay competitive in their markets. The need to dominate the cycle (DTC) of value was emerging. Moving to a DTC customer strategy, Dow Corning now was recognizing the need to deliver several different customer values as the cycle of value evolved and changed over time within its customers' markets and businesses.

For a company with a history of success through innovation, this change in customer value and needs represented a contradictory message for Dow Corning's business model. It had built a *Form Follows Value*™ *

---

* *Form Follows Value* is a trademark of Eric W. Balinski and *SYNECTION.*

business model to serve customer innovation effectively, but the model did not serve the changing customer values emerging in the market. *Form Follows Value* is the systematic structuring of back office resources and operations to deliver the promise of the front office customer value. This framework aligns the business *form* (the resources, people, processes, and systems — the *back office*) to the *front-office value* that is most important to customers and to what they *will pay*. With *Form Follows Value,* every cost is aligned within the company to elements from which the targeted customers will derive value. Additionally, it was becoming clearer that some competitors who did not invest in innovating with customers were willing to buy the customer's business with a lower price.

HOW DID DOW CORNING TACKLE THIS CHALLENGE?

In the spring of 2000, Dow Corning Corporation's electronics industry and advanced engineering materials business unit began to explore resegmenting its market with the intent of developing a more customer-focused strategy. "We just knew from our customer research and from direct customer feedback that we were missing the point somewhere," recalls Ian Thackwray, the unit's general manager. "We were doing the right things in terms of getting the customer feedback and we had a mountain of knowledge in the organization, but we were struggling to know what to do with it."

The business leadership team went through an extensive strategy review, during which it realized a need to involve more people who had direct customer interface. "Our attitude had been that we didn't require needs-based segmentation in order to develop a strategy. How wrong we were," says Thackwray. "That strategy review meeting was a milestone in changing our thinking to the realization that customer needs and a true, full, and deep understanding of customer needs [are] fundamental to developing a meaningful and profitable business strategy."

A second meeting was convened in September, 2000, with 36 people from the business team; technical; marketing; sales; supply chain; and new business groups. The objective was to reevaluate implications of customer value segmentation as a basis for reviewing the business strategy.

"The really exciting thing was that no one had a preconceived idea of what the outcome would be and everyone went in with an open mind," remembers Babette Pettersen, then responsible for marketing and new business development in the electronics industry sector. "The idea was to stimulate an open-minded reappraisal of our customer value segmentation, formulating our intimate customer knowledge alongside frameworks and segmentation approaches from both theoretical models and practical examples." The resulting set of customer value commitments was simple, but Dow Corning's electronics business had never developed its strategy from this customer needs-based perspective before.

"We defined and profiled each segment and we assigned customer applications into each segment, enabling us to quantify and evaluate each segment in terms of attractiveness and our ability to compete as a basis for targeting," Thackwray explains. Based on the success of applying the value-based marketing principles in the electronics industry business, similar sessions were conducted by each of the global business units. Scott Fuson, global executive director of marketing and sales, relates,

> This is where the real insight came. After applying the customer needs-based segmentation methodology, we began to realize that there [were] a significant [number] of existing customers who buy for very different reasons. This led us to develop an enterprise-wide look at our customers, then creating distinct and compelling value propositions and business models for each of the customer needs-based segments we identified.
>
> We were particularly excited about how this also better took advantage of our market-based structure and operations. These new business models resulted from converting the needs-based segmentation into customer-focused value that better aligned our resources and structure to improve business model performance with our customers.

Dow Corning recognized that its customers sought additional real value. "A critical outcome of the reevaluation is that it forced us to reappraise our entire market positioning and brand presence," Fuson explains. This included the essence, attributes, and hierarchy for the Dow Corning brand and creation of an entirely new business model for customers that required a price-reliable supply. This new brand positioning became the company's XIAMETER brand.

APPLYING VALUE-BASED MARKETING AT DOW CORNING

Step 1: Discovering and Understanding the Customer

As a company built on developing customer innovation, Dow Corning had a substantial amount of customer information from numerous sources: purchased studies of its customer base; regular customer satisfaction studies conducted by an outside research firm; and regular customer feedback through its customer relationship management (CRM) process. All of this contributed to a full and deep understanding of its customers' needs and value expectations. Yet when Dow Corning started to look at its information from a segmentation and customer value perspective, the information started to reveal new things. For example, three broad customer value segments were identified:

- Customers who innovate into new markets
- Customers in fast-growing markets
- Customers looking to reduce costs and improve productivity in large, highly competitive markets

Innovation-focused customers are defined as those committed to being first to the market with new technologies and state-of-the-art products, and who seek advanced innovation and creation of unique technical or market positions. Dow Corning's customer value commitment for this group of customers is to provide innovative solutions based on cutting-edge technologies and services and expertise in assisting customers to get their products to market faster with better value differentiators for the customers' customers. For example, the company helped Reliance Industries reformulate its fiber-optic cable conduit inner lining to improve the lining's slipperiness, thus allowing fiber optics to go into conduit faster and at longer lengths. This enabled Reliance Industries' customers to install fiber-optic cables significantly faster and for 30 to 50% lower cost. In another instance, Dow Corning helped a consumer products company get its new household cleaner to market faster by taking on manufacturing of the cleaner in its own facilities.

Customers in fast-growing markets are defined as those looking for easy, drop-in solutions that give them speed, efficiency, convenience, and reliability to meet growth demands. Their value drivers are lower-cost offerings with proven performance and demonstrated use. For them, Dow Corning's customer value commitment offers proven performance in technology, manufacturing, and supply chain management. Dow Corning helped a customer's global sealants and adhesives business by working with its larger customers to convert to bulk delivery systems. The change from 55-gallon drums to a new 8000-gallon storage facility reduced handling and labor costs, dropped waste 7%, and freed up 10,000 square feet of space in the customer's operation.

Customers in large, highly competitive markets, typically with products in the mature stage of the product life cycle, form the third segment. These customers expect improved process efficiency and effectiveness in manufacturing to help them achieve maximum profit by reducing costs. They are looking for such things as ideas from suppliers; outsourcing capabilities; inventory control and supply-chain services; and disposal assistance. Dow Corning's customer value commitment for this customer value segment is to offer cost-effective solutions that drive overall costs down. One tool that the company developed for these customers was software that could more precisely pinpoint lubrication for critical plant equipment. The integrated oil analysis software enabled plant operations to perform a complete oil and lubrication analysis on vital equipment to optimize maintenance programs rather than follow routine scheduled maintenance.

As Thackwray makes clear, "We could define and profile each segment and we could identify customers in each segment, enabling us to quantify and evaluate each segment in terms of attractiveness and our ability to deliver a superior value to these customers." Building upon the three broad segment groupings, the electronics business identified seven new customer value segments based on the needs and values of the company's customers.

The key was to take all the various inputs about customers from multiple sources and to integrate them in an interactive and creative thinking process to deliver an insightful output that helped the business better understand what really mattered to its customers' success. Dow Corning developed a summary matrix of customer value for its business. Exhibit 3.1 presents a generic segmentation framework that can be adapted by other businesses to assess customer value segments.

Step 2: Commit to the Customer

Once Dow Corning's business units had identified the key customer value segments it wanted to target, it was a relatively straightforward process for them to proceed with defining the customer value commitments for the company's respective target customer value segments. Each customer value commitment represented a change in the way Dow Corning approached these customers. For the first time, the company moved from assuming that all customers equally valued Dow Corning's innovation to figuring out what was relevant to and valued by specific customers in each customer value segment. The company learned more clearly the real and superior value points with its customers. An important additional insight from the work conducted was the realization that one or more of the needs-based customer value segments cut across the traditional industry sector structure around which Dow Corning had been organizing its business and the corporation.

The value propositions, called customer value commitments, are derived from the individual customer value segment profiles. In most cases, the biggest challenge initially was to identify a truly unique, superior element in the offering because of the strong product innovation focus in the group. Once minds at Dow Corning opened to value differentiators beyond product features and benefits, the ideas started to flow.

"We have spent the past 5 years transforming Dow Corning into a customer-directed organization," comments Dow Corning executive vice president Stephanie Burns. "The result has been our ability to commit better and deliver historic change to the marketplace by offering silicon-based solutions tailored to specific customer needs. The introduction of the new XIAMETER brand reflects a key element of our revitalized and precision-focused company."

The specific value propositions for each customer value segment, according to Dow Corning, "became linked to what really mattered most to our customers' success in each segment through a more focused understanding of each segment's different needs and value drivers." Equally important was recognizing that innovating not only the product, but also the way in which business was conducted with customers, could develop a successful business and deeper relationships with customers. Additionally, the company's core customer value commitments remained true to providing a "full range of services and innovative technology expertise for customers who want to leverage them to give their products a competitive edge. Value-added services are also available with the purchase and use of Dow Corning's other product lines, and include technical innovation, product application, and development support."

According to Dow Corning's experience two key lessons of the second step in value-based marketing are:

- It is necessary to be open minded and completely rethink what the customer considers as superior value commitments and ultimately organize (*Form Follows Value*) around the value needs and expectations of the customer value segments.
- Long-entrenched structures and perspectives need to be examined critically and challenged.

Step 3: Create Customer Value

After creating clear segmentation based on customer need and differentiated value propositions for each customer value segment, making Dow Corning's customer value commitments real to its customers was a relatively easy next step. This involved its need to create resources and infrastructure aligned to the target customer value commitments. Dow Corning defined clear customer value commitments to deliver the desired value to its customer value segments and this enabled management to define the needed resources in terms of people, infrastructure, and financing. Its new emerging form would now follow and be aligned to the distinctive value that it identified in each

	Segment 1: Innovators	Segment 2: Optimizers	Segment 3: Operationalizers	Segment 4: Economizers
Behavior of customers in segments	First to market, risk takers; reputation for the latest ideas	Fast followers; let someone else prove, then exploit market	Best at optimizing total acquisition and use costs	Focused on best pricing; tradeoffs to drive cost out
Value need in segment	Leading ideas or technology to create edge	Fast and responsive support to make transitions	Supply chain optimization support	Continually drive costs out of business
Typical customer cost drivers	R&D; marketing; engineering	Marketing; production; purchasing	Supply chain; production	Production; logistics
Customer profit model	Profit generated through a stream of innovation	Profit generated by quickly capitalizing on opportunities	Efficiency of operations drives profits	Selling as much stuff as cheaply as possible drives profit
What do these customers measure?	Time to market; market response; development costs	Market share and its growth; price/cost variances	Share protection; purchasing costs; supply chain costs	Purchasing costs; market share; operation costs
Customer's market drivers/ situation	Unique ideas are valued in market; few competitors can match	Customer sees opportunity and battles over growth in market	Market is mature, need to win the race to run efficiently	Market declining but these customers hang on
Leading competitive offering/ situation	Competitor wants to play one-upmanship	Variable offerings with high differentiation to attract customers	Unbundling of offerings and a la carte purchasing	Suppliers are exiting, but some will streamline operations to survive

(continued)

Your strategic value commitment	Centered on driving innovation in ideas, products, and solutions	Centered on helping customers capture growth opportunities	Centered on streamlining supply chain, ease of doing business	Centered on driving every possible cost out

Exhibit 3.1   Generic Customer Value Segment Matrix

customer segment, with the ability to manage the changing customer value (DTC) occurring in the marketplace.

Also, one new segment was identified in which the customers valued a low-price cost of doing business and the guarantee of on-time shipments. Dow Corning also backed up the shipment guarantee with a 3% financial reimbursement to the customer if the company missed a shipment commitment time. These customers tended to value research and technical support less. It was also recognized that customers in this segment tended to make large purchases, but not necessarily of a wide variety of products. This customer value segment became the basis for establishing a new business model and channel to market, which was launched in March of 2002.

To serve this new segment, the business model and channel needed to be streamlined; tied to Dow Corning global manufacturing and supply chain capability; and simplified for customers and Dow Corning. Internally, this meant focusing operations to supply the most popular customer products; favoring a Web-based channel; and leveraging the SAP systems to manage order entry and inventory commitments with customers. The changes for customers led to more clearly defined and transparent business practices on such things as pricing, delivery, and order quantity; the best way for the customer to order; and communications practices. This helped guide customers to a better way for them to conduct business with Dow Corning based upon the way those customers might want to conduct business rather than on how Dow Corning wanted to conduct business.

Services and customer processes director Tom Cook remembers,

> What's really amazing is that with this level of clarity and simplicity it was easy to explain similarities and, more importantly, differences in what we should be offering to different customers to best meet their needs. For the first time it was also easy to explain WHY! And, more importantly, customers could understand how they could more easily meet their needs with us.

A bonus benefit was the widespread level of understanding and commitment derived by involving people from many of the implementation functions in the original development work. Bob Schroeder of Dow Corning's construction industry states,

> Involving people from a complete cross section of our global business paid real dividends when it came to rolling out the results. We had our own group of apostles to go out and tell the story to their own colleagues and peers in their own language. The adoption of our new customer value commitment has been immediate and the skepticism is more along the "show me" line of thinking vs. "have you lost your mind?"

These new insights led Dow Corning to redesign its organization from a focus on business sectors to aligning with the newly identified customer value segments. This included the appointment of a customer value segment manager with a specific focus on the newly defined customer value segments and responsibility for delivering the newly defined customer value commitments across all the industry sectors that Dow Corning serves.

According to Dow Corning, the third step of value-based marketing offers two key lessons:

■ You can only define your organization and your infrastructure when you know the value that you want to deliver and to whom you want to deliver it.
■ Involving a broad cross section of the organization builds stronger commitment and buy-in to the end results and speeds implementation.

Step 4: Obtain Customer Feedback

After a long history of succeeding with customers primarily through product innovation, Dow Corning now more than ever needs to assess feedback from its customers on many new dimensions important to them. The new segmentation also establishes a business rationale for changes and can help sort out voices from the customer into specific segment groups. The company's review of its customer value commitments was instigated by feedback from customer research from an outside, independent research firm and from specific situations documented through its customer relationship management (CRM) process. Dow Corning also encourages all staff with customer interface to pose questions about customer satisfaction and obtain direct feedback from the customer using its customer relationship management process.

"Using our customer relationship management process, service level management provided our customer interface people with a methodology to capture specific customer needs and issues in a one-on-one situation," explains Jamie Moore, CRM business process manager. "We can capture and address with each specific customer their insights and then later aggregate these inputs for analysis in order to act upon them across the entire customer base."

An important insight from Dow Corning's experience is that it is difficult for the company to become complacent with the responses to these feedback data. It continues to assess by conducting research on a regular basis and is looking constantly for pointers to the next needed change in its customer value commitments. As Moore describes it,

> Dow Corning's commitment to satisfying customer requirements resulted in the use of needs-based segmentation methods to deepen our understanding of what mattered most to their success. The use of these methods has resulted in the proactive segmentation of customers, each with unique value propositions; improved behaviors in our business units in how we treat customers; and better aligned resource development options in anticipation of customers' changing needs.

> For instance, using customer needs analysis in a structured manner with our CRM process, we specifically know where and how we can provide improved service to customers. This approach to CRM also provides the ability to aggregate information; identify trends with customers and markets; and make better focused decisions and actions. This is because we have a factual and quantified mechanism for communicating customer needs throughout the organization and use this as the basis for responses.

According to Dow Corning, the three key lessons of the fourth step of value-based marketing are:

■ Customer feedback must be obtained from a variety of sources, but at least one must be independent and objective.
■ The sum total of the customer feedback may be greater than the individual feedback when creatively and critically reviewed, integrated, and analyzed.

■ Never be complacent — always look for the next change in a value affecting customers.

Step 5: Measure and Improve Value

Preliminary results of the Dow Corning customer value commitment have been very positive and encouraging. However, it is a story in development and in transition. Fuson affirms that

> While we do believe that some of our latest customer value commitments put us ahead of our competition, we recognize that delivering superior value to our customers is not about beating our competition. Focusing on the competition as the basis of improving our business with customers could and would prevent us from truly understanding our customers and discovering unique insights about how we can help them succeed better. Also, focusing on the competition would trap us in a common shared point of view about customers and our markets rather than developing the breakthrough ideas.

Fuson also points out that,

> If we measured ourselves primarily against competitors, then it would lead most likely to a marketplace of similar offerings for customers, which in the long run would mean poorer responsiveness to changing customer value. Establishing regular and rigorous reviews of our customer interfaces and feedback programs fosters the continued development of our customer value commitments, maintaining the best value for our chosen target customers. The final realization is that providing superior value for customers is profitable for customers and also profitable for us.

The other interesting aspect of the new Dow Corning is how the company is leveraging its existing capabilities better and developing new customer capabilities that utilize the Web, although its focus was not to get on the Web per se. Having gone through the segmentation work first, Dow Corning better understood the value drivers of its customers and, in some value segments, realized that the Web was a better way to provide this value than traditional channels.

A number of Internet-based business start-ups sought to service the same customer segments upon which Dow Corning focused. Although these Internet businesses may have recognized this customer segment, they failed to succeed in this marketspace because they lacked the necessary infrastructure and supply chain investments. Dow Corning already had a $100 million investment in a SAP system — the world's largest manufacturing and distribution system for silicon-based products, with 40 locations worldwide — in place and operating. The company also had a great deal of information about buying habits and behavior of customers. Therefore, it knew it had a global back-office operation that could support the global front-office operations with which their customers interacted. Dow Corning practiced *Form Follows Value*. In contrast, most Web-based companies trying to serve the same customers focused on getting customers to their nice virtual front-office Web sites, but had few capabilities in place to deliver their value propositions.

Dow Corning's challenge was to see value from the customer perspective, rather than only product innovation value, and then sort out its customer information to create the business processes and build channel strategies, including customer touch points like the Web. According to Dow Corning, the fifth step offers two key lessons:

- Rigorous and regular strategy and customer performance reviews are essential to maintaining a leadership position with customers.
- Customer value is not simply telling the customer that you bring them value, but first making the commitment, resource changes, and leadership choices that enable a business to deliver what it says it can do for its customers.

QUESTIONS

1. Critique Dow Corning's segmentation planning process and the resulting three broad customer value segment groupings. Which target market(s) should Dow Corning pursue and why?
2. Compare and contrast Dow Corning's market targets to the four customer value segment profiles in Exhibit 3.1.
3. How typical are the customer value segments (innovators, optimizers, operationalizers, and/or economizers) in Exhibit 3.1 in today's B2B markets? Consider customer attraction and retention in your response.
4. Applying the five-step customer value approach described in this case, provide a specific example of how another company can improve its market analyses and strategies.
5. What role does the Internet play in creating and delivering value for: (a) Dow Corning, and (b) the company that you have chosen in question 4?

BIBLIOGRAPHY

Debonis, J.N., Balinski, E.W., and Allen, P. (2003) *Value-Based Marketing for Bottom Line Success: 5 Steps to Creating Customer Value,* New York: McGraw–Hill and the American Marketing Association, 2003.

http://www.dowcorning.com/content/announce/xiameter_backgrounder.asp.

CASE 4: EDWARD JONES — MANAGING CUSTOMER RELATIONSHIPS*

BACKGROUND

Founded in 1922 with a history traced back to the 1870s, Edward Jones, the privately held St. Louis-based securities broker, has become America's storefront stock brokerage. The company now has over 9000 one-broker offices across the U.S. located almost equally between urban settings and rural strip malls. Managing over $370 billion in U.S. client assets has earned the company over $2.3 billion in revenue in 2002; however, this company does not resemble the typical Wall Street investment firm. In fact, it is not located on Wall Street; Edward Jones' corporate offices are located in Missouri and a majority of its storefront offices are nestled somewhere between the dry cleaner and barbershop in their communities.

With over 28,000 total employees and no layoffs during the tumultuous stock markets of 2001 through 2003, Edward Jones continues to grow and garner attention. The company is the only major financial services firm advising individual investors exclusively, Edward Jones has twice been ranked number one by *Fortune* magazine on the "100 Best Companies to Work For" list (2002 and 2003), despite the fact that the firm does not offer employees any written job descriptions. Employees function essentially as owners — over 25% of Edward Jones' employees have ownership stakes and 100% of all employees receive a portion of company profits. Edward Jones also finished number one in *Kiplinger's Personal Finance* 2003 ranking of the nation's full-service brokers.

---

* This case was prepared by Trevor Fried, doctoral student, H. Wayne Huizenga School of Business and Entrepreneurship at Nova Southeastern University, Ft. Lauderdale, Florida.

RISK AND RELATIONSHIPS

Investing is viewed by many as a risky proposition. Edward Jones uses storefront offices and door-to-door local IRs (investment reps, the only self-referring term used by Edward Jones' brokers) to make investing less intimidating and to build personal relationships based on trust. Moreover, the firm offers no risky products such as stocks under $4 per share, including penny stocks, IPOs, options, or futures, which are often deemed profit engines for other investment firms. Instead, the company stresses a buy-and-hold strategy, even though such behavior limits the transactions that would generate profit for it. Although Edward Jones does not shun profit, it does recognize that building trust and working to make its middle-class clientele comfortable with buying investments creates enduring relationships. This conservative yet proactive investor relationship formula works to reduce the dissonance associated with buying stocks or bonds in potential and existing clients.

One key difference in the Jones sales strategy is apparent right away. Rather than finding new accounts by telephone prospecting, each new broker with Edward Jones begins by knocking on at least 1000 doors. Using this organic approach to building a client base, Edward Jones' IRs serve those most like themselves and build face-to-face relationships within an industry that is otherwise overwhelmingly electronic. Jones' philosophy is "find a community and join it." Its remarkable growth since 1980 is shown in Table 4.1.

CUSTOMER SATISFACTION VS. CUSTOMER LOYALTY

Edward Jones recognizes that, although customer satisfaction is important, the far superior customer loyalty implies a two-way relationship. In the

Table 4.1 Edward Jones Revenue and Brokerage Data

Year	# of Edward Jones' Offices	Revenues (in thousands)
1980	378	$41,517
1985	968	$171,069
1990	1664	$319,791
1995	3188	$720,014
2000	7042	$2,200,000
2001	8079	$2,141,997
2002	8838	$2,261,839
2003	9000+	?

Source: Edward Jones, 2003.

Spring of 1999, during the height of the Internet stock frenzy, company CEO John Bachmann spent over $2 million to send letters and magazine articles warning of the coming stock market implosion to over 6 million customers, referring to the then-present environment as a "dot-com fad." Most organizations measure their marketing or sales successes by the potential revenue contribution of each exercise, but as the top-rated full service broker in J.D. Powers and Associates 2002 customer service rankings, Edward Jones understands that building lasting customer relationships is a precursor to customer loyalty.

Because Edward Jones is a full-service broker, its fees and commissions are much higher than discount brokers such as E*Trade and TD Waterhouse; however, its customer base continues to expand while discount brokerages and other full-service brokerages continue to shed clients. Edward Jones' value-driven marketing strategy focuses on a high level of service quality using strong interpersonal communications with their clients, which builds strong customer loyalty. This strategy has created high perceived value for its customers, helping drive the company over the 6 million customer account mark. The customer intimacy and relationship building used by Edward Jones has created a strong consumer franchise.

RELATIONSHIP MARKETING

Edward Jones understands that long-term customer relationships are the key to building a successful business. The personal relationships that Edward Jones' IRs continue to build are largely based on trust and it is not unusual for customers to invite their Edward Jones IR to family weddings, parties, or even an occasional lunch. Edward Jones customers have come to expect a proactive approach to managing their investments and it is not unusual for these customers to hear from their Edward Jones IRs several times a month, if for no other reason than simply to keep in touch.

Although most brokerage firms offer special benefits or pricing for active traders, Edward Jones treats all customers equally. Because it is a privately held company, there is no external shareholder pressure to meet earnings expectations. Jones' core relationship-based strategy does not believe in switching clients in and out of different funds in order to make a commission. In fact, compared to its major competitors, Edward Jones' compensation system is quite unique. Each investment representative is a profit center instead of creating separate profit centers for each product. Edward Jones pays its bonuses based mostly on the firm's overall performance above a minimum threshold. Rather than offering incentive travel to, say, the top 10% of its investment reps, it offers such travel to anyone who achieves a predetermined level of success. In 2002, 3500 out of 9000 total investment reps earned such awards.

This allows IRs to cater to their clients needs instead of offering an array of services that may not suit the individual customer. The Edward Jones personal IR–customer relationship motivates the IR to build the level of trust by following through on promises and relaying a sincere interest in the welfare of the client's investments.

COMPETITIVE DIFFERENTIATION

Edward Jones operates a service business in a service industry and in reality; its core products are exactly what the competition is also offering. Edward Jones' competitive edge is based on: (1) earning the customer's trust; (2) building customer relationships; and (3) strengthening and maintaining those relationships. Success in these three areas is driven by the quality of the investment broker. Being named a "best company to work for" in the U.S. has not only helped raise the level of brand awareness, but the recognition has also provided the needed stampede of quality applicants to Edward Jones to help fuel present and expected growth.

Just as going door-to-door for new customers requires plain talk and no illusions, Edward Jones' marketing materials and stock reports are written in plain English, intentionally avoiding cumbersome wording and a lot of industry jargon. Reading a stock report from any other brokerage company requires a background in financial industry parlance and technical analysis. Because customers deal only with their local hometown Edward Jones IR, they are not an account number, but rather individuals who are on a first-name basis with their broker. Customers consequently expect face-to-face transactions that conclude with a handshake instead of a "log off" button.

The Midwestern conservatism of Edward Jones is evident throughout much of its business model. The one-broker storefront office might be more costly to operate than a local branch with 60 brokers, but this entrepreneurial set-up does not allow "hot" stock tips, which usually burn investors, to permeate through an office from broker to broker. This contributes greatly to the corporate culture, another key differentiator enjoyed by Edward Jones. Edward Jones employees do not just grow relationships with their clients; they are motivated to grow relationships with their communities through civic involvement, local sponsorships, and other community projects. Additionally, the Edward Jones culture focuses on volunteerism, not only within the community, but also within the organization. In fact, Edward Jones' compensation system encourages employees to help other employees by recruiting, hiring, and mentoring new investment representatives. This ensures that the corporate culture remains intact and consistent with each new generation of representatives.

Top competitor Charles Schwab conducts almost 85% of its brokerage business online, yet Edward Jones continually refuses to consider offering online trading to its customers. Although this has left the company open to criticism from analysts who refer to it as a dinosaur, Edward Jones spends more than 11% of its annual revenue on IT (information technology), which includes over $200 million for data centers, unmatched satellite networks, and a Web site that offers online banking and balance information. Edward Jones actually spends more than the industry average on IT, but will not implement any technology that might sever the relationship between the customer and the IR. In fact, despite having over 1100 employees in the company's IT department, Edward Jones' IRs do not use e-mail to communicate among themselves or with their clients. An Edward Jones client must use the telephone or walk into the office to communicate with his broker. Schwab and other competitors offer the standard online trading complements of touch-tone, voice-activated and wireless trading; streaming quotes and news; and extended hours trading; Edward Jones offers only personal trading through its brokers.

Although Edward Jones' business strategy may seem like an anachronism in today's fast-paced markets, Bachmann's timeless advice still serves the company well:

- Decide who your customer is.
- Know how your company creates unique value for that customer.
- Choose not to perform activities that do not create value for that customer.
- Align all your company's activities to create that value.
- Recognize that meaningful change takes time, so take the long view.

FUTURE STRATEGY

Consultants, pundits, and industry experts have derided Edward Jones' anti-Internet strategy; lambasted its "inefficient" single-trader offices; laughed at its lack of interest in going public; and frequently questioned the strategy of knocking on doors to find clients, yet this company continues to succeed with a face-to-face, low-key conservative strategy. Competitors are cutting employees, but Edward Jones is adding 200 new brokers per month. Employees are key to its future success. Spending almost 4% of its payroll on employee training, with hundreds of hours of annual training per employee, Edward Jones believes that employee education and training are a key to staying sharp in this industry.

With Bachmann headed for retirement, incoming managing partner Douglas Hill is already targeting Canada and Great Britain, with Great

Britain as the eventual launching ground for Europe. Within the U.S., Edward Jones is aiming for 10,000 single-broker offices by the end of 2004 and 25,000 worldwide brokers by 2010, a task buoyed by the fact that Edward Jones now receives over 1 million broker applications per year. While recognizing that European customers may not be as receptive to door-to-door investment brokers, Edward Jones still plans on holding true to what has worked in the U.S. The company believes that even if European expansion is slower than in the U.S., the market can be just as profitable in the long run by paying attention to the same clients that helped it achieve U.S. success: the nonwealthy, middle-class investor.

ACKNOWLEDGMENT

The author would like to acknowledge Jennifer L. Ray, Edward Jones IR in Hunstville, Alabama, for her invaluable assistance in providing information for this case.

QUESTIONS

1. What impact does Edward Jones' investments in its employees have on customer service and loyalty?
2. How does Edward Jones use relationship marketing to achieve success? Cite some examples that reflect the view of relationship marketing as defined in Chapter 11.
3. Can Edward Jones continue to create customer value if it eschews online trading? Should the company eventually give in and offer its clients the same technological advancements that the competition offers? Why or why not?
4. Table 4.1 shows a marginal increase in revenue since 2000, despite the continued rapid expansion of new offices. Will Edward Jones need to deviate from its conservative policies and limited offerings in order to keep revenue moving upward? What would you suggest to management? Develop a strategy for Edward Jones for the next 3 years in order to keep its revenues trending upward.

CASE 5: FEDEX CORPORATION — A CUSTOMER VALUE FUNNEL ASSESSMENT*

"When it absolutely, positively has to get there overnight." Living up to a value proposition like "absolutely, positively" — guaranteeing great service — is not an easy task. FedEx provides high-quality service and has such a great image that it can charge premium prices for that service because customers know that it will deliver. The company's innovative tracking procedures, added to a corporate culture that demands excellence, gives it an additional edge over other overnight delivery firms.

FedEx is a global giant today; however, the early days were filled with great uncertainty about the company's survival. Michael D. Basch, senior vice president of sales and customer service at Federal Express, explained that optimistic forecasts of delivering 300 to 3000 packages the first night were not manifested in the gloomy reality of only six deliveries (and four were from salespeople testing the system) (Basch, 2001). Imagine this nightmarish scenario as of Monday, March 12, 1973: a company with 23 airplanes; hundreds of employees; a Memphis hub/facility; no money; and two customers. By that Friday, only one package was in the system at a calculated cost of half a million dollars to ship! This situation led to an immediate mandate and vision for the company dubbed GET THE PACK-AGES. Over time, as corporate users learned about Federal Express's customer obsession; tracing system; systems and technology; and high-level service experience, the company's fortunes quickly turned. Today, FedEx delivers more than 4 million express air packages on a daily basis.

---

* Case prepared by Jerry Johnson, a supervisor for the U.S. Postal Service for more than 25 years. He currently manages plant operations in Tallahassee, Florida. For further information, contact him at jerryjohnson1@comcast.net

In August 2001, FedEx started handling express mail for the U.S. Postal Service. This partnership gives the Postal Service a guaranteed lift capacity for mail and allows FedEx to gain additional daytime utilization for its air fleet — a marriage that helps both partners. This writer observed day one of the U.S. mail being loaded onto the FedEx jet prior to take off at the Tallahassee, Florida, airport. Amazingly, loaders sprinted across the tarmac between jobs. Here were people making just above minimum wage, but so immersed in the culture of "time is money" that they were doing everything possible to get that plane off the ground on time. In the movie *Castaway*, Tom Hanks plays a FedEx executive who goes to Moscow to convince the FedEx team there that delays are inexcusable; his "tick–tock, tick–tock" as he points to his watch is an accurate portrayal of the importance that everyone in the company gives to quality and on-time service.

FedEx delivers what it promises; communicating that promise is another area in which the company shows its marketing prowess. Its first-rate promotional initiatives feature creative advertising such as the 2001 "don't worry" ad campaign by BBDO, New York, aimed at small businesses. Innovative sponsorships include supporting a team in the Simba Telecon Rally in Uganda and the Southern Heritage Classic, a college football game held between traditional black college football powers every fall in Memphis. Quoting from the FedEx 2001 annual report:

> During a period of challenge and change, only FedEx remains focused on a unique business model — to operate each company independently, focused on the distinct needs of each customer segment, but also to compete collectively, leveraging our greatest strengths, the power of the FedEx brand and information technology. That's why FedEx continues to deliver value for our shareholders, meaningful solutions for our customers and continued opportunity for our employees.

How did FedEx achieve that perceived level of excellence? More importantly, how does it keep that perception intact? The customer value funnel can help show how FedEx maximizes economic value while also responding to the needs of its stakeholders.

GLOBAL BUSINESS COMMUNITY (MACROENVIRONMENT)

Perhaps you have heard the classic tale about how Frederick W. Smith designed the basic idea of a "hub and spoke" delivery system for a class paper at Yale, was given a "C," and told by his professor that his concept would not work. This concept, now known as logistics, is the key building block and process management technique for every major delivery firm in the world.

When Federal Express was founded 30+ years ago, the market for overnight delivery was not large. The Postal Service was dominant in that field at that time and no other national delivery firms of any size existed. Society moved at a slower pace, and "I need it yesterday" was not heard 15 times a day from the CEO's office. How things have changed! As the speed of business changed, particularly in the 1990s, the overnight delivery business boomed and FedEx started earning considerable profits.

FedEx's first customers were the large businesses that provided large volumes of time-sensitive mail and supplies that needed quick delivery. As "just-in-time" inventory strategies started taking hold, FedEx got into the supply-chain business and succeeded so well that the firm was given supplier of the year awards by Dell Computer, General Motors, and Wal-Mart. The Dell award was for superior performance in moving material between Dell's manufacturing facility in Panang, Malaysia, and distribution points in the U.S — an example of FedEx's current growth strategy. Management believes that growth potential is higher overseas than in the U.S. market and the firm is constantly expanding worldwide. Trade barriers have fallen in Asia and FedEx's presence across the European continent is rising.

Organizational demographics also show a growing small business market whose needs are not currently met by UPS; FedEx is working hard to grab that market niche. As an example, Kristin Krause relates the experience of Tracy Melton, the owner of Melton Tackle:

> I sat down with UPS and FedEx and said, "Here I am." ...I needed to be competitive and couldn't use list rates. FedEx was willing to take a chance on me when UPS wasn't. We ship 150 to 200 packages a day — not IBM, but they aren't letters either and that adds up. UPS wants to back up a 40-foot trailer, load it up and drive it to a distribution center. That isn't what we are about.

The economics of starting and running an enterprise like FedEx are staggering. Smith went to several cities before Memphis agreed to help him with the logistics he needed at the airport. Even now, with the firm turning big profits annually, economic downturns and events such as September 11 terrorist attacks can cause major economic problems. In the firm's 2002 annual report, Smith says,

> How did FedEx continue to increase revenue and yields in this difficult economy? With prudent financial management through

pricing as well as customer and product mix. In addition, we deferred or cut capital spending and imposed very diligent internal cost controls on travel, entertainment, outside services, new hires and other discretionary spending. Given the slow-down in volume, we began to "right-size" our transportation networks, making sure that we don't carry excess capacity any more than our customers carry excess inventory.

The natural and physical problems associated with such a business are interesting. For overnight service, one major determinant is distance — how far can you go, and get back, in one night? FedEx flies the fastest cargo jets it can get and still must adjust clearance times on the East and West Coasts to ensure that the planes can get in and out of Memphis within the sortation window at its hub. One physical problem is noise, which ties into the political and legal issues for the firm. In the late 1980s, this case writer was sent to a business meeting in Memphis and stayed in the Sheraton Airport Hotel — a great place, until FedEx planes started to land in the middle of the night. We ended up working all night because none of us could sleep. FedEx is now putting a "minihub" in the High Point, North Carolina, airport. Residents living in close proximity to that airport are putting up a major fight against potential noise pollution, including lawsuits.

Another legal problem is access to markets and airports. As *JoC Week* (2002) reports, examples that affect FedEx are China's assertion that China Post has monopoly control over all international and domestic shipments of documents weighing less than 17 ounces and Japan's decision to reverse its previous ruling allowing FedEx to obtain slots at Tokyo's Narita airport (replacing Delta). It is interesting that fierce competitors UPS, DHL, World-wide, and TNT are joining FedEx in fighting the attempt by the Chinese to gain jurisdiction over the international express market.

The technological aspect of the global business community is one area in which FedEx really shines. The firm has always been a leader in the business of tracking packages and was using optical scanners and barcodes long before those were industry standards; now it is even partnering with AT&T Wireless and Nextel Online to track shipments. FedEx has announced its purchase of the Airbus A380-800 high-capacity, long-range aircraft, taking delivery in 2008. The company has also instituted a com-petition among three firms to develop a hybrid diesel–electric delivery vehicle to replace the current 30,000 vans used. FedEx has partnered with the Alliance for Environmental Innovation to help develop the new deliv-ery vehicle, which is targeted for a 50% improvement in fuel mileage and a 90% reduction in exhaust emissions (*Business and the Environment*, 2002). Another very impressive FedEx technology is what employees call their "secret decoder rings" — a pinkie ring that scans and records a package barcode as the employee picks it up for sortation.

MARKET (MICROENVIRONMENT)

FedEx is constantly seeking collaborative relationships to help grow the firm, as previously noted in the discussion of the U.S. Postal Service, AT&T, and Nextel. According to the *Financial Times* (2002), another example is a partnership with Kodak in which FedEx will provide express service to Kodak stores in China. As Dunham (2002) reports, to help handle security issues after 9/11, Fred Smith and the other CEO members of the Business Round Table have established a secure phone system to help improve communications in case of another emergency situation.

FedEx is handling competition from its two biggest competitors, UPS and Deutsche Post World Net, by zigging when the competition is zagging. In *JoC Week*, Armbruster (2002) explains:

> Specifically, UPS and Deutsche Post World Net have both moved aggressively and publicly into the rapidly growing third-party logistics business. FedEx, while dabbling in logistics, has spent the last few years diversifying away from its core U.S. express business, assembling a large ground transportation network in the U.S. that now accounts for 22% of its total revenue.

"Ground is exceeding our expectations," according to FedEx senior vice-president Bill Margaritis. On February 5, 2002, FedEx opened an additional 31 FedEx home delivery centers, giving FedEx ground coverage for 90% of the country.

FedEx has been given awards for its role as an integral part of other supply-chain networks, so is it any wonder that the company is very picky about its suppliers? In June, 2002, FedEx awarded a 20-year contract to GE Engine Services to perform engine maintenance on FedEx's fleet of planes (*Air Transport World*, 2002). GE Engine is known in the industry as the best contract maintenance firm of its kind. Regarding the night flying noise issue, FedEx has contracted with Really Quiet, Inc. for "hush kits" for FedEx's plane engines (Wastnage, 2002).

The U.S. does not have much regulation of the package delivery business. The Department of Commerce and the Department of Transportation ensure that FedEx meets the minimal safety requirements for transporting cargo. Overseas, customs issues need to be overcome, as well as the previously mentioned political and legal issues.

ORGANIZATION

FedEx knows that the way to remain profitable is to take care of its customers and it does this in many ways: keeping guarantees in place during the holiday season; wining and dining best customers; and bundling services to create value. FedEx won the Web Marketing Association's best transportation Web site award for two straight years, in 2000 and 2001, and *eWeek* ranks FedEx number two in its annual list of e-business innovators. According to Laurie A. Tucker, senior vice-president of global product marketing at FedEx, "FedEx leads the industry in developing valuable interactive services that help customers access, manage and secure transportation services. We are proud of the team of professionals that continues to develop the innovative technologies that enhance the customer experience on FedEx.com."

The business culture at FedEx has already been discussed to some extent. Any firm that can motivate its lowest paid employees to run between work stations, just to ensure that a plane leaves on time, and can get over 10,000 volunteer hours at St. Jude's Hospital in Memphis from its employees every year, knows how to instill the firm's mission in its employees. The company encourages innovation and rewards employees handsomely for suggestions that are adopted. Because employees are treated well, it is easy to understand how the attention to needs is carried over to the treatment of FedEx customers.

FedEx's organizational structure is fairly typical for a firm of its size, with a board of directors, VPs handling functional areas, and station managers in charge of each remote hub site. The firm likes to promote from within and turnover among white-collar employees is very low (and only a 10% annual turnover of all employees). Fred Smith likes to quote President Roosevelt, "Find good employees, and turn them loose."

Smith has discussed growth strategies in recent annual reports. The five-point growth plan is to grow:

■ Core transportation business
■ Internationally
■ Logistics and supply chain offerings
■ e-Commerce
■ New services or alliances

FedEx is also growing through acquisitions. FedEx acquired American Freightways and Viking Freight, "rebranding" them as FedEx Freight (*Logistics Management*, 2002). American Freightways serviced most of the country east of the Rocky Mountains, and Viking covered 17 western states, giving FedEx additional freight firepower across the country.

FedEx obviously provides superior customer value, which means excellent people dedicated to delivering value. FedEx customer representatives have a $2000 allowance that they can spend on any customer, at any time, to make that customer happy (anything from dinner to shipping refunds). As an example, this case writer went to the airport to observe a plane being loaded and was offered a jump seat ride to Memphis to watch the hub operation; the offer shows the pride that these employees have in their company. In sum, FedEx's delivered value meets and, at times, exceeds its perceived value. FedEx is truly a value winner because it has a strong value proposition based on service, quality, image, and price components.

CUSTOMER VALUE AND BUSINESS PERFORMANCE

FedEx is a customer-focused company that believes in making it simple for users to do business with it. Whether via its telephone number (1-800-GOFEDEX); Web site (www.fedex.com); or corporate name (Federal Express repainted its trucks to read FedEx because that is what its customers called the company), a "customer first" mind-set dominates. This approach has contributed to top-of-mind awareness for the company as millions of customers daily say, "let's FedEx this package." Customers appreciate its easy-to-use forms and package tracking procedures, as well as its commitment to high quality and excellent service.

Do FedEx's customers receive superior value? The firm's business performance indicates that it is successful in execution. FedEx earned $120 million in the third quarter of 2002, ending February 28. This is up 11% over the same quarter in 2001 and represents a better business performance than any of its major competitors in a sluggish economy. As mentioned earlier, FedEx had the second highest EPS growth in the U.S. over the last 10 years. The company has found ways to maintain market share in a volatile express market; expand to other market niches (small business logistics, supply chain operations, and ground freight transportation); and become a technological leader in the package tracking field.

STRATEGIC CHANGES

What can FedEx do to improve in the 21st century? Although the steps toward bundling services are a move in the right direction, additional efforts need to be made in that area. The firm needs to do a better job of differentiating and marketing the quality level of its services — stressing the fact that the FedEx value proposition is not just a tag line from an ad. Also, it needs to use its technological firepower to work more towards individualizing the services available to its customers. Individualized service is the wave of the future and FedEx needs to ride that wave into increased value, added care for customers, and increased profitability.

QUESTIONS

1. Critique the FedEx value proposition (VP). How does this VP lead to customer satisfaction; loyalty; retention; long-term relationships; and enhanced business performance?
2. What marketing/business strategies should FedEx pursue to improve its market position in e-commerce?
3. Identify a specific company and detail the lessons it can learn about customer value based on the FedEx business model.
4. What are the critical success factors for FedEx and the industry? How likely are these to change in 3 to 5 years? In the next 10 years?

REFERENCES

Anon. (2002) FedEx Express looks at hybrid vehicles to replace delivery vans, *Bus. Environ.*, 13 (April), 9.

Anon. (2002) FedEx, UPS face China dispute, *JoC Week,* 3 (May 6 pF1), 10.

Anon. (2002) *Fortune* 500: how the companies stack up, *Fortune,* April 15 .

Anon. (2002) GE engine services, *Air Transport World,* 39 (June), 12.

Anon. (2002) Japan to reverse policy, allow Narita slots to FedEx, *Financial Times Inf. Limited,* March 22 .

Anon. (2002) *Logistics Manage. Distribution Rep.* 41 (March), 3.

Armbruster, W. (2002), Going its own way: FedEx charts a different course from competitors Deutsche Post and UPS, *JoC Week,* 3 (May), 11.

Basch, M.D. (2001) *Customer Culture: How FedEx and Other Great Companies Put the Customer First Every Day*, Upper Saddle River, NJ: Financial Times/Prentice–Hall.

Dunham, R.S. (2002), How business is buckling up: security concerns pose big, expensive challenges, *Bus. Week Online,* June 6.

FedEx Corporation Annual Report (2002) Retrieved online June 5, 2002.

FedEx Corporation (2001–2002), Various press releases: October 2001 through May 2002, www.fedex.com.

Krause, K.S. (2002) Serious about small: FedEx sheds image as provider for corporate giants, *Traffic World,* April 15, 25.

Levering, R. (2001) Going places, *Fortune,* January 8, p. 162.

Wastnage, J. (2002) Hushkits: FedEx aids really quiet, *Flight Int.*, May 21, 31.

CASE 6: THE GRATEFUL DEAD — CREATING DEADHEADS BY PROVIDING DROP-DEAD CUSTOMER SERVICE*

What does it take to retain customers and create loyalty in them? This critical question faces all organizations today because customers have a multitude of choices for satisfying their needs and wants. Some valuable lessons can be learned — not from a *Fortune* 500 company or a company with considerable public data, but, instead, from an unlikely organization in an unlikely industry: the legendary rock band, the Grateful Dead. This choice is made because of the volatility of the music industry in which bands come and go on a daily basis and in which response to rapid change is a requirement and has been for many years. The Grateful Dead was also chosen because the author has been actively observing this band for about 30 years and is well acquainted with its unique history and customer service.

Throughout its career starting in 1965, the Grateful Dead grew in popularity until 1995 when it disbanded after the death of lead guitarist Jerry Garcia. It started out playing in a pizza parlor in Palo Alto, California, for $50 a night; in 1973, it played to the largest crowd in U.S. history (estimated at 600,000) at Watkins Glen, New York. This was nearly twice as large as the crowd at Woodstock 4 years earlier. In 1991, total attendance at its concerts was 1.8 million with over 99% occupancy rate. Demand for tickets was always strong, and sales reached $52.5 million in 1994, the band's last full year of touring.

---

* This case was prepared by F. Barry Barnes, Ph.D. Dr. Barnes is an associate professor of management in the H. Wayne Huizenga School of Business and Entrepreneurship at Nova Southeastern University, Ft. Lauderdale, Florida.

Although these numbers are impressive, they do not capture the remarkable fan loyalty that lies behind them. The bond between the Grateful Dead and the Deadheads (as its fans are known) was often a *lifetime relationship*. Some Deadheads even changed their lifestyles to better match the 1960s values of music, peace, and harmony. Many Deadheads moved to the San Francisco Bay area, where more concerts were played each year than anywhere else. Others planned vacations to match the band's touring schedule. As many as 2000 Deadheads ordered tickets for *every* concert during the summer tours of 20 to 25 shows. Over the years, a virtual community of friends developed among the Deadheads as they moved from concert to concert year after year and became a "professional audience." Many fans saw *hundreds* of Dead concerts over the years. Bill Walton, former basketball great and sportscaster, saw 600.

What could lead to this level of customer loyalty? What were the expectations of the Deadheads? How did the Dead match or exceed those expectations with the concert experience? Deadheads, like all consumers, have a set of expectations that determines their level of satisfaction with any product or service and the process of obtaining it. This set includes such things as:

- Reliability or consistency of the product/service
- Availability and accessibility
- Standards regarding tangible aspects of the product/service
- Concerns about empathy and understanding shown regarding the process of obtaining the product/service
- Responsiveness to customer needs and wants

How this set of expectations is met initially determines whether a customer is satisfied and retained and, over time, it determines how loyal the customer will be for the long haul. If each of these expectations held by Deadheads for the Grateful Dead is examined, it may be possible to begin to understand the remarkable bond that developed between them.

RELIABILITY

Deadheads were looking for more than a canned performance that sounded just like the most recent record of the Grateful Dead. They wanted live, improvisational music, music that required their attention in the here and now, music that was adventurous. The Dead was happy to oblige. Its music was an amalgam of folk, bluegrass, blues, reggae, country, jazz, and rock that had been born in the heart of the 1960s hippie revolution, yet continued to develop and grow through the years. No two concerts were ever the same, and the songs played never followed a predictable sequence. Its active musical repertoire was 150 songs at any one time. Each song performance was different from every other performance due to the improvisational nature of the playing. In 1991, this author attended six concerts in seven nights and saw more than 100 different songs performed with only two songs repeated. Thus, the live Grateful Dead concert experience could always be relied on to offer a unique product, which continued to keep demand high and fans coming back for more.

Reliability for Deadheads also meant the quality and consistency of the performances. When things went just right at a Dead concert, a remarkable synergy existed between the band members as they played, and between the audience as well, that created a feeling of joy and ecstasy that is difficult to describe. This was often referred to as the *X-factor*. The band was always seeking this special synergy or X-factor, and although it did not always find it, Deadheads wanted to be there when it did. As concert promoter Bill Graham said, "The Grateful Dead aren't the best at what they do, they're the only ones who do what they do."

Reliability of performances was also demonstrated by the attitude of the band members, who were dedicated to playing as well as they possibly could at every performance. During an interview in 1988, band members said, "We're just now starting to get good at this. We're just now where we wanted to be musically 20 years ago. Even an off-night it isn't too bad these days, but in the past it could be really bad." Rhythm guitarist and vocalist Bob Weir said, "We chase the music just as hard and as fast as we can." Fans knew this was true and respected the continual effort by the band to excel in every concert.

Finally, reliability was demonstrated by the constancy of the musicians in the band. When the band was formed in 1965, the founding members were Jerry Garcia, lead guitar and vocals; Bob Weir, rhythm guitar and vocals; Ron "Pigpen" McKernan, keyboards and vocals; Phil Lesh, bass and vocals; and Billy Kreutzman, drums. A second drummer, Mickey Hart, was added in 1968. During the band's 30-year career, the personnel stayed remarkably constant. Only on keyboards did it have any turnover in personnel. In 1995, during the last concert tour, five of the musicians had been playing together for 27 years, a remarkable achievement for any organization, and a further guarantee of consistency and reliability of performance.

AVAILABILITY

Because the Dead's music was so varied and each performance unique, many Deadheads were not content to simply see the band perform once every few years and then fill in the time between concerts by listening to its records. They wanted the live experience and the possibility of the X-factor, and they wanted lots of it. The Grateful Dead again obliged them. For 30 years the Dead played an average of 77 concerts a year, more than 2300 in all. This is completely unlike other successful rock bands that tour only every few years to support a new album. Moreover, Dead concerts were typically $2^1/_2$ to 3 hours long, but sometimes ran 4 hours or more. On a few occasions, the band played all night long and breakfast was served to the audience at dawn.

Recognizing that fans were spread across the country and around the world, the Dead concert schedule typically included three tours across North America every year. The Dead also toured Europe several times and even played at the Great Pyramid in Egypt. With this kind of availability, it is easy to see why fans could see so many shows.

TANGIBLES

In order to continue to satisfy customers, tangible aspects of any product or service must improve over time. This is another aspect of customer satisfaction at which the Dead excelled. They aimed to create the best possible sound at every concert; to reproduce its music as faithfully as possible; and to minimize listener fatigue produced by noise and distortion in concert sound systems. As a result, the Dead always had the most technologically advanced sound system in the world. In 1968, it helped establish a research and development group, Alembic, that constantly pushed the sonic envelope and created many innovations now used in all concert sound systems.

In the early 1970s, the Dead pioneered the first stereo concert sound system, the "wall of sound," which used no stage monitors. The wall of sound weighed 38 tons, took as many as 40 employees to maintain, and required four tractor trailers to transport. It was so cumbersome and expensive to maintain ($100,000 per month) that the band took its only extended break and did not tour in 1975. In 1991, the Dead pioneered the first fully digital concert sound system. The result of its efforts was the best concert sound in the world and the establishment of new industry standards. Deadheads quickly came to expect this high level of sound quality from all concerts, but were often disappointed at concerts of other bands.

Another tangible aspect to the Grateful Dead concert experience was the lighting. The Dead was never concerned with creating a show or spectacle in its performances. There were no costumes, smoke, explosions, or giant props that might distract from the music. However, with its roots in the psychedelic 1960s, light shows were always a part of its concerts. The lighting effects were always subtle and sensitive to the music.

Another unique characteristic of the tangibles associated with the Dead was its tickets. When it began selling tickets via mail order (see Responsiveness section), the Dead began to add artwork to its tickets. Each concert bore a different Grateful Dead symbol, ranging from roses to dancing bears to skeletons. Each ticket thus became a piece of memorabilia for the fans. New Year's Eve concerts with the Grateful Dead became an annual party in San Francisco hosted by concert promoter Bill Graham for Deadheads. The tickets for the New Year's Eve shows evolved over the years into spectacular pieces of art (see Exhibit 6.1).

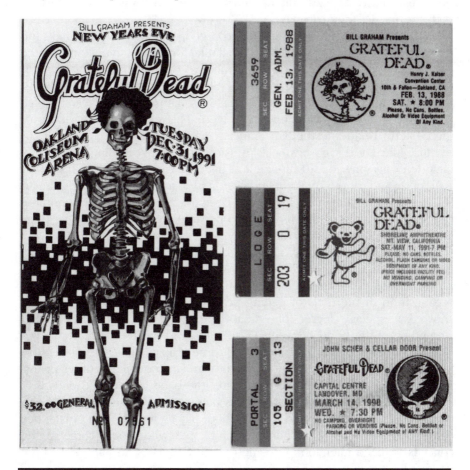

Exhibit 6.1 New Year's Eve Grateful Dead Concert Tickets

EMPATHY

A unique situation with the band's fans arose very early in the career of the Grateful Dead. Due to the improvisational nature of its music and the quest for the X-factor, fans began to record its performances clandestinely and then share them with friends. Although the band recorded its songs on record albums, the studio never managed to capture the dynamics of the live performances. The band recognized this and for many years turned a blind eye to the covert taping. Finally, in 1984, the Dead officially recognized the "taping community" and set aside a "taping section" at each concert with the stipulation that "audio taping is for noncommercial home use only." As lead guitarist Jerry Garcia said, "When we're finished with the music, they can have it."

The sanctioned (and unsanctioned) recording of the band's performances has led to tapes that are available for nearly every one of the band's concerts and has made it the most recorded band in history. It is not uncommon for fans to have tape collections of hundreds of concerts. A huge community of tape traders has arisen through the years, which trades the tapes with no money involved. This embodies the values of the Grateful Dead and the San Francisco psychedelic scene of the 1960s because the band gave away its music despite a recording career that included only one top 10 hit single. This customer-friendly taping policy is a clear indication of the band's empathy toward Deadheads, again strengthening customer loyalty. It has been adopted by a growing number of bands starting in the 1990s and also became the precursor for the huge amount of online music trading today.

The Dead also established a trouble line, which gave Deadheads a real person to talk to about problems with tickets, venue security, or any problem related to the band. This understanding by the Grateful Dead organization of the trials of getting tickets and traveling to see the band showed a special degree of empathy and was another element that strengthened the bond between Deadheads and the Dead.

One decision by the Dead intended to be empathetic to Deadheads led to extremely challenging situations for the band as the number of fans grew. Before 1987, when there were fewer fans, the band allowed Deadheads to sell food and T-shirts in the parking lots before and after shows. Fans freely used Grateful Dead logos and icons without paying royalties. An unintended consequence was growing numbers of people who would come to the concerts with no intention of seeing the show but just to hang out in the parking lot vending area. This created logistical nightmares for the band and local officials who had to manage and police the crowds. A second unintended consequence was the band's loss of tens of thousands of dollars in merchandise sales and licensing fees. Members of the Dead organization worked closely with local officials to minimize problems with the crowds and urged fans not to come to concerts without tickets. In 1992, it began to protect its trademarks and logos carefully and began an ambitious licensing program, often enlisting vendors from the parking lot scene.

RESPONSIVENESS

As the Dead's popularity increased over the years, it became more of a challenge for Deadheads to obtain tickets. This was especially true if a fan wanted to see a concert in a city other than his own. In response to the concern expressed by many traveling Deadheads regarding purchasing tickets, the Dead set up a telephone hotline and established Grateful Dead ticket sales (GDTS) in 1983 (years before the Internet). The hotline was a recording of information about upcoming concert tours, special events, and band member information. This allowed Deadheads to determine easily when and where the Dead would be playing next and how to obtain tickets. GDTS quickly became responsible for selling up to 50% of the tickets for each venue directly to Deadheads via mail order, usually a month or more before they went on sale at the local venue. The hotline and GDTS combined to allow Deadheads to find out when the band was playing and then easily order tickets in advance, a very responsive move by the band.

The Dead was also responsive to fans in many other ways. Many Deadheads believe that the music and even the X-factor were elements of responsiveness to the fans at concerts. Sometimes the music was clearly changed in response to Deadhead requests. One particular song, "Keep Your Day Job," was not well liked by fans and, after 4 years, it was dropped from the repertoire in 1986 at the request of Deadheads.

The Grateful Dead continue to be responsive to its fans even today, years after it disbanded. It continues to release live recordings from its concert archive at the unprecedented rate of three or four albums every year. These live performances from its 30-year career continue to be in great demand, and one ongoing series of recordings is Dick's Picks. For this series, the Grateful Dead tape archivist seeks considerable input from Deadheads, then chooses three or four concerts from the tape vaults to release each year. The Dick's Picks series is sold only through mail order from Grateful Dead Merchandising. Sales estimates for these albums range from 30,000 to 50,000 copies each, demonstrating an ongoing desire by the fans to continue listening to the music.

RECENT DEVELOPMENTS

In 2002, the four surviving original band members reunited after 7 years apart and, in early 2003, they adopted the name "The Dead." They are now touring again and attempting to reestablish the phenomenal bond of loyalty with their fans. This may be no easy task, however, because many new "jam bands" have emerged to fill the void left by the original Grateful Dead. Bands such as Phish, Dave Matthews Band, String Cheese Incident, moe., and Leftover Salmon learned many lessons from the success of the Grateful Dead. These bands play improvisational music, tour frequently, allow taping, and sell tickets via the Internet; they are well on their way to creating a high degree of customer loyalty.

SUMMARY

Today, more than ever, retaining customers and gaining their loyalty is the key to business survival and profitability in the new millennium. People often look to large organizations like Microsoft, Ford Motor Company, or Southwest Airlines when they seek models for loyal, satisfied customers. However, one organization that, at its peak employed only 70 full time employees, had a level of retention and loyalty in its customers that is only dreamed of by most organizations. Deadheads, like all customers, weighed their experiences and compared them to their expectations. What they found for 30 years was a continually surprising level of reliability, availability, tangibles, empathy, and responsiveness in their dealings with the Grateful Dead. Jerry Garcia once said, "I'd like to see what can be created from joy." Having attended 193 Dead concerts over 21 years, this author believes the Grateful Dead consistently created superior customer value and memorable performances for its fans. Whether or not the new incarnation of The Dead can reestablish this same level of customer loyalty remains to be seen.

QUESTIONS

1. How would you rank order the importance of the five service quality characteristics exhibited by the Grateful Dead? Why?
2. How can these characteristics be used effectively by other organizations?
3. Visit the new Web site for The Dead at http://dead.net/the-dead/main/index.html. Examine the various links and assess how well you think The Dead is now exhibiting (a) reliability; (b) availability; (c) tangibles; (d) empathy; and (e) responsiveness. Based on your assessment, do you think The Dead will be able to reestablish its remarkable level of customer loyalty? What steps must it take?

CASE 7: HARRAH'S ENTERTAINMENT, INC. — LOYALTY MANAGEMENT*

BACKGROUND

Harrah's Entertainment, Inc. is one of the most recognized and respected brand names in the casino entertainment industry. The company was founded in 1937 when Bill Harrah opened a bingo parlor in Reno, Nevada. Harrah's grew quickly, building and acquiring properties throughout Nevada and beyond. In 1973, it became the first casino company listed on the New York Stock Exchange.

Gambling is very big business in the U.S.; 2001 saw $50 billion in annual gambling revenues — up from $17 billion in 1976. Harrah's Entertainment, Inc. is a major player in the industry with 26 casino locations in 13 states (Exhibit 7.1). The company tripled the number of casinos it opened between 1990 and 1997, due in part to changes in state and federal gaming laws. Over the last 60 years, the Harrah's name has become synonymous with customer-focused, high-quality casino entertainment in more locations than any other competitor in its industry.

Today, Harrah's is a $4 billion company, and has been recognized by *Forbes* and *Business Week* as a market leader, due in large part to its mission to "build lasting relationships" with its customers. Largely on the strength of its new tracking and data mining system, Harrah's has emerged in recent years as the second-largest casino operator in the U.S., behind MGM Mirage. Harrah's achieves its mission through operational excellence and technological leadership, which enables Harrah's to manage each customer relationship individually.

* This case was prepared by William C. Johnson, professor of marketing, H. Wayne Huizenga School of Business and Entrepreneurship, Nova Southeastern University, Ft. Lauderdale, Florida.

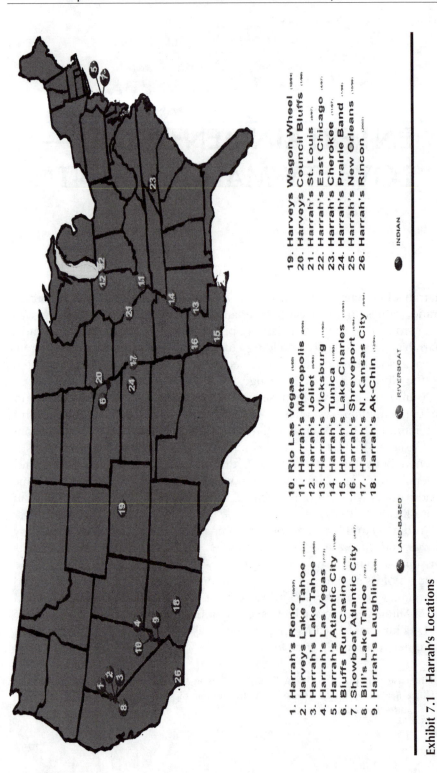

1. Harrah's Reno (1937)
2. Harveys Lake Tahoe (1944)
3. Harrah's Lake Tahoe (1955)
4. Harrah's Las Vegas (1973)
5. Harrah's Atlantic City (1980)
6. Bluffs Run Casino (1985)
7. Showboat Atlantic City (1987)
8. Bill's Lake Tahoe (1987)
9. Harrah's Laughlin (1988)

10. Rio Las Vegas (1990)
11. Harrah's Metropolis (2993)
12. Harrah's Joliet (1993)
13. Harrah's Vicksburg (1993)
14. Harrah's Tunica (1993)
15. Harrah's Lake Charles (1993)
16. Harrah's Shreveport (1994)
17. Harrah's N. Kansas City (1994)
18. Harrah's Ak-Chin (1994)

19. Harveys Wagon Wheel (1996)
20. Harveys Council Bluffs (1996)
21. Harrah's St. Louis (1997)
22. Harrah's East Chicago (1997)
23. Harrah's Cherokee (1997)
24. Harrah's Prairie Band (1998)
25. Harrah's New Orleans (1999)
26. Harrah's Rincon (2002)

LAND-BASED   RIVERBOAT   INDIAN

Exhibit 7.1   Harrah's Locations

HARRAH'S STRATEGY

Harrah's attempts to differentiate itself from its competitors by generating loyalty in customer gambling behavior. Rather than competing on the traditional casino attributes of location and facilities alone, it focuses on providing assurance to gambling customers that they will enjoy an experience that they have come to know, trust, and appreciate. With this brand identity, Harrah's strives to provide consistent value and a reliable, predictable experience for its customers. Unlike the other major casinos, the company derives the lion's share of its revenue — 87% in 2001 — from its casinos. Harrah's focuses on creating lasting relationships with its core customers, slot players, which has led to greater and more sustainable profit growth.

Using a multimarket strategy, Harrah's focuses on customers who visit more than one market annually. It targets the 70% of its customers who play in more than one market per year. These multimarket players have higher budgets than single market players, and they make more trips to casinos. To implement the strategy, Harrah's invests significant time and resources in identifying the best gaming customers and what it can do to give them a more satisfying gaming experience.

For example, when a high roller at a Harrah's casino in Las Vegas walks into a Harrah's casino in Lake Tahoe, he or she expects to be recognized as a good customer. Harrah's can easily handle this situation with the huge database that links all of its casinos. Using this vast database, it identifies customers who gamble regularly and lose a lot of money because a casino's success depends on how much money the average guest leaves behind. The ability to track these data and develop targeted offers includes, for example, direct mailings to customers who visited one of its casinos in the last 30 days. Harrah's then invites them back with special offers. It can also sort players by earning potential (approximately how much they spend and lose) and create a marketing campaign to lure them back. The database can also identify someone who has visited Harrah's casino in the past year and lost a lot of money each time.

A culling of Harrah's customer base showed that 26% of the gamblers who visited Harrah's generated 82% of its revenues. Harrah's discovered that these "heavy users" were not the gold-plated, high rollers, but rather doctors, bankers, and machinists with discretionary time who enjoyed playing slot machines. The majority of these individuals did not stay in a hotel, but visited the casino on the way home or during a weekend night out.

Harrah's also came to understand how the lifetime value of its customers would be critical to its marketing strategy. Instead of focusing on how much people spent during a single visit to a casino, Harrah's recognized the need to focus on their potential over time. Harrah's also discovered that happy customers are more loyal. In fact, customers who indicated that they were happy with their experience at Harrah's increased their spending on gambling by 24% per year; those disappointed with Harrah's decreased their spending by 10% a year.[1] Encouraged by these results, the company now links employee rewards to customer satisfaction.

Harrah's expects that competitors will have difficulty duplicating its strategy because its many locations give it more opportunities to build relationships with customers. Beyond its strategy based on geographic distribution, Harrah's has the technological tools, knowledge, relationships, and experience with customers to offer a value proposition fundamentally different from those of competitors. That gives customers a unique reason to choose Harrah's, not just in one market, but across its entire network of casinos.

CREATING LOYAL PATRONAGE

Prior to 1997, Harrah's operated and marketed itself separately from its other properties, creating a system of "fiefdoms" according to John Boushy, Harrah's senior vice president, information technology and marketing services. Then, in 1997, Harrah's introduced its Total Gold (later renamed Total Rewards) system for tracking, retaining, and rewarding its 25 million slot players, regardless of which casinos they visited over time. For example, a frequent guest at Harrah's Atlantic City, New Jersey, casino will be immediately recognized upon presenting a Total Rewards card in the company's Las Vegas casino and duly rewarded for his or her repeat business.

Traditionally, casinos have treated customers as though they belonged to the single property they visited most often. However, Harrah's has found that customers who visit more than one of its properties represent a fast-growing segment of its revenue. "We want to encourage and reward these customers," said Boushy. "Repeat customers at any one of our Harrah's properties should be recognized and rewarded for their loyalty."

The patented Total Rewards program entitles Harrah's repeat customers to free entertainment, vouchers for food and accommodation, and points redeemable for merchandise. These rewards encourage customers to remain loyal to the Harrah's brand across the country and over time. The Total Rewards program has increased traffic and retention for Harrah's. (where just a 1% increase in retention is worth $2 million in net profit annually). Harrah's also places at each of its casinos touch-screen kiosks at which customers can check on their points or print vouchers redeemable for cash or other goods.

Harrah's is borrowing from the airline industry's frequent-flier model to reward loyalty. Loyalty cards are swiped on the casino floor to monitor the sums gambled and time spent at slot machines and card tables. Players can earn gold, platinum, and diamond status based on their gambling levels. Platinum and diamond cardholders receive higher levels of service, such as not waiting in lines and instant check-in at the front desk. Harrah's also introduced its own Visa card that funnels points, as a percent of purchases, directly into a member's Total Rewards account. By using the card, the customer provides Harrah's with a detailed record of gambling and purchasing preferences, enabling it to solicit that person in more sophisticated ways with its databases.

"Many of our customers have an opportunity to visit our properties just once or twice a year. To find important trends and measure repeat business, we must maintain and analyze a large amount of detailed data over a long period of time," Boushy said. Using the magnetic strips on these Total Rewards cards, Harrah's is able to build records for an unlimited number of customers, and offer "comps" and other incentives based on the amount of money inserted into machines, not the amount won. Harrah's has the capability of analyzing hundreds of customer attributes to determine likelihood to visit, predicted spending, opportunities for cross sell, and much more. This allows the company to target promotions and mailings to individual customer preferences. For example, Harrah's might award hotel vouchers to out-of-state guests, while free show tickets would be more appropriate for customers who make day trips to the casino.

Today, Harrah's network links more than 40,000 gaming machines in 12 states and operates on the belief that, given the right inducements, customers will become "brand loyal" to Harrah's. In just 2 years after introducing the Total Rewards program, the company saw a $100 million increase in revenue from customers who gambled at more than one Harrah's casino. At the time, Harrah's was receiving $0.36 of every dollar that its customers spent in casinos. Harrah's current "share of wallet" now stands at 42%. Since 1998, each percentage point increase in Harrah's share of its customers' overall gambling budgets has coincided with an additional $125 million in shareholder value.

MIGRATION TO THE WEB

Initially, Harrah's Web presence was dull and static and did little more than house communications and financial investment information. Furthermore, several of the company's individual properties had developed their own marketing-oriented sites, leaving the company without a unified face on the Web. All that changed as the company relaunched the Harrahs.com site featuring Harrah's eTotal Rewards program, which offers customers at the company's Harrah's, Showboat, and Rio properties comprehensive account information, benefits, and complimentary offers in real time. In late 2000, Harrah's updated its site further by enabling customers to log on and find out how to earn a higher level rewards card that entitled them to various privileges at the company's properties.

Harrah's seeks to lure business away from competing casinos by personalizing relationships with customers online. By integrating with its Web site a yield management system used by call center agents, Total Rewards members will be able to take advantage of various benefits based on their gambling and spending patterns.

Harrah's wants to discourage gamblers from patronizing other casinos, said David Norton, vice president of loyalty marketing. "Our competitors focus on branding, but our strategy is to extend the relationship with our best customers, using the Web site," he said. "Basically, it's bringing a lot of our Total Rewards functionality, i.e., the offline customer benefits program, to the Web."

The revamped site also leverages the company's internal call center environment and enables hotel customers to access their information on the Web site. Part of Harrah's Web efforts involved linking its call center — used for making hotel reservations — to the new Web site. Web visitors can now send e-mail to the call center; edit customer profiles; provide information such as physical and e-mail addresses; request nonsmoking rooms; and receive special offers at the casinos. "What we really wanted was to use our CRM back-end technology to integrate that onto the online channel," said Tim Stanley, vice president of IT development at Harrah's in Las Vegas. Now the company boasts of having some of the more leading-edge CRM management capabilities and providing a single view of the customer for more than 25 million Total Rewards participants. At an online gaming portion of the new site, customers can play games for fun and to receive credits toward reward levels rather than for money.

ONLINE GAMING?

Although still in its infancy, the Internet gaming sector is expected to continue to grow. Christiansen Capital Partners estimates the Internet gambling industry will top $6.3 billion by 2003. Much of that wealth will come from bets placed by American gamblers.

In a bold move, MGM Mirage, Harrah's major competitor, recently announced a deal with Silicon Gaming to create a new subsidiary called WagerWorks. Silicon Gaming specializes in the design and manufacture of real-world gambling machines, and the new venture aims to launch an online site promoting MGM Mirage brands such as the Bellagio, Treasure Island, and New York–New York casinos. However, it will pull up short of taking wagers online because that would violate Nevada law. Instead, company officials said WagerWorks will be a free hub where visitors can vie online for cash and coupon prizes based on the length of play.

For now, the online casino sector is in a rough-and-tumble phase of evolution taking place largely outside the U.S. Various Caribbean countries play host to cyber parlors, including Casino-On-Net and Golden Palace Online Casino. Australia is also experimenting with licensing and regulating online gaming companies. That leaves marquee U.S. gambling houses such as MGM Mirage, Harrah's Entertainment, and Park Place Entertainment with their foundations firmly stuck in the sand: the Nevada Gaming Commission frowns on Internet-based wagering because it violates state law against placing bets over the telephone. Regulators are particularly worried about minors gambling and are not convinced that any safeguards exist in the Internet arena to verify age.

For that reason, the leading U.S. gambling houses have largely avoided partnering with Australian gaming companies for fear of antagonizing state regulators in Mississippi, Nevada, and New Jersey. Nevertheless, the lure of the Net is proving irresistible. Recently, Harrah's announced that it was taking a minority stake in the sweepstakes site Iwin.com in a deal described by company executives as purely an affinity marketing opportunity. Harrah's hopes to draw Iwin contestants to its brick-and-mortar parlors. "What we have done with this partnership has very little to do with Internet gambling," said Richard Mirman, senior vice president of marketing at Harrah's. "When Internet gambling becomes legal, it's something we'll look into." Harrah's spokesman Gary Thompson was more forthcoming: "Cyberspace is simply another venue, like Vegas or Atlantic City. We think that it will be very difficult to prohibit Americans from participating in online gambling. Every major gaming operator, including Harrah's, is looking at it closely."

QUESTIONS

1. How does the Pareto principle relate to Harrah's market situation?
2. How does Harrah's practice customer relationship management (CRM)?
3. Visit Harrah's Web site (harrahs.com). How can it use this site to practice CRM more effectively?
4. Suppose you were hired as a consultant to Harrah's. How would you advise the company in terms of its presence and activity online?

REFERENCE

1. Loveman, G. (2003) Diamonds in the data mine, *Harvard Bus. Rev.*, May, 111.

CASE 8: "HERDING CATS" ACROSS THE SUPPLY CHAIN*

Customer relationship management is a set of business strategies to get new customers, keep existing customers, and provide additional value added products/services to current customers. A major objective of customer relationship management (CRM) programs is to provide customized products and services at a cost that customers are willing to pay. The premise of CRM processes and supporting systems is that interactions with customers — all interactions, not just sales interactions — should be consciously managed to optimize the value of relationships with customers. Furthermore, CRM should provide a "360° view" of the customer in terms of frequency of interactions and how favorably customers' view those interactions. The CRM system challenge is that this requires a realignment of business processes around the customer — within the original equipment manufacturer (OEM) and across its supply chain. Loosely based on actual events, this case study from the automotive sector highlights the difficulty in designing and implementing necessary business process changes within the firm and across its supply chain in support of realizing CRM objectives.

BACKGROUND

A large OEM supplier (call it ACME) makes and supplies customized car seats to multiple automobile manufacturers. The manufacturing requirements for ACME's customized car seat components change frequently, based on user satisfaction surveys and quality-related warranty work. For

---

* This case was prepared by Ram Reddy, president of Tactica, a technology and business strategy consulting firm (www.tacticagroup.com), and William C. Johnson, professor of marketing of the H. Wayne Huizenga School of Business and Entrepreneurship, Nova Southeastern University, Ft. Lauderdale, Florida. Adapted from Reddy, R. (2000) *Intelligent Enterprise*, 3(14), 44–48.

example, if a significant number of customers express dissatisfaction with a particular feature of a car seat, ACME will change its engineering and manufacturing specifications to remove the irritant. Thus, the primary objective of the ACME CRM initiative was to implement processes and supporting systems that could sense and respond rapidly to changes in customer (and thus manufacturing) requirements.

Before the project, it took 2 to 3 months for a change in customer requirements to "trickle down" to all participants in the supply chain. Because of this time-lapse view of customer requirements, every participant in the supply chain had a different view of what the requirements were at any given time. This view forced participant companies to stock up on various combinations of components to meet current and future requirements of ACME. Not having a current real-time view of the requirements resulted in the supply chain participants incurring unnecessary costs. These costs ranged from inventory holding costs to excessive working capital requirements.

In this supply chain environment, implementing a CRM solution focusing on delivering customized solutions, at an affordable price and with reduced cycle time, was like trying to put out a fire with gasoline. Runaway inventory holding and working capital costs inflated the cost of customized products, turning customers off. The customers of ACME in this case were automobile manufacturers and that enforced a cap on what they would pay for a car seat.

The project goal, therefore, was to realign business processes and supporting systems across the supply chain to enable cost-effective CRM systems. Throughout the 5-month reengineering effort, the project team was constantly pulled in different directions by various functional groups within the OEM and its suppliers. However, the focus on customer requirements; creation of a business process realignment team charter (derived from an actionable definition of the business problem); and executive sponsorship helped overcome these problems.

DEFINING THE PROBLEM

The business problem needed to be defined clearly before processes and systems could be realigned to support the CRM initiative — a quite challenging task. The first attempt at getting a clear definition of the business problem resulted in a simple statement: "We need a CRM system!" This goal was obviously too vague to be actionable, so key personnel from the OEM and its supply chain partner were interviewed to get a clear definition of the problem.

Each interviewee was asked to describe the problems he faced in his particular operational area, without any thought to upstream or downstream processes. Interestingly, although all of them emphasized the need to increase the internal efficiencies of their particular functional groups, none described the problem in terms of the customer. Rather, the business problems described were inward facing and involved streamlining existing processes. Eventually, the executive sponsor from the OEM (the VP of manufacturing operations) became disappointed about the disjointed problem definitions arising out of the one-on-one interviews.

Consequently, all the key stakeholders — such as the VPs of sales, comptrollers, and directors of purchasing from the OEM and across the supply chain — were invited to a one-day "visioning session." The objective was to define the problem collectively from a customer standpoint and use it as the basis for developing a CRM system. During this session, two main business problems were identified:

- Reduce cycle time for communicating customer requirements across the supply chain.
- Reduce costs — working capital requirements, inventory holding, and unplanned shipping costs — across the supply chain to make the product more affordable for customers.

Now, with the business problem clearly defined, the suggestions for solutions arrived fast and furious. The OEM executives wanted to implement an ERP (enterprise resource planning) system across the supply chain, but were reminded of the difficulty that they were already having realigning internal processes in an ongoing internal ERP implementation. That experience highlighted the enormous difficulty of implementing a complex integrated ERP-type solution within a single firm, let alone across multiple firms.

Furthermore, the OEM's infrastructure consisted of a hodgepodge of legacy and client/server systems across which various pieces of customer information were distributed. These systems were unable to store and communicate customer requirements reliably within the firm or across the supply chain. Multiple systems of record contained customer requirements and changes; no single system could access customer information inside the OEM or from supply chain partners. Unfortunately, this situation is all too common. Data warehouses and data marts may aggregate information from various systems of record, but by definition they do not support the level of customer detail needed for CRM efforts.

PROPOSED SOLUTION

The stakeholders who had articulated the business problem were asked to define a high-level solution. This experience turned out to be very educational. The stakeholders had no problem defining a high-level process flow that addressed communication issues across the supply chain. The challenge in implementing the solution became evident as each individual component of the solution was examined in greater detail. At first glance, each item seemed relatively easy to implement; however, the domino effect on the entire supply chain would be substantial. For example, real-time changes in customer requirements for an existing order would lead to a lengthy analysis on the disposition of work-in-process inventories, intermediate goods in shipment between suppliers, and so on.

The OEM had brushed aside previous discussions on these details and deemed them "a supplier problem." However, these details could no longer be overlooked and the company was forced to consider implementing a channel partner relationship management system. Selecting and implementing partner relationship management would require many infrastructure changes across the supply chain. Thus, the OEM decided to pilot the business process changes initially with a Web-based workflow system before considering a partner relationship management system.

Next, the complex task of implementing all facets of CRM — product and service information, field service management, etc. — forced the stakeholders to prioritize different areas of functionality for implementation. They based this prioritization on the business benefits and operational feasibility of each CRM deliverable. For example, although the proposed CRM solution covered areas such as marketing automation; sales; product and service information; and product and service configuration, the stakeholders drilled down and defined only small pieces of functionality that addressed the most pressing business problems. This task became relatively painless, given that the same group of stakeholders had defined the common business problems initially. Eventually, each process and system deliverable was allotted a 2- to 4-month cycle time from the visioning session to implementation.

THE 800-LB GORILLA APPROACH — ROLE OF THE CHANNEL MASTER

The business process alignment and functional specifications for the CRM effort nearly became victims to the 800-lb gorilla, the channel master. When the channel master (in this instance ACME) for the supply chain began to develop the processes and systems for the solution, it assigned groups from different functional areas of the company that were not represented in the initial visioning and prioritization sessions to help define the solution. These assigned groups from ACME did not share the same vision as the original stakeholders; rather, they focused on addressing their immediate operational needs.

As it turned out, these groups wanted to change system functionality and process alignment specifications arbitrarily. For example, the more powerful functional areas pushed changes in processes out of their areas to less powerful ones, ensuring that the status quo was maintained for their respective parent departments. They also asked for automated system workarounds instead of changing their processes to support CRM objectives. For example, the customer service department opposed any change in the way in which it recorded information about warranty work authorizations. The manager was reluctant to add any additional data capture tasks to his staff and wanted an automated workaround instead.

When these functional areas then began to push the majority of the changes out to the suppliers, it was the last straw; the resulting business process realignment and system specifications became disjointed and unattainable. Furthermore, the less powerful departments within the OEM and the supply-chain partners were alienated from the project and did not believe the solution would truly address their business problems.

Fortunately, the original stakeholders were required to review and sign off on the proposed solution. During this review, it became clear that the group's vision was not reflected in the proposed solution. Stakeholders from less powerful departments and the supply chain were very vocal about the lopsided nature of the business process alignment and system changes. It was evident that attaining the project objectives required the willing participation of the entire supply chain and all OEM departments. If some of these groups did not participate in the process design and take ownership of the solution, the CRM implementation would never fulfill its business objectives. As a result, the stakeholders decided to build a team that could define a solution acceptable to the entire supply chain.

COLLABORATIVE TEAM APPROACH — A WIN–WIN FOCUS

The initial attempt at process alignment was unanimously characterized as trying to "herd cats." Fortunately, a new team was formed that was committed to getting the right membership, charter, and executive access for success. The team leader came from outside the OEM; this element would be critical in gaining the trust of the supply chain partners. Furthermore, team members who were nominated from across the supply chain had operational knowledge of the processes to be realigned. They were also empowered to make process decisions — a critical step, in that they were expected to sell the redesigned processes to their respective organizations. In contrast, in the initial failed effort, the most expendable people with minimal operational knowledge were assigned to participate on the design team.

The time allotted for process design and developing functional specifications was a single, focused, 2-day work session. Because each prioritized deliverable's cycle time was 3 months on average, the solution was not very difficult to design. Given the previous resistance to process change across the supply chain, the team members were expected to deliver a CRM solution acceptable to the entire supply chain. Thus, they were chartered to use the agreed-upon business problem definitions to guide their process redesign efforts. They were also empowered to evaluate whether a process change or functional specification contributed to solving the business problem; for example, they considered and discarded many functional specification requests that were cosmetic in nature and found to be lacking in any real business value.

All proposed changes to process or functional specifications were subject to a change-control process managed by the team. This approach helped protect the credibility of the team members in selling the process redesign and solution to their respective firms.

WHAT HAPPENED?

A rather surprising fate awaited the newly chartered team as it embarked on its mission. ACME's various departments found innovative ways to define hitherto non-CRM functions and features as critical to the project's success. An imaginative sales manager insisted that this project could not succeed without upgrading ACME's contact management software. Closer examination revealed that the proposed changes did not directly interact with any component of the contact management process.

Seeing the trend, the supply chain partners wanted to get some of their stalled projects implemented under this initiative. Suddenly, the IT departments from the OEM and supply chain partners needed new hardware and software upgrades. In essence, sensing that the team would successfully develop and implement a solution, the whole supply chain tried to add "pork" to it. Ultimately, the team overcame these distractions and completed its mission successfully. Clear definition of the CRM problem in measurable and actionable terms acted as a filter in keeping the pork-barrel projects at bay. Success was also due in no small part to access to executive leadership within the OEM and across the supply chain.

LESSONS LEARNED

Based on this experience, it seems clear that executive sponsorship and access are mandatory for implementing solutions that cut across the OEM and supply chain. This access is the most important element in implementing process redesign solution deployment. The team leader must insist on weekly face-to-face meetings with key executives, especially those at ACME. This weekly "face time" helps keep "scope creep" in check.

For example, the project team's attempts to explain impending process changes can be preempted by direct reports from managers who have regular operational contact with the executives. Often, these reports do not present proposed process changes in the best possible light. Without regular face time with the team leader to discuss impending changes in an objective way, the executives can and do become alienated from the team's objectives. Moreover, the team leader should also have direct access to the executive sponsors, not to an intermediary acting on the team's behalf. Perception turns out to be more important than reality when successfully selling process changes to the executives of each supply-chain partner.

The team leader also needs immediate access to executives on an as-needed basis to address sudden showstoppers, most of which come from the operations area during process redesign. In such situations, people who are good at operations tend to overanalyze and fail to make decisions quickly. In contrast, executives usually evaluate problems from a big-picture standpoint, take decisive action, and then communicate with their respective organizations. Similarly, the executive sponsors must communicate project status, features, and functionality to their respective organizations with staff support from the team. This makes the final executive sign-off on the CRM solution easy and predictable.

Succeeding and surviving the implementation of such process changes requires deft maneuvering. It is all too easy to become dazzled by technology but ignore the organizational changes that come along with its implementation. If people and perceptions are managed effectively during process realignment, the process and technology components will be relatively easy to implement. Consider:

1. The team leader must learn and work within the organizational culture of the firm. A team leader may be brilliant technically, but a lack of sensitivity to organizational culture can stall the process changes associated with CRM. Rather, the leader must possess a sense of empathy and understanding of challenges facing group members before asking them to change their processes.

2. The members of the process redesign team should constantly remind themselves that people dislike change, not the team or its leader. Getting defensive or confrontational is a natural response to change; it is necessary to listen patiently to people who do so. Agreeing that they have legitimate concerns and then shifting their focus to the long-term benefits involved will usually cause their resistance to change to decline. In fact, on a couple of occasions,

dissenting voices raised legitimate concerns that were not evident during the process design. The dissenters then became advocates for the proposed process and solution within their respective departments. These advocates helped ACME gain credibility for the proposed solution and organizational buy-in across the supply chain.

3. Ensure that non-IT executive sponsors and stakeholders get credit for defining and deploying the solution. It is the team's job to ensure that the day-to-day operations staff who will work with the CRM solution take ownership of the realigned processes. CRM across the supply chain requires multiple individuals across different organizations to work in unison to support a customer with whom they do not directly interact. For key operatives within the ACME organization and across the supply chain, an incentive structure to use the solution must be instituted to ensure success of the realigned processes.

4. Implementing CRM across the supply chain requires a fundamental shift in the way in which the dominant channel partner interacts with its supply chain. Implementing limited process realignment across the supply chain lays the foundation for this new relationship, or supply chain, community. In such a community, everyone works together as peers, despite the presence of a dominant OEM, collaboratively squeezing waste out of the chain, optimizing processes, and sharing the gains equitably among all members. Without this change in mind-set, supporting CRM across the supply chain will be impossible. The traditional "arm's length" relationship between suppliers and the dominant channel partner cannot support processes to sense and respond to the customer with products and services at an affordable price.

QUESTIONS

1. Explain how CRM should *ideally* function.
2. What are some of the challenges to implementing an effective CRM system that are highlighted in the case and typical to many companies considering a CRM system?
3. Discuss the pros and cons of the "channel master" taking the lead in building supply chain integration.
4. Discuss the "human element," particularly the role that trust plays in process alignment across the supply chain network.
5. What are the key success factors for successful supply network integration?

REFERENCE

1. Reddy, R. (2000) Herding cats across the supply chain. *Intelligent Enterprise*, 3(14), Sept. 44–48.

CASE 9: JETBLUE AIRWAYS — ADDING VALUE*

Keep an eye on JetBlue. That could prove to be a successful operation.

Herb Kelleher, cofounder, CEO, Southwest Airlines[1]

We've started to hear that people aren't just saying, "Oh, I flew to Florida." They say, "I took JetBlue to Florida." What that means to us is the JetBlue experience is special to customers.

Chris Johnson, senior VP, Magnet Agency[2]

JetBlue Airways took to the air on February 11, 2000, with the inauguration of service between New York's John F. Kennedy Airport and Ft. Lauderdale, Florida. Since launching its operations, the airline has served more than 12 million passengers with a fleet of 41 new Airbus A320 aircraft and is scheduled to place 12 more into service by the end of 2003. JetBlue currently operates 164 flights a day and serves 20 destinations in nine states and Puerto Rico (Exhibit 9.1). In the face of a challenging industry environment, consistent nine-quarter profitability, including five consecutive quarters of double-digit operating margins, has earned it remarkable loyalty among its customers and has grown the JetBlue family to 4970 employees.[3]

JetBlue Airways is the best-funded start-up airline in U.S. aviation history, with an initial capitalization of $130 million. The company's strategy is to combine common sense with innovation and technology; it set out with the goal of "bringing humanity back to airline travel and

---

* Case prepared by Nicholas W. Bodouva and Jamie J. Bodouva, Principals of Bodouva & Associates, New York, NY, and Doctoral Candidates – H. Wayne Huizenga School of Business and Entrepreneurship, Nova Southeastern University. They can be contacted at nickjamie@msn.com.

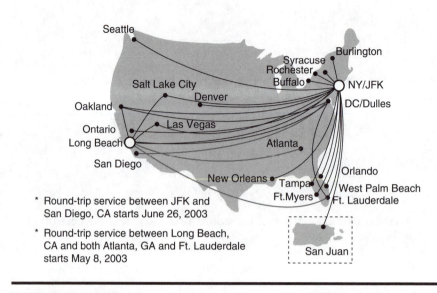

Exhibit 9.1   JetBlue Airways Route Map (From JetBlue Web site [May 14, 2003] — www.jetblue.com.)

making flying more enjoyable."[4] To accomplish this, JetBlue aimed to be the first "paperless" airline by substituting computers and information technology in all areas of its operations, from flight planning to maintenance to the sole use of e-tickets. However, the company is not about efficiency only; it is also focused on service.[5] In the words of the airline's founder David Neeleman, "We like to think of ourselves as customer advocates. We believe that all travelers should have access to high-quality airline service at affordable fares."[6]

FOUNDER AND CEO DAVID NEELEMAN

David Neeleman got his start in the airline business in 1984 when he partnered with June and Mitch Morris to run the Southwest Airlines look-alike, Morris Air. Herb Kelleher, CEO of Southwest Airlines, watched the growth of Morris Air and in 1993 purchased the airline. David Neeleman joined Southwest's top management team as an executive vice president and was rumored to be Kelleher's successor. Neeleman's aggressive, restless, hands-on personality, which was always seeking ways to innovate, created tension and jealousy in Southwest's top management team. In 1994 he was let go from Southwest after a discussion with Kelleher about "why this particular marriage would not work."[7]

After leaving Southwest Airlines and waiting for his 5-year noncompete agreement to expire, Neeleman launched WestJet, a successful Canadian carrier, and developed a new e-ticketing reservations system called Open

Skies, which he sold to Hewlett-Packard in 1998.[8] Neeleman decided to capitalize on his earlier industry experience and develop a new airline. He realized that markets and customers' tastes change and that it is necessary to adapt continually to these changes. Neeleman wanted to follow the successful Southwest model, stimulating demand in underserved markets with low fares. This plan was achieved through the highly productive use of employees and aircraft; this included flying larger planes over longer distances and providing an improved overall passenger experience.[8]

For his new airline, Neeleman began with the strategy of excelling in the attributes that really distinguish the brand at a relatively low cost, such as *comfort, punctuality,* and *courtesy*, while dispensing entirely with airline meals. Three principles (also known as the "golden rules") that followed this strategy include: (1) flawless execution at every customer contact point; (2) making matters right with customers if the execution is not flawless; and (3) treating employees well. These guiding principles have been extended to all levels of JetBlue's operation, internally and externally, and have created unique customer appeal.[9]

COMPETITIVE STRENGTHS

In recent years, passengers have become increasingly dissatisfied with airline travel due to flight delays and cancellations; overbooking of flights; complicated fare structures; mishandled baggage; and lack of customer care. The potential to stimulate demand through low fares coupled with the high level of dissatisfaction among airline customers has provided an opportunity for JetBlue. This airline seeks to provide a high-quality flying experience, emphasizing safety; security; reliability; customer service; and low fares.[10] JetBlue's principal competitive strengths are:

- Low operating costs. The company's cost per seat mile of $0.643 for the first quarter of 2003 is the lowest of any major U.S. Airline (see Exhibit 9.2).
- New all Airbus A320 fleet. With a strong capital base, JetBlue was able to acquire a fleet of new aircraft that sets them apart from most other low-cost airlines.
- Strong brand. JetBlue has made significant progress in establishing a strong brand that helps to distinguish it from the competition. It seeks to be identified as a safe, reliable, low-fare airline that is highly focused on customer service, provides an enjoyable flying experience, and is constantly evolving.
- Strong company culture. JetBlue has created a strong and vibrant service-oriented company culture. The company reinforces this culture by explaining to its employees the importance of customer

	Three Months Ended March 31		Percent Change
	2003	2002	
Operating Revenues			
Passenger	$209,903	$129,091	62.6
Other	7,227	4,278	68.9
Total operating revenue	217,130	133,369	62.8
Operating Expenses			
Salaries, wages, and benefits	56,901	33,561	69.5
Aircraft fuel	35,966	12,984	177.0
Sales and marketing	11,427	9,850	16.0
Landing fees and other rents	16,288	9,939	63.9
Aircraft rents	13,079	9,491	37.8
Depreciation and amortization	10,322	4,712	119.0
Maintenance materials and repairs	3,332	1,905	74.9
Other operating expenses	35,362	27,549	28.4
Total operating expenses	182,677	109,991	66.1
Operating Income	34,453	23,378	47.4
Operating margin	15.9%	17.5%	(1.6) pts
Other Income (Expense)			
Interest expense	(6,194)	(4,187)	47.9
Capitalized interest	1,021	1,297	(21.3)
Interest income and other	772	1,802	(57.2)
Total other income (expense)	(4401)	(1088)	
Income Before Income Taxes	30,052	22,290	34.8
Income tax expense	12,694	9,266	
Net Income	$17,358	$13,004	33.5
Earnings per Common Share			
Basic	$ 0.28	$ 1.90	
Diluted	$ 0.25	$ 0.23	
Weighted average shares outstanding			
Basic	62,627	4,216	
Diluted	68,523	57,470	

Source: From JetBlue First Quarter Report, March 31, 2003.

Exhibit 9.2   JetBlue Airways Corporation Consolidated Statements of Income

service and safety and the need to remain productive and keep costs down.

■ Well positioned in New York. JetBlue's primary base of operations is at New York's JFK airport, which provides access to a market of approximately 21 million potential customers in the New York metropolitan area and about 6 million potential customers within 15 miles of the airport.

■ Proven management team. CEO David Neeleman was the president and one of the founders of Morris Air (later acquired by Southwest Airlines) and a founder of WestJet. David Barger, COO, was vice president in charge of Continental Airlines' Newark hub. The CFO, John Owen, spent 14 years as the treasurer of Southwest Airlines.

■ Advanced technology. JetBlue makes use of advanced technology throughout its organization. All the pilots use laptop computers in the cockpit to calculate the weight and balance of the aircraft and to access manuals in electronic form during the flight. JetBlue was also the first to install cabin security cameras on each aircraft with a live feed to the cockpit crew and, when on the ground, to a central operations center at JFK airport.

VALUE-ADDED SERVICES

JetBlue is a new kind of airline that focuses on people; modern aircraft; great personal service; state-of-the-art revenue management systems; and a single class of service with fares averaging 65% less than those of the competition. The approach is straightforward, with a radical application of common sense that aims to give customers what they want and nothing that they do not want. JetBlue has created many value-added services for its customers by offering low fares with high style, a high quality of service, and friendly crewmembers who believe in service. This includes:

■ Leather seats
■ An uncommon amount of legroom
■ Free satellite TV at every seat
■ Airplane yoga cards (Exhibit 9.3)
■ Assigned seats
■ Ticketless travel
■ No discount seats
■ A "TrueBlue" loyalty program

All fares are one way with a Saturday night stay-over never required; discounts for booking online; reliable performance; high-quality service; and safety.

Exhibit 9.3 Yoga Card (From JetBlue Web site, May 14, 2003, www.jetblue.com.)

JetBlue strives to be customer friendly: computer terminals rotate to show the customer what the agent is looking at; whenever a flight is delayed for more than 4 hours for reasons other than weather or traffic, customers receive a free flight voucher; and a $25 voucher is issued when bags are misplaced.[11] According to Amy Curtis-McIntyre, VP of marketing for JetBlue, "people do not necessarily point to one thing that gives them value, but it is all part of the effort to make everything feel sort of generous and interesting and valuable."[12]

In addition, the value JetBlue offers its customers extends to its corporate culture, which is differentiated by the high-quality service all employees provide to their customers. JetBlue is a value-based company built on the principle that to be extraordinary on the outside you must first be extraordinary on the inside. Every airport employee, from the supervisors on down, is considered an equal player in the company's success and referred to as "crewmembers" (see Exhibit 9.4). JetBlue hires the very best people and treats them exactly the way it expects them to treat its customers. It is important that everyone at JetBlue view the business as the customer does; the company believes this will allow the airline always to provide a superior delivery system that continually evolves to meet the needs and wants of its customer base.[13] As testament to these beliefs, CEO David Neeleman takes two flights a week to hear first-hand passenger feedback, good or bad, and apologizes for or explains any inconveniences the passengers may or will experience. Neeleman can often be seen serving snacks or wrestling carry-on bags out of the overhead bins for passengers. It is also his practice to be "beeped" when any flight is experiencing a delay or any situation occurs that prevents a "flawless delivery" by the airline.[14]

JetBlue believes that values drive all other activities and are the basis for development of an organization. Ann Rhoades, former VP of human resources for JetBlue and Southwest and now on the company board, states that "JetBlue did not want a mission statement nobody reads. They want words that allow everybody to talk together. Having shared values makes decision-making much easier."[15] JetBlue's values are defined in behavioral terms (Exhibit 9.5) and are intended to drive other activities. Management does not attempt to control employees with rules and supervision, but simply to show how its decisions fit with corporate values. The five core values that characterize the airline are: *safety, caring, integrity, fun* and *passion.*

JetBlue's solid commitment to customer value is also demonstrated by its exceptional operational performance (Exhibit 9.6). As of May, 2003[16]:

■ JetBlue's completion factor of 99.8% was higher than any of the major U.S. airlines.

Exhibit 9.4   JetBlue Airways Customer Value (From *Company Prospectus,* June 2002.)

- JetBlue's on-time performance (defined by the U.S. Department of Transportation [DOT] as arrivals within 14 minutes of schedule) of 85.7% was higher than all major U.S. airlines.
- JetBlue's incidence of delayed, mishandled or lost bags of 2.33 per 1000 customers was lower than any of the major U.S. airlines.

SAFETY

*Supports compliance with all regulations
*Sets and maintains consistent
high standards
*Committed to "safety first"
*Ensures sense of security for co-workers
and customers
*Never compromises safety in making
business decisions

CARING

*Maintains respectful relationships with
each other and customers
*Role model at work and in community
*Embraces healthy balance between
work and family
*Takes responsibility for personal and
company growth

INTEGRITY

*Exhibits honesty, trust and mutual respect
in all aspects of the job
*Gives the values a heart beat
*Unwillingness to compromise the values
for short term results
*Possesses and demonstrates broad
business knowledge
*Committed to self-improvement

FUN

*Exhibits a sense of humor and ability to
laugh at self
*Adds value to "customer's" experience
through humor
*Demonstrates/creates enthusiasm
for the job
*Converts a negative situation into a
positive customer experience every time
*Creates a friendly environment where
taking risks is OK

PASSION

*Celebrates diverse needs of co-workers
and customers
*Champions team spirit
*Craves and delivers superior performance
*Shows excitement and eagerness to break
down and eliminate barriers to service
*Colors outside the lines to solve business
issues

Exhibit 9.5   JetBlue Airways: Five Core Value Definitions (From Company Crew Member Handbook [2003], *Blue Book*)

■ JetBlue's rate of customer complaints to the DOT per 100,000 passengers was 0.43, compared to an average of 1.22 for the major U.S. airlines and was second only to Southwest Airlines.

THE CHALLENGES AHEAD

Despite the triple constraints of simultaneous recession, terrorism, and war, JetBlue Airways continues to report profits. This airline has committed

	April 2003	April 2002	% Change
Revenue passenger miles (000)	898,119	496,870	80.8
Available seat miles (000)	1,068,415	592,230	80.4
Load factor	84.1%	83.9%	0.2
Revenue passengers	750,882	447,565	67.8
Departures	5,601	3,418	63.9

	YTD 2003	YTD 2002	% Change
Revenue passenger miles (000)	3,272,965	1,801,145	81.7
Available seat miles (000)	3,986,486	2,206,900	80.6
Load factor	82.1%	81.6%	0.5
Revenue passengers	2,761,499	1,628,482	69.6
Departures	21,012	12,857	63.4

Source: JetBlue, First Quarter Report, March 31, 2003.

Exhibit 9.6   JetBlue Airways Traffic Results

50% of its revenue to growth, which includes: purchasing new planes; expanding number of flights; increasing route destinations; expanding the employee base; opening new facilities; and the recent purchase of LiveTV.[17] There are questions whether JetBlue can maintain its success through a long period of sustained growth while remaining true to its core beliefs.

JetBlue's success also stems from its ability to keep costs low by limiting cabin service (like Southwest, JetBlue has no meals during flight, although it does offer blue chips, blueberry muffins, and blue M&M snacks). Furthermore, JetBlue controls costs by using point-to-point flights (as opposed to hub-and-spoke); employing reservation staffers that work from home; booking reservations online; keeping a new fleet of aircraft; flying to smaller airports; using a nonunion workforce; and offering profit sharing and higher wages to keep employees from joining unions.

As JetBlue expands, will the very things that make it so lean and profitable start to weigh the company down? Four years from now, maintenance costs on the aircraft will increase 25% to $1.6 million each year per year. As the staff becomes more senior, it will demand more tangible benefits and pensions. If the workforce becomes unionized, labor costs will rise (cutting profit by 28%). As the flight legs become longer, the need to provide meals may be necessary and with growth the involvement of the executive staff will be limited.[18] Even Neeleman admits "growth comes with a price, which is why I am so focused on maintaining loyalty and customer value."[19]

Competition from other airlines is also looming and each has its own take on cheap and chic. Ironically, JetBlue's biggest competitor may prove to be Southwest. Profitable for 30 straight years and with the lowest cost per passenger mile of $0.633, it has a pretty comfortable lead over JetBlue. However, according to Gary Kelly, Southwest's CFO, "we do not discount them; we have already automated our baggage-handling and boarding-pass processes, ideas Neeleman pushed when he worked for us. We have got to be prepared for intense competition."[20] For now, the two airlines do not compete directly in many markets.

THE FUTURE

Although JetBlue is experiencing enormous success, the company is not complacent. It realizes that it is only as good as its last arrival. That is why the company focuses on every aspect of the customer experience, from the first interaction of making a reservation to the last of ensuring on-time delivery of the final piece of baggage at the flight's destination. CEO David Neeleman plans for continued success comprise three key goal categories: *people, performance,* and *prosperity.* In other words, great people drive solid operating performance, which yields continued prosperity.[21]

JetBlue's future is dedicated to providing the best airline experience, always striving to surpass expectations and build on brand loyalty. Its success in retaining customers allows the airline to count its loyal base as one constant in a climate overrun by variables. The company has about 600,000 people signed up for its TrueBlue program, which rewards passengers who repeatedly fly the airline. About 1500 to 2000 people register for TrueBlue daily, and the program's members account for about 20% of online sales. Last quarter, 15.6% of JetBlue's revenue came from TrueBlue members.[22]

According to Michael Boyd, an airline industry consultant, "any idiot can get an airplane, fill it with people and charge low fares, [but] getting people to come back again — that is the magic, and that is where JetBlue's strength is for the future."[23]

QUESTIONS

1. JetBlue is at a crossroads at which other airlines have stalled before. Can its formula — efficiency, low costs, and high levels of customer value — remain undiluted as the company continues to grow?
2. Discuss the relationship between JetBlue crewmembers and customers and how this adds value for the company.

3. Compare and contrast the JetBlue and Southwest approaches to creating superior customer value. How does JetBlue's company model of value represent a change agent for the airline industry?
4. How likely is it that JetBlue's competition (excluding Southwest) will be able to duplicate its delivery system and change customers' perceptions of value? How should other airlines respond to Jet-Blue's strategy now and by 2010?

REFERENCES

1. Moore, M. (2001) The top entrepreneurs, *Bus. Week*, January 8.
2. Johnson, C. (2002). Campaigns: JetBlue soars on strength of branding, *PR Week*, September 23, (U.S.), 23–30.
3. JetBlue Airways Corporation (April 2002) www.jetblue.com
4. Neeleman, D. (August 3, 2002) Live Interview - Headlines. MSNBC.com.
5. JetBlue Airways (March 31, 2003) *Third Quarter Earnings Report.*
6. Neeleman, D. (August 3, 2002) Live Interview - Headlines. MSNBC.com.
7. Wells, M. (2002) Lord of the skies, *Forbes,* 170(8), 130.
8. Gajilan, A. (2003) The amazing JetBlue, *Bus. 2.0*, May, 1–7, business20.com.
9. Labetti, K. (2002) Motivating a blue streak, *Potentials*, 35(9), 75.
10. JetBlue Airways (December 31, 2002) *10k Report.*
11. Leavenworth, S. (2002) Assessment of business strategy, student paper, CUNY, New York, 1–15.
12. Goldwasser, A. (2002) Something stylish, something blue, *Business 2.0*, February, 1–4.
13. Labetti, K. (2002) Motivating a blue streak, *Potentials,* 35(9), 75.
14. Wells, M. (2002) Lord of the skies, *Forbes*, 170 (8), 130.
15. Rhoades, A. (September 24, 2002) Interview, Kew Garden, New York.
16. JetBlue Airways Corporation (May 6, 2003) www.jetblue.com.
17. JetBlue Airways (March 31, 2003) *First Quarter Earnings Report.*
18. Beyer, M. (2003) aviation consultant, Morten Beyer & Agnew, Arlington, VA.
19. Phan, M. (2003) Fasten your seat belt. *Newsday*, April 7.
20. Gajilan, A. (2003) The amazing JetBlue. *Business 2.0,* 1–7, business20.com.
21. JetBlue Airways (2003) *Flight Plan — Annual Report.*
22. Barnett, C. (May 23, 2003) Pleasant, profitable, nearly perfect. *In The Media*, jetblue.com. 1–3.
23. Michael Boyd (2003) airline industry consultant, chief executive of the Boyd Group, Interview.

CASE 10: LEXMARK INTERNATIONAL — CREATING NEW MARKET SPACE*

Creating new market space is an approach that forward-thinking companies can use to achieve a competitive marketing advantage. This case addresses, individually and collectively, the six components of new market space: substitute industries; strategic groups within an industry; redefining buyer groups; complementary products and services; functional and emotional industry orientation; and time. The discussion will explain how Lexmark International utilized (and might have utilized) several of these strategic differentiators as it went head to head with the leading manufacturers in the global printer industry.

INTRODUCTION

A cohesive strategy is essential for understanding and improving a company's business performance. This strategy should include a clear approach designed to outthink and outvalue rivals. Many companies are overwhelmed by fierce competition. Some companies lack the ability to recognize and adjust to trends. Others are unable to acquire and exploit

---

* Case prepared by Jude Edwards, DIBA, and Art Weinstein, Ph.D. Dr. Edwards is a market analyst at Lockheed Martin, aircraft traffic management, and an adjunct professor in the graduate school, Capitol College of Engineering, Laurel, Maryland. An earlier version of this case was published in *Proceedings of the Association of Marketing Theory and Practice Annual Meeting,* Ponsford, B. (Ed.), Hilton Head, SC (March 27–29), 2003 2.3: 5–9.

market intelligence that is readily available. Others simply do not have the wherewithal to stay in the market, let alone leapfrog the competition.

Rather than focusing on building market share, market-driving firms such as Amazon.com, CNN, Dell, FedEx, and SAP have revolutionized their industries. These innovative companies have created new markets or redefined their businesses to make competitors inferior or obsolete.

Creating new market space (hereafter abbreviated as NMS) is a marketing response and strategic model for extending growth in maturing or matured markets. This may be best understood from the perspective that specific markets are already saturated with products and suppliers; nevertheless, creative entrepreneurial companies can redesign the competitive landscape by redefining markets to find new business opportunities.

This case study examines the components associated with new market space as a fresh approach to market definition/segmentation strategy. The Lexmark International case demonstrates how NMS ideas can be employed to gain a competitive advantage in the printer industry. Finally, this case concludes by offering guidelines for marketing professionals and managers on how to compete in new market arenas.

WHAT IS NEW MARKET SPACE?

Kim and Mauborgne state that innovation is the only way that companies can break free from the pack when faced with cutthroat competition.[1] It is essential that organizations stake out a fundamentally new market space by creating products or services for which no direct competitors exist. This suggests that the best companies have developed processes and/or strategies for cornering the market or nailing down particular market niches.

Defining markets is not a one-shot effort; rather, it requires fine-tuning and periodic reviews. Guidelines for defining market spaces have been provided by Vandermerwe[2]:

- Take an integrated view of the customer.
- Look for arenas that are greater than the sum of the core items.
- Find market spaces that can be expanded over time.
- Bridge product lines.
- Cut across industry boundaries.
- Span customer activities over a lifetime.

As Kim and Mauborgne explain,[1] creating new market space consists of six areas of comparative opportunity for managers to evaluate in making effective market decisions (see Exhibit 10.1). This approach can work well for early entrants as well as latecomers in the marketplace. (Note that

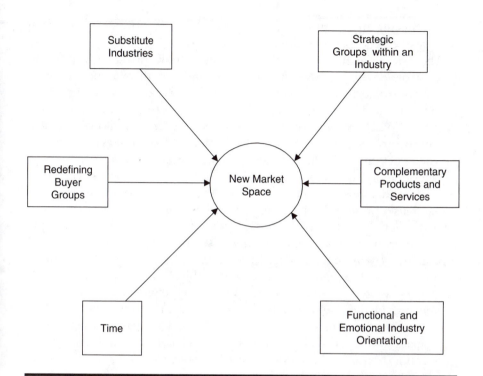

Exhibit 10.1   The Six Parameters of New Market Space (Adapted from Kim, C.W. and Mauborgne, R. [1999], *Harvard Bus. Rev.*, 77(1), 83–93.)

Lexmark International was a late entrant into the global printer industry.) The next section details how Lexmark employed new market space initiatives in its market planning.

LEXMARK INTERNATIONAL: NMS AS A COMPETITIVE MARKETING TOOL

Lexmark International is a 12-year old company that began as an IBM spinoff. The company develops and owns innovative technologies that have won more than 800 awards from technology and business publications worldwide. Lexmark has grown to become a global leader in printing solutions (printers, supplies, and services). In 2000, the company generated more than $3.8 billion in revenue, earned a half a billion dollars in profit, and obtained 56% of its business from international markets.[3]

Clearly, a key ingredient in the Lexmark success formula was its ability to apply ideas that reside in the domain of new market space. Were these NMS principles executed in a deliberate way, i.e., as part of Lexmark's global strategy? It is difficult to know the answer to this query for sure.

It is interesting and worthwhile, however, to examine how several of these elements became part of Lexmark's global marketing strategy.

The first element associated with creating new market space is the concept of *looking across substitute industries*. As an extreme example, one might argue that postage stamps, e-mail service, long-distance telephone calls, videoconferencing, and airline tickets are all competitive offerings. To achieve and sustain an effective presence in global markets, it is necessary to design and execute an integrated strategy that covers the full spectrum of market entries across a variety of industries.

Undoubtedly, Lexmark employed this strategy by using its typewriter products and industry contacts to pave the way for its dot-matrix and low-end laser printers. With the market well established for these products, Lexmark then moved on to the next stage of its overall strategy — tapping market segments for its top-of-the-line laser printers. From the onset, it appears that Lexmark intentionally used a substitute industry (typewriters) to develop a viable market for its emerging high-end laser printer sector. Early generation Lexmark products such as typewriters and dot-matrix printers provided brand recognition, price leadership, and quality signaling to the marketplace; this yielded a competitive advantage over less diversified mass and niche market players in the global printing industry.

Second, Lexmark created new market space by targeting *strategic groups within each industry*. Strategic groups are companies within an industry that pursue a similar strategy, often based on price and performance dimensions. Initially, the company's market included users of laser printers, dot-matrix printers, and typewriters. Lexmark competed in a strategic group that targeted end users that did not have an immediate need for high-end laser printing (the firm created a new market segment in the industry). These customers were located in many different industries and came from various geographical areas around the world.

Lexmark divided the international market into three regions spanning the global market horizon: (1) the U.S.; (2) Canada, Latin America, and Asia Pacific; and (3) Europe, the Middle East, and Africa. In emerging markets, prospects often lacked the purchasing power to buy expensive equipment and necessary training to maximize the printing power of advanced technologies. Because many developing countries lacked the technological infrastructure to absorb its laser and color inkjet printers, Lexmark formulated a strategy to capture the typewriter and dot-matrix business; later, it introduced more sophisticated printers as the economies of each country allowed. Thus, Lexmark targeted these buyers as long-term (lifelong) strategic customers.

Third, Lexmark achieved a competitive advantage by *redefining buyer groups*. It exploited information by collecting market intelligence about end users. As Porter's value chain theory suggests, the bargaining/purchasing power of the buyer is a fundamental market consideration.[4] Lexmark clearly recognized the importance of buyers. As an example, the company provided low-end, but high-quality, laser printers to specific customers whose needs were not met by Hewlett-Packard. (Note: HP laser printers were often priced beyond the purchasing power of average consumers). Since its entrance into the printer market, it had been Lexmark's strategy to introduce a variety of laser printers to meet market needs previously untapped by the competition. As a result, Lexmark outperformed Hewlett-Packard and other rivals in many key segments of the laser printer market.

Fourth, it can be shown that Lexmark obtained a competitive advantage, particularly for it high-end laser products, by offering *complementary products and services* to its typewriter and dot-matrix customers. Lexmark developed channel relationships by providing quality goods and services that met immediate customer needs. Strategic alliances were created with local distributors in host countries that allowed the distributors the freedom to design their own effective marketing strategies and programs. Lexmark also provided training to enable intermediaries and customers to utilize their products better. Later, the company rolled out upgraded products and services for the international markets, as needed. Thus, Lexmark created new market space by providing complementary products and service where the competition had failed to do so and achieved a global competitive advantage in the process.

In considering Lexmark's overall marketing strategy and performance, a fifth point can be stated: the company achieved a competitive advantage over *time*. The company's objective is to develop and keep customers for life. Initially, Lexmark acquired new business by meeting customers' basic printing needs, using dot-matrix printers, other low-end printer types, or services. Many of these customers were located in developing regions of the world with limited funds or capacity to absorb high-end laser products. Over time, as these countries, companies, and customers expanded their capacities and economic and technical infrastructures, Lexmark introduced state-of-the-art laser printers into those markets. A variety of other customer-specific services and products was also provided. This strategic planning process was fine-tuned with the introduction of each new version/product into designated market segments.

In sum, five approaches for creating new market space were effectively utilized by Lexmark International, a late market entrant, to forge a competitive marketing advantage in the global printer industry. (Note: information was insufficient to be able to comment on the functional and emotional orientation of the industry). When existing domestic or international markets are saturated with competitors and their associated products, NMS techniques may provide the needed competitive edge to win

NMS Dimension	Lexmark Strategy	Lexmark Performance
Substitute industries	Typewriters	4 — Successful
Strategic groups	Matched corporate printer line to country-specific needs	4 — Successful
Buyer groups	Low-end, quality laser printers	3 — Somewhat successful
Complementary products and services	High-end laser printers; training and services	5 — Very successful
Time	Develop and keep customers for life	5 — Very successful

Exhibit 10.2   How Lexmark Captured New Market Space

customers and build market share. Lexmark's business performance relative to the five NMS elements discussed is summarized in Exhibit 10.2.

LEXMARK AND NEW MARKET SPACE: SOME LESSONS LEARNED

How can NMS concepts be used as a strategic business tool by managers and marketing professionals to gain a competitive advantage in international markets? As a starting point, the marketing strategy should enhance the business performance. Consider Lexmark's global expansion into new regions. For example, Lexmark recently entered the subcontinent of India through a joint venture with a local Indian partner. It will be noteworthy to observe Lexmark's performance in the world's second largest country over the next few years. Thus, multiple business strategies (some NMS based and others not based on NMS) in different parts of the world need to be executed to achieve marketing advantages.

In addition, the proposed new market space concepts are useful as a complementary competitive tool to strategies that are currently used by companies in any market. Although it is not necessary that all six components of creating new market space be utilized, the right combination may prove sufficiently effective in penetrating and expanding a market base. Five additional implications of creating new market space are suggested:

- NMS advocates that a company extend its competitive reach by looking across substitute industries. In contrast, niche marketing narrows an organization's scope by focusing on a single segment of a market.

- Strategic groups within industries or markets can be cultivated to build new competitive alliances.
- Creating new market space recognizes and effectively manages the tradeoffs between the bargaining power of buyers and end users.
- A product development culture is nurtured. This competitive strategy extends product life cycles and fosters relevant new product and service offerings.
- The concept of time is based on building long-term relationships and creating customers for life. The different ways in which various cultures deal with the idea of time must be carefully assessed.

FUTURE PROSPECTS

Finally, the recent Dell–Lexmark alliance, whereby Lexmark will manufacture low-end, Dell-branded inkjet and laser printers and supplies, threatens Hewlett-Packard's market leadership and is worthy of careful analysis. Although HP currently has about a 43% share of the world's printer market, followed by Epson (22%) and Lexmark (14%), the Dell–Lexmark team led by Dell's PC marketing muscle may alter this competitive landscape considerably.[5] An in-depth study of relevant new market space concepts in this context may be enlightening.

QUESTIONS

1. How can your company apply the market-driving idea of *new market space* to create value for customers?
2. Compare and contrast new market space concepts to niche marketing, segmentation, differentiation, and positioning. What role does the value proposition play in communicating value to customers in a new market space?
3. What impact does the size of the company have in using the NMS guidelines?
4. What changes would be called for if Lexmark International applied new market space thinking to the European Union, Japan, or Latin America? How should Lexmark market its products in cyberspace?
5. Critique the Dell–Lexmark joint venture from a segmentation and market space perspective.

REFERENCES

1. Kim, C.W. and Mauborgne, R. (1999) Creating new market space, *Harvard Bus. Rev.*, 77(1), 83–93.

2. Vandermerwe, S. (2000) How increasing value to customers improves business results, *Sloan Manage. Rev.,* Fall, 27–37.

3. *Lexmark International Annual Report* (2001) Lexington, KY: Lexmark.

4. Porter, M.E. (1986) *Competition in Global Industries,* Boston: Harvard Business School Press.

5. Pimentel, B. (2002) Dell Computer signs printer deal with Lexmark, *San Francisco Chronicle*, September 25, online edition.

6. Root, F.R. (1994), *Entry Strategies for International Markets,* San Francisco: Lexington Books.

CASE 11: NANTUCKET NECTARS — PERCEIVED QUALITY*

BACKGROUND

Nantucket Nectars began rather inauspiciously, when two freshmen from Brown University forsook the corporate world and moved to Nantucket to chart their own course. Shortly after graduating from Brown in 1989, Tom Scott and Tom First, cofounders and copresidents of Nantucket Nectars, started *Allserve*, a boat business servicing visiting yachts in the Nantucket harbor. Nantucket is a small island in Massachusetts located 30 miles off Cape Cod and known for its famous whaling history and rich New England culture.

Watching the daily flow of traffic in Nantucket harbor resulted in Scott's brainstorm: why not take supplies to the moored yachts on a boat? To eat, refuel, and restock, boaters needed to make their way from their boats to the shore to pick up life's little necessities. Everyday chores of washing laundry, grocery shopping, and buying dinner were a hassle. Scott envisioned a service that would offer boat-to-boat service in the harbor. Rather than making the laborious trip to town, boaters could radio Scott on his 19-foot, red Sea Way to place their orders. He described the plan to First and soon the two were in business with their company called *Allserve*, which began delivering newspapers, laundry, and other necessities not readily available to visiting boatmen.

---

* This case was prepared by William C. Johnson, professor of marketing, H. Wayne Huizenga School of Business and Entrepreneurship, Nova Southeastern University, Ft. Lauderdale, Florida, and Edward Schwerin, associate professor and director of disciplinary studies, College of Liberal Arts, Florida Atlantic University, Boca Raton, Florida.

The first summer, the partners delivered a lot of groceries, especially ice, because most of the boats did not have adequate refrigeration systems. They went out each morning and served coffee and donuts and at night they loaded up the boat with fresh lobster dinners from a local restaurant. However, *Allserve* was not merely a delivery service. The cofounders were willing to do anything to get the business off the ground, so they cleaned boats and shampooed dogs for visitors who traveled with their pets.

The service became so popular that soon the founders expanded the *Allserve* fleet to include three boats. The business expanded from its floating store to extending services to land dwellers out of a little shore-side shack that the owners converted into the *Allserve General Store*, which is still located on the harbor's Straight Wharf.

During their first winter in business, while mixing fruits in a blender, the partners created peach juice based on Tom First's memory of a peach nectar that he had tasted while traveling in Spain. They perfected the peach nectar recipe and planned to offer the Nantucket Nectars juice at the *Allserve General Store* and onboard the *Allserve* boats. Bottling the juice offered a challenge. Because they could not afford a professional bottler, the two men improvised, using empty milk cartons and soda, beer, and wine bottles. Their juice was an immediate success; however, their business was not. The all-natural juice, although easy to sell, was difficult to store and spoiled quickly. Six months into their venture, having already pooled their combined savings of $17,000, they contracted with an independent bottler in upstate New York to handle the process. Costs for their first batch topped $14,000, and the partners knew they had to sell a lot of juice just to cover their expenses.

MARKETING

The founders discovered quickly that the most effective way to market their juice was to get people to taste it. However, consumers had to be able to buy the juice at their local stores, so this presented a "catch 22" of sorts. Because the duo spent most of their initial budget on labels and production, they undertook distribution themselves. They met with store owners; took orders; loaded and unloaded trucks; stocked shelves; collected money; and ran the warehouse. In short, they did it all. They quickly discovered to their dismay that they were becoming a distribution company, rather than focusing on improving the juice and creating new flavors. In time, they would sell the distribution side of the business and hire outside distributors to sell the product, now available in over half the states, Latin America, France, Korea, Canada, and Britain. Although Nantucket Nectars initially distributed its products through health food and specialty stores, today it sells its line of products in convenience stores and supermarkets.

As customers flocked to the product, early sales figures were encouraging; yet the company was losing money. Scott and First eventually identified the problem: they were charging less for a bottle of juice than it cost them to produce it, grossing less than 5% a case. Not only did they learn a valuable lesson in cost accounting, but also that customers "buy quality." The price of the product was not as important as the quality they provided; customers are attracted to value, not simply low prices.

The company's promotional strategy was centered almost exclusively on its origins, with the founders telling their story in folksy radio spots. Radio was a perfect medium to showcase not only their products but also the unique culture of Nantucket Nectars. Scott and First became almost instant media stars, using a natural, laid-back approach to tell the story of their company and its products. In each of the spots, the founders offered a bit of inside information on the company. For example, in one ad, they talked about the early days of selling the peach nectar off the *Allserve* boat. The bulk of their advertising is still in radio in cities across the country, although they do a limited amount of print advertising and maintain a Web site (www.juiceguys.com).

The hallmark of their marketing strategy continues to be the product. The company sells only fruit juice drinks, enabling it to combine soft-drink marketing with rising health awareness. Consumers are looking for high-quality beverages with high percentages of real fruit juice and pure ingredients and are willing to pay for them. To that end, Nantucket Nectars determines to create the best quality product in the juice market. In fact, through an internal program called the Quality Juice Evolution, it follows a strict set of standards to guarantee that each bottle of its juice is high quality and the best tasting that it can be. The Nantucket Nectars line now has 36 flavors, including fruit juices, iced teas, and lemonades. The company has introduced a line called Super Nectars that are iced teas and fruit juices containing herbs, vitamins, and minerals, thus capitalizing on the growing "neutraceutical" market. The products are mixed and bottled in four bottling plants located strategically across the country. Each location was carefully chosen to facilitate the distribution network.

Although the products represent a key differentiation, so does the company's packaging. Glass plays a big part in Nantucket's strategy, conveying the message of quality. Nantucket uses rather unique proprietary packages: a 12-ounce bottle, a 17.5-ounce bottle, and, most recently, a 36-ounce bottle. Even the bottle caps are unique. Each purple bottle cap features a real fact about Nantucket Island and Nantucket Nectars. The stories featured on the bottle caps help customers understand the philosophy and character that distinguishes Nantucket Island and Nantucket Nectars.

CORPORATE CULTURE

Nantucket Nectars has developed a unique corporate culture, which plays a major role in its marketing success and has shaped its management style and work environment. The corporate culture is reflected in its mission statement and core values; community service commitment; support of environmental causes; and corporate image.

The corporate image is created around the story of the cofounders, Tom First and Tom Scott. Tom and Tom are "juice guys," blonde beach boys who represent fun, a laid-back lifestyle, and the Nantucket Island mystique. These juice guys wear jeans and T-shirts to work and bring their dogs, Becky and Pete, to work with them. However, Tom and Tom are also hardworking, free-spirited young entrepreneurs whose core values include providing a quality product and quality service to their customers, as well as a quality work environment for their employees.

As part of the local business community, the juice guys wanted to become involved in local environmental issues and to support causes for health and wellness. Therefore, Tom and Tom have recently launched Juice Guys Care, their social responsibility program, by teaming up with the city of Cambridge and donating seven recycling bins to be placed in and around their Harvard Square headquarters

The corporate image of the juice guys and the Tom and Tom story are communicated to the public and customers via slogans, folksy radio ads, a colorful Web site, and bottle cap facts about Nantucket lore and the cofounders. Many of the cap facts are simply memories and fun island stories from Tom and Tom's early years on Nantucket. Many of the facts refer to old island legends and characters that make Nantucket unique and colorful. The bottle caps are designed to tell the story of Nantucket Island and Nantucket Nectars.

Although Tom and Tom are the original juice guys, they are not the only juice guys. Customers automatically join the juice guy fraternity by enjoying Nantucket Nectars. According to Tom and Tom, if you buy Nantucket Nectars, you are a juice guy. If you sell Nantucket Nectars, you are a juice guy. If you make Nantucket Nectars, you are a juice guy. Because the term *juice guys* is not gender specific, women are included; anyone can be part of the juice guy team. The juice guy story, philosophy, and credo shape Nantucket Nectars' corporate culture and management style. A positive corporate culture is vital to the survival and success of all companies, but this is especially true for start-up companies where hard-driving employees typically put in long hours for relatively low pay.

The lack of a clearly defined positive corporate culture can keep a new company from ever getting off the ground.

A company's culture should communicate to everyone in the company, from bottom to top, what business it is in and who its customer is. A company's culture is reflected in its employees' behaviors, values, and expectations. When employees understand and share their company's mission and values, they are more likely to be enthusiastic about achieving its goals and therefore the company becomes more prosperous.

A company's culture is typically articulated by its founders early in its existence. At Nantucket Nectars, First and Scott deliberately set out to foster an entrepreneurial, freewheeling corporate culture, with no hierarchy, no dress code, and few job titles. Like Tom and Tom, the employees do not wear suits and ties to work and many of them regularly bring their dogs with them. According to the company's mission credo, the stated purpose is

> ... to create a work environment that promotes entrepreneurship, honesty, mutual respect, fairness, orderliness, diversity and conscientious hard work. Juice Guys will be given a clear definition of their responsibilities and will be expected to meet those responsibilities in a creative, energetic, and timely manner. The work atmosphere should positively impact each of our lives, support, but not intrude upon our private lives.

The Nantucket Nectar participatory management style combines a dual emphasis on individual empowerment as well as teamwork and collaboration. Nantucket Nectars tries to recruit entrepreneurial types who believe in the American Dream, hard work, and success and prosperity. Employees are empowered by being given the opportunity to make decisions; use their judgment; and make mistakes and learn from them. Employees have a vested interest in the success of the business that stems from being given free rein, creating their departments and seeing the difference that they can make. Tom and Tom regularly communicate their dreams and the importance of setting individual goals, as well as company goals, and accomplishing them. Constant communication is used to keep employees involved and passionate about the quality of the product and success of the business.

The company's participatory management style stresses the importance of teamwork. Weekly staff meetings include employee guest speakers who stand up and talk about their lives and what inspires them. The purpose of this exercise is to encourage respect for what other people do and an understanding of who they are and how they are helping the company.

Employees are urged to maintain an even balance between work life and family life. They are encouraged to stay physically active; to continue educating themselves in areas of interest to them; to stay informed; and to make suggestions about company policies and procedures. Nantucket Nectar employees are also encouraged to help improve the community by volunteering on a regular basis to work on community issues and problems of interest to them. To facilitate community involvement, all employees are given two paid volunteer days per year for community service.

One of the biggest challenges currently facing Nantucket Nectars is how to maintain its unique, positive corporate culture during a period of explosive growth. As a company grows rapidly, it becomes more difficult to maintain a team atmosphere and to communicate company values and goals to those who work in the field. Now, as its juice sales exceed 50 million, Nantucket Nectars is outgrowing its free-spirited fraternity house culture and Tom and Tom are grappling with how to manage that growth without destroying the entrepreneurial spirit and participatory management style that have made the company special.

INDUSTRY AND COMPETITION

The beverage industry (all beverage categories, carbonated and noncarbonated) continues its uninterrupted growth, growing just over 3% to 30 billion gallons in 1997. Breaking this down in per capita terms, every man, woman, and child consumed 111 gallons of beverages during that year. According to *Beverage Digest*, a leading beverage trade publication, the soft drink industry (including carbonated and noncarbonated alternative soft drinks) grew less than 1% from 1996 to 1997; sales of shelf-stable (single-serve glass bottles) juices and juice drinks grew 21.6% during the same period. Juice and juice drinks, the primary market for Nantucket Nectars, represent a small but healthy category of the total soft drink market (see Exhibit 11.1). Since 1992, the category has averaged nearly 20% annual growth rate (see Exhibit 11.2).

As the decline in consumption of carbonated beverages continues, consumer research has found that 38% of those surveyed are drinking fewer carbonated beverages than they were a year ago. Instead of those carbonated creations, consumers are drinking water and fruit juices, whose sweetness appeals to many consumers. Of those who had reduced soft drink consumption, 65% reported that they now drink water, while 40% now substitute juice for some or all of those drinking occasions. Another 18% have opted instead for tea or iced tea. All of these alternatives share a common attribute — stronger positive health benefits than soft drinks.

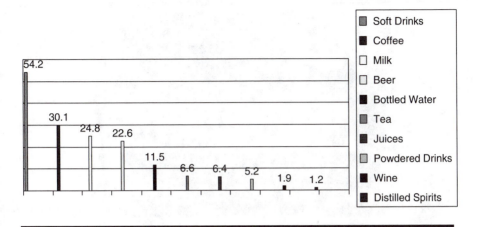

Exhibit 11.1   Per Capita Beverage Consumption, 1997 (Gallons Per Person)

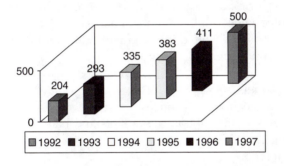

Exhibit 11.2   Fruit Juice and Juice Drink Sales, 1992 to 1997 (in Millions of Cases)

Nonetheless, sales of fruit juices and juice drinks dropped 2%, from $10.8 billion in 2001 to $10.5 billion in 2002. Juices account for 60% of sales, with the remainder going to juice drinks. Projections are for less than 1% growth from 2002 to 2007, although this could be higher by increasing per capita value through more product introductions and convincing consumers that juices are a convenient beverage (i.e., the use of aseptic packaging; see Exhibit 11.3). Given Americans' battle with obesity and the rising rate of diabetes, the current trend is toward lower-calorie (especially lower-carbohydrate) drinks, which has resulted in a growing market for sugar-free, fruit-flavored beverages. In addition, considering the growing Hispanic population, tropical juice flavors such as guava, mango, and pineapple are growing in popularity.

The $53 billion soft drink industry is highly segmented according to product type and channel. The major retail soft drink categories include:

Exhibit 11.3   Example of Aseptic Packaging

carbonated soft drinks; ready-to-drink (RTD) teas; sports drinks; bottled water; and juice/juice drinks. With annual sales volume of nearly $60 billion, the carbonated soft drink segment still dominates the industry. Major retail channel segments include

- Supermarkets
- Convenience stores (C-stores)
- On-premise consumption (restaurants and bars)
- Vending
- Club stores
- Food service
- Drug/mass merchandisers

Although supermarkets, convenience stores, and health food stores have long carried fruit juices and juice drinks, these products are increasingly available in mass merchandisers, drug stores, and other retail outlets. In 1997, the amount of fruit juice sold through convenience stores increased 7% to 75.1 million gallons. In the drug/mass merchandiser channel, volume grew 3.6% to 72.7 million gallons.

Nantucket Nectars competes directly against other fruit juice and fruit drink (new age) producers such as Snapple, Mistic, Fruitopia, Arizona Ice Tea, Ocean Spray, and Odwalla, to name a few. The company's revenue growth has far outstripped its chief rivals, however (see Exhibit 11.4). Profit margins have become increasingly squeezed, especially in the supermarket and C-store channels, where price competition is the norm. In fact, the retail price per ounce of carbonated soft drinks is the same

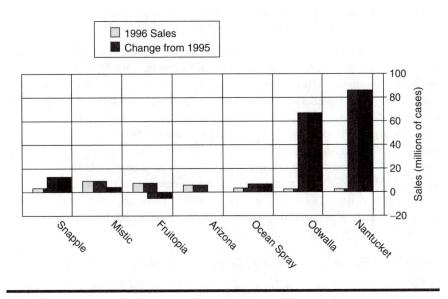

Exhibit 11.4   Nantucket Nectars' Competitive Position

today as it was in 1975, underscoring the nature of price competition in the soft drink industry. Nantucket has been able to maintain premium pricing over its competitors due to the higher juice content and natural ingredients that it offers in its products. Other product–market competitors include

- Carbonated soft drinks
- Fresh and juice products made from concentrate
- Sports drinks (isotonics)
- Energy drinks (e.g., Red Bull)
- Iced coffees
- Smoothies
- Ready-to-drink iced tea products

The primary battleground in the soft drink industry continues to be the retail shelf. Failure to secure retail facings and warehouse slots can often doom an otherwise good product. The industry heavyweights, such as Coke, Pepsi (including its Gatorade brand), and Ocean Spray tend to dominate the retail beverage aisle, often squeezing out smaller rivals. This will become a major challenge to Nantucket as it expands distribution beyond health food and specialty stores to more traditional retail outlets.

GROWTH AND PERFORMANCE

Nantucket Nectars has been a true entrepreneurial success story, growing from a start-up delivery business to a company with $50 million in revenues in 1997. The company's early expansion was fueled by the owners' pooled investments; however, additional capital was required if the company wanted to move to the next level. Former Alamo Rent-a-Car chairman Michael Egan eventually invested $500,000 and took 50% ownership in Nantucket Nectars. In early 1998, Ocean Spray bought a substantial interest in the company, essentially replacing Michael Egan as its financial partner. The partnership with Ocean Spray allowed Nantucket to remain a private company independently run by its cofounders. However, Nantucket Nectars did not stay independent for long; it was acquired by Cadbury Schweppes in May, 2002.

Nantucket Nectars' sales have risen steadily; 1998 revenues were estimated at $60 million, making it one of Inc magazine's 20 fastest-growing private companies (see Exhibit 11.5 for annual sales since 1993). The company continues to seek attractive growth opportunities, such as the Nantucket Nectars Fall Harvest creation available in three varieties: apple cider, cranberry apple cider and peach apple cider. Unlike traditional apple juice, these cider products are coarsely filtered to allow more apple into the bottle. The Fall Harvest line-up is 100% not-from-concentrate fruit juice and, like all Nantucket Nectars, is pasteurized and all natural, with no artificial colors, flavors, or preservatives. Other new product introductions include Nantucket Nectars Summertime and its recent product hit Nectar-Fizz, a healthy, lightly carbonated juice drink offered in six flavors (Exhibit 11.6).

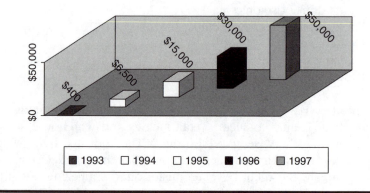

Exhibit 11.5   Nantucket Nectars' Revenues, 1993 to 1998 ($000)

Blackberry
Lemonade
Pink Grapefruit

Cranberry
Orange Mango
Raspberry Lime

Exhibit 11.6   Nantucket NectarFizz (New Product)

QUESTIONS

1. Suppose you were hired as the director of marketing communications for Nantucket Nectars. Write out a statement that conveys Nantucket Nectars' unique selling proposition.
2. Evaluate Nantucket Nectars' positioning strategy. On what is its brand positioning based?
3. Discuss how Nantucket Nectars has raised the perceived quality for its brand. Does the Nantucket Nectars brand represent a good value? Why or why not?
4. What is unique about Nantucket Nectars' corporate image and culture? What are some of the possible advantages and disadvantages of its corporate culture?

5. How has Nantucket Nectars' corporate culture shaped its management style and work environment? Describe its management style in detail. Does this particular style make a contribution to overall customer value?

6. In what ways is corporate culture useful or necessary to the survival or success of a start-up company? of a mature company?

7. As a company grows and develops, how does (should) the corporate culture evolve?

CASE 12: RUBBERMAID — MARKET ORIENTATION*

The Rubbermaid Division of Newell Rubbermaid, Inc. is a multinational company that manufactures and markets a wide array of food storage and preparation products; children's products; casual furniture; organized storage; and waste containers for consumer, commercial, and industrial use. Rubbermaid continues to be a successful American company despite the economic downturns and stiff competition it has faced throughout its history.

Rubbermaid's vision is to grow as a leading global business by creating the best value solutions as defined by its customers. Throughout its heyday in the 1980s and early 1990s, its customer solution orientation set it apart from a market made up of "humdrum" products. For three consecutive years in the 1990s, the company made *Fortune* magazine's list of one of America's 10 most admired corporations. It even won the coveted number-one spot in *Fortune's Survey of America's Most Admired Companies*. In 1999, the Home Furnishing Network's brand study found Rubbermaid to be the number-one name in home and food storage. According to Newell/Rubbermaid's own research at the time, the Rubbermaid brand also had an unprecedented 90% consumer loyalty rate.

Rubbermaid's mission is to be the leading marketer under a global umbrella of brands of products and services that are responsive to customer needs and trends and make life more productive and enjoyable. It endeavors to achieve this mission by creating the best value for the consumer, commercial, and industrial markets. See Exhibit 12.1 and Exhibit 12.2 for a 20-year summary of Rubbermaid's financial performance.

---

* This case was prepared by William C. Johnson, professor of marketing, Huizenga School of Business and Entrepreneurship, Nova Southeastern University; Ft. Lauderdale, Florida, and James Barry, adjunct professor of marketing, Florida Metropolitan University, Fort Lauderdale, FL and Florida Atlantic University, Boca Raton, Florida.

Year	Sales ($M)	Operating Income ($M)	Net Income ($M)	EPS
2002	$2,592	$215	a	a
2001	$2,566	$201	a	a
2000	$2,809	$326	a	a
1999	$2,907	$208	a	a
1998	$2,462	$251	$132	$1.15
1997	$2,305	$235	$143	$0.95
1996	$2,355	$273	$152	$1.01
1995	$2,344	$268	$60	$0.38
1994	$2,169	$356	$228	$1.42
1993	$1,960	$346	$211	$1.32
1992	$1,805	$294	$184	$1.17
1991	$1,667	$257	$163	$1.02
1990	$1,534	$233	$144	$0.90
1989	$1,452	$217	$125	$0.78
1988	$1,292	$183	$107	$0.67
1987	$1,096	$169	$91	$0.57
1986	$865	$143	$75	$0.47
1985	$748	$119	$62	$0.40
1984	$677	$99	$54	$0.34
1983	$556	$86	$45	$0.29

[a] Not separately reported from consolidated Newell Rubbermaid.

Exhibit 12.1   20-Year Summary of Rubbermaid's Financial Performance

BACKGROUND

In 1920, five local businessmen formed the Wooster Rubber Company in a rented building in Wooster, Ohio, to manufacture the Sunshine brand toy balloon. Horatio Ebert and Errett Grable then purchased the company in the mid-1920s. During the early 1930s, while shopping at a department store, Grable noticed a line of houseware products that had been developed by James Caldwell. Caldwell's product line, which he named Rubbermaid, included rubber dustpans, drain board mats, soap dishes, and sink stoppers. Grable contacted Caldwell and the two men agreed to join their businesses. In 1943, Wooster Rubber began producing Rubbermaid brand products. During the 1950s, Wooster Rubber produced its first plastic product, a dishpan, along with a line of commercial goods aimed at hotels,

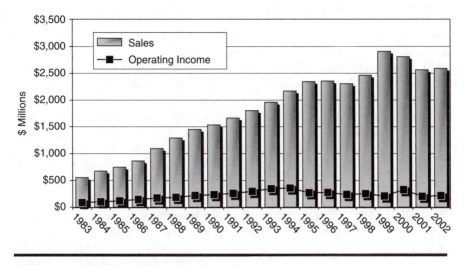

Exhibit 12.2   Rubbermaid Financial Performance

restaurants, and institutions. The company went public in 1955 and 2 years later changed its name to Rubbermaid.

During the decade of the 1980s, Rubbermaid experienced phenomenal growth; sales increased fivefold from just over $300 million to over $1.5 billion. Rubbermaid also went on an acquisition binge, acquiring Cont-Tact (decorative coverings) in 1981; Little Tikes (plastic toys) in 1984; Gott leisure and recreational products in 1985; SECO floor products in 1986; Microcomputer Accessories in 1986; and Viking Brush (cleaning supplies) in 1987. Rubbermaid then formed a joint venture with the French company Allibert in 1989 to produce resin furniture and, the following year, established a joint venture with the Curver Group (purchased Curver in late 1997) of the Dutch chemical company DSM to market housewares in Europe, Africa, and the Middle East (Rubbermaid ended the joint venture with DSM in 1994).

Growth through acquisition continued in the 1990s with Rubbermaid's purchase of EWU A.G., a Swiss floor care supplies company. It also acquired Eldon Industries, a producer of office accessories, and formed a joint venture with the Hungarian Group CIPSA, the number-one housewares company in Mexico. In 1992, Rubbermaid purchased Iron Mountain Range, a manufacturer of playground equipment along with Carex, Inc., a producer of walkers and canes, giving Rubbermaid a toehold in the home health-care market. Finally, Rubbermaid acquired stroller-maker Graco Children's Products in order to shore up its juvenile products business.

Beginning in early 1997, Rubbermaid began to extend its highly respected brand name through a series of licensing agreements as well.

It partnered with Town & Country Living — a 40-year-old family mass-market supplier of table linens, decorative pillows, and bath products — to produce a line of shower curtains, bath rugs, liners, curtain rings, and tension rods. This move allowed Rubbermaid to expand its presence from retailers' houseware departments into their home textiles departments that would carry Rubbermaid's new bath products line. Moreover, this agreement was part of Rubbermaid's strategy to offer consumers a total room approach. Since 2000, Rubbermaid has licensed its Graco and Little Tikes lines through The Beanstalk Group as a way to further penetrate the market for juvenile furniture and products. Finally, the company granted a license to Amway Corporation in 1997 to market a line of food storage items under an exclusive arrangement.

Surprisingly, Rubbermaid began to falter in the late 1990s, in part because of its inability to meet the service demands of a major retail customer, Wal-Mart (primarily in not meeting Wal-Mart's stringent on-time delivery schedule). Wal-Mart also significantly cut back Rubbermaid's shelf space and gave it to smaller competitors after Rubbermaid insisted on passing along higher raw material costs. In early 1999, expecting to turn things around, the Newell Company acquired Rubbermaid. Newell knew that declining customer service was an area of chief concern, but was confident that it could correct this.

PERFORMANCE

During the 1980s, Rubbermaid routinely posted double-digit sales growth. Over the past 20 years, sales had grown at a compounded annual growth rate (CAGR) of 8.4%/year, while operating income grew at a CAGR of 5%/year. Prior to the integration with Newell, CAGRs for sales, income, and EPS were 10.4, 7.5 and 9.6%/year, respectively. Operating margins have averaged 13% of sales over the past two decades, an exceptional return for a predominantly commodity-oriented product line. Not long after the merger, Newell Rubbermaid cut profit forecasts three times. For 2001, sales were off 2.4% and new income was down 42%, with fall share prices reflecting this.

ENVIRONMENT

Rubbermaid has responded to changing public attitudes regarding the environment by using recyclable plastic whenever possible and designing its containers for easy recycling. It introduced a "litter-less" lunch box that can carry food and drink without the need for throwaway sandwich wrappings, paper bags, and juice containers. Rubbermaid annually conducts surveys of the needs and preferences of consumers and recycling coordinators before designing new products. It also sends out recycling kits to retailers and recycling-related educational materials to public schools, as well as using product labels to inform consumers about the environmental benefits of using recycled goods.

TECHNOLOGY

Rubbermaid continuously invests in state-of-the-art equipment in order to remain a high-quality, low-cost producer. It uses a chemically advanced mixture of polyethylene as well as an intricate injection molding process for its plastic products. Between 1980 and 1991, Rubbermaid invested over $600 million to expand manufacturing and distribution facilities; modernize equipment; install process control systems; automate packaging systems; upgrade tooling for new products; and increase capacity for producing new products. In 1992, Rubbermaid invested over $132 million to purchase molds for new products, expand production capacity, add new equipment, and keep facilities efficient and productive. The company also upgraded its computer systems to track inventory and improve service to retailers. By 1996, Rubbermaid had spent $62 million alone on computer technology to meet Wal-Mart's demands. However, even with this significant technology investment, Rubbermaid was barely achieving an 80% on-time delivery service at Wal-Mart.

Rubbermaid has relentlessly pursued quality. Stanley Gault, the former CEO for Rubbermaid, visited several retail stores weekly to see how Rubbermaid products were displayed and to inspect the quality of workmanship. Gault once remarked, "No one surpasses our quality...we use more and better resin...we don't buy cheap resin...and we use a thicker gauge."

STRATEGY

Before retiring in 1991, Rubbermaid's CEO Gault outlined six basic strategies for "leap" growth:

- Develop new products (with 30% of its revenues to come from products introduced in the previous 5 years).
- Enter new markets every 18 to 24 months.
- Acquire new companies.
- Diversify through joint ventures with outside partners.
- Establish stronger bonds with its suppliers.
- Create specialized goods for its customers.

Creating high-quality, functional plastic products for housewares, the office, and industrial and farm markets represents a great deal of Rubbermaid's success. Part of this success is continually to improve the design of existing products; for example, the company revised the design of its ice trays to make it easier to remove the cubes. Its Lid-Access Tool Box was designed to deliver added convenience with compartments built directly onto the lid, allowing a person to keep the parts for a project in reach. Rubbermaid's genius lies in its ability to satisfy customer needs precisely and to make the small changes they demand, as well as its ability to imbue otherwise ordinary kitchen and household products with fashion.

Rubbermaid has diversified by producing storage for clothing, and videocassette and computer disks. Rubbermaid makes nearly a half-million different items, boasts an amazing 90% success rate on new products and obtains at least 30% of its sales each year from products less than 5 years old. Rubbermaid is practically a new product development machine cranking out 400 new products a year.

Most of Rubbermaid's new products have come from cross-functional teams, each with five to seven members (one each from marketing; manufacturing; R&D; finance; and other departments, as needed). Each team focuses on a specific product line so that someone is always thinking about key product segments. However, innovation at Rubbermaid is not limited to teams. Individual employees are geared toward creating new products as well. Rubbermaid has taught its employees to think in terms of letting new products flow from the firm's core competencies, thus encouraging managers to find out what is happening in the rest of the company by continually looking at processes and technologies. Employee brainstorming sessions yield up to 200 to 300 product ideas in one sitting.

Rubbermaid's new product strategy ultimately begins with the consumer and thus is market driven rather than technology driven. Rubbermaid relies extensively on focus groups and consumer marketing research to assess needs and to identify new product opportunities. Customers phone, fax, write, or e-mail more than a dozen or so new product ideas daily. Researchers at Rubbermaid have been known to conduct home visits — 2-hour inspections of randomly selected consumers' homes in which they photograph closets and ask about how people live. These visits have yielded about 100 new product ideas. Another part of Rubbermaid's marketing intelligence includes studying its competition. Yet rather than benchmark its competitors, it benchmarks against the standards set by their customers. It runs focus groups to test color and style preferences and confirms those preferences by conducting surveys in shopping malls.

Rubbermaid also obtains a great deal of feedback from customer complaints. Each complaint received from comment cards or the toll-free number is documented by marketing and is widely distributed, even to the company's executives. Rubbermaid makes good on every customer complaint as well, replacing its products without charge to the customer. The company also runs a day care program where researchers can observe children having problems with toys and test the company's new toys. This input from the customer is then used to modify existing products or develop totally new ones.

New products are launched at Rubbermaid with record speed, sometimes within 20 weeks of the birth of the idea. New-product cross-functional teams, consisting of a product manager, an R&D manager, a manufacturing manager, and a financial analyst, manage the entire process from spotting a need to commercialization. These product development teams, which have considerable autonomy and authority to carry out their objectives, are also rewarded based on achieving those objectives. Rubbermaid bypasses traditional test-marketing because of its careful homework with customers to develop the right product and its wish to avoid exposing new products to competitors.

Rubbermaid moved away from a product and price focus in its ads to pitching its products as problem solvers in myriad areas — homes, offices, backyards, gardens, and playgrounds. According to former CEO Wolf Schmitt, "Ours is the only product portfolio that literally spans from cradle to cane." Rather than focus on selling individual items, like garbage cans, Rubbermaid increasingly is trying to sell "solutions." Rubbermaid even promoted an 89-page book entitled, *1001 Solutions for Better Living*, that offers tips on how Rubbermaid's products can help consumers deal with problems in their homes and home offices. The book, which was free with three proofs-of-purchase of Rubbermaid products, also came with coupons with a face value of as much as $101 for the company's products. Several of the booklet's tips are practical, such as putting Rubbermaid Ultra Grip plastic liner under a computer keyboard to keep it from slipping or keeping a Rubbermaid ice cream scoop to fill cupcake tins with cake or muffin batter. Others are more blatantly aimed at increasing sales, such as a suggestion to use laundry baskets in different colors for sorting whites, darks, and delicates.

As far as pricing, Rubbermaid's prices tend to be higher than those of its competitors, due to its products' higher quality content and stellar reputation. Rubbermaid products command a 5 to 10% premium over competitors due to the high-grade plastic used in the manufacture of its products. However, rising resin costs continue to create added pricing pressures.

Rubbermaid's products have been marketed primarily through mass merchandisers and home center stores such as Home Depot, as well as through specialty stores and the Internet. Rubbermaid teams up with its trade partners, such as Wal-Mart and Target, to jointly develop displays, merchandising plans, promotions, and logistics. In fact, the company has already redesigned many items to make them easier for retailers to handle, such as plastic picnic tables produced by Little Tikes that are now collapsible. Rubbermaid also provides generous allowances to retailers to help support price promotions and co-op advertising in local markets.

Finally, Rubbermaid has shown its trade partners how to increase sales of its products by displaying them in its Best Practices Center. Retailers who visit this center can see how Rubbermaid products can be most effectively merchandised. The company's field salespeople are organized around categories instead of products, allowing them to work closely with retailers to decide what goes on the shelves. For example, Rubbermaid is working with fast-food concern McDonald's Corporation to look at how its products could be used in commercial kitchens. Rubbermaid believes that this channel specialization allows for more intensive management involvement with its trade customers. This strategy seems to be paying off; the company has increased its penetration of its served retail market from 60,000 outlets in 1980 to well over 100,000 outlets today.

For promotion, Rubbermaid supports its products with national television and radio ads. It also supports products at the local retail level with trade allowances and co-op advertising. At one time, Rubbermaid partnered with its retailers in a project called *Earth View*, sponsoring programs geared to retail management that reinforced its longstanding commitment to recycling and utilizing recycled materials in its products. Rubbermaid also showcases its products over the Internet, where visitors to its Web site can click on an image of a kitchen and see before and after pictures of how Rubbermaid products can be used to organize a refrigerator or a space under the sink.

INTERNATIONAL OPERATIONS

Presently, an increasing share of Rubbermaid's sales is coming from its foreign operations. Foreign revenues from international operations accounted for 27% of sales in 2002, compared with 18% in 1995. Rubbermaid achieves this high international penetration by establishing a strong brand image and developing extensive distribution networks in its international markets.

Rubbermaid is also moving away from a strictly export-based strategy to one of direct foreign investment. For example, Rubbermaid entered a joint venture with French company Allibert to produce resin furniture in 1989. The company formed a strategic alliance with Sommer–Allibert of France to manufacture and distribute resin casual furniture in the French market. Rubbermaid also established a joint venture with Curver Group of the Dutch chemical company DSM to market housewares in Europe,

Africa, and the Middle East. It purchased Curver, Europe's leader in plastic housewares, in late 1997. Its acquisitions continued in the 1990s with the purchase of EWU A.G., a Swiss floor care supplies company. In 1992, Rubbermaid acquired CIPSA of Mexico, a leading plastics and housewares company. In 1994, Rubbermaid formed a joint venture with Richell of Japan, in which the company currently holds a 40% equity interest. Another joint venture took place with Royal Plastics Group, Ltd. of Canada for manufacture and marketing of modular plastic components and kits to build storage sheds for consumer, commercial, and industrial markets. Also in 1994, Rubbermaid broadened its portfolio further by acquiring Ausplay, an Australian maker of playground equipment.

Rubbermaid is trying significantly to boost its presence in Europe. The company introduced a new retail concept called Everything Rubbermaid in key European cities and is working more closely with host country partners to gear its products more effectively to European tastes. For example, when Rubbermaid saw that European parents were not buying novelty children's beds, like its sports car-shaped bed, the company discovered that the standard European mattress did not fit the beds. The company then approached a European company to design an appropriate mattress.

"NEWELLIZING" RUBBERMAID

Under Stanley Gault, Rubbermaid seemed to pop out a new product every day, helping the stock routinely return 25% annually. However, after Gault retired, Rubbermaid's customers started complaining about lousy service. The company had to hand over the profits to retailers on its best new products just to stay in the game. Wal-Mart finally purged most of its stores of the company's Little Tikes toy line, clearing lots of shelf space for competitor Fisher Price. With Rubbermaid's stock down 40% from its 1992 high, it was ripe for a takeover.

In May 1999, Rubbermaid was acquired by Newell Co., a housewares concern specializing in sales to discount retailers, for $6.3 billion (two times current sales). Newell sells a range of household products from pencils and combs to window blinds. In 10 years it bought 75 mediocre, smallish companies and polished them up by eliminating the least valuable products, employees, factories and customers. Most of its targets had strong brand names (Sharpie markers, BernzOmatic torches, Burnes picture frames), but bad customer service.

With the acquisition of Rubbermaid, Newell brought to the table a strong back-office support system, placing a premium on on-time deliveries and customer service. It also recognized its contribution to Rubbermaid as one of shoring up its channel relationships. According to Newell executive Denton, "Rubbermaid understood the consumer but didn't understand the customer." Denton proceeded to apply the philosophy known as *Newellizing*. In essence, the philosophy at Newell was to acquire attractive brands, first squeezing costs and then boosting profit margins. Specific initiatives at Rubbermaid included major capital investments; changes in Rubbermaid's distribution system; conversion to Newell's operating system; and personnel restructuring.

Over the past few years, Rubbermaid has slowly been integrated into the more streamlined operations of Newell. During this time, deliveries have improved in large part because of the production and distribution strengths of Newell. The company's dismal performance in 1995 with Wal-Mart and Target has begun to turn around under Newell management. Rubbermaid appears to be rebounding well from a slow economy, rising resin prices, and Kmart bankruptcy. Nonetheless, sales and operating income remain well below the growth rates of the 1980s and mid-1990s.

QUESTIONS

1. Discuss how Rubbermaid is market oriented. Discuss customer orientation, competitor orientation, and interfunctional coordination in your response.
2. How does Rubbermaid use quality function deployment in its new product development?
3. How does Rubbermaid practice "relationship marketing"?
4. In what ways can Newell management help or hurt Rubbermaid's market orientation?
5. In what way did the market environment affect Rubbermaid's market orientation?

CASE 13: OFFICE DEPOT® GOES ONLINE — E-SERVICE QUALITY*

BACKGROUND

Office Depot, Inc. is the world's second largest supplier (behind Staples) of office products and services. The company's selection of brand name office supplies includes business machines, computers, computer software and office furniture; its leading-edge business services encompass copying, printing, document reproduction, mailing, and shipping. Office Depot's customers include small office/home office (SoHo), medium-sized, and large businesses located in the U.S. and in 17 other countries.

The company sells its products through multiple distribution channels, including more than 960 office supply stores, direct mail, global Internet sites, business-to-business e-commerce, and sales forces. Office Depot operates under the Office Depot, Viking Office Products®, Viking Direct®, and 4sure.com brand names. This S&P 500 company generates revenues of nearly $12 billion annually and has 48,000 employees worldwide. *Business Week* ranked Office Depot fourth among S&P 500 firms in overall shareholder returns during 2001. Today, Office Depot is one of the world's largest sellers of office products and an industry leader in every distribution channel, including stores, direct mail, contract delivery, the Internet, and business-to-business electronic commerce. (See Exhibit 13.1)

Although Office Depot is clearly a powerful organization today, the company's beginnings were quite modest. Office Depot was founded in Florida in 1986 and opened its first store in Ft. Lauderdale. In late 1987, David I. Fuente assumed the post of chairman and chief executive officer

---

* This case was prepared by William C. Johnson, professor of marketing, H. Wayne Huizenga School of Business and Entrepreneurship, Nova Southeastern University, Ft. Lauderdale, Florida.

357

(Dollars in millions)	2003		2002		2001	
Sales	$12,358.6	100.0%	$11,356.6	100.0%	$11,082.1	100.0%
Cost of goods sold and occupancy costs	8,484.5	68.7%	8,022.7	70.6%	7,940.1	71.6%
Gross profit	3,874.1	31.3%	3,333.9	29.4%	3,142.0	28.4%
Store and warehouse operating and selling expenses	2,802.2	22.7%	2,338.1	20.6%	2,331.0	21.1%
Segment operating profit	1,071.9	8.6%	995.8	8.8%	811.0	7.3%
General and administrative expenses	578.8	4.7%	486.3	4.3%	445.5	4.0%
Other operating expenses	22.8	0.1%	9.8	0.1%	12.1	0.1%
Operating profit	$ 470.3	3.8%	$ 499.7	4.4%	$ 353.4	3.2%

Note: Our overall sales increased 9% in 2003 after an increase of 2% in 2002. The increase in sales in both periods is attributable to increased sales from our International Division and our Business Services Group, partially offset by declining sales in our North American Retail Division. Positively impacting sales in our International Division during 2003 was our acquisition of Guilbert in June.

Source: From SEC Filings, Feb. 26, 2004 (10-K Report).

Exhibit 13.1   Office Depot Financial Data

of the fledgling company and took Office Depot public in 1988. Fuente immediately began to execute an ambitious plan to expand the company's footprint in key U.S. markets. The results were dramatic: by the end of 1990, Office Depot had 173 stores in 27 states. That same year, the company merged with The Office Club, Inc., becoming the largest office products retailer in North America.

Domestic growth, however, was only one aspect of Office Depot's expansion in the company's early years; the management team had its sights set on penetrating international markets as well. Early 1992 marked the company's acquisition of H.Q. Office International, Inc., which included the Great Canadian Office Supplies Warehouse chain in western Canada. Growing steadily, the company also opened new retail stores in Israel and Colombia under international licensing agreements.

As Office Depot expanded geographically, the company also began to extend beyond its traditional markets. In 1993, it entered the rapidly consolidating contract stationer business by acquiring two market leaders: Wilson Stationery & Printing Company and Eastman Office Products Corporation. The merger with six additional contract stationers followed these purchases during 1994. These moves positioned Office Depot to take advantage of industry trends that would come to play a central role in the company's success.

In the meantime, the company continued its steady international growth. Between 1995 and 1998, it opened stores in Poland, Hungary, and Thailand under international licensing agreements, and in Mexico, France and Japan under joint venture agreements. Later, the company acquired the interests of its joint venture partners in France and Japan.

In 1998, Office Depot merged with Viking Office Products, a public company and the world's leading direct mail marketer of office products. The addition of Viking to the Office Depot organization not only vastly expanded Office Depot's international presence, but also made the company the leading provider of office products and services in the world.

That same year, Office Depot began to leverage the Internet aggressively, launching the first of a number of new Web sites, www.officedepot.com. The award-winning site established the company as the industry's technology leader; expanded its domestic e-commerce capabilities; and, ultimately, extended the range of products and services the company could offer its customers. The following year, the company launched its first European e-commerce site, www.viking-direct.co.uk, in the U.K. Today, the company has 15 international Web sites in nine countries, with worldwide e-commerce sales in 2001 at approximately $1.6 billion (see company financial data in Exhibit 13.1)

The company recently signed an agreement with Albertsons, one of the world's largest food and drug retailers, in which Office Depot initially will provide office and school supplies to 18 Albertsons' stores in three markets (Chicago, Los Angeles, and Phoenix). As part of the pilot program, Office Depot's "store within a store" environment will feature an assortment of more than 700 products — ranging from ink jet cartridges, copier paper, and writing instruments to mailing and school supplies. The company also plans to open 25 to 30 "superstores," dubbed *Millennium*, with an average of 20,000 to 36,000 square feet, by the end of 2003.

CREATING A MULTICHANNEL STRATEGY

Most retailers are quick to profess their loyalty to an integrated selling model that gives customers freedom to make purchases online, offline, or over the phone. Office Depot, a leading company in the $90 billion consumer market for office supplies, is marshaling its resources in its most ambitious push to unify its channels: superstores, catalogs, toll-free numbers, and Web site. Next month, it will launch Millennia, a project that, for the first time, gives in-store employees real-time information about inventory, pricing, orders, and customer accounts over the Web. Although many other office-supply retailers set up Web operations independent of their stores, Monica Luechtefeld, Office Depot's senior vice-president of e-commerce, insisted the Net operations be woven into Office Depot's existing business. Unlike other bricks-and-mortar retailers, Office Depot chose not to spin off its e-commerce operations. "We chose from day one to make this an integral part of the company," said Luechtefeld, whose goal is to push 50% of Office Depot customers onto the Internet. "We felt our strength was in having the Internet be another door."

"Experience has proven that having an overall multichannel approach is the way rather than to spin it off," said Julian Chu, executive consultant for IBM Global Services e-business strategy and change practice consulting group, "That way, you address politics within the organization so folks in the stores don't have the incentive to undermine the Internet business."

Office Depot executive vice-president and CIO Bill Seltzer, who leads a 500-person IT staff, spearheads the channel integration strategy built around Web connectivity. "When my order entry system gets an order, it doesn't care if it comes from the Web, an 800 number, or a store owner," Seltzer says. "We're totally integrated; it treats everything the same."

Building Office Depot's online offering presented a considerable challenge. Luechtefeld had to persuade senior management not to spin off the online effort as a separate silo, but rather to incorporate it as the backbone of the company's supply chain. Salespeople were terrified, fearing that the Web would take away their jobs. To win their support, Luechtefeld offered reps bonuses for steering corporate customers to do some of their buying online. At the same time, every sales applicant must pass a test about the Net and create a video pitching Office Depot's online sales system to a potential customer.

Office Depot workers were not the only skeptics. Luechtefeld signed up only 500 customers during the venture's first 2 years. To break down the resistance, Luechtefeld followed a grassroots educational campaign with purchasing managers, many of whom she knew personally from her 20 years in the office-products business. She convinced many of these businesses that online shopping would reduce costs, increase control over who bought what, and eliminate tedious work. After these initial successes, Office Depot introduced the "business in a box" strategy, which aims to push more customers into online buying, now an important growth engine in a market where growth has been limited in recent years.

Office Depot's Internet operations initially focused primarily on its business-to-business accounts, setting up customized Web pages for 37,000 corporate clients. For each customer, the company has designed a site with parameters that allow different employees of its customers various degrees of freedom to buy supplies. For example, a stockroom clerk might only be able to order pencils, paper, and toner cartridges, while the assistant to the CEO might have carte blanche to order everything the company sells. Also, according to Luechtefeld, Office Depot learned an important lesson about Web site design: customers care more about ease of use than about new technologies.

The cost savings to Office Depot have been impressive. Processing an order taken over the Net costs the company less than $1 per $100 of goods sold, vs. twice that for phone orders. Because no customer service representative needs to key in the transaction, order-entry errors are virtually eliminated and returns are cut in half.

Not only Office Depot wins by moving to the Web — so do its customers. The company's Web operations help its corporate clients reduce their need for costly purchase orders because billing is handled electronically. The average order for supplies is about $125 at Office Depot; however, many customers report costs of more than $100 simply to process a purchase order and pay an invoice. Using the Web can slash that cost to $15 to $25.

Office Depot owes a great deal of its success online to efficient back-end operations. It processes Internet, catalog, and business contract orders out of 25 distribution centers, including one in Weston, FL, that handle up to 100,000 orders a day. A separate network of 10 warehouses services the stores. Unlike some land-based retailers or a host of failed pure e-retailers, it processes enough Internet orders to cover distribution and delivery expenses. Although Internet customers can choose to have items delivered from the nearest store, more than 90% elect to have them shipped, according to Office Depot's senior vice president of distribution,

Dennis Andruskiewicz. Furthermore, the company is making it easier to return goods purchased online by having its delivery trucks pick up goods that customers wish to send back.

The other ingredients that Office Depot leveraged for its success in cyberspace were a solid brand name and hefty purchasing power. The company uses its considerable purchasing power to match — or undercut — discount-minded cyber rivals.

Office Depot's multichannel strategy has other key elements as well. The company recently began rolling out in-store kiosks in many of its stores, allowing customers to order items not found in the store online. The company is also expanding beyond selling supplies to selling services as well. For example, it is adding free and fee-based services online for its small business customers, including help with tax preparation and debt collection.

The company earned $1.6 billion in e-commerce sales in 2001, making it the second largest retailer on the Internet behind Amazon.com. This figure represents an increase of 58% over 2000 e-commerce revenues. Also, unlike most other online firms, Office Depot's e-commerce venture has been profitable since it was launched in 1998. For 2002, Office Depot expects e-commerce revenues of $2 billion. e-Commerce sales represented nearly 15% of total company revenues in 2001. Several analysts believe that the company will increase that to 20% within the next 3 years.

Two years ago, 30% of Office Depot's large- and medium-sized business customers and 10% of small-business customers ordered online; by the end of this year, the company expects those percentages to grow to 50 and 30%, respectively. Office Depot Chief Executive Bruce Nelson said the company has no intention of reining in the galloping growth of its Internet operations and no fear that Internet sales will siphon off portions of in-store sales. According to Nelson, "You have to offer the customer the way they want to buy and when they want to buy and let them choose."

QUESTIONS

1. What were some of the key success factors for Office Depot's online venture?
2. What lessons can be drawn from the Office Depot experience that might assist future online ventures?
3. Explain how Office Depot performs some of the value chain functions (i.e., buying, selling, outbound/inbound logistics) more efficiently and effectively in the marketspace. (Note: *marketspace* is the digital, networked, virtual world of information that parallels the tangible world of goods and services.)

4. You were just hired by Monica Luechtefeld to improve the customer service at Office Depot. Prepare a two-page report addressed to her on how you would effectively integrate online and offline service; also, as part of your report, visit Office Depot's Web site (http://www.officedepot.com) and suggest how to make it more "customer friendly."

CASE 14: PIZZA HUT® — A CUSTOMER LOYALTY PROGRAM*

"I can't figure it out," Rick, the Pizza Hut delivery area manager, commiserated to Jean, an area manager on the dine-in side of the business. "I've got stores with double digit sales growth. Their bottom lines are as strong as they've ever been. Yet the managers of these stores aren't meeting their quarterly bonus targets so they're quitting. In the past few months I've lost many of my best managers. Some have gone to work for Papa John's and one now works for Domino's. Two of them have even taken voluntary demotions to become delivery drivers saying that driving pays more than managing. This is all because their customer loyalty scores are not very good."

"I've got the opposite problem," replied Jean. "My dine-in restaurants are showing negative sales growth, yet have very high customer loyalty scores. My managers are happy because they're making their quarterly bonus targets; however, my boss is breathing down my neck wondering where the sales growth and profit are."

"It wasn't like this in previous years," Rick said. "In those days, all the management bonuses were based on store profitability. If you weren't making a profit, you weren't getting a bonus. Then, in 1995, the company began its customer satisfaction/loyalty initiatives. The company was jazzed about it. All my

---

* This case was prepared by Alan Seidman, associate professor of hospitality at Johnson and Wales University, North Miami, Florida.

managers were jazzed about it. Instead of receiving bonuses based on their stores' financial statements, managers now qualified for bonuses based upon how loyal and satisfied their customers say they are when surveyed. It seemed to make sense. Loyal customers were going to patronize us more and tell their friends about us. That meant extra business. Extra business meant extra profits."

"And extra profits are going to mean big bonuses for the managers," agreed Jean. "But somehow that never happened. Somewhere, somehow, the system broke down. Maybe we can figure out why."

OVERVIEW

In 1958, the Carney brothers in Wichita, Kansas, borrowed $600 from their mother and opened the first Pizza Hut restaurant to great success. Within a year, the first franchise was opened. By 1977 the company had grown to nearly 3200 units and was acquired by PepsiCo. With over 12,300 units, Pizza Hut has become the largest pizza restaurant chain in the world, operating in 84 countries and territories.

Providing carry-out, dine-in, and delivery service, Pizza Hut features a variety of pizzas as well as pasta, salads, sandwiches, chicken wings, and other food and beverage items. Its list of awards includes the Best Pizza Chain in America in a survey conducted by *Restaurants & Institutions* magazine, as well as the January 1997 winner of the *Consumer Reports* best pizza chain in America. Its recognition is tremendous and hardly anyone in the U.S. has not tried a Pizza Hut pizza.

In 1986, the company began offering delivery service. Special Pizza Hut delivery units were constructed, separate from the smaller, traditional "red roof" restaurants. Because of their relatively low cost and easy construction, delivery units began to proliferate in strip malls and other centralized locations, competing directly with Domino's Pizza, the leading pizza delivery company in the country at that time.

Although delivery was a huge success, the company continued to search for new products and ideas that would keep Pizza Hut at the forefront of an increasingly competitive pizza delivery segment. In 1993, BIGFOOT™ pizza was introduced, followed by stuffed crust pizza in 1995 and triple-decker pizza in 1996. All three pizzas were instrumental in providing short-term increases to sales; however, they lacked the ability to increase sales over a long term.

In 1996, worldwide system sales exceeded $7.4 billion. Although this was a record sales figure, it was due primarily to system growth. Same-store

Top Five Pizza Chains	U.S. Systemwide Food Service Sales (in $ millions)		
	1997	1996	1995
Pizza Hut	4700	4927	5300
Domino's	2480	2300	2100
Little Caesar's	1375	1400	1450
Papa John's	868	619	459
Sbarro	422	400	395

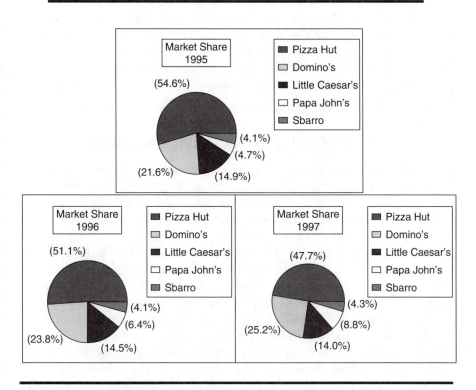

Exhibit 14.1 Pizza Hut's Declining U.S. Market Share (From Rubenstein, E. [1998], *Nation's Restaurant News*, April 6, 8.)

sales in company-operated stores decreased 4%, reflecting fewer transactions within each store. In the first half of 1997, same-store sales of company-owned restaurants dropped an additional 7%. Clearly, the company was headed in the wrong direction (see Exhibit 14.1).

Pizza Hut's role as a PepsiCo subsidiary ended in 1997 when the parent company spun off its three major fast-food holdings (Pizza Hut, KFC, and Taco Bell) in an effort to concentrate solely on its beverage and snack food (Frito Lay) business. Consisting solely of fast-food restaurants, the new company, TRICON Global Restaurants, focused solely on the needs of its three restaurant holdings. The major challenge facing Pizza Hut and TRICON was to remain competitive in today's global environment by keeping old customers happy while trying to attract new ones.

CUSTOMER LOYALTY

In response to increasing competition and declining sales, Pizza Hut began a comprehensive customer loyalty initiative in 1995. Through marketing research, the company aimed to improve guest satisfaction and unit-level execution at over 3700 company-owned stores and about 200 franchised restaurants. By presenting restaurant managers with weekly feedback from their customers, Pizza Hut hoped to strengthen operations within the control of each restaurant manager. The plan comprised two components: a customer service toll-free number and a customer satisfaction/loyalty survey.

TOLL-FREE CUSTOMER SERVICE NUMBER

For the first time in its history, Pizza Hut introduced a customer satisfaction hotline. Composed of a toll-free number visibly posted inside stores and on individual pizza boxes, the customer satisfaction hotline was designed to answer all questions, problems, and/or complaints a customer might have about the product or service.

Because many issues and concerns were handled by an outside marketing agency, the hotline was able to reduce the time a manager spent handling customer complaints, thereby giving him or her more time to devote to running the store. Additionally, the hotline operator was able to listen and respond to each situation from a neutral perspective.

The customer service hotline provided another benefit. It became a forum for those who chose not to complain to a store manager or employee during a face-to-face encounter. Many customers who normally did not like to complain, now had an opportunity to do so. This was very important for Pizza Hut. Consider the following findings from *Consumer Complaint Handling in America*, a study by Technical Assistance Research Programs, Inc. (TARP):[2]

- About 50% of the time, customers who have a problem with a product or service are not likely to tell the company about it.
- Nine out of ten of these "silent critics" will probably take their future business to a competitor.
- Even when a customer does complain, one out of every two will not be thoroughly satisfied with the company's efforts to solve the problem.

These findings have a large impact for Pizza Hut as well as all other service firms. Because dissatisfied customers typically tell between seven to nine other people when they have had an unsatisfactory experience with a company, it is imperative that companies do all they can to try to get a dissatisfied customer to complain. If a customer's concern goes unresolved, the likelihood of that customer returning is greatly diminished.

When a call was made to the hotline, the operator would try to find out which Pizza Hut was in question (landmarks and other relevant information could be used to help identify individual stores in case a customer was unsure). The operator would make notes of the incident and send the customer free pizza coupons as an apology. All incidents were sent to each affected store manager and area manager via a computerized download. More severe incidents would be presented to people further up the chain of command. These incidents did not affect a manager's bonus opportunity in any way. The customer service hotline was merely a tool for Pizza Hut managers to listen to customers who might not normally complain. It was a great resource for the customer and the company.

CUSTOMER SATISFACTION/LOYALTY SURVEY

Identifying loyal customers became a necessity for many service businesses. In the early 1990s, articles in the *Harvard Business Review* detailed the impact loyal customers can have on a business.[3,4] Simply stated, if a customer is satisfied with the product and service, he or she stands a good chance of returning to that business. Keeping the customer loyal to a business has obvious implications. A loyal customer will return to the business time and time again. Often times, he will bring other customers along. Almost certainly, he will tell other people about his good experiences. Such positive word of mouth will bring other customers. Over time, they, too, become satisfied and loyal, telling their friends as well. Over time, the business becomes more profitable because of repeat business and positive word of mouth of loyal customers.

The questions asked were constructed in such a way as to analyze the relationships between repeat customer visits and the operational components within each restaurant that would affect customer loyalty. Such components included product quality, service quality, and overall restaurant appeal. Each interview was conducted by an outside marketing agency. Brief telephone interviews were given only to customers who purchased a Pizza Hut pizza within the preceding 36 hours. After that time, it was deemed that the survey results would lose some degree of accuracy. Because delivery stores and dine-in restaurants had unique customer relationship characteristics, separate survey processes were developed for each.

Delivery Restaurants

Capturing and quantifying loyalty is by no means an easy task for any business. Pizza Hut (in the delivery side of the business) did have a distinct advantage. An in-store database, which contained customers' names, addresses, and phone numbers, as well as a record of what they had ordered in the past, tracked carry-out and delivery customers.

The satisfaction/loyalty initiative for the delivery stores worked as follows. A name at random would be drawn from the store's database and contacted by the marketing research representative. The customer was asked if he or she had ordered and eaten the pizza within the last 36 hours. If the answer was yes, the following questions would be asked (in this order):

1. On a scale of 1 to 5, if you had a chance to return to this Pizza Hut in the next 90 days, would you do so? (1 = definitely not; 2 = probably not; 3 = may or may not; 4 = probably would; 5 = definitely would.)
2. Did you have any type of problem with your last order? (yes or no)
3. Did you receive the correct order? (yes or no)
4. How valued did we make you feel as a customer? (did or did not feel valued)
5. On a scale of 1 to 7, how would you rate the topping amount on your pizza? (1 = hardly any toppings; 7 = toppings were plentiful)
6. On a scale of 1 to 7, how would you rate the temperature of your pizza? (1 = very cold; 7 = very hot)
7. On a scale of 1 to 7, how would you rate the appearance of your pizza? (1 = did not look appealing at all; 7 = looked very appealing)
8. On a scale of 1 to 7, how would you rate your overall experience? (1 = terrible, 2 = unsatisfactory; 3 = average; 4 = above average; 5 = good; 6 = very good; 7 = excellent)

On average, nine customers per store per week were polled, regardless of the store's volume. Generally, delivery stores' order volumes would range from about 800 up to 2000 orders a week.

Survey data were then brought into Pizza Hut's mainframe computers where they were organized, analyzed, and sent or downloaded to individual stores. Each delivery store manager and area manager (as well as every other level of management up the chain of command) received a tabulation of these scores on a weekly basis. Tabulations were kept on a running 4-week basis. In other words, all scores and data were the reflection of 4 weeks of customer surveys (approximately 36 surveys). When results from a new week were downloaded, the earliest week's scores would drop off so that the scores now reflected the preceding 4 weeks' worth of surveys.

Questions 1 and 8 determined customer loyalty. A customer needed to answer the first question with a 5 (definitely would return to this store in 90 days) *and* a 6 or 7 (very good or excellent) for question 8, dealing with his overall experience. If question 1 received a 5 and the eighth question a 6 or 7, Pizza Hut considered the respondent a loyal customer. The percentage of loyal customers was regularly tabulated and considered to be the leading index of that store's performance. For example, if 36 customers were surveyed in a month and 20 answered question 1 with a 5 *and* question 8 with a 6 or 7, that store would have a loyal customer reading of 56%.

Dine-In Restaurants

The dine-in restaurants, or "red roofs" as they were known, did not have the computerized database information that the delivery stores did. As a result, the red roofs had a different approach toward the survey process. In these cases, loyalty/satisfaction measurements were based on voluntary surveys taken by customers. At random, certain customer receipts were issued asking the customer to participate in a loyalty survey. The customer was to call a special 800 number (within 36 hours after his visit); give a coded identification number (provided on the receipt); and answer questions about the quality of food and service identical to those asked of delivery customers. The only question that differed was one dealing with a lunch buffet, if applicable.

Customers were encouraged to participate by incentives described on each receipt, e.g., a free soft drink or free order of breadsticks with future purchases. Although the questions were basically the same between delivery and red-roof stores, the one major difference was that the dine-in surveys involved the customer calling the survey company, while the survey company called the delivery customers.

THE BONUS PROGRAM

Weekly salaries of managers of all company-owned Pizza Hut stores were competitive with the salaries of fast-food managers of other companies. Every 3 months (quarterly), however, all store managers became eligible to receive a bonus. Bonuses generally ranged from 0 to $4000 per store manager a quarter. The bonus program was a major incentive for all store managers.

Traditionally, store bonuses were based on a store's sales growth and profitability. With the advent of the customer satisfaction/loyalty initiatives in 1995, that index was changed. Bonus potential for store managers now depended solely on their overall quarterly customer loyalty percentage. The minimum percentage a manager needed to achieve so as to receive a bonus was 60%. A loyalty rating below 60% meant that the manager was automatically out of the running for a quarterly bonus.

Managers who received a bonus were given a flat dollar rate for each loyalty percentage point they received. Managers scoring between 60 and 64% loyalty would receive one amount; those scoring between 65 and 69% would receive a larger amount and a bigger bonus was warranted by 70 to 75%, etc. Pizza Hut perceived that a direct relationship would exist between a store's overall operational strength and its percentage of loyal customers.

TODAY

Phil Crimmins, vice president of customer satisfaction for Pizza Hut and founder of its loyalty program, claims the loyalty initiatives have made many positive inroads. "We noticed our rating on the abundance of toppings wasn't where it should be about a year ago," Crimmins recently told a group of restaurant operators at a multiunit technology conference in March, 1998. As a result, the company increased food costs by $50 million by adding more toppings to each pizza. Since then, Crimmins claims that topping amounts are no longer an issue.

Crimmins also claims that the customer loyalty initiative has helped Pizza Hut identify underperforming stores. By visiting and studying the stores with high loyalty scores and comparing them to the underperforming stores, Crimmins and his team were able to develop a blueprint for success. Many underperforming stores were slowly transformed from "marginal" or "breakdown" stores into "excelling" or "standard" stores. Today, over 60% of its participating stores are considered to be "excelling" or "stable," as opposed to only 40% when the loyalty process started in 1995.

Unfortunately, some setbacks have occurred. High loyalty scores have not always translated into high-performing stores. Conversely, many low loyalty stores continue to be extremely profitable. Area managers and store managers alike continue to discuss and evaluate the system and its deficiencies. Pizza Hut has listened to such discussions and continually strives to improve the process by making modifications. Pros and cons of the customer loyalty initiative continue to be evaluated.

QUESTIONS

1. In what ways did Pizza Hut benefit or not benefit from its customer satisfaction/loyalty initiatives?
2. In your opinion, what were the causes behind the issues in your response to the preceding question?
3. Identify the breakdowns in the process as they affected delivery restaurants and dine-in restaurants.
4. Where was the breakdown in the quarterly bonus program? What changes (if any) would you make to this system?
5. What else can Pizza Hut learn from its customers using its marketing research/loyalty process?
6. Evaluate the wisdom of the company's introducing the loyalty programs the way that it did and the "law of unintended consequences" that soon followed.

REFERENCE

1. Rubenstein, E. (1998) Research prompts Pizza Hut to listen to its customers, *Nation's Restaurant News*, April 6, 8.
2. TARP (1986) *Consumer Complaint Handling in America: An Update Study* Washington: White House Office of Consumer Affairs.
3. Heskit. et al. (1994) Putting the service-profit chain to work, *Harvard Bus. Review,* Mar.-April.
4. Reichheld, F. (1993) Loyalty - based management, *Harvard Business Review*, March-April.

CASE 15: PUBLIX SUPER MARKETS, INC. — ACHIEVING CUSTOMER INTIMACY*

Publix Super Markets, Inc. is a Florida-based grocery chain with approximately 120,000 employees and annual sales in 2002 of $15.9 billion. Presently, Publix serves over 1 million customers every day. The company has no immediate international expansion plans at this time. Named after a chain of motion picture theaters, Publix is one of the largest employee-owned companies in the world with annual sales of approximately $12 billion. It was the first supermarket chain to install electric-eye doors; Muzak; fluorescent lighting; and air-conditioning in its stores. It was also one of the first companies to offer water fountains; self-service shopping; shopping carts; and computerized scanning technology. Since 1997, Publix has been rated as one of the best companies to work for in America as reported by *Fortune* magazine.[1]

Everything that Publix does revolves around pleasing the customer; this is why it has enjoyed success since the 1930s. Publix's goal is to make every customer feel personally valued in such a way that he sees himself as *one in a million*. This profile focuses on the company's customer-intimate philosophy and how Publix satisfies and delights its customers daily in order to become the "premier quality food retailer in the world."

---

* This case was coauthored by Dr. Bahaudin Mujtaba, director of institutional relations, planning, and accreditation for the H. Wayne Huizenga School of Business and Entrepreneurship and formerly a senior management development specialist at Publix Super Markets, Inc., and Dr. William C. Johnson, professor of marketing at H. Wayne Huizenga School of Business and Entrepreneurship, Ft. Lauderdale, Florida. The information here is based on the authors' opinions and does not necessarily represent the views of Publix management.

BACKGROUND AND COMPANY PHILOSOPHY

As of September, 2003, Publix was operating 769 stores: 577 in Florida; 143 in Georgia; 32 in South Carolina, 10 in Alabama, and 7 in Tennessee. In terms of financial success, during 1991 through 1996, Publix outperformed the S&P 500 Index and the customer Peer Group Index with regard to return on investment. The Peer Group includes A&P; Albertsons; American Stores; Bruno's; Food Lion; Giant Foods; Hannaford Bros.; Kroger; Safeway; Smith's Food & Drug; Weis Markets; and Winn-Dixie.

A key differentiating factor in Publix's success formula can be attributed to the philosophy of its founder, George W. Jenkins, who stated that

> ... some companies are founded on policy. This is wrong. Philosophy, the things you believe in, is more important. Philosophy does not change frequently... and is never compromised... we attempt to adapt a philosophy in such a way as to allow ordinary people to achieve the extraordinary... to reach higher... to look upon average with disdain.

Employee Training Material, 1990 Publix Philosophy

The philosophy of caring for people has been embedded in Publix's corporate culture throughout its stores in the four states. Publix associates understand that they are not just in the grocery business but also in the people business. Therefore, taking care of associates, customers, suppliers, and community members is important to Publix people and the communities that they serve.

George Jenkins once said that "Publix will be a little better place to work or not quite as good because of you." A philosophy of employee appreciation has been embedded in the culture of the organization, so when upper echelon managers visit retail stores, especially during appreciation week, they make it a point to see and thank every associate personally. They understand that people need recognition and sincere thanks for their hard work and commitment to the company. According to Howard Jenkins, member of the Publix board and retired CEO, "growth is the end result of a simple equation. As each of us continues to please our customers, more customers will look to Publix for their shopping needs. We must never lose sight of exactly what those needs are." Keeping its sight on the changing needs of its customers and effectively filling those needs have paid big dividends for Publix's consistent growth and achievement over the years. See Exhibit 15.1 for an evolution of Publix's growth since its inception.

Publix associates are encouraged to interact with their customers on an hourly basis; they constantly attempt to assess the customer in order to get

Year	Accomplishments
1930	First Publix Super Market opened in Winter Haven, Florida
1940	First store known as the "marble, tile, and stucco food palace" built in Winter Haven, featuring such revolutionary retail concepts as air conditioning, wide aisles, and electric-eye doors
1945	Bought 19-store chain of All American Food stores in Lakeland and moved headquarters to Lakeland
1950	New 70,000-square foot grocery warehouse built in Lakeland; today this warehouse occupies over 2 million square feet
1957	Publix Employee Federal Credit Union opened in a Lakeland warehouse
1959	Opened its first store in Miami and bought seven stores
1963	Opened southeast coast headquarters and distribution center in North Miami
1971	Two stores opened in Jacksonville
1973	Opened bakery plant and constructed produce distribution center in Lakeland
1974	Sales passed $1 billion annually; opened distribution center and division office in Jacksonville, Florida
1975	Publix Employee Stock Ownership Trust (ESOT) started this year
1980	Celebrated 50 years of "shopping pleasure"; dairy processing plant opened in Lakeland; chain-wide checkout scanning implemented; in early 1980s, started opening on Sundays
1984	Sales passed $3.23 billion; according to *Progressive Grocer*, Publix's 2.36% before-tax net was highest of top 10 supermarket chains — 2.5 times better than Safeway, the industry leader
1986	Opened its first food and pharmacy stores in Orlando and Tampa
1987	Opened dairy processing plant in Deerfield Beach
1990	400 stores and 74,000 associates in Florida
1992	Announced plans for expansion to Georgia and South Carolina
1993	Implemented company-wide quality improvement process (QIP) and work improvement now (WIN) tools for fact-based decision-making and employee empowerment
1994	Sales of $8.66 billion; implemented chain-wide customer intimacy program
1998	Sales of over $12 billion and 120,000 associates; almost 600 stores in four states
2000	Ranked 132 on the *Fortune* 500
2001	Charlie Jenkins Jr. replaced cousin Howard as CEO
2002	Began opening stores in Nashville, Tennessee

Exhibit 15.1   The Publix Spirit over the Years (Compiled from the Publix Website in late 2003 by B. Mujtaba.)

immediate and local feedback. One of the district managers in the Central Florida region used to encourage, and in some cases require, his department managers to learn at least two customers' names every day through face-to-face introductions and interaction. This is important because Publix employees serve their own communities and through this face-to-face interaction they can determine customers' needs, wants, and desires better and faster than any research firm could ever do. Also, research shows that nearly 75% of supermarket shoppers shop and visit supermarkets on a weekly basis. Thus, building a relationship with customers is a necessity, rather than a luxury, in order to stay aware of their needs and expectations.

It is through these types of programs and committed people that Publix is able to offer its employees an environment "where *working* is a pleasure" and its customers an environment "where *shopping* is a pleasure." Publix associates' success with customers originates from their belief that no sale is final or complete until the meal is eaten and fully enjoyed; then, they have made a positive and lasting impression. Publix's guarantee, of which every associate is aware, reads that "we will never, knowingly disappoint you. If for any reason your purchase does not give you complete satis-faction, the full purchase price will be cheerfully refunded immediately upon request." These are not just words to live by but moral imperatives for retailers that have made Publix a successful and innovative giant.

KEY SUCCESS FACTORS

Competition in the supermarket industry is strong; for example, Wal-Mart, now the number one retail grocer in the world, is opening major super-centers throughout Florida. However, Publix is not willing to concede its customers to the competition. Bill Fauerbach, vice president of the Miami division, said, "only we can give our customers a reason to shop elsewhere. As long as we take care of our customers better than anyone else, we will defeat our competition." The new generation of Publix leaders under-stands that complacency is their number one enemy; therefore, they continue to focus and improve on factors that have made them successful in the past.

They further understand that delivering superior customer value is a race without a finish line in today's fast-paced world. Therefore, they never lose sight of caring for people and delivering quality products, service, and excellence in everything they do. Ed Crenshaw, the president of Publix, during his first year in the office in 1995, introduced four success drivers for the company: *knowing the business*; *knowing the product*; *knowing the customer*; and *continuously training people*. Therefore, every department has implemented different means of doing a better job with these four success drivers.

Publix has instituted a world-class training program for its perishable departments like deli, bakery, produce, and seafood. The goal of getting to know the customer has made Publix better than ever with regard to understanding customers and fulfilling their needs in a timely fashion. Publix's customer intimacy program has enabled managers to keep their fingers on the pulse of the customer on a daily basis. This focus on customers has encouraged management to gather feedback, not only from their own customers but also from their competitors' customers. They gather data from satisfied as well as dissatisfied customers because they understand that using biased data to make generalizations regarding all customers is more dangerous than not using them at all.

Publix continuously collects data from its store associates using a program called Associate Voice Survey (AVS). For example, during 1997, over 90,000 retail and support associates completed this survey and, as a result, Publix learned that communication was the dominant factor in associate satisfaction; customer service, loyalty, and positive coworker attitude ranked as the next top three satisfaction drivers. Another positive outcome of AVS was that many departments and stores created cross-functional and ad hoc teams to discuss opportunities for improvement. Furthermore, Publix has invested heavily in developing an internal professional development curriculum to develop associates' skills and help them assume greater responsibility and leadership roles at Publix. Howard Jenkins once told employees that "we envision Publix as a world player. And there will be bumps in the road as we grow larger and spread further. I need each of you to help me uphold our mission to be the premier quality food retailer in the world." This type of a statement from a top company representative can be very influential and encouraging with regard to teamwork; taking personal responsibility for results; and overall financial performance.

A major factor contributing to Publix's ongoing success is the company's loyalty and commitment to employee training. Most employees begin working for Publix at a young age and tend to stay there after college as well.

> One story is about a young man who had recently graduated from college and was hired by a supermarket. On his first day on the job, the manager greeted him with a warm handshake and a smile, gave him a broom, and said, "Your first job will be to sweep out the store and then we will begin mopping."
>
> "But I'm a college graduate," the young man replied indignantly.
>
> "Oh, I'm sorry. I didn't know that," said the manager. "Here, we do have on-the-job training so give me the broom — I'll show you how!"

Although a college education is very important for leadership and management positions, Publix provides many executive development and on-the-job training opportunities for its associates.

INDUSTRY RANKINGS AND AWARDS

A customer satisfaction survey conducted nationwide by *Consumer Reports* revealed that Publix Super Markets was ranked third among 46 chains. Publix scored 82 out of a possible 100, meaning that customers were very satisfied on average, according to the magazine. *Consumer Reports* surveyed more than 25,000 of their readers during 2001 and early 2002, asking them to rate the various chains on prices, check-out speed, service, and cleanliness. Raley's, an 83-store chain in the West, and Wegmans, a 65-store chain in the Northeast, topped the survey. Raley's scored an 84, while Wegmans had an 83. Differences of fewer than four points are not meaningful, according to the survey, so the top three chains essentially are even. Raley's, Wegmans, and Publix each received neutral ratings on prices but excelled in check-out speed, service, and cleanliness. Many customers say they do not mind paying a little more to shop in Publix's clean stores staffed with well-trained and friendly employees. "Service is what Publix built its reputation on," said Chuck Gilmer, editor of *The Shelby Report*, an industry newsletter based in Gainesville, Georgia.

Publix is consistently ranked the highest among its competitors in the *American Customer Satisfaction Index* or ACSI (see Exhibit 15.2).

	1994	1995	1996	1997	1998	1999	2000	2001	2002
Supermarkets	74	75	74	73	73	74	73	75	75
Publix Super Markets, Inc.	81	82	80	79	79	82	77	81	81
SUPERVALU Inc.	77	77	75	74	77	75	75	76	77
Safeway Inc.	72	73	73	70	71	72	76	75	76
The Kroger Company	76	76	74	74	73	74	71	75	75
Albertsons, Inc.	74	77	77	72	70	73	70	72	73
Winn-Dixie Stores, Inc.	74	75	75	74	74	71	74	72	73

[a] Fourth-quarter rankings by year.

Exhibit 15.2 American Customer Satisfaction Index[a] (From The American Customer Satisfaction Index. http://www.theacsi.org/ fourth_quarter.htm#sup.)

Established in 1994, the ACSI consists of uniform and independent measures of how households rate various consumption experiences. ACSI tracks trends in customer satisfaction and provides valuable benchmarking insights of the consumer economy for companies, industry trade associations, and government agencies. The ACSI is produced through a partnership of the University of Michigan Business School; the American Society for Quality (ASQ); and the international consulting firm, CFI Group, ASCI questions also assess perceptions of value and how well the products or services live up to customer expectations and whether customers are willing to pay more for them.

The National Quality Research Center polled more than 50,000 customers on 200 companies. The University of Michigan measured the responses according to six quality indices and scored the companies on a 100-point scale. Publix received a score of 80, with its closest competitor on the list, Albertsons, receiving a score of 77. In another ranking by *Fortune*, Publix moved up to the number two spot in the Food and Drug Store Industry for America's most admired companies; Walgreens took first place. Although Publix has had its share of success and recognition as a tough competitor, it is still relatively small compared to other supermarket giants with regard to the number of stores and yearly revenues (see Exhibit 15.3).

Publix has received various rankings and awards for being a caring employer, an industry leader, and socially responsible in the community. As a caring employer, Publix has been:

■ Named by *Child* magazine as one of the top 10 child-friendly supermarkets (2003)

Company Name	No. Stores (2003)	2002	1996	1995	1994
Kroger Co.	2519	51,700	25,170.91	23,937.80	22,959.12
Winn-Dixie Stores, Inc.	1073	12,200	13,218.72	12,955.49	11,787.84
Food Lion	2520	15,000	9,005.93	8,210.88	7,932.59
Safeway, Inc.	1702	32,400	17,269.00	16,397.50	15,626.60
Albertsons Inc.[b]	2287	35,620	13,776.68	12,585.03	11,894.62
Publix	769	15,900	10,525.97	9,470.71	8,742.49

[a] Revenues in millions.
[b] Albertson's acquired American Stores in 1998.

Exhibit 15.3 Comparison of Publix and Competitor Revenues[a]

- One of the top companies in *Fortune*'s list of 100 best companies to work for (2003)
- One of *Jacksonville Magazine*'s top 25 family friendly companies (2002)
- One of the nation's outstanding employers of older workers, according to Experience Works (2002)
- One of BestJobsUSA.com's employers of choice 500 (2001)
- One of *Central Florida Family* magazine's top companies for working families (1999)
- One of the top 10 companies to work for in America in the book, *The 100 Best Companies to Work for in America* (Currency/Double-day, 1993)
- Awarded the 1996 United Way Spirit of America award

COMPANY EARNINGS

Publix announced its 2002 annual results on March 3, 2003. Sales for the fiscal year ended December 28, 2002, reached $15.9 billion, a 4.2% increase from the preceding year's $15.3 billion. Comparable store sales for 2002 decreased 0.7%. Net earnings for 2002 were $632.4 million, compared to $530.4 million for 2001. Earnings per share increased to $3.25 for 2002, up from $2.62 in 2001. On March 5, 2003, Publix announced that its board of directors declared a cash dividend on its common stock. The 2003 dividend is $0.40 per share, up from $0.33 per share in 2002. Publix CEO Charlie Jenkins Jr. said, "I'm pleased that our strong earnings growth resulted in a stock price increase at a time when the market continues to struggle." According to Howard Jenkins, these positive results come as no real surprise to the people of Publix:

> Publix people have been working hard, preparing for an even grander vision of our future. Earlier in this decade, we committed ourselves to a mission to become the premier quality food retailer in the world. We introduced our own quality improvement process and later adapted a discipline of *Customer Intimacy*, which is helping us to listen more effectively to our customers. All of these initiatives have engaged the resourcefulness of thousands of associates from every area of our company. Together we are discovering powerful new methods for delivering customer value.

SERVICE WITH A SMILE: THE PUBLIX STYLE

The author of the slogan "where shopping is a pleasure," the late William (Bill) Schroter, became a legend within the Publix culture as the spirit of the statement spread throughout the company and became part of the Publix culture. Schroter started working for Publix in 1949 and served the company for over 40 years; he retired in the early 1990s and died in 1998. Schroter's slogan replaced an older slogan, "Florida's finest food stores" that, according to Schroter, was self-congratulatory, offering no promise to customers. The current slogan tells Publix employees that their customers want more than just groceries. Publix people know that customers want good quality, excellent prices, and a good shopping experience. Although quality products and good prices are very important to creating customer value, they are not enough to keep customers coming back. Therefore, Publix associates are always receiving training on relationship-building techniques in order to understand customers better and take care of their needs quickly.

Publix's mission statement very clearly states that Publix is passionately focused on customer value. Publix is committed to satisfying the needs of its customers as individuals better than its competition does. Although competitors can offer good prices and quality products, Publix wants to stand out in the customer's mind for providing *delightful* customer service in every shopping experience. Competitive prices and quality products must exist in order for a business to be successful and are easily duplicated; however, providing delightful customer service comes from the culture of an organization that creates superior customer value. This is why Publix associates closely align their daily work habits to stay focused on customers.

Publix people understand that they cannot be casual about achieving *customer intimacy*. They realize that such intimacy needs an intimate, professional, thorough, consistent, and disciplined method of serving customers that will become a normal way of doing business. In fact, the goal at Publix is to build customer intimacy in all of its stores by creating an environment that is sensitive and responsive to the wants and needs of all customers. Publix spends considerable time studying the best practices of other companies and incorporates a practical and comprehensive plan for developing customer intimacy in all Publix stores. Developing customer intimacy means working through four phases again and again. Each phase is critical for success of the program and feeds the next phase:

1. Understand customers' wants and needs (with respect to food acquisition and the accompanying quality and service levels).

2. Understand customers' and competitors' perceptions of the company.
3. Establish and maintain a strong customer intimacy program throughout the company.
4. Continually improve the customer intimacy relationship program.

The philosophy of Publix is not to satisfy and delight customers one time; customers must be satisfied, delighted, and excited every time they visit or shop at the store. Publix associates are taught that customers are their most valued assets, who must be welcomed, cherished, and appreciated for choosing to shop at their stores. Associates are often asked to reflect on some of the following facts about customers, as well as other similar facts:

■ The average customer spends $5000 on groceries each year and lives in one geographic area for about 10 years (total spending = $50,000).
■ Attracting a new customer costs companies five to six times more than keeping one who already shops with them.
■ Of complaining customers, 95% will continue to do business with the company if their problems are properly taken care of and resolved on the spot.
■ Of customers who quit shopping at a particular store, 86% do so because they feel the company or an associate was indifferent to a problem they expressed.
■ One dissatisfied customer tells eight to ten potential customers about a problem or bad experience that was not addressed in the store. It has been said that each of the eight to ten potential customers is likely to tell at least five more people about the problem or bad experience.

Publix associates understand that if they cannot satisfy customers' requirements and meet their demands, customers will shop at other retailers. They remember that if they, as Publix associates, do not offer a great shopping experience for their customers, someone else will. Therefore, all retail associates are taught the *10-Foot* and *10-Second* rules to help them quickly acknowledge customers. The *10-Foot* rule states that one must acknowledge all customers within 10 feet of one's surroundings and the *10-Second* rule states that these customers must be acknowledged within 10 seconds of entering the service counter area or the 10-foot zone.

Research in the supermarket industry indicates the factors that affect customer loyalty:

- The largest percentage of customers (68%) leave if they perceive an attitude of indifference.
- Some customers (14%) leave because they feel they can find better quality products and services elsewhere.
- Customers (9%) shop elsewhere because they think a store's prices are higher than its competitors' prices.
- A few of the customers (5%) become friends with people who work for a competitor and take their business there.
- Some customers (3%) leave because they move to a different area.

Publix associates are also encouraged to use their daily observations, customer feedback, survey evaluation, and other data to improve their jobs, better serve their customers, and make Publix a better place "where shopping is a pleasure." Associates can use Publix's quality improvement process (QIP) or work improvement now (WIN) tools to improve their jobs, based on fact-based decisions and data. These statistical tools are available for everyone to learn and use during their work hours in order to deliver more than what they promise.

Publix teaches the principle of "deliver plus 1%," which states that an associate must consistently meet his or her customers' shopping needs and then exceed their expectations by improving service 1%. The company believes in positively surprising the customer by overdelivering on what customers value. This principle further states that when a promise is made to a customer, the one making the promise must be consistent and deliver *all* the time. It means that, before exceeding customers' *expectations*, it is necessary to be meeting their *needs* satisfactorily. If any extra services are promised, make sure that they are delivered as promised.

Finally, Publix rewards top-notch service by implementing an awards program that shows associates how much management values their efforts to provide *delightful* service to customers. Delightful Service Awards are given for customer service over and above the minimum standards listed on the observation sheet for the area. Associates are expected to provide great customer service as part of the job requirement, so the awards are given to associates who make the extra effort to delight customers at Publix. To receive a Delightful Service Award, associates must provide delightful service to a customer in a way that is formally recognized by the customer, a "mystery shopper" appointed by district management, or a member of the store management team.

Associates are trained and encouraged to set personal goals with regard to serving customers better and exceeding their expectations. They are asked to find out what they can do to increase and improve their personal commitment to customer intimacy. They are encouraged to set goals to increase their awareness of customers as well as customers' wants and needs — and rewarded for doing so. For instance, associates may set goals such as:

- Learn the names of two or more "regular" customers every week.
- Identify new or unusual products in the store, noticing when a customer has selected the product for purchase and using the new item to start a conversation.
- Notice at least four customers in a week's time who may need help locating a product and take them to it.
- Volunteer to demonstrate a new product in the store in order to develop or improve people skills with customers.
- Conduct an unofficial mystery shopper evaluation when shopping at a Publix store, which will help increase awareness of a personal definition of delightful customer service when a customer.

PUBLIX GOES ONLINE

A recent study revealed that by 2007, 20 million households in the U.S. will purchase groceries, food and other household items online (see Exhibit 15.4). They will spend approximately $85 billion dollars, mainly for food items.[2] However, to date none of the major grocery chains has mastered the online arena. Peapod, Inc., which began as a start-up with no money, was first. The company took phone calls and faxes for orders. Employees filled them at local supermarkets and delivered them to the homes of customers. Peapod was initially profitable, but eventually began to fail when, by 1999, the company had incurred losses of $29 million on sales of $73 million. (Peapod was acquired outright by the Dutch giant retailer Royal Ahold NV in late 2001.)

California-based Webvan entered the scene in 1999 with much fanfare, planning to revolutionize grocery retailing. Webvan utilized a "central fill" model in which large distribution centers costing $35 million each were dedicated to filling online grocery orders. Customer demand never reached anywhere near levels required to recoup its huge fixed-costs investment and the company lost from $5 to $30 on every order it handled. Webvan filed for bankruptcy protection in early 2001 and ceased operations later that year.

Profits for Internet grocers were scarce, affected primarily by high shipping costs and regular distribution centers, which were not well suited to handle order fulfillment. Not a single online grocer in the U.S. has been able to turn a profit; however, U.K.-based Tesco has reported a profit in its online operations. Tesco, as well as Safeway and Albertsons, utilizes a "store pick" model (see Exhibit 15.5), in which orders placed online are simply drawn from goods on store shelves and delivery costs tacked on

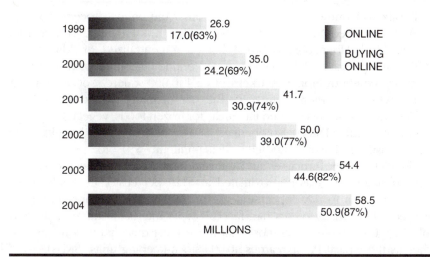

Exhibit 15.4   U.S. Households Online and Online Buying Trends

Exhibit 15.5   Store Pick Model

to the cost of the groceries (as opposed to Webvan's emphasis on central warehouses). The warehouse system can be cheaper in the long run, but it requires a huge amount of initial capital and a well-developed infrastructure to get the goods to the shopper. Distribution logistics are a "make or break" proposition in online grocery retailing.

Publix was one of the latecomers to enter the online grocery business when it launched PublixDirect in September, 2001. Unlike competitors Safeway and Albertsons, Publix followed a centralized or "direct fill" fulfillment approach. PublixDirect served online customers over a 35-mile radius in the South Florida market from a 140,000 square foot distribution center, which was more than twice the size of many Publix stores.

The warehouse was divided into areas for frozen foods, vegetables, meats, and poultry. PublixDirect also operated its own bakery devoted solely to the online business. For a $7.95 fee and a minimum $50 order, PublixDirect would pick up the groceries and deliver them to a customer's doorstep. Average order size was approximated at $120 per customer. PublixDirect took 18 months to develop a strategy for the Internet venture, hoping to succeed where many others had failed. For its Internet venture, it stocked only 12,500 items, selecting those that move most quickly off store shelves, whereas the typical Publix carries 40,000 stock-keeping units (SKUs).

The company benchmarked earlier grocery online operations to fine tune and perfect its processes, including order taking, order fulfillment, outbound logistics, and payment. Orders placed at www.publixdirect.com would be downloaded at midnight to a central computer, which organized them for pick-up in the warehouse and for delivery by truck. Orders could be made 7 days in advance and were filled starting at 6 a.m. Each order was distilled into a bar code and attached to a plastic box. When a PublixDirect employee scanned the bar code, a shopping list came up on a tiny computer attached to his or her wrist. The order also appeared on a handheld computer given to each truck driver. When the goods were delivered, the customer signed for the delivery on the computer screen, using a stylus.

Payment was made in advance at the Web site, using a credit card. Customers were issued a paper receipt and were sent a back-up via e-mail. If a customer had ordered beer or wine, the driver was prompted on the computer screen to check his age. Drivers were even asked to cover their shoes with footsies when they entered a house.

PublixDirect believed that the average income of its online target customer would skew higher than its regular store shoppers. Although initially anticipating that its primary target market would be dual income families with household incomes exceeding $75,000, much to the company's surprise, the typical shoppers attracted to PublixDirect turned out to be single-income households with stay-at-home moms.

PublixDirect strongly felt that its prospect for survival in the online grocery business would be based on a well-conceived value proposition that included:

■ Convenient solution to grocery shopping
■ Prices similar to local supermarkets

- Superior product quality
- Superior customer service

The company benchmarked earlier grocery online operations to fine-tune and perfect its processes, including order taking, order fulfillment, outbound logistics, and payment.

CURRENT TRENDS

Change is constant and ubiquitous throughout the supermarket industry because customers are becoming more knowledgeable and demanding. In today's market-based economy, customers want a variety of ethnic foods made with quality ingredients and representing their culture; therefore, quality service must be aligned accordingly with the best prices in order to deliver superior value. Over 20,000 new items hit the market every year and understanding the value of each product to each customer is no easy task. Therefore, the value of understanding, anticipating, and determining consumer preference cannot be overestimated. Changing effectively is a matter of keeping up with the demands of consumers; offering more value for the customer's dollar; being competitive; and creating fans of the supermarket.

Food safety is becoming a major issue in the grocery industry. According to a *Better Homes and Gardens* panel study, only 20% of the panelists were very confident that the food they buy is safe to eat. Global activist group Greenpeace has joined two other coalitions — True Food Now and GE-Free Markets — trying to convince two supermarket operators in California to stop using genetically engineered ingredients in their private label food lines. According to a NBC Dateline investigation, seven of the nation's largest grocery-store chains, operating more than 7000 stores in nearly every state, admitted to redating meats and fish after they had reached their original "sell-by" date. In the food retailing industry, leaders are paying more attention to ensuring that food products are safe and produced in a clean environment. According to Todd Rossow, corporate quality assurance lab coordinator at Publix, its associates are constantly looking at all the risk factors associated with food quality as well as food safety while attempting to eliminate them.

Today's customers are increasingly concerned and vocal about the quality and nutrition of the food they purchase. According to research, 70% of women and 54% of men say they consider nutrition to be an important factor in their consideration of food purchases. Once a niche category, organic foods are becoming increasingly mainstream as small, regional, organic food-producing companies have been acquired by major manufacturers. Demand for organic foodstuffs is growing 20 to 24%

annually; according to the U.S. Department of Agriculture, Americans spent $460 billion on groceries and $9.4 billion on organic items in 2001. Today's nutrition-conscious supermarket shoppers are checking labels as never before. The Food and Drug Administration is requiring that *trans* fat content appear on all food labels by January 1, 2006. (*Trans* fats are found in foods ranging from partially hydrogenated oils to fried foods, cookies, pastries, dairy products, and meats.) Finally, some manufacturers are considering the idea of offering "functional foods" fortified with a growing number of popular herbs, vitamins, hormones, and other healthy additives.

Technology that allows customers to be their own cashiers and check out their own groceries has been around for many years. However, it is only recently that some food retailers are toying with its implementation as a strategic tool to enhance their competitive position and offer better service to the time-impoverished customer. This is because self-checkout technology, which allows shoppers to scan their own items, offers savings to the shopper and the retailer, along with an added convenience. Self-checkouts can serve only the segment of the market that wants to scan its own groceries and has a debit card to pay for them. Check-out efficiency has also been improved by widespread use of debit and credit card payment systems.

The days of preparing complete meals at home are becoming a distant memory for most working people in the U.S. Today's time-poor shoppers are opting for prepared foods such as precut produce, cooked dinners, and prepared takeout foods. According to a *Better Homes and Gardens* 1997–1998 consumer panel survey, 37% of respondents buy prepared products at least once each week, compared with 27.3% in 1992. About 22% of the panelists use more convenience foods than they did 2 years earlier and 76.1% buy convenience products such as salad mixes and precut vegetables. Also, 77.4% of the respondents purchase prepared foods to eat at home and 49% of those who eat at home said they do so because they are more careful about what they eat. It has been said that over 40% of all consumer spending on food is for meals eaten away from home.

CONCLUDING REMARKS

Publix's history shows that it bought 19 All American stores in 1945 and 7 Grand Union stores in Miami in 1959 to expand its market share. According to Publix leaders, currently no plans for mergers or acquisitions exist. However, the company is not against the idea of acquiring another company that fits Publix's culture and philosophy. "If the right opportunity came up we could acquire another company... we may or may not find another company we like.....we believe in internal growth, building our own stores."

The supermarket industry is becoming increasingly concentrated as large regional chains such as Kroger, Safeway and Albertsons dominate their markets. The rapid growth and development of "supercenters" as evidenced by Wal-Mart's grocery industry ascendancy is testament to the viability of hybrid formats (i.e., grocery and general merchandise). Super-centers' sales exceeded $100 billion in 2000 (half of which was accounted for by the grocery side of the store). Therefore, more companies are being forced to grow faster, partner, or merge in order to survive long term. Publix's current strategy is to grow steadily from within and expand the Publix culture throughout its stores. (Postscript: PublixDirect discontinued operations in August, 2003, just short of 2 years after it was launched. Its Broward County, Florida, and surrounding area pilot programs failed to meet management's projected revenue and profit levels for the business.)

QUESTIONS

1. What factors are currently involved in successfully competing in the supermarket industry and how will these factors change in the next 10 years?
2. What can Publix do to strengthen its market position with regard to its suppliers, customers, competitors, and employees?
3. What are the values of Publix's organizational culture; employees; customers; shareholders; suppliers; and competitors? Which ones do you consider to be value adders and which do you see as value destroyers as Publix attempts to become the premier quality food retailer in America?
4. What factors are currently influencing a customer's decision to shop at Publix? Why have competitors been unable to duplicate such success factors successfully? How will these factors change in the next decade?
5. Analyze how PublixDirect's processes were used to add value. In hindsight, what should the company have done differently to keep PublixDirect a viable business model?
6. What were the factors that led to the demise of PublixDirect? What does it take to create a successful online operation in the U.S.?

REFERENCES

1. Moskowitz, M. (2003) 100 best companies to work for, *Fortune*, 147, 127.
2. Smith, J. (1999) On-line grocery shopping on track for rapid growth, *Food Consumer Packaged Goods News Inf.*, September 15, 1.
3. The American Customer Satisfaction Index, http://www.theacsi.org/fourth_quarter.htm#sup.

CASE 16: STATEPRIDE INDUSTRIAL LAUNDRY — VALUE CHAIN ANALYSIS*

The rental laundry industry (SIC categories 7213 and 7218) is highly competitive and in the midst of consolidation. Laundries generally rent industrial uniforms and entrance mats with a service of periodically (once or twice a week) picking up the dirty uniforms and mats. These are then laundered and returned clean.

To survive and generate a reasonable profit, locally owned StatePride Industrial Laundry must outperform the larger national chains. The general manager, Mr. Don McDonald, wants to develop a market advantage. He believes that *value chain analysis* is the right tool to help him provide to customers the benefits that they want at prices that are reasonable. If StatePride can do this effectively, the firm will discover the basis for a competitive edge.

WHAT IS VALUE?

Mr. McDonald first needs to understand how customers such as the local Ford dealership, dairy plant, or plumbing supply firm perceive the value of StatePride's offerings. Each of these companies purchases goods and services on the basis of the value that it believes it receives. A simple mathematical formula expresses this:

$$Value = Benefits \div (Price + Associated\ Costs)$$

---

* This case was prepared by Dr. Hilton Barrett, associate professor of business, Elizabeth City State University, Elizabeth City, North Carolina. He may be contacted at hbarrett@mail.ecsu.edu

This customer value formula can be explored in more detail. The potential customer looks at the *benefits* he receives from products — not the physical characteristics. The customer does not rent a uniform or a mat; he pays a service fee to reduce the maintenance costs of keeping his workers and workplace clean, healthy, and presentable. The entrance mat fiber description *nylon 6,6* has little or no meaning to the customer. The words *clean, presentable*, and *healthy* have a great deal of meaning. If the mat is at the entrance to a laboratory, the customer receives little additional benefit from a mat with the company's logo; however, if the mat is at the front door of a car dealership, the customer may perceive a large additional benefit of the positive image generated from a logo mat. Thus, increasing benefits increases value — if it helps the customer. However, simply providing more product features does not necessarily mean that the customer places an increased value on the additional offering. The objective is to meet customer requirements or needs. The customer will expect to pay for benefits that satisfy needs, but nothing more.

The product is more than the mat. It also includes the mat's cleanliness, timeliness, and service delivery, as well as StatePride's response to requests for additional mats or replacing dirty mats in an emergency. Furthermore, "product" means office functions such as invoicing and flexibility on contract responsibilities. It also includes the attitude and helpfulness of the laundry's customer service representatives, as well as clarity of communications between these people and the customer.

The emphasis today is on *total* costs and long-term relationships. This is more than simply the *price paid* to StatePride. It includes *associated costs*, which are costs incurred by the customer using this service. For example, these costs may include the square footage within the customer's facility required for uniform lockers. After all, the area devoted to lockers cannot be used for production machinery or related profitable activities. Associated costs include normal business functions such as personnel time needed to check in the product and account for returns; accounting department time to process invoices; or workers' time to fill out repair tags. Often, neither the customer nor the supplier recognizes the various associated costs. The key to success is to drive down *total* costs. If a customer's *total* costs over the long term are reduced, the resulting *value* to StatePride is increased.

Price can be confusing. The uniform rental price may be quoted as "per change." However, normal pricing within rental laundries can include loss and abuse charges; wastewater surcharges; name and emblem charges; or set-up charges. The customer is relatively unconcerned about State-Pride's costs. He simply wants a viable, profitable supplier who can provide a long-term, ongoing solution to his needs. He is concerned only about the invoiced price coupled with his company's associated costs and the supplier's continuing ability to provide the required quality level of service.

The value formula math is simple and straightforward: (1) increase the benefits and increase the value; (2) decrease the price paid and/or associated costs and increase the value. The customer will pay up to the perceived value — not a penny more — if the price paid is less than the value received, so much the better.

CREATING VALUE: THE VALUE CHAIN ANALYSIS

Value chain analysis is a powerful management tool used to understand how to drive down costs; provide greater benefits to the customer; and understand the generation of value. This technique is the most useful weapon in the marketing arsenal for increasing the value of StatePride's products to its customers. A value chain follows the generation of value from design through operations to the final product or service delivered to the customer. It can then be expanded to include StatePride's suppliers' development, delivery of its goods/services, and finally into the customer's system as the products are used. Each phase of the chain provides an opportunity to increase the customer's benefits or decrease costs. As shown earlier, either or both of these can increase the value of StatePride's offering as perceived by the customer. Remember that value, quality, and beauty are in the eye of the beholder (the customer).

Michael E. Porter, an economics professor at Harvard Business School, discusses the value chain concept in his book *Competitive Advantage* (1985). A generic value chain is depicted in Exhibit 16.1. At this stage, the core question is: what activities add value within your firm? To use value chain analysis fully, the generic chain needs to be expanded and redefined to include the supplier, firm, and customer. As an example, follow the value chain for a uniform program that StatePride Laundry is renting to a regional plumbing company, DownEast Plumbing.

Three separate levels of activity are depicted in Exhibit 16.2. In value chain analysis, the middle phase is always the analyst's firm. If a uniform manufacturer performs the analysis, the supplier might be a textile mill and the customer might be a rental laundry. By tracing the activities of each phase and the generation of value, management can evaluate possibilities for increasing benefits and lowering costs within each of the

Design → Materials management → Operations and sales→ Marketing → Distribution → Service

Exhibit 16.1   The Generic Value Chain

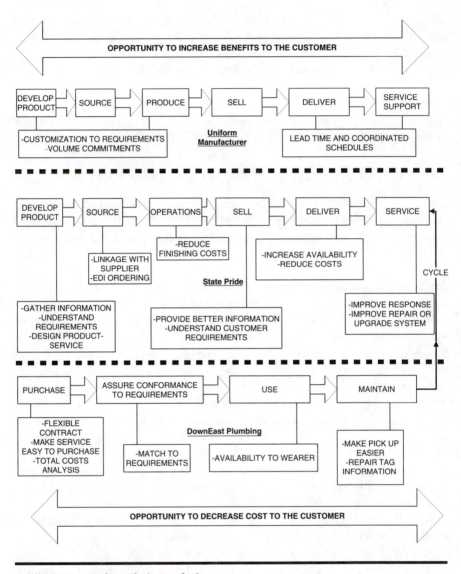

OPPORTUNITY TO INCREASE BENEFITS TO THE CUSTOMER

| DEVELOP PRODUCT | SOURCE | PRODUCE | SELL | DELIVER | SERVICE SUPPORT |

-CUSTOMIZATION TO REQUIREMENTS
-VOLUME COMMITMENTS

Uniform Manufacturer

LEAD TIME AND COORDINATED SCHEDULES

| DEVELOP PRODUCT | SOURCE | OPERATIONS | SELL | DELIVER | SERVICE |

-REDUCE FINISHING COSTS

-LINKAGE WITH SUPPLIER
-EDI ORDERING

-INCREASE AVAILABILITY
-REDUCE COSTS

State Pride

CYCLE

-GATHER INFORMATION
-UNDERSTAND REQUIREMENTS
-DESIGN PRODUCT-SERVICE

-PROVIDE BETTER INFORMATION
-UNDERSTAND CUSTOMER REQUIREMENTS

-IMPROVE RESPONSE
-IMPROVE REPAIR OR UPGRADE SYSTEM

| PURCHASE | ASSURE CONFORMANCE TO REQUIREMENTS | USE | MAINTAIN |

-FLEXIBLE CONTRACT
-MAKE SERVICE EASY TO PURCHASE
-TOTAL COSTS ANALYSIS

DownEast Plumbing

-MATCH TO REQUIREMENTS

-AVAILABILITY TO WEARER

-MAKE PICK UP EASIER
-REPAIR TAG INFORMATION

OPPORTUNITY TO DECREASE COST TO THE CUSTOMER

Exhibit 16.2   Value Chain Analysis

phases. These possibilities are shown in this exhibit figure by the comments given under the various activities.

The more the analyst understands the processes and real needs within the customer's internal value chain, the easier it is to develop products and related support services that increase the benefits or drive down the associated costs. Value chain analysis is a multipurpose tool. It can be used in numerous applications, as listed in Exhibit 16.3.

Cost reduction through reengineering your processes (changing the way you run the business)

Cost reduction through reengineering processes with suppliers

Cost reduction through reengineering processes with customers

Developing a competitive advantage by restructuring the value chain (supplier–firm–customer) to offer greater benefits, lower total costs, and increased value of your goods and services

Benchmarking an activity in your value chain; for example, FedEx is often benchmarked (compared to) for its world-class logistics systems.

Competitive analysis — analyzing strengths and weaknesses of key competitors; this learning experience can help find a unique market advantage

Evaluation and control — objectively critiquing the performance of business strategies and tactics

---

Exhibit 16.3   How to Use Value Chain Analysis

APPLYING VALUE CHAIN ANALYSIS

DownEast Plumbing is a large regional firm with many service vehicles. Its major competitor is a nationally franchised firm with a similar number of service vehicles in the targeted market. Competition is intense (where is it not today?). DownEast's marketing tactics emphasize the professionalism of its people and its service response time. Management wants company personnel always to wear appropriate uniforms and to wear them appropriately because this enhances the company image. StatePride's salesperson is working with DownEast on developing an image-oriented program. The uniform will be basic navy pants and a striped work shirt unique for DownEast Plumbing. The uniform program is an important part of DownEast's marketing activities; a series of local cable television commercials is built around its friendly and professionally uniformed plumbers.

Mr. McDonald's initial use of value chain analysis is to examine the activities within his firm. This evaluates the intrafirm or horizontal linkages between value-generating activities. The first step is to review possible alternatives for increasing value by increasing benefits or lowering costs. For example, more durable uniforms will increase StatePride's initial purchasing costs, but will lower the replacement, repair, and average-per-week costs.

Next, Mr. McDonald assesses the interfirm, or vertical, linkages among supplier, StatePride, and the customer. What are the requirements of each within the process? The greater the understanding of buyer needs and

requirements, as well as the uniform supplier's capabilities and requirements, the better the ability to generate greater value for customers. A
working relationship with supplier and customer will allow evaluation of
capabilities and requirements, as well as possible alternatives with the
objective of increasing benefits and reducing costs.

DownEast Plumbing emphasizes comfort as much as appearance for
its personnel. It anticipates redefining the image of its workforce in about
18 months. On the basis of the StatePride salesperson's knowledge and
support from the uniform manufacturer, this could lead to a proposal of
100% cotton shirts and pants. Although these garments do not last as long
as 65/35 fabrics, the plumbing firm does not need the longer wear-life,
nor does it increase the benefits of StatePride's products for them. Further
discussion may indicate that wrinkle-resistant cotton shirts and pants
provide an acceptable appearance. The laundry then can forego pressing
and decrease labor and energy costs. Such savings can be passed on to
its customer.

StatePride can work with the uniform manufacturer on a shirt unique
to DownEast. Perhaps Mr. McDonald can use a base fabric already in the
manufacturer's stock. He can work with the manufacturer to look for ways
to reduce his costs while still meeting the objectives of DownEast Plumbing. Good manufacturing suppliers welcome the opportunity to work with
their customers on this objective. Thus, value chain analysis helps the
manufacturer in the same way that it assists StatePride. An overengineered
shirt may be a great shirt; nevertheless, StatePride will only pay for a shirt
that meets its requirements, and nothing more.

Mr. McDonald can easily use value chain analysis to evaluate his
marketing options. It is typical for a manufacturer to require volume
commitment and lead time commitments. The value chain shows that,
once again, this is an area of opportunity. Working with the customer,
StatePride can develop forecasts for its uniform needs. This benefits the
production planning for the manufacturer and leads to a delivery schedule
agreed to in advance by all participants. It reduces inventory vulnerability
by all concerned — another cost reduction. These "win–win" solutions
benefit all parties.

Communication is the key to success in the development of any value
chain analysis program. What are DownEast Plumbing's requirements for
the uniform and servicing? What are the uniform manufacturer's requirements for volume and lead time? What are the laundry's requirements for
receiving garments so as to provide adequate time for preparation for
initial placement? Each participant has its own requirements and capabilities. Armed with value chain analysis knowledge and understanding, the
process from uniform manufacturer through laundry to customer (and the
service cycle back through the laundry) can be evaluated. Properly

assessed, the opportunities for increasing benefits, lowering costs, and increasing value are readily apparent. When it is successfully implemented, satisfied customers receive greater value and StatePride builds customer loyalty and retention and increases profits.

QUESTIONS

1. What are some ways that StatePride can reduce price paid without changing its regular list prices for services?
2. How can StatePride's advertising campaign affect a customer's perceived benefits and the resulting perceived value?
3. Explain how service firms should apply value chain analysis to create, deliver, and maximize customer value.

BIBLIOGRAPHY

Porter, M. (1985) *Competitive Advantage*, New York: The Free Press.

CASE 17: TIME INSURANCE — A STUDY OF PROCESS QUALITY IMPROVEMENT*

A longtime industry leader in providing health insurance to individuals and small groups, Time Insurance Company had always enjoyed an excellent reputation with its network of independent agents. However, increasing costs, added product complexities, and uncertainty in the health-care industry threatened Time's ability to maintain its track record of profitable growth. In the second and third quarters of 1992, the company's management undertook a fundamental review of its business strategy, which included a 6-month reengineering effort in the individual medical underwriting unit. Dramatic improvements in quality were achieved through a combination of strategic context, methodology, teamwork, and commitment.

FORMING A TEAM

The company's main challenge was to increase effectiveness in dealing with an increasingly uncertain and changing environment in which local and regional differentiation requires rapid and flexible competitive actions. This meant the organization had to become more nimble in identifying and taking marketplace initiatives, while simultaneously achieving substantial improvements in operating costs and service. A critical element involved the identification and redesign of Time's key business processes to minimize cycle time and waste while simultaneously providing superb quality service to policyholders and agents.

---

* This case was prepared by John Feather, partner, Corporate Renaissance, Inc., and William C. Johnson, professor of marketing, H. Wayne Huizenga School of Business and Entrepreneurship, Nova Southeastern University, Ft. Lauderdale, Florida.

Phase I	Phase II	Phase III	Phase IV
Planning 0.5 months	Analysis 2 months	Design 2.5 months	Implementation

Exhibit 17.1 Phases of the Project

It had become quite apparent that Time's medical underwriting department was in trouble. Policy issuance for the preceding 2 years remained flat; unit costs were increasing; and policy reissues had reached an alarming 10%. Moreover, help-desk calls for application-related problems were increasing 50% a year. Incremental improvement would not help; radical change was needed.

A project team was formed with nine Time employees and two consultants. The consultants acted as reengineering czars, providing project management guidance while facilitating process analysis. The team was charged with developing and testing a new process design. Exhibit 17.1 illustrates the phases of the project and the approximate time spent on each phase.

PLANNING THE PROJECT

First an organizational readiness assessment was conducted to determine the company's climate for change. The assessment was done by the consulting firm using a questionnaire and interviews. The results indicated that the organization was ready for change, meaning that most employees recognized the need for and welcomed change. Next, biweekly divisional meetings were held to inform the entire organization about and include it in the project. Monthly communication forums were also established, as were daily mechanisms for employee involvement, including a newsletter; an electronic mailbox for questions and ideas; a suggestion box; and a "living list," which included ideas that employees thought should be incorporated into the design.

ANALYZING THE SITUATION

As part of the analysis, the team developed:

- Customer segmentation analysis (needs assessment by customer type)
- Workload profile (volume and mix of work)

- Activity value analysis (steps in the process that add value for the customer)
- Design specifications (specific customer demands, such as 24-hour turnaround)
- Design options (range of options used to customize the design)

It then constructed a business process map that detailed work flow to the customer.

From the start, the team felt it needed to look at the new policy issue process from the perspective of its customers: the agents. To gain this outside–in view, it developed a business process map. In this map, the flow of work required to issue a new policy was described in terms of blocks of activity. For example, as applications go through the process, each underwriting request gets quoted, sold, processed, delivered, and serviced. By mapping work flow, the team uncovered startling information about the underwriting process. First, it learned that contact between the company and the customer was minimal, with lengthy gaps between each intersection. At the time, the process required the underwriter to wait for requirements to arrive, and it took an average of 37 days of internal processing time to issue a policy. Often as much as 60 days had elapsed by the time the policyholder received the policy.

Mapping the existing process also revealed that a new policy application went through 284 process steps, only 16 of which actually added value for the customer. These 16 steps accounted for only 9% of the process time (the actual hands-on time that a person spends working on the application being processed). About 95% of the time that was not defined as hands-on was attributed to work waiting in queue.

In addition to mapping the existing process and quantifying the workload, the project team performed documentations of customer specifications and of design options. Questions about service were developed and circulated to gather broad input from agents. This survey was supplemented by a series of customer focus groups. The data collected by the team were categorized by four performance dimensions: quality, delivery, cycle time, and cost. From this research, a set of process specifications was developed to guide the process redesign.

DESIGNING THE NEW PROCESS

The design of the new process had two stages: high-level design and detailed design. In the initial high-level design, team members strove to think out of the box to create a conceptual model that would exceed the already ambitious design specifications. The driving specifications for the design were to improve responsiveness to customer needs dramatically and to reduce cycle time drastically.

Subteams worked in parallel to design the new business. The best attributes of each subteam were integrated into one cohesive vision of the new process and supporting structures. The resulting high-level design envisioned a work team approach. Each work team would be aligned regionally with agents. Some of the key features of the high-level design concept were:

- The high-level conceptual design provided guidance for designing the details.
- The Time team created a new detailed business process map as the primary documentation of the new design.
- The new process contained only 85 process steps, and more than 60% of these added value for the customer.

A NEW ORGANIZATIONAL STRUCTURE

The new process called for new roles and responsibilities throughout the organization; the traditional vertical organizational structure with first-line supervisors was replaced with a flatter organizational structure. Considerable responsibility was assumed by teams under this new organizational structure. Employees were then matched with the skills required in the newly identified roles and intensive training began. The entire division participated in planning and implementing the transition to the new process. A new organization was to be structured around core teams regionally aligned with agents. A technical resource center would be used to train people continually. Teams would pull resources from the technical resource center when trends indicated a higher volume of work or, if the volume was high enough, new teams would be formed.

SUCCESSFUL RESULTS

The new design has resulted in significant process improvements that have in turn had a substantial impact on Time. The process improvements have increased quality and delivery to agents while reducing Time's unit cost and cycle time. Revenue growth has been significant due to the exceptional service given to the agents. The increased flexibility with the new team structure gives the company a competitive advantage and also permits quick changes to accommodate regulatory constraints along with providing Time with a solid base for transition in the new health-care environment. Other results are:

- A 60% reduction in policy reissuances
- A 50% increase in measured customer satisfaction ratings
- A 10% reduction in cost per policy issued
- An 80% reduction in process cycle time for fast-track applications
- Significant increases in revenue from higher customer retention

QUESTIONS

1. Using the Deming Cycle, evaluate Time Insurance's process improvement efforts.
2. What are some other quality tools that Time Insurance could have used to better understand and improve its service levels?
3. What were the key success factors in this case, particularly with regard to process redesign?
4. Discuss the relationship between process improvement and customer-added value.

CASE 18: WALGREENS — CUSTOMER ORIENTATION*

How could a company that started with one store over 100 years ago become the number one drugstore by sales; the number two drug retailer by store count; and rank as one of the world's most admired companies according to *Fortune* magazine? The answer is simple: a focus on creating value for its customers.

BACKGROUND

Walgreen Corporation was started in 1901 on the south side of Chicago by Charles R. Walgreen and it has seen tremendous success over the last century. Mr. Walgreen worked as an apprentice at a drugstore in Chicago and became a pharmacist in 1893. With over 1500 drugstores competing in Chicago and very limited customer service, Walgreen saw an opportunity. He recognized the need for friendlier stores, good customer service, and better quality products and was convinced that, by providing all this, he would succeed as a young entrepreneur.

Walgreen purchased a store from a former boss for $6000 and immediately started the transformation. New, brighter lights were installed in the store; he widened the aisles to make them more inviting; reduced the prices on many items; and started to greet each customer personally at the door. Soon Walgreens became known for a very high level of customer service through its "two minute drill." Walgreen would take an order over the phone from a customer who lived nearby and then repeat it loudly so that one of the apprentices could prepare the order and rush it over to the customer's house. Many times the customer was still on the phone

* Case prepared by Mariana Ilca, Pharm. D/MBA, a pharmacist for Walgreens, who interviewed a district manager and store manager in writing this case. For further information, contact her at milca41907@aol.com.

when the doorbell rang and the order was delivered. Customers were very impressed with the way in which they were treated and the speed with which they received their orders.

The next thing that Walgreen added to the store was the soda fountain; however, unlike competitors, he saw a need for hot food during the winter. Instead of closing the soda fountain in the winter, he started serving soups, sandwiches, pies, and cakes prepared in the kitchen by his wife Myrtle. This way, the fountain was turned into a profitable venture all year round. He also began to add diverse items to the general product mix. He reasoned that if customers came in to get a soda or a snack, they would likely take a couple of minutes and look around the store. If he stocked items that customers might need, even if they were not pharmaceutical goods, customers would buy them there. As a result, Walgreens grew to nine stores by 1916. In 1922, Walgreens distinguished itself from competitors again with the milkshake (see Exhibit 18.1). Ivar Coulson invented the malted milkshake, which was priced at only $0.20 — no minor accomplishment. Walgreens became the place to "hang out" and by the end of 1929 there were 524 stores open around the country.

Walgreen was not satisfied with the company and its success, however; he had an even higher vision. He saw the importance of advertising and in 1931 his was the first company to advertise on the radio. He was also running the largest promotional campaign at a cost of over $75,000. Good customer service; high-quality products; competitive pricing strategy; and advertising kept Walgreens from closing its doors during the Great Depression.

Walgreen recognized that all his success was due to his customers, so it was time for him to give back to the community and further make the company's name known. In 1937, he donated $500,000 to the University of Chicago to form the Foundation for the Study of American Institutions. During World War II, Walgreen opened a nonprofit drugstore in the Pentagon

Use a frosted malt can
1 1/2 oz. of chocolate syrup
3 #16 dips of vanilla ice cream
5 1/2 oz. of cold milk
Add malt powder (one heaping tablespoon)
Place on mixer only until mixed — do not overmix
Use a generous portion of whipped topping in a #1808 10-oz. glass
Pour malted milk in glass approximately 2/3 full
Serve remainder of malted in a shaker along with the glass to the guest
  with straws and package of fountain treat cookies

Exhibit 18.1   How to Make an Old-Fashioned Chocolate Malted Milk

to serve military personnel and the President later recognized him for his good deed. Walgreen also recognized the need for good employees loyal to the company. In order to reward his staff and to attract new talent, he was the first to give profit sharing and pension plans to his employees.

GROWTH, TECHNOLOGY, AND ALLIANCES

By 1984, Walgreens had opened its 1000th store. Today, Walgreens has 3818 stores in 43 states and Puerto Rico. Florida has the highest concentration of stores (570), followed by Illinois (440); Texas (387); and California (313). No other state has more than 120 stores. Walgreens stores were opened strategically with freestanding stores in high-traffic areas accessible to customers. Currently, 20,000 people live within a 5-mile radius of a store, providing a vast pool of customers that can use Walgreens' services. The company is looking to expand and penetrate new markets. Although 50% of the U.S. population lives within a 5-mile radius of the stores, Walgreens' goal is to have 80% of the population within a 1-mile radius. The company has no immediate plans to expand outside the U.S., but plans to open 6000 stores by 2010 and perhaps 10,000 by 2020.

Not only is the company planning to expand and open more stores, but Walgreens is also looking into remodeling older stores and keeping up with new technology. With 7474 pharmacist positions remaining unfilled by the end of 2001, Walgreens needs a plan to help achieve its goals despite the national pharmacist shortage. The only way to beat the pharmacist shortage and still operate almost 4000 stores is by having the best technology and improving work flow in the pharmacy so that each store will be able to fill more prescriptions.

Walgreens invests in technology and is considered to have the best computer information system in the industry. In 1994, Walgreens introduced IntercomPlus, a pharmacy computer system that links all the stores via satellite. This indeed makes it very convenient for customers to be able to travel across the country and have their prescriptions filled or refilled at any Walgreens store in minutes. The system allows the pharmacist to pull up the patient information and profile from any other store and does not require making phone calls to transfer the prescriptions. The system also links the pharmacies to insurance companies, thus enabling them to submit all the claims electronically and get necessary approvals within seconds.

Another innovation that Walgreens introduced to the pharmacy was Pre-scribe. This allows physicians to enter new prescriptions directly into the Walgreens system. If refills are requested, they can also be transmitted through Pre-scribe. This eliminates the need for the prescriptions to be retyped into the system by the technicians; reduces the number of errors; and reduces the time needed to process a prescription. Most importantly, it makes transactions very convenient; the patient does not need to get a written prescription, bring it to the pharmacy, and then wait for it. Once the physician types the script from the office, the prescription is incorporated into the work flow; conceivably, the prescription could be ready by the time the patient gets from the doctor's office to the pharmacy. Walgreens is one of the largest users of the satellite, second only to the U.S. government.

Walgreens enjoys the success that it has earned for over 100 years, but retail is a very competitive industry. The top five drug chains by store count are

1. CVS (4191)
2. Walgreens (3818)
3. Rite Aid (3497)
4. Eckerd (2646)
5. Albertsons (2126)

The top five drug chains based on billion-dollar sales volume as of 2001 are:

1. Walgreens ($24.6)
2. CVS ($22.2)
3. Albertsons ($17.9)
4. Rite Aid ($15.1)
5. Eckerd ($13.8)

CVS recently penetrated the Florida market. In 2001, CVS closed 563 stores, only to reopen others that are modernized in freestanding locations.

SUPPLY CHAIN INTEGRATION

When competition is intense, collaboration with suppliers and other organizations is absolutely necessary. Walgreens is doing just that. Its strategic inventory management system (SIMS) is used by the stores to keep inventory. Based on the demand, SIMS creates forecasts for the next week's or month's demand. The system is linked to the supplier and directly transmits the order. Every item scanned at the register is listed in the SIMS. At the end of the week, the SIMS details how many items were sold and what is left in stock and creates the order list for the next week based on what was sold. The system allows the stores to have a complete inventory with minimum storage requirement. Adjustments for seasonal goods and specialty items are also possible; these are done manually.

Walgreens has seven distribution centers in the U.S., with approximately 800,000 square feet. Most of the merchandise within the stores comes from the distribution centers. The company has contracts with manufacturers and is able to purchase large volumes at lower prices. The pharmacy and the store each get a major weekly order, but also have the option to place daily orders. If a customer needs a specific item that is not in stock, the item can be ordered through Cardinal (a major supplier) and is delivered the next day. Because the customer can always count on Walgreens to get items as soon as possible, the store does not need to keep rare products in stock.

Recently, Walgreens formed a partnership with Universal to sell more than 100 licensed products in over 3400 Walgreens stores. Universal merchandise such as Jurassic Park, Woody Woodpecker, and Chilly Willy will be integrated with typical Walgreens products such as ice cream, toothbrushes, and certain beauty products.

Walgreens has also established major partnerships with two leading drug manufacturers, Pfizer and Eli Lilly. The partnerships were formed to benefit senior citizens over age 55 who do not have prescription coverage. These patients can enroll in a membership program to get Pfizer products for only $15 or Lilly products for only $12 at any Walgreens store. Walgreens also realizes how important it is for customers to have adequate information about their disease status or prescription medications. The company formed a partnership with Mayo Clinic that allows customers access to medical information via the Internet through Mayo Clinic databases.

SERVICE INNOVATION

The main objective of Walgreens is to serve customers better and make shopping more convenient for them. The new millennium brings higher demands from customers. With changing times, customer needs are changing as well, and retailers must be willing to accommodate those needs. Walgreens strives to go the extra mile for its customers. For example, because many pharmacy customers are working parents, Walgreens opened over 800 24-hour stores and over 2600 stores with drive-through lanes. By 2006, Walgreens is hoping to have 90% of its stores with drive-through lanes and over 1300 24-hour stores. This enables customers to do their shopping at any time, day or night. For the disabled person or the mother with an infant in the back seat, the drive-though is a great convenience. Customers never need to get out of the car, but are still able to drop off or pick up prescriptions.

To make it even easier for pharmacy customers, Walgreens introduced touch-tone refills and an online pharmacy. Using the telephone, a customer can input the refill numbers and when he wants to pick up the filled prescription. The online pharmacy gives customers the opportunity to fill in their medication histories with any over-the-counter medication that they might be taking. It also allows them to request refills for existing prescriptions that can be delivered or picked up. Currently, Walgreens has three mail-order centers that will allow customers to fill prescriptions for up to a 3-month supply. Walgreens gives its customers the option of getting their prescriptions filled without leaving home.

In some areas, such as South Florida, language barriers can be a problem and present health risks if the patient does not understand how to take the medication properly. Because it is virtually impossible to employ pharmacists who speak multiple languages, Walgreens is using a computer system that translates the directions and medication information into eight different languages. Besides English, customers can request prescription instructions to be printed in Spanish; Chinese; French; Polish; Portuguese; Russian; and Vietnamese. By complying with medication needs, patients can reduce hospital admissions by 10%.

Another program that Walgreens offers to benefit customers is Express Pay. Instead of sending students to college with a credit card, Walgreens offers parents the option of putting the credit card information on file. This way, children who need to fill a prescription while away from home can pay using Express Pay instead of a credit card; then they simply pick up the prescription. Elderly customers can use Express Pay if they need someone else to pick up the prescription for them.

Walgreens has launched a program that will benefit customers over age 55 who do not have prescription coverage. The Senior Dividends program credits senior customers with 10% of the dollar amount of the prescription, which they can use to pay for any other purchase throughout the store. This program attracts customers to the pharmacy department and the store. Giving customers credit for using the pharmacy makes them more likely to shop at Walgreens for household items as well as medications.

Store layouts are inviting for female shoppers. The wide aisles are made to accommodate mothers with children and strollers. The pharmacy department gives waiting families the option of watching children's movies. Frequently, if children are waiting at the pharmacy, the clerks offer them coloring books. If the kids are entertained, parents are willing to wait for the prescription even if it takes a little longer. Beauty supplies are strategically placed at the front of the store in order to attract more female shoppers. To attract children, all children's merchandise and colorful items are placed at their eye level. The stores are well lit and the clerks are trained to help the customers and be the eyes and ears of the store.

THE SEVEN SERVICE BASICS

Walgreens instills seven fundamentals concerning customer service and how important customers are to the company in each of its employees. Every store has this "list of seven" placed by the registers or by the time clock, thus reminding each employee how to treat the customers. These fundamentals are intended to win and keep customer loyalty:

- *No one waits at Walgreens* — This teaches employees to get customers in and out as soon as possible. If more than three customers are in line, the register clerk is supposed to call IC3 code and another register will be opened. Customers do not like to wait in long lines, so Walgreens is committed to serving them as fast as possible.
- *In your aisle, get a smile* — Customers like welcoming, friendly stores. Walgreens' employees should always look friendly and welcome each customer with a smile.
- *It is no problem* — Customers should not feel that it is a problem to ask employees for help. Anything that the customer wants should be taken care of with no problems.
- *The phone is for you* — The phone should not ring more than three times at Walgreens before someone answers it. Customers do not like to be placed on hold for prolonged periods of time or to have the phone ring with no one answering it.
- *The company is coming* — The stores should always be clean and well stocked. Every day at Walgreens should be like a day when the district manager or the vice president is coming to visit. Clean and organized stores make good impressions and customers will return for other purchases.
- *See you soon* — Employees should personally thank each customer for shopping at Walgreens and find a way to tell the customer that they look forward to seeing them again.
- *Surprise* — Employees should always go the extra mile for the customer and surprise him or her with the good service that Walgreens has to offer.

INTERNAL, INTERACTIVE, AND EXTERNAL MARKETING

Walgreens recognizes the need for good employees in order to achieve corporate goals. Its employees are the ones that have first-hand interaction with the customers. If the employees are not friendly and not loyal to the company, great customer service is not possible. In order to have great talent and loyal employees, Walgreens offers very competitive salaries along with excellent benefits. Besides the above-average salaries, Walgreens offers comprehensive medical and dental benefits for employees and their dependents. Employees are entitled to a 15% discount on any store purchase at any location and a 10% discount on prescriptions.

Profit sharing is another benefit; a Walgreens pharmacist can invest 2% of his or her paycheck and Walgreens matches $3.28 for every $1 invested. Employees are eligible to buy stock shares at a 10% discount with no broker fees. With Walgreens stock splitting seven times within the last 15 years, the option to buy stock is a great benefit. The fringe benefits that Walgreens offers are very competitive and make the employees think twice before leaving the company. Because the employees are given a part of the company, they will work hard to ensure a profitable company.

In addition to benefits and salaries, Walgreens offers employees the opportunity to improve the company. If an employee has a suggestion on how to improve certain things he or she can submit the idea. The best three ideas win prizes such as $1000, $500, and $250. Names and pictures of prize-winning employees are also published in company newsletters. Employees are also encouraged to be creative with the displays in the stores. When new promotions are needed or seasons change and displays are to be put up, the whole district is involved in a contest. When displays are up, the district managers and supervisors go from store to store and vote for the best display. The employee with the best display receives gift certificates at local restaurants and gift certificates at Walgreens.

As stated on the Walgreens Web site (www.walgreens.com), the strategy is "not fancy but rock solid." The Walgreens strategy is to enter new markets; "dense up" the existing markets; relocate; remodel; invest heavily in high-tech store and distribution systems, which drives service up and costs down; and offer an online drugstore Web site totally integrated with the retail stores.

Walgreens knows the power of promotion. Creating attractive displays attracts customers. Walgreens offers a weekly circular advertising new products as well as the sales going on that week. In 2001, Walgreens had 43 million inserts; by the end of 2002, it plans to have 50 million inserts. Television is another advertising medium that Walgreens uses. However, by far, the best advertising is produced by providing great customer service and thus favorable word-of-mouth promotion.

WALGREENS' BUSINESS PERFORMANCE

Walgreens sales for the fiscal year 2002 were $28.7 billion up 16.5% from 2001 figures. August pharmacy sales increased 18.5%, while comparable

Fiscal Year Ended Aug. 31	Sales (in billions)	Percent Increase	Earnings (in millions)	Percent Increase	Earnings per Share	Percent Increase
2001	$24.6	16.1%	$886	14.0%	$0.86	13.2%
2000	$21.1	18.9%	$777	24.5%	$0.76	22.6%
1999	$17.8	16.6%	$624	22.2%	$0.62	21.6%
1998	$15.3	14.5%	$511	17.2%	$0.51	15.9%
1997	$13.4	13.5%	$436	17.2%	$0.44	17.3%

Exhibit 18.2   Five-Year Sales and Earnings

pharmacy sales rose 13.8%. Total prescriptions filled at comparable stores increased 6.0%. The net earnings in 2001 were $886 million compared to $777 million in 2000. (Exhibit 18.2 presents key 5-year financial performance measures for the company.)

Walgreens ranked 66th in sales; 88th in profit; 56th in market value; and 316th in assets in the *Forbes* "500" published in April, 2002. The company was also ranked number one among food and drug chains in *Fortune* magazine's "Most Admired Corporations in America" issue published in March, 2002 (see Exhibit 18.3 for numerous industry rankings and corporate ratings for the company). Finally, Walgreens was listed as one of only 11 "great" companies based on 15-year stock performance in Jim Collins' book (2001) *Good to Great* (the others were Abbott; Circuit City; Fannie Mae; Gillette; Kimberly-Clark; Kroger; Nucor; Philip Morris; Pitney Bowes; and Wells Fargo).

QUESTIONS

1. How does Walgreens create value for its customers? Specifically, how is it better than its competitors? What areas need improvement?
2. Comment on how Walgreens uses technology and collaboration to gain a competitive advantage in the retail marketplace. What other initiatives should the company pursue?
3. Explain how a company in another industry might adopt or adapt Walgreens' "Seven Service Fundamentals."
4. Is Walgreens really a "great" company? Why or why not? What does it take to become a truly superior company? (Go beyond financial performance in your response.)

Largest drugstore chains based on previous 12-month sales (through July 31, 2002)

Walgreens — $28.4 billion
CVS — $23.5 billion
Rite Aid — $15.5 billion
Eckerd — $14.3 billion

Largest drugstore chains based on store count

CVS — 4007
Walgreens — 3818
Rite Aid — 3446
Eckerd — 2642

***Fortune* magazine "World's Most Admired Companies" (published Oct. 2, 2000)**

Ranked no. 1 among food- and drugstores

***Fortune* magazine "Most Admired Corporations in America"
(published March 4, 2002)**

Ranked no. 1 among food- and drugstores and is listed for ninth consecutive
year

***Fortune* magazine "500 Largest U.S.-Based Companies"
(published April 15, 2002)**

Ranked 78th overall in revenue; 4th among food- and drugstores

***Fortune* magazine "Global 500 Largest Companies" (published July 22, 2002)**

Ranked 183rd overall in revenue

***Forbes* "500 List" (published April 15, 2002)**

Ranked 66th in sales, 88th in profit, 316th in assets, and 56th in market value

***Forbes* "Platinum 400 List" (published January 7, 2002)**

Walgreens again made this list of the best-performing big companies in the
U.S.

***Business Week's* performance rankings of the S&P 500 (published spring, 2002)**

Ranked 66th overall; 13th in the health-care industry (first among drugstores)

Moody's

Current rating is Aa3

(continued)

Standard and Poor's

Current rating is A+

10-Year Walgreens Stock Performance

On July 31, 1992, 100 shares of Walgreens stock sold for $3587; 10 years later, on July 31, 2002, those 100 shares, having split three times, had grown to 800 shares worth $28,264, for a gain of 688%

Number of customers served daily chainwide

3.0 million

Employee count, 2001

130,000

Total prescriptions filled, 2001

323 million

Exhibit 18.3   Walgreens' Ranks and Ratings

BIBLIOGRAPHY

Anon. (2002) *Chain Drug Rev.*, June 10, 24(10), RX1, 30.
Collins, J. (2001) *Good to Great: Why Some Companies Make the Leap ... and Others Don't*, New York: HarperBusiness.
Anon. (2002) *Drug Store News*, March 25, 24(4), 30.
www.walgreens.com

INDEX